MODERN HUMANITIES RESEARCH ASSOCIATION

TEXTS AND DISSERTATIONS
(formerly Dissertation Series)

VOLUME 18

Editor
R. M. WALKER
(Hispanic)

EPIC AND CHRONICLE
The *Poema de mio Cid* and the
Crónica de veinte reyes

TO MY PARENTS

EPIC AND CHRONICLE

The *Poema de mio Cid* and the *Crónica de veinte reyes*

BRIAN POWELL

Lecturer in Hispanic Studies,
University of Hull

LONDON

THE MODERN HUMANITIES RESEARCH ASSOCIATION

1983

Published by

The Modern Humanities Research Association

Honorary Treasurer, MHRA

KING'S COLLEGE, STRAND
LONDON WC2R 2LS
ENGLAND

ISBN 0 900547 84 7

Printed in England by
W. S. MANEY & SON LIMITED
HUDSON ROAD LEEDS

CONTENTS

1-24, 94-107

PREFACE

This book contains a revised version of a doctoral dissertation submitted to the University of Cambridge. The revision has not been fundamental, although changes have been made at many points in the text. The study has two main aspects. The first two chapters deal with critical problems concerning the background to the *Poema de mio Cid* and the *Crónica de veinte reyes*, while the remaining chapters study in detail the incorporation of the former into the latter. The hitherto unpublished text of the relevant section of the *Crónica* is included in an appendix. I should like to thank Professor D. W. Lomax of the University of Birmingham and Dr D. G. Pattison of the University of Oxford for their help and advice in the preparation of this work. Above all, I wish to express my gratitude to Professor C. C. Smith of the University of Cambridge for his invaluable guidance and encouragement throughout the time that I have been engaged upon these studies.

ABBREVIATIONS

1. Texts

CAI	*Chronica Adefonsi Imperatoris*
C1344	*Crónica general de España de 1344*
CMC	*Cantar de mio Cid*
CRC	*Crónica de los reyes de Castilla*
CSZ	*Cantar de Sancho II y cerco de Zamora*
CVR	*Crónica de veinte reyes*
DRH	*De Rebus Hispaniae*
EE	*Estoria de España*
GE	*General Estoria*
HR	*Historia Roderici*
LR	*Liber Regum*
MR	*Mocedades de Rodrigo*
PCG	*Primera crónica general*
PMC	*Poema de mio Cid*
TCG	*Tercera crónica general*

2. Journals and Series

AEM	*Anuario de Estudios Medievales*
AS	*Acta Salmanticensia*
BAE	*Biblioteca de Autores Españoles*
BH	*Bulletin Hispanique*
BHS	*Bulletin of Hispanic Studies*
BRABLB	*Boletín de la Real Academia de Buenas Letras de Barcelona*
BRAE	*Boletín de la Real Academia Española*
BRAH	*Boletín de la Real Academia de Historia*
CHE	*Cuadernos de Historia de España*
FMLS	*Forum for Modern Language Studies*
HBalt	*Hispania (U.S.A.)*
HR	*Hispanic Review*
KRQ	*Kentucky Romance Quarterly*
MA	*Le Moyen Age*

MLR	*Modern Language Review*
NBAE	*Nueva Biblioteca de Autores Españoles*
NRFH	*Nueva Revista de Filología Hispánica*
PLPLS	*Proceedings of the Leeds Philosophical and Literary Society: Literary and Historical Section*
PMLA	*Publications of the Modern Language Association*
RABM	*Revista de Archivos, Bibliotecas y Museos*
RFE	*Revista de Filología Española*
RH	*Revue Hispanique*
RLC	*Revue de Littérature Comparée*
RPh	*Romance Philology*
RR	*Romanic Review*
Sc	*Scriptorium*
ZRP	*Zeitschrift für Romanische Philologie*

3. Manuscript Collections

Ac. Hist.	Real Academia de Historia, Madrid
B.N.	Biblioteca Nacional, Madrid
Esc.	Biblioteca del Monasterio de El Escorial
Pal.	Palacio Real de Oriente, Madrid
Paris	Bibliothèque Nationale, Paris
Pelayo	Biblioteca de Menéndez Pelayo, Santander
Salamanca	Biblioteca de la Universidad de Salamanca

4. Place of Publication

M.	Madrid

CHAPTER 1

THE *POEMA DE MIO CID* AND REFERENCES TO THE CID BEFORE THE COMPOSITION OF THE POEM

I. THE *POEMA DE MIO CID*

The *Poema de mio Cid* (*PMC*) is the most complete epic poem of the Spanish medieval period now known to us in a form close to that in which it was originally written down. It is also one of the oldest extant literary works in Castilian, and one of the important landmarks in the tradition of epic poetry in Western Europe.[1] It has survived in only one manuscript, which is of no more than fair quality, having a number of scribal errors and corrections, some passages which are barely legible, and folios missing at the beginning and at two points within the text. It is generally agreed, however, that not a great deal of the poem is missing.[2] The date of composition of the poem and the date of the extant manuscript are both topics of critical debate, although the manuscript does have an *explicit* which states that it was written down 'En era de mill & C.C. xL.v. años', that is, in A.D. 1207.[3] These matters are discussed in the following section.

The theme of the *PMC* is the progress of its hero, Rodrigo Díaz de Vivar, known as the Cid, from the condition of penurious exile to that of conqueror of Valencia, from disgraced vassal to honoured father of princesses. Perhaps within his lifetime, and certainly from shortly after his death, and well before the composition of the *PMC*, the figure of the Cid had taken on heroic proportions. He became a figure worthy of literary praise, and the stories told or written about him began to confuse the facts of his life with elements of fiction. The *PMC*, in fact marks only one stage in a process which has meant the development of the heroic legend of the Cid, and its survival, in various forms, up to the present day. The Cid became and has remained the national hero of Castile.[4]

Consequently, the importance of the *PMC* in the whole history of the legend should not be exaggerated. Before the poem was composed, tales about the Cid appeared in a variety of texts, mainly in Latin and hence by learned men. Some of these references are brief, but imply that the Cid's name had great prominence outside the circles of the learned. After its composition, the *PMC* was used as a source by the chroniclers of the thirteenth and fourteenth centuries, but they also included stories of the Cid's youth, adult life, and death from other sources, now lost, some of which present him as a man whose character is far removed from that of the protagonist of the poem. Later, when the poem seems to have been virtually forgotten, ballads, chronicles, and the theatre provide many and various portraits of the man, and evidence of the attraction that his figure has held for centuries. Even now, when the poem is well known, the majority of the people who are familiar with the Cid's name know nothing of the poem, although it remains the greatest single work of literature inspired by the hero.[5]

The subject of this first chapter is the stories about the Cid that appear, or are referred to, in texts prior to the *PMC*, and their relationship to the story of the *PMC* itself. In particular, the origins, diffusion, and interrelationships of the stories will be discussed. As far as the source of the stories is concerned Menéndez Pidal believed that the most important source was history, both for prose texts and for the *PMC*. In the case of the *PMC*, he believed that accurate preservation of the historical facts was intended and achieved by epic 'juglares', and talks of 'el carácter verista, concretamente histórico de las primitivas gestas castellanas', amongst which he includes the *PMC* (*EDC*, p. 48). However, in recent times, many studies have shown the lack of historical accuracy of the *PMC*, enabling Horrent, for example, to write 'même dans ses parties les plus historiques, le *Cantar*, quand on le serre d'un peu près, finit par contredire l'histoire', while Smith has observed that accurate history was not the concern of the poet but that realism, 'the impression of verisimilitude', was an essential part of the artistry. In other words, the *PMC* may be convincingly 'real', but it is not historical.[6]

As far as the texts that predate the *PMC* are concerned, the historicity of their stories about the Cid is not easy to confirm or deny. The history of eleventh-century Spain will always be partially hidden from us, particularly when it concerns the details of the life of a non-regal personage such as the Cid, however distinguished that personage might have been. One can attempt to make an objective judgement about any particular 'fact', taking into account the chronological distance between the supposed event and its first known record, and the inherent probability of the 'fact', but frequently one cannot be certain, since no independent corroborative evidence exists. In any case, in this study it is not intended to concentrate on the historical or non-historical nature of the stories about the Cid that can be shown to have existed. Rather, the available material will be considered from the point of view of what it tells us about the development in the twelfth century of the figure of the Cid as hero, and how this is related to the protagonist of literary fiction who appears in the *PMC*. The historical value and reliability of some of the texts dealt with will inevitably be touched on when they are discussed, but historicity will be of relatively little importance in the chapter as a whole.[7]

A. The Date of the 'PMC'

In his fundamental *CMC*, Pidal argued for a date of composition for the *PMC* of about 1140, modifying it slightly to 'entre 1140 y 1150' in the additions to the second edition (pp. 19–28, 1165–70). Some earlier critics had proposed similar dates, but others differed. Andrés Bello suggested the 'primera mitad del siglo XIII, aunque con más inmediación al año 1200', an idea that foreshadows recent theories. Pidal supported his dating with arguments based on several references within the text of the poem and with more general observations about the antiquity of its language. However, critics have since argued strongly against his deductions from the textual references, and Bello in the last century and Pattison recently both used linguistic evidence to argue positively for a later date than Pidal's.[8]

In fact, most new contributions to the debate on the date of the poem since the second edition of Pidal's *CMC* have argued for a date later than 1140. Russell used diplomatic details to argue that the poem could not have been composed before about 1185. Ubieto employed historical arguments in support of the date on the *explicit* of the manuscript. Pattison, as mentioned above, used linguistic material, principally suffixes, which suggested an early thirteenth-century date, while Gicovate and Smith both pointed out that considerable time must have passed before the content of the poem could have been developed in its present form. Very recently, Lomax has shown that there are weaknesses in most positive arguments for the dating of the poem, but he concludes that there is a lot more to be said for 1207, the date of the *explicit*, than for 1140.[9] It is also worth noting that in 1965, when well into his nineties, Pidal himself put forward the theory that the *PMC* was conserved orally from composition in 1140 'hasta que a fines del siglo XII se puso el poema por escrito', which implies that there are aspects of the text which Pidal had begun to believe did not square with its being written down in 1140.[10]

It is clear, then, that the date of 1140 for the composition of the *PMC* is no longer really acceptable, although it is still commonly assumed to be the date by many critics, particularly within Spain.[11] Instead of 1140, various approaches have produced a date of composition of around 1200, with some critics arguing positively for 1207, the date apparently given in the *explicit*. The *explicit* reads:

> Per Abbat le escrivio en el mes de mayo,
> En era de mill &.C.C   xL.V. años.

> (ll. 3732–33)

There is a gap between the second C and the x of sufficient size to permit the insertion of another letter in the number, or for another letter to have been erased from it. Now, as far as Pidal was concerned, there had indeed been another letter erased from the space in the manuscript, and this letter had been a C. In other words, the date should be read as 'era de 1345', that is A.D. 1307.

The problem that faced Pidal when he elaborated this theory was that for him a date of 1207 made no sense. It was neither the date of composition, 1140, nor the date of the extant manuscript, which was and still is considered to be of a fourteenth-century date. With an extra C, the explicit could be referring to the date of the extant copy. However, there is no positive evidence that a letter has been erased. There is, for example, no trace of any ink in the gap. In fact, once it is accepted that 1207 is a possible date of composition, the need to presuppose a missing C vanishes. The way is then open for the obvious date of 1207 to be accepted as the date referred to in the last lines of the *PMC*.[12]

It is safe to conclude, therefore, that the *PMC* was written down by someone called Per Abbat in the year 1207. The extant copy is descended from the text of 1207 via a manuscript tradition of uncertain length. The circumstances surrounding the writing down of the poem in 1207 demand further consideration. Questions about how the poem was composed and whether Per Abbat was an author, transcriber of an oral performance, or copyist of a written text are dealt with in the next section. Suffice it to say now that for the purposes of this study the *PMC* is assumed to have been composed in or shortly before 1207. This later date for the poem means that certain texts of the twelfth century, which refer to the Cid, and which could reasonably have been assumed to be familiar with the poem when it was dated to 1140, could not, in fact have known it. These texts are the *Chronica Adefonsi Imperatoris* (*CAI*), *Crónica Najerense*, *Liber Regum* (*LR*), and *Linaje del Cid*. The implications of this change of chronology are discussed when these texts are considered later in this chapter.[13]

B.   The Composition of the 'PMC'

It was pointed out towards the end of the preceding section that deciding when the *PMC* was written down was only one aspect of the question of the origins of the poem. Now, I intend to consider how the poem was composed, and related matters such as whether composition and writing down took place at the same moment and whether they were carried out by the same person. These problems are the subjects of complex critical debates, and it is not pretended that any definitively conclusive statements can be made here. However, it seems worthwhile reviewing the current state of criticism, in the particular context of this study, and it is, of course, desirable to outline the reasons for some of the assumptions that are later implicit in it.

There are two extremes in the current range of theories about the composition of the *PMC*, which might be termed the oral theory and the learned theory.[14] Proponents of the oral theory believe that the *PMC* is an example of a flourishing tradition of epic poems which were composed, performed, and transmitted orally by highly skilled and experienced poets or 'juglares'. All the other poems of this tradition have been lost in their original form, but the *PMC* has survived because it was copied down by a scribe, who was listening to an oral performance, probably dictated by the poet specifically for transcription by the scribe. And, of course, a copy of the text has survived. There may well have been other epics transcribed, but these have been lost, like many manuscripts of medieval Spain. Evidence for the existence of other poems, it is argued, exists in overt references to singers of stories in contemporary texts, and, in a specific way, in chronicles which used them as historical sources, as they used the *PMC*, and in the later tradition of ballads, some of which are said to derive directly from epics through oral transmission.[15]

Broad anthropological considerations, in fact, do support the idea of the existence of oral poetry. Illiterate societies or illiterate sections of societies in most parts of the world cultivate oral poetry, often of an epic type, which can flourish and survive over centuries, sometimes ignored by more 'cultivated' levels of the society concerned, as was the case with the Spanish ballads.[16] But what has given particular impetus, in recent years, to the study of orality, and to the detailed development of the oral theory in the context of the medieval epic, is the work carried out by Parry and Lord on the living oral tradition of Serbo-Croatian heroic songs. Particularly in *The Singer of Tales*, features of orally composed narrative poems of the modern tradition were analysed and described, and the results revealed certain similarities with features that are present in the *PMC*. These include the use of characters taken from history as protagonists, the fact that the requirements of dictation tend to upset the poet's rhythm and hence the rhyme-scheme of the poem, a distinct lack of enjambement in the composition, and, on a more technical level and most importantly, the regular employment of set-pieces, motifs, and formulaic language in identifiable recurrent patterns which have a crucial role in assisting oral composition.[17] Studies deriving from Lord's conclusions have shown that the *PMC* undoubtedly has a large amount of material in it that can be best accounted for by the influence of the techniques of oral composition. Such studies confirm the existence of a tradition of oral narrative verse in twelfth-century and thirteenth-century Spain, by demonstrating its influence on an extant text.[18]

What such studies have not been able to show conclusively is that the *PMC* is an orally composed epic. Some have demonstrated the amount of formulaic or other oral material in the poem and have concluded that it is a transcribed oral text. Others have agreed with the quantities of oral-related material, but have argued that the total in percentage terms is not as much as one would expect to find in a purely oral poem.[19] Moreover, it seems to me that the *PMC* cannot be a 'purely oral poem' for the simple reason that it is written down. The problems raised by the concept of the dictation of an oral composition have not yet been satisfactorily accounted for by the supporters of the oral theory. Lord describes some of the difficulties involved in writing down an oral performance and the difficulties faced by the poet performing for dictation. Such difficulties must have been much greater in the medieval period, when illiteracy was the norm and literacy was the exception, when reading and writing were laboriously learned skills, and not the fluent, rapid processes which we today take for granted. It is very hard to imagine the *PMC* being composed and dictated at a speed slow enough for it to be copied down in a thirteenth-century hand.[20] The oral theory, then, is only a partially successful explanation of how the *PMC* was composed. It has not been able to show that the poem is an oral composition, but it has shown that it has debts of some importance to methods normally used in oral composition.

At the other end of the spectrum of theories about the composition of the *PMC* is what I have called the learned theory. The proponents of this theory argue that the poem was composed in writing by a poet who was possibly a cleric, and who certainly had had legal training. He was highly literate, familiar with French and Latin texts, and strongly influenced by them. Smith, who has developed the most detailed arguments, goes further, and claims that the poet consciously uses French literary works and Classical Latin historians as direct sources for a number of episodes in the poem. Moreover, he argues, the *PMC* was a unique work, quite different from any tradition of epic poetry, oral or written, that might have existed.[21] His view, supported by Walker, of the way in which sources have been used in the poem supposes great subtlety on the part of the author, who selected or rejected large or small sections or even details of his source, in a manner which Smith has referred to as 'de una complejidad asombrosa'.[22] Other studies have identified probable influences on the *PMC* without claiming that they represent directly used sources. Walsh suggested parallels between the poem and legends of the deaths of martyrs which would have been widely known at the time; Adams has shown comparable usage of certain linguistic phrases in the *PMC* and contemporary French texts; Deyermond and Chaplin point out a considerable number of folk-motifs in the poem, while observing that the presence of the same motifs in the poem and elsewhere is not proof of direct influence or dependence of one text upon another. It is, rather, a demonstration of the analogues that exist between different cultures, particularly contiguous ones.[23] Indeed, what all these studies show, including those of Smith and Walker, in my view, is not that the *PMC* was composed on the basis of direct borrowing from sources, but that its poet had a wide range of influences working on him. These influences were those present in the cultural milieu of northern Spain in A.D. 1200. They included ecclesiastical traditions, and they included elements derived from the superior culture of France to the north, although most important was probably native Spanish culture, with all that that implies. The *PMC* is a richly textured work, and the man who composed it was highly intelligent and highly skilled.

The evidence does seem to suggest that he had some specialized legal knowledge, but there is no convincing proof that he read French or Latin texts, nor is there any need for him to have done so. The learned theory, then, like the oral one, is only partially successful in explaining how the *PMC* was composed. What this theory has done is to stress the importance of the individual author in the creation of the poem. It has demonstrated that the individual poet had characteristics which, of course, left their mark on the poem, making it unique. What it has not succeeded in showing is that the poem is a highly learned composition, with more debts to French and Latin traditions than to Spanish ones.

With the composition of the *PMC*, as with many problems in the study of medieval literature, it is easier to spot flaws in others' theories than to propose a coherent theory of one's own. But it is worth re-examining just what the poem itself is like. It is a long narrative heroic poem with a complex but identifiable structure. Its general artistic excellence and its verbal subtlety would seem to argue against any possibility of oral composition. It is certainly a more consummate work of art than any of the recorded Serbo-Croatian songs, and its use of epic epithets, for example, is much less automatic than theirs appears to be.[24] But the complex artistry of the poem is a double-edged sword, for it implies a poetic tradition in which the techniques of the poem were developed. The techniques cannot all have been invented by the author of the poem, and they certainly do not all come from French and Latin sources. The metre of the poem and its use of tenses are just two features which, though problematical to us, were sufficiently familiar to the poet for him to employ them with apparent ease.[25] There must, therefore, have been either an oral or a written tradition of narrative poetry, or both, in which features familiar to us from the *PMC* were regularly employed; and it is this Spanish tradition that was the most important influence on the author. It has already been pointed out in discussion of the oral theory of composition that the *PMC* clearly uses techniques associated with oral poetry. It is logical to assume, then, that a Spanish genre of oral heroic poetry existed in the period prior to the composition of the *PMC*, and that it was well known to the author of the poem. A tradition of written poems employing oral techniques may have existed, too, but the evidence for this is more tenuous.[26] Now, although the *PMC* makes great use of techniques copied from oral poetry, it is not an oral poem. Rather, it must have been composed in writing by one poet, familiar with oral poetry, but an educated, literate man. This poet may well have written his poem in 1207, and his name may well have been Per Abbat. Smith has established some very strong links between the characters of the poem and one man of that name; but, inevitably, the case is not proven.[27]

The *PMC* was written in the first decade of the thirteenth century by one poet. This poet composed his work principally influenced by the methods of the oral genre of narrative poetry with which he was familiar. He borrowed techniques from the oral tradition, and he may also have borrowed his story from that same tradition. It is reasonable to assume that the Cid and his exploits were one of the subjects of oral poems, and it would not be surprising if at least part of the story of the *PMC* had been related in such poems. This supposition is given support by the way in which the poet seems to assume that his audience is already familiar with events he refers to and with characters whom he brings into his story. However, the evidence of the twelfth-century tradition of stories about the Cid, and the relevance of this to the story of the *PMC* are principal themes of the remainder of this chapter.

There is, finally, the question of how the *PMC* was diffused, whether only in written form or also orally through 'juglares' who learned the text. In the case of the *Mocedades de Rodrigo* (*MR*), the extant text most comparable to the *PMC*, Deyermond has argued strongly that the form and content of the poem can only be satisfactorily accounted for by learned composition, oral diffusion, and later dictation by a 'juglar' to a scribe to produce the surviving text. This argument depends principally on the view that the opening prose section of the *MR*, which turns gradually into verse, and the very inconsistent metrical forms of the verse throughout must be the result of dictation. Harvey, of course, had already suggested dictation as the explanation for the inconsistencies of the metre of the *PMC*. Hence, Deyermond's theory could apply to the *PMC* too. But a comparison of the *MR* and the *PMC* shows that the lines of the former are far more inconsistent than those of the later, and it is easier to explain the variations in the latter's verses by supposing a flexible metre not dependent on a count of syllables. It is not necessary to suppose dictation to account for the extant *PMC*. Its apparent irregularities can be explained by a fairly free verse form, and some careless work in places by one or more copyists. In addition, it will be shown in later chapters that the vernacular chroniclers who use the *PMC* knew the poem in a version or versions very similar to the extant one, so similar, in fact, as to suggest a relationship through a manuscript tradition rather than in any other way. There is evidence, then, to suggest the *PMC* was diffused in manuscript, but no convincing evidence that it circulated in oral form. This does not affect the possibility that oral poems about the same period of the Cid's life as the one treated in the *PMC* did circulate widely, telling a similar story, or one showing many differences from the one that has survived.[28]

II. BEFORE THE *POEMA DE MIO CID*

A. *Carmen Campidoctoris*

The earliest surviving account of events involving Rodrigo Díaz seems to be a remarkable poetic composition in Latin, which briefly recounts the hero's early prowess, his closeness to King Sancho, the break with King Alfonso, the defeat of Count García at Cabra, and finally the preparations for battle with the Count of Barcelona and Alfagib of Lérida, at which point it breaks off abruptly. The poem survives in only one manuscript, which is of thirteenth-century date. In its present incomplete state it consists of thirty-two four-line stanzas plus one line. There is an erasure of some eighteen lines, which has been covered by other writings, on the remainder of the last folio of the poem, but whether this would have been the original end of the work is uncertain. Pidal seems to think it was, but it seems safer to say, with Horrent, that it is impossible to know.[29]

Most scholars have agreed on a very early date for this work, within Rodrigo's lifetime in fact. This dating is based mainly on two references in the work. The first is to a town reconquered in 1093: 'castrum / quod adhuc Mauri vocant Almenarum' (ll. 97–98). The early dating here rests on the interpretation of this line as meaning that the Moors still hold or have just lost Almenar. This interpretation seems rather strict; it could simply mean, 'whose Moorish name is . . .'. The second piece of evidence is in line 19: 'qui eius freti estis ope'. The present tense is taken as meaning that the hero is alive and protecting the poet and his audience. However, it seems at least possible that the support provided by Rodrigo was more spiritual than material, that it came from the inspirational qualities of his life and image rather than his physical presence.[30]

More in keeping with a later date are some of the attitudes and perspectives in the *Carmen*. Many of these are later at the heart of the developing heroic image of the Cid. The relationships between Rodrigo and the two royal brothers, Sancho and Alfonso, are those found in much later accounts. Sancho loved Rodrigo, who played a vital role in the transfer of power to Alfonso (1072), and then Alfonso turned against him. The jealous courtiers who have the King's ear, and who later are sinister figures in the *PMC* (ll. 9, 267), are present in the *Carmen*, as is García, 'comitem superbum', defeated at Cabra. Other interesting points are the Cid's youthful prowess in defeating the Navarran, and the rivalry with the Count of Barcelona. The Campeador of the *Carmen* is a figure of historical magnitude worthy of comparison with the heroes of antiquity:

> Tanti victoris nam si retexere
> ceperim cuncta, non hec libri mille
> capere possent, Omero canente
> summo labore.
>
> (ll. 9–12)

All this seems somewhat exaggerated to have been written during Rodrigo's lifetime, let alone in years before the capture and defence of Valencia. Moreover, even in Pidal's terms, the historical accuracy of the author is not very strong for someone as close to the deeds of the Cid, as he suggests. The poet has confused the order of events in Castile, and though Pidal says, 'el poeta conoce exactamente los pormenores relativos al combate del Cid y del conde Berenguer' (*EDC*, p. 880), on examination these details prove to be few in number, and refer principally to the dressing of the Cid before battle. There seems no convincing reason for saying that the poet had to be a contemporary of the events described in order for him to be able to know what he tells us.[31]

On a reconsideration of the available evidence, then, it is difficult to accept the idea that the *Carmen* was written as early as has normally been said. There is no reason to think it ended originally without recounting the Cid's later exploits. There is little to suggest that the historical information of the poet is exceptionally detailed or accurate. Moreover, the historical perspective shown in the lines that have survived would be remarkable in a contemporary. It is more logical to see what this Latin poem tells us as a reflection of the fame of the hero after his death, when the popular image has begun to overlay historical 'fact'.[32] Really, there is no way to date the poem on the basis of detailed internal evidence. It is the broad view that the work adopts that is most striking. It is a view that probably required a period of time after the death of the Cid to have been so fully formed.

B. *Historia Roderici*

The second early text to be considered is the *Historia Roderici* (*HR*), or 'Gesta de Roderici Campi Docti' as it calls itself. Written in Latin prose, it is a much more substantial piece of work than the *Carmen*, but, like it, it is essentially an account of events in the life of Rodrigo Díaz, and is eulogistic. It has survived in two manuscripts, which seem to be from the same original, and which have formed the basis of several modern editions from 1792 onwards.[33]

Pidal's study of the *HR* remains the most substantial, his edition the most thorough, and his views the most widely accepted. His most important claims for the text are that it dates from less than eleven years after the death of the hero, and that it was written by one of his followers, who had access to notes and documents, and who gives us accurate historical information. The history, according to Pidal, is based on three fully detailed sections, for which the author had sources and which are historically accurate; these sections are joined together by brief linking passages, which reveal a certain haziness in the historical knowledge of the writer, although documents also contributed to parts of these passages. For example, 'algún apunte de un familiar del héroe' (*EDC*, p. 913) is suggested as the source for the genealogy of the *HR*, 2. The variety to be found in the language of the text is due, according to Pidal to differing sources or differing methods of compilation. Even the three fully detailed sections are not perfectly matched in manner of composition. For the first of these sections, the 'primer destierro', 'el autor se funda en notas tomadas con un criterio distinto del que sirvió para anotar los sucesos del fragmento cuarto' (*EDC*, p. 913). To add another element to this variety Pidal sees possible poetic influence on two episodes in the history. Firstly, the *HR* deals with the early exploits of the Cid rather imprecisely; 'pero nunca con falsedad manifiesta. Acaso en estas páginas iniciales se hallen restos de algún canto épico breve sobre hazañas particulares del Campeador' (*EDC*, p. 908). Secondly, some similarities between the *PMC*, ll. 986–1004, and the *HR*, 37–41, lead Pidal to suggest a common poetic source, in Latin, rather strangely (*EDC*, p. 382, note 2, and p. 908).

Pidal's faith in the historical accuracy of the *HR* relies on a combination of factors. The documents quoted are too detailed to have been invented, and the variation of terminology points to a variety of sources. The amount of detail and the phraseology persuade him of the authenticity of the letters exchanged between the Cid and the Count of Barcelona, the four oaths sworn for Alfonso, the lists of places given by Alfonso to Rodrigo, the latter's gifts to Valencia Cathedral, and so on. The volume of information and the mundane nature of some of it indicate, for Pidal, the trustworthiness of accounts of certain events. The way in which the vernacular chronicles of the thirteenth and fourteenth centuries have blended the *HR* in with their other sources, especially the lost text of the Arabic historian Ben Alcama, further strengthens his belief; for he argues that the Arabic history must be accurate, the chronicles match the *HR* with it, and therefore 'la *HR* muestra una veracidad de coetáneo igual a la de Ben Alcama' (*EDC*, p. 912). Finally, Pidal claims that the author was interested in Zaragoza, but does not report an important event of 1110 connected with that city. Therefore, he must have written the *HR* before this date, which would obviously make him a contemporary of Rodrigo's, and the parts of the jigsaw fit into place. In short, Pidal saw the *HR* as a reliable, historical account of three periods in the life of the Cid, written by a follower who was with him during these periods — 'clérigo aventurero y soldado, natural de tierras aragonesas o mejor catalanas, poco docto según el mal latín que emplea' (*EDC*, p. 917).

Other studies of the *HR* have not always concurred with Pidal's conclusions, which are heavily dependent on his dating; for there is often no independent proof as to the historical 'truth'. If the date of the work is placed much later, although documents may still have been used, the information generally lacks the 'veracidad de coetáneo' so important to Pidal. In fact, before Pidal's study Dozy and Menéndez y Pelayo had suggested 1150 and 1140 respectively as the date of composition. Bonilla tended towards the former year, and Lang chose an even later date, 1170, without presenting any evidence in support of it. Between the first and second editions of the *EDC*, a cautious note was struck by Kienast, who was mainly concerned to warn against definitive conclusions on the scanty evidence offered by the work. Then, in 1961, in a valuable contribution, Ubieto Arteta offered four deductions based on internal wordings, which placed the *HR* respectively, after 1144, between 1144–48, after *c*.1137 and after 1117, and he tentatively suggested 1144–47 as the likely date of composition. This accumulation of textual evidence does seem more persuasive than Pidal's intuitive feelings about historicity, and his one negative observation about Zaragoza. It now seems reasonable to accept Ubieto's dating, which means that the history of the Cid has had almost half a century since his death in which to develop.[34]

Let us consider, therefore, possible legendary aspects of the *HR*, and the state of any poetic legends it may reflect. As mentioned above, Pidal suggested possible poetic influence on the *HR* and its opening sections and in its accounts of the battle of Tévar. For Pidal, of course, the fact that a section may have been based on a poetic, epic source would in no way reduce its trustworthiness as history, given his view of the 'carácter verista, concretamente histórico' of early Spanish epic. Smith also sees poetic overtones in the Tévar incidents when he speaks of 'a Latin poem or an oral chant in Romance . . . of which there is a strong echo in the *HR*'. From a different viewpoint, evidence of possible vernacular epic influence on the language and style of the *HR* has been suggested.[35]

In an examination of the early sections of the *HR*, where Pidal saw a possible poetic source, the first feature to attract the attention is the genealogy (*HR*, 2). The oral preservation of genealogies is a feature of primitive societies; here, the chronicler himself says 'Hec esse videtur' which suggests an uncertain, so perhaps unwritten, source. At the head of Rodrigo's lineage stands 'Flaynus Calvus', without any explanation. It is not until much later, in the *Linaje del Cid* (see below) that he is identified as one of the 'judges' of Castile. Other parts of the family tree involve Pidal in some problematical explanations to justify their accuracy. For example, Laín Núñez is named as the Cid's grandfather. The documented person of the same name, whom Pidal identifies, has to have been almost fifty years of age before he began to follow the royal court, and moreover he outlived his son, the hero's father (*EDC*, p. 682). These details are not impossible in themselves, of course, but neither do they present a very strong case for trusting the genealogy. Section 3 of the *HR* tells us of the prowess of the Cid's father 'Didacus Flaynez' in opposing the Navarrese: 'nunquam contra eum potuerunt prevalere.' The strength of the father is thus foreshadowing the career of the son, a repetition of family characteristics typical of literary technique. Section 5 has Rodrigo defeating fifteen Zamorans single-handed, and quotes details worthy of a poem:

VII autem ex his erant loricati, quorum unum interfecit, duos vero vulneravit et in terram prostravit, omnesque alios robusto animo fugavit.

This section also recounts Rodrigo's two single combats, 'cum Eximino Garcez' and 'cum quodam sarraceno'; the first of which is mentioned by the *Carmen Campidoctoris* as well.[36]

More intriguing, perhaps, are the accounts of the events leading to the hero's exile (*HR*, 7–11). Like the genealogy and the duels, these events have left little or no historical evidence outside the *HR*, and the *Carmen* in the case of one of the duels and the Cabra story. Some details seem to be in conflict with what historical evidence there is available. As regards the Cabra incident there is an error regarding the kingship of Sevilla and Córdoba, and the characters named are not very precisely documented, with the exception of García Ordóñez. 'Didacus Petriz' certainly does not seem to have been 'unus ex maioribus Castelle' (*EDC*, pp. 733–36). Considered objectively, the whole incident seems rather unlikely. It is difficult to see how Alfonso's ex-commander-in-chief, García Ordóñez, would be able and willing to help one Moorish vassal against another, who was actually accompanied by an official messenger from the King. If this did take place, it does not seem to have affected the position of either man in the royal court. The story was, however, promulgated in fiction, and the relationship between Rodrigo Díaz and García Ordóñez, stemming in part from the Cabra incident, is an important factor in the *PMC*.[37] In the language of this account, 'gener Garsiae regis Pampilonensis' and 'unus ex maioribus Castelle' stand out as interesting epithets. There are a number of pairs of words of which 'tam sarracenorum quam christianorum' is the most reminiscent of a poetic pair, 'moros et christianos' (*PMC*, ll. 107, 145, 1242, etc.). There are three hours of battle, and three days of capture; 'tentoria et spolia' are collected, and 'munera et dona' received. The hero returns 'honorifice', but the passage closes with dramatic foreboding, 'causa invidie, de falsis et non veris rebus illum apud regem accusaverunt', reminiscent of literature.

Similarly, the incursion into Toledan lands, which is briefly recounted in the *HR* after the Cabra incident, has possible poetic features. Word pairs, especially 'inter viros et mulieres' (compare *PMC*, ll. 17, 541), some direct speech, a dominant feature of epic, and an unlikely number of seven thousand captives suggest a fictional source, while the mention of Gormaz is an interesting coincidence with the geography of the *PMC*. There is no independent evidence recording or hinting at such an event as this outside the *HR*, but as far as the history is concerned, this adventure is the direct cause of the exile of the hero. Unlike the Cabra incident, however, the Toledan incursion does not seem to have left any visible reflection on known later poetic versions of this period in the hero's life. It is not possible to say for certain whether it featured in the lost part of the *PMC*, though Pidal thinks it did not (*CMC*, p. 1024, note 1).

Beyond these opening sections, possible poetic features become less frequent. One small point, which evokes interesting thoughts, is raised by the first sentence of *HR*, 12, the beginning of the hero's exile: 'Ille autem de regno

Castelle exiens Barcinonem venit, amicis suis in tristicia relictis.' There is no more about this visit to Barcelona, for in the very next sentence Rodrigo has moved on to Zaragoza. To draw any dramatic conclusions from this, with its rather strange, unexplained 'amicis . . . relictis' would of course be foolish, but it does bring to mind the unexplained reference in *PMC*, ll. 962–63:

> dentro en mi cort tuerto me tovo grand
> firiom el sobrino e non lo enmendo mas.

These words of the Count of Barcelona obviously refer to an incident sufficiently well known for the *PMC* not to have to explain it at all. This reference in the *HR* is the only one surviving to any visit by the Cid to Barcelona, and the poem offers one reason for the briefness of the visit.[38]

The enmity between Rodrigo and the Count of Barcelona itself provides the climax of the first 'cantar' of the *PMC*. It is to all appearances the same incident which is related in the *HR*, 37–41, though of course rather differently from the poem. As stated above, Pidal saw possible influence of a poetic tradition on this section of the *HR*. He saw this in coincidences in the *PMC* and the *HR* resulting from a common source, a 'canto noticiero', and in one phrase of the *HR* 'dentibus suis cepit fremere' (*EDC*, p. 382, note 2). Other linguistic detail could be added, such as the list of booty: 'multa vasa aurea et argentea, et vestes preciosas, mulos et equos, palafredos, lanceas, loricas, scuta et omnia bona quecumque' (*HR*, 40). However, in general terms, it is clear that a tradition of enmity between the Count and the Cid and the blustering figure of the Count, repeated in the *PMC*, are present in the *HR*. Other elements, too, later to become firmly established in the poetic tradition are present. These include the separation and reunion of Rodrigo and his family, and the battle of Cuarte, though much of the *HR* is concerned with political matters which do not seem to have inspired the popular imagination.

The purpose of this study of the *HR* has been to see what features of the poetic tradition are traceable in the work, and to examine how the work supports the faith in its historical veracity which has been previously affirmed. What is clear is that there are elements present which do form part of the legendary and poetic tradition at various stages of its development. The historicity of the work is a more difficult question. It seems obvious that great care needs to be taken before placing trust in what the text says. It is clearly based on a variety of sources, including legendary tradition, documents, perhaps Arabic accounts or texts in Latin prose, and so on. The source material used, however, is patchy and unreliable, or at least it is used unreliably. Pidal himself unconsciously documents the case for doubting the veracity of the text. There are its omissions, which he conscientiously lists, some of them hard to explain in his own terms: the siege of Zaragoza by Alfonso, for example, in an author who mentions much about the city. The attack by Alfonso on Valencia is an 'omisión que no pudo existir en el original', if, that is, Pidal's conclusions are correct. There are errors, or signs of inadequate knowledge, such as in the account of Cuarte, or in the misplacement of the interview between Rodrigo and Pedro of Aragón. There are inconsistencies, such as the long account of the ambush at Rueda, which Pidal calls 'chocante', and the varying techniques found in the 'segunda parte' and 'cuarta parte' (see *EDC*, pp. 906–20).[39]

This text with its confusion of sources and styles cannot be shown to be inaccurate except in a few instances, but to accept what cannot be shown to be inaccurate as historical fact seems a dubious procedure. The evidence for saying that the chronicler actually uses a poem is admittedly weak. The linguistic evidence cited above is, at the very most, only suggestive. Nevertheless, the mixed nature of the text and the lack of historical support for events which fit so well into the poetic, legendary tradition at least persuades one of a likely manipulation of history by imaginative minds, if not of the complete fabrication of stories. Moreover, Pidal's views on the date and the reliability of the *HR* are readily challenged, and once they are undermined, a revaluation of the whole text is clearly needed.

It seems most satisfactory to see the *HR* as a tribute to Rodrigo Díaz based on respect and admiration, but composed at some distance from the events. It is logical to consider that the appearance in the *HR* of elements of the popular tradition is due to the direct influence of that tradition on the author, and that the author used this tradition together with the other sources at his disposal to fashion his intriguing but unsatisfactory biography. The tales known to the composer of the history were obviously not those best known to us. To approach the tradition known to him we can only extract what seem to be probable features of the legend from his text, and place them in the context of what we do know. It does seem that there were more stories than those reflected in the *PMC*, but that much of the background structure of relationships surrounding the poem was already being created. A date of forty or fifty years after the death of Rodrigo would allow time for a tradition to have developed and become known over a wide area of Spain, but of course what is history and what is tradition is not easily identifiable. The *HR*, then, allows us to glimpse the developing legend of the hero, though this is heavily disguised and only partially employed by the admirer of the hero who composed the chronicle.

C.   Chronica Adefonsi Imperatoris

Apart from the *Historia Roderici* and *Carmen Campidoctoris*, in which Rodrigo Díaz is the protagonist, there are two other Latin works of the twelfth century in which the hero is mentioned. Although in both the references to him are only brief, they are of considerable interest.

The first of these, the *Chronica Adefonsi Imperatoris* (*CAI*) is an account of the reign of Alfonso VII of León and Castile, and a prolonged eulogy of the king and his court. Written about 1148, the work is in three clearly divided sections, parts one and two in prose and part three in verse. It is in part three, which is written in hexameters, and is normally known as the *Poema de Almería*, since it recounts the siege of that city in 1147, that the mention of the Cid occurs. The author of the work is now thought to be Arnaldo, Bishop of Astorga, though various other suggestions have been made in the past. He was, in any case, well-educated and a cleric. Biblical influence on the language has been clearly demonstrated, epic in Latin has been suggested as an influence, and features later found in vernacular epic style have been noted in the work.[40]

The mention of the Cid in the *Poema de Almería* occurs in the context of the eulogy of a member of the royal court, one 'Alvarus Roderici'. He is a descendant of Alvar Fáñez, and is honoured by the nobility and distinction of his ancestor, with whom the Cid is associated, beside the famous heroes of French epic poetry. The relevant lines are these:

> Tempore Roldani si tertius Alvarus esset
> post Oliverum, fateor sine crimine verum,
> sub iuga Francorum fuerat gens Agarenorum . . .
>
> Ipse Rodericus, Meo Cidi saepe vocatus,
> de quo cantatur quod ab hostibus haud superatur,
> qui domuit Mauros, comites domuit quoque nostros
> hunc extollebat se laude minore ferebat
> sed fateor verum quod tollet nulla dierum:
>
> Meo Cidi primus fuit, Alvarus atque secundus,
> morte Roderici Valentia plangit amici
> nec valuit Christi famulus ea plus retinere.
>
> (*Poema de Almería*, ll. 215–17, 220–27)

This passage enables us to confirm some conclusions which were strongly implied in the *HR*, and to approach others about the state of popular diffusion of stories of the Cid at the time of this text; for the dating of the *CAI* to 1147–49 is in no doubt, making it contemporaneous with the *HR*, a mere half-century after Rodrigo's death and well before the surviving *PMC* was written down.

The most obvious and most important observation is that there undoubtedly was a popular poetic tradition about Rodrigo Díaz well established by this time. There were stories of him sung, and sung in the vernacular, and sung frequently. This can be concluded from the oft-quoted 'Meo Cidi, saepe vocatus, de quo cantatur'. The vernacular name is strong evidence of popular diffusion. It is the first time it appears in any text, and its appearance in a Latin text of some erudition is clear testimony to its widespread use and acceptance. It can be deduced, too, that the tales had circulated sufficiently widely and for a long enough period for these brief references to be enough for the chronicle's readers to know what the author had in mind. Not even the surname is required, simply 'Ipse Rodericus, Meo Cidi saepe vocatus', and everyone must have understood. Similarly, the easy mention of the Cid and Alvar Fáñez beside the great French heroes of epic legend, Roland and Oliver, who had done great deeds for the Christian faith, deeds which had survived for centuries in legend, shows the heights of popularity and esteem to which our hero's reputation had already climbed.[41]

As to the content of the stories known by the *CAI*, some features are referred to by implication, though not many. Not surprisingly, Valencia must have played an important part as it is singled out for mention. No doubt, its capture is seen as an inspiration for the besiegers of Almería. More interestingly, there was clearly established by this time a close link between the Cid and Alvar Fáñez: 'Meo Cidi primus fuit Alvarus atque secundus.' This association survives strongly into the *PMC*: 'Cavalgad, Mynaya, vos sodes el mio diestro brazo' (1. 753). In the poem, the two men rely on one another to a great extent, so that the relationship is like the one the *CAI* implies. The invincibility of the hero already mentioned in *HR*, 74, is reiterated here. Finally, the hemistich 'comites domuit quoque nostros' reveals another theme in the stories, though one which is slightly obscure. 'Comites nostros' may refer to the Counts of Barcelona or to the nobles of León and Castile with whom the Cid had disagreements, or it may refer to a combination of both. The use of 'nostros' in a work centred on León (see Sánchez Belda) would suggest it was not referring to Catalan nobles, so it is probably the enmity of the Cid towards the Castilian and Leonese nobility that is brought out as one of his well-known attributes. At first sight, it seems strange to see an author praising someone for defeating his own side, but this is obviously due to the exaltation of the hero in the legendary tradition to a level at which defeat by him is not regarded as a disgrace to the descendants of the defeated.

This brief Latin text reflects the legend of the hero half a century after his death, and little more than half a century before the *PMC*. The most notable feature of what is reflected is the sheer breadth of the tradition revealed at this early stage: a vernacular tradition, a well-known tradition, and yet a tradition respectfully cited in a work of erudition written to please the Emperor of León and Castile himself.

D. *Crónica Najerense*

The other mid-twelfth-century historical work to mention the Cid is the *Crónica Najerense*. First published as the 'Chronique léonaise' by Cirot, it survives in the same two manuscripts in which the *HR* survives. Studies by Pidal and others show that the work was compiled at Santa María de Nájera in La Rioja in the decade following the composition of the *CAI*. It is an annalistic chronicle, probably written by a French monk of the monastery. It is the first general history of the León and Castile area which was not written under the auspices of the royal court of its time, and, although it does use the main series of Asturian–Leonese official chronicles as sources, it uses other sources as well, including local stories from Nájera, and tales taken from heroic legends. As Pidal says, 'la *Najerense* aparece como la primera historia castellana, y ella hace la primera catalogación de la floreciente épica castellana' (*Reliquias*, p. xliii). This 'catalogación' consists of mention of five heroic tales, which are distinguished from the rest of the dry annalistic history by the introduction of direct speech, presumably under the influence of epic presentation, by the interest of the characters that appear, and by the intrigue and drama of the events recounted. The stories are not told at any great length, for the whole work is concisely written and not very extensive.[42]

Fortunately, the epic tale afforded most space in the *Najerense* is one in which Rodrigo Díaz plays a part. If the conclusions reached above about the sources of the *HR* are correct, then the *Najerense* is not the first history to use heroic tales of the Cid as sources. But the two texts are very different in that the *HR* is really a biography, while the *Najerense* is a national chronicle; in addition, the *Najerense* clearly uses other poetic tales showing that the Cid was not the only topic of interest to the poetic tradition of the time. In fact, in the story in which Rodrigo appears in the *Najerense*, his role is a subsidiary one. The lost epic, which is believed to lie behind this part of the *Najerense* and behind the corresponding sections of later chronicles in varying forms, is normally known as the *Cantar de Sancho II y cerco de Zamora* (*CSZ*). This tale recounted the internecine struggles which took place in northern Spain after the death of Fernando I (1065) and his 'partición' of his kingdom between his three sons, and which ended in 1072 with the emergence of Alfonso VI after the death of his elder brother Sancho II, 'el fuerte' or 'el bravo'.[43]

In the version provided by the *Najerense*, the Cid, who is always referred to as Rodericus Campidoctus or simply Rodericus, plays a minor role compared to the royal protagonists. He does, however, appear at vital moments, as will be seen. He first appears in an intriguing set-piece with King Sancho in the Castilian army camp, on the night before the battle of Golpejera against Alfonso and his Leonese army. Sancho is in boastful mood: 'Si illi numerosiores, nos meliores et forciores. Quin immo lanceam meam mille militibus, lanceam vero Roderici Campidocti, centum militibus comparo' (*Najerense*, 34). Rodrigo modestly demurs, so Sancho suggests fifty of the enemy as a suitable comparison, then forty, thirty, twenty, and finally ten, while Rodrigo declines to say more than 'cum uno se cum Dei adiutorio pugnaturum, et quod Deus permitteret facturum.' Reig pointed out the 'fortitudo-sapientia' contrast in the relationship between the two men. Moderation and wisdom are characteristic of the Cid's heroic persona, at least until the wilder stories of his youth begin to appear. Following the account of the debate, the day of the battle of Golpejera arrives. Both Kings are captured by their enemies, but Rodrigo confronts the fourteen Leonese who are leading Sancho away. Very reasonably, he offers a straight exchange of monarchs, which the Leonese rudely reject. He then dares them to give him a lance to challenge them. They do this, and he puts them to rout, 'ut de illis XIIII non evaderet nisi unus gravissime sauciatus' (*Najerense*, 36). Sancho is freed, Alfonso is in captivity and victory is achieved. The Cid's role is vital, for it is he who makes the difference in the battle; through him the kingdom is won and lost. It is interesting to note the similarity of this act of prowess by Rodrigo to the one related in the *HR* where he defeats fifteen Zamorans single-handed. In both, the numbers are similar and there is precise numerical information about the fate of the vanquished. It is tempting to suggest they are variations of what is basically the same tale adapted by a poet to suit the context, but there is, of course, no further evidence in support of this. The third and final intervention of the hero in the tale told by the *Najerense* is at a very dramatic moment in the siege of Zamora. 'Quidam filius perditionis Bellidus Ataulfus' has just foully murdered King Sancho. As he is making his way coolly through the Castilian camp, Rodrigo speaks to him, asking where the King is. The traitor spurs his horse and dashes for Zamora. Rodrigo leaps on to a horse and gives chase; but the city gates open and, 'arrepta lancea, illum insequitur inter portas semiclausas, lancea proditoris equum percutit fugientis'. Rodrigo returns to the camp lamenting his dead monarch (*Najerense*, 43). He takes no further part in the story told by the chronicle. Sancho is buried and Alfonso returns from Toledo to assume the throne.

All the appearances of the Cid in this chronicle show how he has become a prominent historical personality, despite the fact that he is not of royal blood. His importance in the *Najerense* version of the *CSZ* must reflect his great fame in the minds of the people of this time. He is introduced as 'Rodericus Campidoctus' without any explanation of who or what he is. His participation in events, when considered objectively, is almost superfluous. His role could have been omitted, certainly in the pursuit scene, where it produces no result, similarly in the pre-battle debate, which is unnecessary; and even the occasion on which his intervention wins the day might have been left out, reflecting, as it does, so little credit on the monarch. As can be seen, no part of Rodrigo's adventures, when Alfonso is on the throne, has been included by the compiler of the *Najerense*, though the *CAI*, for example, shows there can be no doubt these stories were widely known. It seems probable, as Pidal suggests in *Reliquias* (p. xlii, note 2), that the chronicler's main concern was the history of the royal house of Castile. Material not connected with this was therefore omitted, however well known. The stories of the Cid which are included are connected with the King, and with the famous hero, hence their justification.

Reig pointed out in her study of the *CSZ* that the version found in the *Najerense* has features which are more fictionalized than later versions. The conversation between Rodrigo and Sancho never appears again, and elsewhere in the story there are extreme novelesque or folkloric features, such as a bastard who kidnaps a queen, which are not found again. This, of course, goes against Pidal's established theory of 'el inevitable avance de las refundiciones épicas desde el verismo inicial a la novelización progresiva' (*Reliquias*, p. xli). In this case, features of 'novelización' appear in the earliest known account, but not in subsequent ones.

As regards the general state of the heroic tradition of the Cid, the *Crónica Najerense* is notable for the evidence it provides of the importance of the figure of Rodrigo in the civil wars. His role is wide in scope. It illustrates how the heroic figure, made famous by tradition, appears in new situations because he is a popular figure. It is Rodrigo whom Sancho chooses to praise. It has to be Rodrigo who happens to meet the King's murderer, and who realizes why the villain flees. It has to be Rodrigo who finds and frees the King at Golpejera. For it is he who is the famous hero, the great and loyal warrior, whose presence at the important moments in the history of his time is expected. He is the protagonist on the stage, on whom the spotlight so often falls. It is apparent from the *CAI* and the *Najerense* that by the middle of the twelfth century, the legendary figure of Rodrigo Díaz was large in stature and had acquired great heroic charisma. He had a central role in traditions which gave him an important position in the history of the reign of Sancho II, which associated him closely with Alvar Fáñez and the city of Valencia, and which were widely diffused in society. This much can be deduced from little evidence; but what a pity it is that we have no more.[44]

E.   The 'Liber Regum' and 'Linaje del Cid'

After the mid-twelfth-century Latin historical works, there is a gap of a few decades before the appearance of new evidence of popular traditions concerning the Cid. This fresh evidence comes in the oldest surviving historical work in a Spanish vernacular dialect, the *Liber Regum* (*LR*). Normally included as part of this work is the *Linaje del Cid*, which seems in fact to be a distinct though related text, of perhaps a slightly earlier date.

The *LR* was first published by Flórez in 1761, under the heading 'Genealogías de los reyes de Castilla, Navarra, Francia y del Cid', though elsewhere he does call it the *Liber Regum*. His text, which is in Castilian, begins with Rodrigo, the last of the Goths, describes the genealogies of the ruling houses of Asturias and Castile, of Navarre, of Aragón, and of France, and concludes with the *Linaje del Cid*, a brief but detailed genealogy-cum-biography of the hero. The next editor of the *Liber Regum*, Serrano y Sanz, called his text the

Cronicón Villarense (*Liber Regum*) after Martínez de Villar, a former owner of the manuscript he used. This version begins at the very beginning, with 'la generacion de Adam troa Ihu Christ', lists the Kings of Persia and the Emperors of Rome before arriving in Spain with the Goths. From Rodrigo the last of the Goths it follows the same pattern as Flórez's *LR*, until it breaks off abruptly, in mid-sentence, in the middle of the genealogy of the royal house of Aragón: 'dierenli muller a la nieta del. . . .' It continues with the 'reyes de Francia', but ends definitively with the last of these. It is in Navarrese dialect. More recently, a third version of the *LR* was published by Ubieto Arteta, from a different manuscript. This is a shorter text, including only the genealogy of the Kings of Aragón, which ends at the same point as in Serrano's manuscript, and the *Linaje del Cid*, and it is found in the *Fueros de Sobrarbe y de Navarra*. It has the same lacuna as in Serrano's version, but does not have the lineage of the Kings of France. Like Serrano's text, Ubieto's is in the original dialect, Navarrese.[45]

Serrano considered that the text published by Flórez, because of its inclusion of the section missing from his and the addition of the *Linaje*, constituted a 'versión aumentada' of the *LR*. Pidal (*EDC*, pp. 973–74) developed this idea into a 'redacción primera' and a 'redacción segunda' for Serrano's and Flórez's versions, respectively; but Ubieto, in his introduction to his edition, points out that they are not different in content, merely in length, though he continues to use the labels 'primera' and 'segunda redacción'. Furthermore, despite what Ubieto seems to imply, his edition and that of Flórez do not differ substantially in their versions of what is not found in Serrano. In the passages that are common to two, or even to all three versions, there are variations in wording and forms of words, abbreviations in one text or another of the content, and many errors of transcription. Moreover, as has been said, Flórez's version is in Castilian, based on a translation from the original Navarrese, which is the dialect of the other two. However, when they coincide, all three cover the same ground in virtually the same way.[46]

In short, there are not two distinct versions of the *LR*, but three manuscripts which contain portions of differing lengths of what is, essentially, the same text. The 'Linaje de los reyes de Francia' is in two of the three manuscripts, but its omission from the third implies it was not an integral part of the *LR*. Moreover two of the three manuscripts include the *Linaje del Cid*. The omission from one implies, again, that the *Linaje* was not an integral part of the *LR*, and indeed the royal genealogies and the *Linaje* have been dated by Ubieto as being a few years apart, though their similarities in language and in content, and their juxtaposition in manuscripts, strongly suggest composition in the same area, or even in the same religious house. For the remainder of this study, the term *Liber Regum* will be used to refer to the genealogies of the royal houses, and the term *Linaje del Cid* to refer to the section devoted principally to the Castilian hero.

The *Linaje del Cid* begins with the ancestors of its subject, from 'Layn Calbo' onwards, on the male side, and naming his mother and maternal grandfather. The ancestry given is substantially the same as in the *HR*. However, the *Linaje* fills a lacuna in the *HR* (see *EDC*, p. 921, note 1), and in addition it places the name of 'Nueno Rasuera' alongside that of 'Layn Calbo', stating 'Et fueron anvos iudices de Castieylla. Del linage de Nueno Rasuera vino l'Emperador. Del linage de Layn Calvo [vino mio Cid el Campiador]'.[47] This reference to the two judges chosen by the Castilians, brief as it is, seems to be the earliest surviving one in any text. Pidal recognizes that this first appearance of the tradition is late, but nevertheless believes the tradition to be historical (see *EDC*, p. 93, note 1, and p. 123, note 3). Laín Calvo is named as the first of the male line in the family tree given by the *HR*, but there is no mention of Nuño Rasura, nor of the judges of Castile. What this particular passage certainly does do in terms of the Cidian tradition is to name the hero in direct association with very distinguished company. His ancestry is compared to that of the royal house of Castile and of the Emperor himself. It proves to be equally distinguished; his blood is as honourable as that of the rulers of Castile. This noble ancestral line does not go well with the view of Rodrigo Díaz expressed by the anti-Cid faction in the *PMC*, but it does seem an acceptable step within a tradition which decades earlier had ranked him in military prowess with Roland and Oliver (see II, *D*, *CAI*, above).

After the genealogy, the *Linaje* moves on to the successes of 'Rodic Diaz' under the auspices of King Sancho, who is said to have knighted him. Here, as in the *Najerense*, Rodrigo frees his lord after his capture in battle by his enemies. But here the battle is at 'Sanct Aren' against King García, not Golpejera against Alfonso as in the Latin chronicle. In the *Linaje*, there are none of the conversational details before the battle, nor are there details about the number of opponents involved. Instead, Rodrigo captures García in addition to freeing Sancho. Golpejera and Alfonso are, in fact, then mentioned, but no special deed is recounted, merely that 'no ovo migor cavero de Rodic Diaz'. At the siege of Zamora, Rodrigo does put to rout 'grant conpanya de cavalleyros' in a way reminiscent of his exploit in the *HR*. Moreover, he pursues 'Belid Alfons' back to the city, as in the *Najerense*, but this time he manages to wound the traitor himself, and not merely his horse.

During Alfonso's reign, the hero fights two duels, as in the *HR*. For the first of these the *Linaje* provides an epithet for the Cid's opponent, 'Xemen Garzeyz de Turrillas', an epithet which Pidal says cannot be historically accurate (*EDC*, p. 693), and for the second, which is only in Flórez's text, the *Linaje* gives the name of the opponent, 'el Moro Harizuno', both new details. There is some interesting linguistic usage in the *Linaje*'s account of the 'destierro' of Rodrigo, 'pues lo yto de tierra el rey don Alfonso a Rodic Diaz a [grand] tuerto asi que non lo merecio que fue mesturado con el rey et yssios de su tierra'. The word 'mesturado' is particularly reminiscent of the *PMC* (e.g., *PMC*, l. 267). The incident at Tévar is recounted, again with some interesting linguistic features. Then after the capture of Valencia, when the *Linaje* begins to use the term 'meo Cid' consistently in place of its previous 'Rodic Diaz', we read that the Cid fought off an attacking army, 'et ovo y XIII reyes et la otra gent non avia cuenta'. The number of kings is an odd one. It seems to have no parallel anywhere else. The death of the hero is placed specifically 'en el mes de mayo', whilst the *HR* gives 'mense julio'. Finally, the *Linaje* sets down, for the first time as far as we are concerned, the fate of the Cid's own family. His son Diego is killed at Consuegra. His daughters, Cristina and María, marry 'l'ifant don Romiro' and the Count of Barcelona respectively. The text closes by explaining the brief descendancy from the daughter of the Cid and 'don Romiro' to King Sancho of Navarre, 'a qui Dios de vida y honra' (which helps to explain the Navarrese origin of the *Linaje*).

The effect of this final linking of Rodrigo with the ruler of Navarre is similar to the juxtaposition of the ancestries of Rodrigo and of the rulers of Castile discussed earlier. It ennobles Rodrigo's family and it enhances the dignity of the King of Navarre by attributing such a famous ancestor to him. The two associations considered together clearly show the high status which the hero has attained. In this context, it is interesting to consider the *LR*; for in the royal genealogies the Cid is mentioned twice, in phrases which seem to be taken directly from the *Linaje*. The first of these is the association of the Cid and the Emperor of Castile, and the second is the marriage of the Cid's daughter into the house of Navarre and the subsequent descendancy. In other words, this elevation of the hero to almost regal rank is found not only in a text devoted principally to him, but also in a text devoted principally to the royal houses of Spain.[48]

The *Linaje* is only some six or seven hundred words in length, but it is indeed a rich text in the corpus of evidence which reveals to us the progress of our protagonist's history at this early, but vital, stage. Pidal uses some of the information provided as historical fact. For example, it seems to be the only independent evidence for the death (and life?) of Diego Ruiz, the Cid's only son, and the best evidence concerning the marriages of the daughters.[49] But, generally, it has been a rather neglected text, whose value has been under-estimated. It stands as the last of those texts which conceivably contain accurate historical evidence. It is the first text in romance rather than in Latin, and we see for the first time in the vernacular the full range of names, 'Rodric Diaz', 'el Canpeador', 'meo Cid'. Inadequate as it may be, it is the only surviving evidence outside the *PMC* of what were the current traditions about the Cid's life between the mid-twelfth-century texts and those of the fourth and fifth decades of the next century.

As regards the development of the legendary figure, the most notable aspects of the *Linaje* are the enhancement of the status of the family already considered, the further twists to the hero's exploits in the civil wars between Alfonso, García, and Sancho, and the general accumulation of odd detail at various points. The number of similarities between the *Linaje* and the *HR* does raise the possibility of direct dependence of the *Linaje*. However, the *Linaje* always adds information to what is in the *HR* even when the similarities are great; moreover, so much of the *HR* is not in the *Linaje* that an extremely discreet use of the *HR* would have to be imagined by the author of the *Linaje*, who, in addition, must have had very persuasive alternative sources. A more satisfactory explanation of similarities would be a common source or sources for the sections in question. The most striking of these is the genealogy (*HR*, 2; *Linaje*, p. 30). If it is accepted that genealogical history is one of the principal primitive motives of oral chant, as Bowra suggests (*Heroic Poetry*, p. 369), as a means of preserving accurate ancestries in non-literate societies, it seems at least possible that this genealogy reflects a piece of the story more accurately preserved than others because of its subject matter. An oral background may also explain the accretion of Nuño Rasura and the accompanying details.[50]

The *Linaje* and the *LR* are important texts. They stand at the turn of the century, one hundred years after Rodrigo's death. They were written down at approximately the same time as the *PMC* was being composed, yet there is no evidence of interdependence. They look back to the *HR* with their verbal parallels, and look forward to the Alphonsine chronicles which use them as sources. Brief, but full of detail, they provide many pieces to be fitted into the puzzle of heroic traditions about the Cid.

III. THE *PMC* AND THE PREVIOUS TRADITION

The *PMC* stands chronologically at the latter end of the series of texts examined in this chapter, and does not seem to have been directly dependent on any of them. It is now appropriate to consider the position of the history of Rodrigo Díaz as told in the *PMC* in relation to the tradition revealed in the earlier texts. These texts, unfortunately give us only glimpses of what stories must have circulated, and only two, the *HR* and *Linaje del Cid*, provide any substantial material. However, within the limitations of the available evidence, it is possible to make some informed deductions.

To begin with, there are many features of the tradition examined above which appear in the *PMC*. The broad structure of the hero's progress in the *PMC* is clearly owed to earlier tales. This involves the banishment from Castile by King Alfonso, the first peak of achievement in the defeat of the Count of Barcelona at Tévar, the capture of Valencia, and finally the death of Rodrigo while ruler of that city. To these essential features could be added the great battle of Cuarte in defence of Valencia. These events appear in earlier texts and in the *PMC*, and clearly formed the outline for any version of this period of Rodrigo's life. Then there is the human setting in which the hero moves, which lasts through to the *PMC*. As regards the immediate family, Jimena and the two daughters, who are so important in the poem, have appeared before as have noble husbands for the two girls. The names of the girls and the identity of one of the husbands are, however, completely different in the *PMC* and in their other appearance, in the *Linaje*. Very close to Rodrigo in a different way from his family is Alvar Fáñez. It has been seen earlier that he is quite categorically named in the *CAI*, in such a way as to imply, most strongly, a relationship with Rodrigo akin to that described in the *PMC*, and current half a century before it was composed. Among the enemies of the hero, García Ordóñez, the arch-villain of the *PMC*, more sinister than the pathetic Infantes, had appeared early in the tradition. Already in the *Carmen Campidoctoris* he is 'comitem super-bum', a quality he retains in the *PMC* (e.g., l. 3279).

Finally, amongst the elements in the *PMC* reflected in earlier texts, there are those episodes which are not actually retold in the poem, but to which reference is made, and which are known to us only in previous versions. The principal references, in this context, are those to Cabra (*PMC*, ll. 3287–88), and to the 'parias' which Raquel and Vidas believe the Cid had embezzled (*PMC*, ll. 109–11). Both the *HR* and the *Carmen* recount an incident at Cabra, and it seems to be basically the same one referred to in the *PMC*, although the famous pulling of Count García's beard appears only in the poem. The reference to 'parias' is also explained by the Cabra story in the *HR*. It is possible, of course, that the *PMC* in its complete form related in its missing initial section the story of Cabra and the insult to García. However, it is difficult to see how this incident could have led directly to the hero's banishment. In this case, another intermediary incident is required. This is provided by the raid on Toledan lands in the *HR*, but there is absolutely no trace of this as a cause for the Cid's exile in the *PMC*. No other explanation for the banishment is offered in early texts. The later chronicles are equally of no help, for they use the *HR* for this section. In them, the 'Jura de Santa Gadea' is the last incident (of unknown origin) before the exile, and it is interesting to note that this 'jura' appears for the first time in the first text after the date of the *PMC*, namely the *Chronicon Mundi* of Lucas de Tuy (1236) (see Chapter 2). However, the 'jura' has not left any visible trace on the poem. The debate over the beginning of the *PMC* will never be fully resolved without new evidence coming to light. But even ignoring its possible content, there are indisputable references in the *PMC* to events only known to us in earlier texts. In short, it is clear that the background to the *PMC* and many details therein had a previous existence of some years standing in the tradition of stories about the Cid. This much is evident, despite our limited knowledge of that tradition.[51]

Nevertheless, there are very important aspects of the *PMC* which leave no trace in earlier accounts. Scores of details, of course, are new. More than details, but equally new to us, are the battles of Alcocer and Castejón, and the battles against the Moors later in the poem, though the *HR* and the *Linaje* each refer to one. More importantly and more obviously, the whole episode of the marriages of the Cid's daughters to the Infantes de Carrión and their ramifications receives no mention at all before the poem. The marriages, the Infantes, the lion, the 'cortes', the duels — none of these is even hinted at in earlier texts concerned personally with Rodrigo. The omission of minor battles is understandable: the *HR* specifically states that it is omitting them for brevity. The omission of the other events is less comprehensible. They include marriages, which the *Linaje* normally finds interesting, and the lion incident, which becomes so famous later. They provide the overriding preoccupation for half the poem, and ultimately the most important theme in it. If they were as prominent in the popular stories about this period in Rodrigo's life as they are in the poem, it is very surprising that there is no earlier sign of them. The obvious implication is that they did not play a part in the traditions and, therefore, that they are the invention of the poet of the *PMC*.

Did the poet, then, use the stories known to him selectively, then create elements of his own? There is one observation concerning relationships in the poem which tends to support this view. It concerns the attitude expressed in the poem that the daughters of the Cid were not worthy partners for the Infantes de Carrión because of the lowly status of their family. This is stated forcefully in the final court scenes by the enemies of Rodrigo, and elsewhere in the poem by the Infantes (*PMC*, ll. 3270 ff., 1376, 2553). It is never challenged by the Cid or his supporters; indeed the Cid seems more or less to admit this (ll. 2084–85), although, at that moment, he is in an awkward situation. However, according to both the *HR* and the *Linaje*, Jimena, mother of the girls, was of royal birth (a granddaughter of Alfonso V of León), and, at least in the *Linaje*, the ancestry of the father himself was of the highest order, worthy of comparison with that of the Emperor of Castile. Royal families were pleased to count him as one of their ancestors, though this was largely due no doubt to his own merits rather than his noble ancestors. Respect for the Cid's lineage is implied in the *PMC* in the line 'Oy los reyes d'España sos parientes son' (*PMC*, l. 3724), which reflects the status given to him in the *Linaje*. The lack of this consciousness of status in the characters in the poem is useful artistically. It gives the Infantes an empty justification to enable them to persuade themselves of the rightness of their action, it underlines the vanity of them and their supporters, and it makes them look all the more foolish, since the audience probably knew what was to come in the very honourable second marriages.

It seems, therefore, that there is enough evidence to suggest that the *PMC* is not truly representative of the mainstream of traditional accounts of Rodrigo's life at the time of its composition. It is implied in the evidence that the poet took from the tradition what he required, added much of his own, probably using non-traditional sources, and glossed over that part of the tradition which did not suit him. What he took from the tradition was the framework of his protagonist's life, some of his personal relationships, and much of his personality, including his wisdom, his magnanimity to the defeated, his strength and valour, and his heroic charisma. What the poet seems to have contributed himself is the less military, more personal side of the work, the essential drama of the honour of the family man embodied in his children, the delicacy of the relationship between the lord, the vassal, and the family, and other basically human elements. What he has chosen to gloss over in the tradition, besides the Cid's third child Diego Ruiz, who appears only in the *Linaje* and would have no place in the *PMC*, is the honourable estate which the hero's family seems to have attained by the end of the twelfth century, as regards ancestry as well as contemporaneous honour.

The poet did well. He used the traditional structure and then applied his artistic judgement in developing his own poem. He seems to have been his own man, and to have gone his own way, as compared to the popular tradition. To judge by our evidence, this tradition was more interested in the period of the Castilian–Leonese civil wars, for which we find many more anecdotes and more variation, than in the period of the Cid's life covered by the *PMC*.[52] However, it is the *PMC* that is the literary masterpiece. It is what survives in the best state of preservation. It may not be at the heart of the tradition, but it is the only extensive example of the poetic tradition that we have. Moreover, as is well known, it was the most persuasive evidence that the Alphonsine chronicles could find when they came to document that section of Rodrigo Díaz's life.

CHAPTER 2

THE *POEMA DE MIO CID* AND THE
ALPHONSINE CHRONICLES OF SPAIN

I. THE LATIN PRECURSORS OF THE
ALPHONSINE CHRONICLES

After the composition of the *PMC* in the opening years of the thirteenth century, it is several decades before Rodrigo Díaz makes an appearance in any surviving text. He is then referred to in two major histories of Spain, both in Latin and both by leading clerics, the *Chronicon Mundi* of Lucas, Bishop of Tuy, and the *De Rebus Hispaniae* of Archbishop Rodrigo of Toledo. These two important chronicles bridge the gap between the earlier tradition of Latin histories by ecclesiastical authors, and the new tradition of vernacular chronicles established by Alfonso X, who used both the above works, and especially the *De Rebus Hispaniae*, as the structural basis for his *Estoria de España* (see below). Both Lucas and Rodrigo seem to have known and used fictional, probably poetic, sources, although sparingly. Pidal suggests that together they used up to eleven epic tales, but, as will be seen, it is unlikely that they knew the *PMC* in a form like that in which it has survived.

A. The 'Chronicon Mundi' of Lucas of Tuy

Lucas of Tuy, known as el Tudense, took his *Chronicon* up to the year 1236, and it was therefore completed in that year or shortly afterwards. The prime mover behind the work seems to have been Queen Berenguela, mother of Fernando III; this is made clear in the prologue: 'Astrictis praeceptis gloriosissimae ac prudentissimae Hispaniarum Reginae dominae Berengariae . . .' (p. 1).[1] The work begins with a eulogy of Spain, listing at length the country's features and its qualities, and this is followed by an account of the creation (pp. 2–6).[2] It is not until the fourth of the four 'libri', into which the history is divided, that we reach the beginnings of contemporary Spain, with the battle of Covadonga and the reign of King Pelayo. The work ends with the conquest of the old Moorish capital, Córdoba, by San Fernando, and the restoration of the bells of the cathedral of Santiago removed from there centuries earlier by Moslem raiders. Compared to previous historical works, such as the *Crónica Najerense*, the *Chronicon* is a big step forward. It is much longer and more ambitious. It uses legendary sources more frequently and more fully. Lucas's most interesting hero is not Rodrigo de Bivar, but the Leonese Bernardo del Carpio, whose feats include the defeat at 'Roscidaevallis' of Charlemagne and his army, in alliance with King Marsil of Zaragoza. Later, Charlemagne sensibly welcomed Bernardo into the ranks of his soldiers (p. 75). For his posthumous fame, Lucas was unfortunate to be followed so closely by Rodrigo Toledano, who was politically and ecclesiastically more important, and, in addition, more productive as a writer. Lucas provided Rodrigo with part of the basic structure of his history of Spain, and with much source material. Once described as 'Roderico praesuli toletano aequalis et in simili conscribendae historiae studio versus ingenio', Lucas has many interesting individual features, as can be seen in his references to Rodrigo Díaz.[3]

In general terms, the appearances of the Cid in the *Chronicon Mundi* are in similar vein to those found in the prose texts discussed in Chapter 1. Attention is centred on events related to the civil wars of 1065–1072 and therefore not within the scope of the *PMC*, although this period is by no means excluded. The hero is first seen at the battle of Golpejar: 'in illis diebus surrexerat miles quidam nomine Rodericus Didaci armis strenuus, qui in omnibus suis agendis extitit victor' (p. 98). The impressive language of this is noteworthy, as is the theme of the Cid's invincibility found as early as the *Carmen Campidoctoris*. Lucas goes on to relate how Rodrigo persuades King Sancho to regroup his forces after being driven from the battlefield by the army of his brother Alfonso. They attack the unsuspecting Alfonso at break of dawn put his men to rout, and capture Alfonso himself in the church of Santa María de Carrión (p. 98). Once more, as in the *Najerense* and the *Linaje del Cid* (see Chapter 1), we see a variation worked on the mode of victory in a civil-war battle, confirming the variability of the tradition. As in the *Najerense*, direct speech is used to report the Cid's advice to Sancho. Rodrigo does not appear at Zamora in the *Chronicon*, but the basic story is the same as elsewhere, with Vellido Dolfos playing his customary role as assassin of Sancho (pp. 99–100). The hero does appear, however, in a new context after the murder of Sancho. When Alfonso returns from exile in Toledo to assume Sancho's crown, the Castilian and Navarrese nobles demand that he swear his innocence of any involvement in the regicide. Lucas continues: 'Cum nullus esset, qui iuramentum a Rege auderet accipere, suprafatus Rodericus Didaci strenuus miles iuramentum a Rege accepit. Quapropter Rex Adefonsus semper habuit eum exosum' (p. 100). This is the earliest extant account of the 'Jura de Santa Gadea' as it is known from its setting in later accounts in the church of that name in Burgos (unless an elliptical reference to such an event is read into *Carmen Campidoctoris*, lines 41–44). As I stated towards the end of the first chapter, it is a fact that this piece of drama appears in the text chronologically next after the *PMC*. It gives a good reason for Alfonso's antipathy towards Rodrigo, and it is repeated and expanded with poetic details in all later chronicles. Pidal thought it an historical event, but there is no proof of this, and it seems unlikely.[4] Moreover, an actual link with the *PMC* is improbable, especially in view of the arguments against Lucas's having known the *PMC* put forward below. Rather, the 'jura' exemplifies the pattern of how the hero becomes more and more prominent in the popular history of his era, and how his appearance in new episodes occurs because of the stature his figure had attained.

The third mention of the Cid in the *Chronicon Mundi* does indeed concern the period covered by the *PMC*. The complete quotation is: 'Eodem tempore Rodericus Didaci miles strenuus pugnavit cum Petro Rege Aragonum in campo, et cepit eum. Post haec obsedit Valentiam et cepit eam. Deinde vicit barbarorum Regem Buchar et interfecit multa millia Sarracenorum' (p. 101). First, the naming of Pedro of Aragón is surprising. He appears where one would expect to find the Count of Barcelona (compare *HR*, *Linaje*, *PMC*). Historically, he seems to have been the Cid's ally (see *EDC*, pp. 812–16), yet here he is opponent and victim of Rodrigo. There is no obvious explanation. Secondly, the other interesting name in the above passage is clearly that of Búcar, king of the Moors. Although this is his first appearance in a chronicle, from the *PMC* onwards, Búcar is a prominent character, and his name becomes inextricably linked with that of the Cid.[5] The obvious deduction is that Lucas took the name of Búcar and the large number of casualties from the *PMC* (see ll. 2311–2427). If he did, however, it is the only piece of the *PMC* that he uses, while the naming of Pedro of Aragón and not the Count of Barcelona is in direct contrast to the *PMC*. The other possibility is that both the poet of the *PMC* and Lucas himself draw separately on a tradition in which Búcar appeared. The independent existence of this tradition is supported by two further considerations. First, the poet of the *PMC* devotes most space, attention, and detail to those episodes he seems most likely to have added to the traditional tales. Examples are the captures of Alcocer and Castejón, and of course the marriage scenes.[6] Búcar, on the other hand is not given much attention, and it is implied he is already famous (l. 2314). Secondly, the strength of the figure of Búcar later, in the chronicles and in the ballads, and his variable fate (compare *PMC*, l. 2425; *PCG*, ch. 931) suggest an independent existence outside the *PMC*. The evidence that Lucas knew the *PMC* is weak. It must be said that the evidence in el Toledano's *De Rebus Hispaniae* tends to confirm the conclusion that he did not use the poem (see below).

It is clear, however, that Lucas did know of Rodrigo Díaz as an outstanding figure of his era. He uses a constant epithet, 'miles . . . armis strenuus, strenuus miles, miles strenuus', suggesting close association in his sources of an epithet with Rodrigo's name, possibly 'Campeador'. Two of Rodrigo's appearances in the *Chronicon* are related to the history of the royal house. The third mention is perhaps more notable, since it does not involve the mainstream history of León and Castile. For the hero's story, the *Chronicon* is not very different from the preceding prose texts. The stories of his exploits still vary and expand his role, and they still suggest a fluid form of existence. It is surprising that the *PMC* has had so little effect. The explanation would seem to be that its diffusion was not yet wide enough for Lucas to know it, or, if he knew it, it was not important enough in his eyes for him to take it into account.

B. The 'De Rebus Hispaniae' of Rodrigo Toledano

A mere handful of years after Lucas completed his history, a second Latin account of similar theme appeared, in 1243. This was the *Historia Gothica* or *De Rebus Hispaniae* (*DRH*) composed by Rodrigo Ximénez de Rada, Archbishop of Toledo, called el Toledano. El Toledano was an outstanding churchman, statesman, and historian, who had already been Archbishop of Toledo for thirty-three years when the *DRH* was finished (see *DRH*, Prologue). Apart from the *DRH*, his works include several other histories, of the Romans and the Moors, for example. Schott gives a succinct biography of him: 'Mater Navarra, Nutrix Castelle, Schola Parisii, Sedes Toletum, Hortus Mausoleum, Requies Caelum.'[7] Since much ground is covered in his other works, el Toledano's *DRH* does not have the universal nature of Lucas's work. Instead, it traces the history of the Goths as direct ancestors of the royal house of León and Castile, and of Spain after the Goths' arrival there. It is divided into nine 'libri'. Covadonga and Pelayo appear in book four, and Sancho II and Alfonso VI in book six. The whole work is dedicated to King Fernando III. El Toledano adds a little legendary material to that found in el Tudense, but tends to suppress some detail. He does make the first direct reference in the chronicles to popular tales and their tellers when he speaks of the 'histrionum fabulis', in order to contradict them.[8] As for the story of the Cid, el Toledano adds some minor details to previous texts, but relies mainly on two of them. For the first time, then, the principal sources used by a chronicler are known and can be identified. It is instructive to examine the compilation of sources as carried out by a thirteenth-century historian. El Toledano's sources in this section are the *Linaje del Cid* and the *Chronicon Mundi*.

The *DRH* first uses the *Linaje* when it gives the ancestry of the Cid from the judge of Castile, Laín Calvo (p. 82). Beside this, the descendants of the other judge, Nuño Rasura, are listed as far as Fernán González, of epic fame, a passage to be found in Lucas. For the battle of Golpejar (p. 101), el Toledano relies on Lucas's account, omitting the direct speech, but adding to Lucas's epithet 'miles strenuus' the vernacular-based 'Campiator', found in the *Linaje* (and in the *PMC*, of course). In other contexts, the *DRH* keeps the vernacular epithet, but drops the Latin one. As the Cid's intervention at Zamora was not mentioned by Lucas, here the *DRH* uses the *Linaje*, apparently glossing the

Linaje's simple text 'dioli una lancada', with 'fere in ipsa urbis ianua interfecit', referring of course to the hero's pursuit of Vellido Dolfos, the assassin (*DRH*, p. 103). Here, he does omit episodes in the *Linaje* not directly of concern to royal history: the defeat by the Cid of a group of Zamorans, and his victorious duel with Ximén Garcíez. He had earlier omitted the Cid's role at the battle of Santarem, probably because he had a better source for the account of this battle, and another version of King García's fate. For the 'Jura' administered by the Cid to Alfonso there was again only one text, Lucas. It is worth noting, however, that el Toledano does include the additional details that the Castilians and Navarrese met to decide what to do, and that they met at Burgos. These may be el Toledano's own contributions.

Thus far, there have been no problems for el Toledano in presenting his information, now from one source, now from the other. It is when we come to the Cid's exile from Castile and the events thereafter that we see el Toledano having to blend his sources more carefully. Here, in brief, are the three accounts:

Linaje del Cid: the Cid is unfairly exiled by Alfonso. He defeats the Count of Barcelona at Tévar and frees him. He besieges Valencia, defeats a relieving army, and takes Valencia. He dies and is taken to Cardeña.

Chronicon Mundi: the Cid fights and captures Pedro of Aragón. He besieges and captures Valencia. He defeats Búcar and kills many Moors.

De Rebus Hispaniae: with a band of kinsmen and followers, the Cid invades Moorish lands. At the Aragonese border, he defeats, captures, and releases Pedro of Aragón. He besieges Valencia, defeats Búcar, who flees, leaving many dead. Valencia falls. The Cid lives there for the rest of his life; Jerónimo is made bishop by Archbishop Bernardo. The Cid dies and his body is taken, amid insults from the Moors, to San Pedro de Cardeña, where it still rests.

The most obvious facts are that the *DRH* account is much longer than the other two and it contains a number of additional details. It does combine the two earlier accounts quite skilfully with the new information. All the material from Lucas's version is included, but his story is not respected entirely, since his chronology of events at Valencia is altered. It is altered to suit the chronology in the *Linaje*, whose account of Tévar is, however, ignored, unless the detail of Pedro's release from captivity can be attributed to it.

We must also consider el Toledano's new information, in the order in which it is found. The Cid's exile is made voluntary, perhaps the author's own alteration to avoid placing Alfonso in a poor light. Companions for the Cid are specified, 'manu consanguineorum et militum aliorum', a phrase which brings to mind phrases of the later vernacular chronicles (see, for example, *PCG*, p. 523.b.7, 'sus parientes et sus amigos'). This scene must have been included in some form in the lost part of the *PMC*. Next, the *DRH* specifies the site of the defeat of Pedro of Aragón as 'versus frontariam Aragoniae', which is perhaps a reaction to the *Linaje*'s precise siting of the defeat of the Count of Barcelona. More interestingly, to Lucas's information about Búcar, el Toledano adds that he escaped 'vix vitae relictus'. This is an assertion in direct conflict with the *PMC*, where Búcar is killed by the Cid himself, and where his death is repeatedly mentioned (see *PMC*, ll. 2425, 2458, 2475, 2522–23, etc.). In the later version of these events as found in the *PCG*, for example, Búcar does escape, albeit wounded, rather as implied in the *DRH* (*PCG*, p. 606.b.26–28). The two conflicting versions of Búcar's fate would seem to show that el Toledano did not know or did not use the *PMC*. Further new information is provided after the capture of Valencia. The bishop, Jerónimo, a character in the *PMC*, is said to have been appointed by Archbishop Bernardo, suggesting an ecclesiastical source for the information. El Toledano's information on the ecclesiastical affairs of Alfonso VI's reign is, not surprisingly, both full and detailed. It is reflected in the vernacular chronicles (for example, *PCG*, pp. 540 ff.). As the Cid's body left Valencia, the *DRH* informs us that it left 'inter insultus Arabum', which may indicate an Arabic source, for Moslem historians were generally unfavourably disposed towards the Christian conqueror of Valencia. Finally, Archbishop Rodrigo adds the contemporary information that the Cid's body still lies at San Pedro de Cardeña.

Overall, the *DRH* version of the affairs of the Cid contains only a few new points of interest. What it adds to the *Chronicon Mundi* is taken mainly from the *Linaje del Cid*. Some of the additional details may come from the compiler himself, as he rewrote and expanded his sources, or they may be reflections of sources known to him in learned or popular form. The most surprising conclusion to be drawn from a close study of the relevant sections of the *DRH* is that the *PMC* was almost certainly not known to el Toledano. Apart from the points raised in the examination of the *Chronicon Mundi* above, it seems impossible that the Archbishop could take Búcar from the poem, and then categorically change his fate, thus robbing the Cid of one of his main personal military triumphs in the poem. Moreover, the *Linaje*, one of el Toledano's known sources, agrees with the *PMC* on the battle of Tévar, but the *DRH* ignores the incident. The mere fact that el Toledano and el Tudense use the name Búcar does not show that they knew the *PMC*. Búcar must have come from another poetic source, whose version of events in this episode establishes itself in the later chronicles.[9]

It was not until a few decades after Rodrigo completed his *DRH* that Alfonso X and his collaborators eventually took up the *PMC* together with all the other texts they could find which might help them to write the history of Spain. Pride of place amongst all these texts went to el Toledano's *DRH*, closely followed by Lucas's *Chronicon Mundi*. Although not so important in those sections dominated by the Cid, a glance through the lists of sources for Pidal's *PCG* shows clearly the Alphonsine debt to his two precursors (see *PCG*, I, pp. lxxiii–cxxxii, II, pp. cxxxix–ccviii).[10] In a way, el Tudense and el Toledano's apparent lack of knowledge of the *PMC* makes the space they devote to the Cid greater evidence of his fame outside the poem. His reputation was clearly far-reaching, and did not depend for its stature on the *PMC* alone. Rather, it was a result of a flourishing tradition on which the poem itself drew.

II. THE ALPHONSINE CHRONICLES

The Alphonsine chronicles form a series of related chronicles of the history of Spain composed in the thirteenth and fourteenth centuries. They are called Alphonsine because their basic structure and much of their content stem from scholarly work carried out under the instructions of Alfonso X, el Sabio, King of León and Castile (1252–84), whose original aim was to write a comprehensive *Estoria de España* (*EE*). As will be seen below, it is doubtful whether this work was completed while Alfonso was alive, but his efforts gave a marked impetus to historiography, and the result was a number of chronicles, related, but distinct.[11] Alfonso's *EE* was to stretch from the Creation, via the history of Rome and the history of the Goths, to the kingdoms of León and Castile up to Alfonso's time. For most of the chroniclers who followed him, and for most people since, the interest is concentrated on the Asturo–Leonese and Castilian periods of dominance. The later chronicles vary in length but fall mainly within this span. All the chronicles are in the vernacular. Alfonso's dedication to the promotion of Castilian as a medium of prose writing gave an important impetus to its development. The chronicles form a series because they are so close structurally and often verbally that they either descend one from another, or have a common principal source in some form. The chronicles in question will be examined below in the following order: *Estoria de España* (*EE*), *Primera crónica general* (*PCG*), *Crónica de veinte reyes* (*CVR*), *Crónica de los reyes de Castilla* or *Crónica de Castilla* (*CRC*), *Tercera crónica general* (*TCG*), *Crónica de 1344* (*C1344*), and a chronicle in the form of summarized chapters, the *Crónica abreviada*. All these works contain the story of Cid at great length, but no two tell it in exactly the same way. Only one uses the *PMC* in its entirety, although the poem's influence may occasionally be seen elsewhere. It is the use of the poem in the *CVR* that will occupy later chapters of this study, but for the moment I will consider these various products of the Alphonsine school of historiography, with particular regard to the constantly developing story of Ruy Díaz of Bivar.[12]

A. *Estoria de España*

The *Estoria de España* is the name used by Alfonso X himself to refer to his projected history of Spain 'desdel tiempo de Noe fasta este nuestro' (*PCG*,

p. 4.a.46–47). The name is used in the heading of the one manuscript thought to be an original copy of part of the *EE*, approved by Alfonso, and it is also found in the monarch's universal history, the *General estoria* (*GE*), where there are references to 'la nuestra Estoria que ficiemos de España', and 'la nuestra Estoria de España'. The past tense in the first of the above quotes, and the statement by Juan Manuel, nephew of Alfonso el Sabio that 'este muy noble rey don Alfonso . . . ordenó muy complidamente la Crónica d'España, e pusolo todo complido', imply that the *EE* was completed by Alfonso. However, the references to the *EE* in the *GE* are all in close proximity and all refer to early episodes in the history; and Juan Manuel in his *Crónica abreviada* summarizes a mixed version of the *EE* (see below).[13] The most prestigious manuscript of the *EE* is generally accepted to be a true product of Alfonso's schools. However, this manuscript, which fills one volume and part of a second, contains the history only up to about the year A.D. 800. At this point, there is a definite change of hand, and, from then on, the second volume, into which the final part of the manuscript is now bound, is a mixture of hands of various dates. Much of the volume can be attributed to work carried out under Alfonso's successor, Sancho IV, but none of it beyond the first hand can be attributed to work done under Alfonso X.[14] In fact, no manuscript exists of the later part of the *EE*, which can convincingly be attributed to the time of Alfonso X. Furthermore, it seems that the early part of the *EE* was not written in the last decade of Alfonso's reign, nor was it revised then. The re-burial of King Bamba in 1274 is not mentioned when his reign is recounted; repairs to the aqueduct of Segovia carried out by Alfonso are not referred to either. In other words, the royal scholar appears to have composed the early part of his *EE* before 1274, and thenceforth made no progress towards completing it.[15]

The most satisfactory explanation of the apparent abandonment of the *EE* lies in the all-embracing nature of Alfonso's other historical project, the mammoth, universal *General estoria*. As the *GE* got under way, perhaps Alfonso began to see that a universal history included and transcended the *EE*. As the *GE* grew in importance, so the *EE* was left behind. The sheer size of the *GE* may have been a factor: its six surviving 'partes' are each longer than a complete *EE* would have been, and yet they only reach the beginnings of the Christian era. Alfonso may not have had the time or resources to devote himself to much beyond the *GE*.[16] So the *EE* was completed by Alfonso only to approximately the year 800. However, the scholarly work of Alfonso's compilers still had an important influence on the later histories of the period after the beginnings of the ninth century. It is clear from the chronicles to be examined below, that a corpus of historical material covering the period after A.D. 800 must have existed in some form; for later writers were able to draw on it to create basically similar versions of the history of that period. The compilation of the source material must have taken place under the impetus given by Alfonso's historical projects. The extent to which the information was organized and synthesized during the reign of Alfonso is uncertain, but the successive versions in the later chronicles do suggest a certain amount of previous structuring of the material, into chapters or into annals perhaps, though the chronicles sometimes disagree on divisions and dates. Uncertain, too, is the source of the information which is new to each chronicle; it may come from outside the Alphonsine material, it may have been present there previously but not been used, or it may often stem from the independence and originality of the individual chronicler's approach.

Pidal was the first person to point out the existence of source material in a form no longer extant. He believed that the material was organized under Alfonso to the end of the *EE*, although in varying stages of completeness depending on the section of history concerned. This lost compilation he called the 'borrador', which he saw as the important element behind the Alphonsine chronicles, which enabled their authors to create their new versions, without being tied to a definitive text. It made possible the growth of 'tradicionalidad', that is, a popular tradition of chronicle writing, in which each version is an 'obra colectiva, nacional, que como toda obra tradicional se transmite en continua variante'.[17] Doubt has been expressed about Pidal's 'borrador' theory. Gómez Pérez pointed out that no 'borrador' survives for any of Alfonso's many works, and suggested that it is merely a convenient way of explaining the confused relationships between the vernacular chronicles without having to sort out the actual relationships between them. The fact remains, however, that the chronicles of the thirteenth and fourteenth centuries have not yet yielded sensible answers to explain their contradictory similarity and diversity, without the supposition of lost texts of early date and of considerable importance.[18] Although the *EE* of Alfonso never appeared in a definitive version, the potential *EE* in whatever form it existed played a vital role in the historiography of central and western Iberia for over a century. The manifestations of this 'potential *EE*' are examined below.

B.   *Primera crónica general*

Crónica General was used from an early date to refer to the Alphonsine chronicles, in preference to Alfonso's own title of *EE*. In *Leyenda*, Pidal referred to the 'primera Crónica escrita en romance castellano', and he expressed preference for two particular manuscripts of this 'Primera Crónica General', which had earlier been selected as best by the Marqués de Pidal, Gayangos, and Caveda (*Leyenda*, pp. 50–52). It was these two manuscripts, Escorial Y-i-2 and X-i-4, that formed the basis for Pidal's edition of Alfonso's chronicle. This edition has been the best known form of the *EE* ever since Pidal produced it, but the *EE*, and the *PCG*, Pidal's edition, are not to be identified with one another. Here, *PCG* refers only to this edition and version of the Alphonsine chronicle and to its few related manuscripts.[19]

(i) The value of the *PCG*

Unfortunately the two manuscripts used by Pidal as the base texts for his edition are not of equal worth. While the first, Esc. Y-i-2, is a consistent, finely decorated volume with every claim to be a genuine product of Alfonso X's workshops, the second volume, Esc. X-i-4, is rather a hotch-potch.[20] As early as 1874, Milá pointed out: 'debe notarse que la parte del "Escurialense" que habla de Bernaldo [del Carpio] es adición más o menos posterior a lo restante del códice, y acaso ya del siglo XV.' More recently, Diego Catalán has made a detailed study of X-i-4, which definitively undermines the validity of the manuscript as a whole, although individual sections, when treated as such, may still be of great value. Catalán's principal relevant conclusions are as follows.[21] X-i-4 is a composite manuscript of a number of originally independent sections, of various dates. The first seventeen folios of X-i-4 were removed from Y-i-2 (in order to divide the two volumes at the Moorish conquest). Y-i-2 with its last seventeen folios intact was copied by B.N. 12837, C, a manuscript of the second half of the fourteenth century. X-i-4 in its present form was copied by B.N. 10314 ter, I, of the late fourteenth or early fifteenth century.[22] Thus, X-i-4 was constituted in its present form towards the end of the fourteenth century. Strangely, despite his own evidence, Catalán suggests 1344–50 as dates for the creation of X-i-4, and, later, that Alfonso XI (1312–50) ordered its creation (*DAX*, pp. 78, 88). However, Alfonso XI cannot both have found two manuscripts in his library, and have ordered them to be created as Catalán seems to argue. The more convincing evidence on dating is that provided by manuscripts C and I. They point to a late fourteenth-century date.[23]

In any case, the date of the final creation of X-i-4 is not the date of its constituent parts, which Catalán has analysed. The oldest sections, apart from the first seventeen folios, are folios 23–198 and 257–320. These sections are in the same hand, and have been subject to the attentions of a 'corrector', who has not left any mark on any other section of X-i-4. On folio 26^r, there is mention of the contemporary 'era', which corresponds to the year A.D. 1289, which means that these sections were written in that year or shortly afterwards, in the time of Sancho IV, son of Alfonso X. These folios, then, were originally part of the same independent manuscript, which I shall call the 1289 text. Folio 23 was probably the first folio of this independent manuscript, since it still has a large illumination suitable for such a position (see *PCG*, facing p. 360). Part of the 1289 text is not extant; there must be a section missing where folios 199–256 are now interpolated. The missing section would have contained in some form exploits of the Cid. The extant first section includes a prose version of the first 'cantar' of the *PMC*, more or less as it is known to us, but very little more of the poem. The second surviving part of the 1289 text contains nothing about the Cid.[24] It was the prose style of the 1289 text that led Pidal to his theory of the 'versión regia' and 'versión vulgar' of the *PCG*. Catalán, however, has shown that it is only the 1289 text that has the distinct style on which Pidal's differentiation depends. Outside the two periods covered by that text, there are not two 'versiones'. Moreover, with regard to the story of the Cid, there is only one manuscript which could represent the 'versión vulgar', Salamanca MS 2628, F, which is of a late date and not of outstanding quality. Between the two parts of the 1289 text, there is the 'Cidian interpolation', folios 200–57, so called because it deals only with the exploits of the Cid, ending shortly after his burial. These folios have been extracted from another chronicle and incorporated into X-i-4 without subtlety. They have, for example, their own chapter numeration, which is unlike that of the preceding folios, and begins with number 52, and they contain none of the chronological data found previously. The hand is of the fourteenth century, and the text has great similarities with that of F.[25] The two sections of X-i-4 other than the part taken from Y-i-2, the 1289 text, and the Cidian interpolation, are designed to link the others to form a continuous compilation, and are probably in the hand of the late fourteenth-century compiler.

Two very important conclusions stem from Catalán's devaluation of X-i-4. The first of these is that the second volume of the *PCG* does not contain the text on which other Alphonsine chronicles depend. It is not the head of the series, particularly since it was not put together until most of the others had already been written. Parts of X-i-4 are important, particularly the 1289 text because of its early date and its royal origins, but even that text is worthy of no more than a place alongside the other chronicles of the period, and should not be placed at their head.[26] The second important conclusion to be inferred from Catalán's work is of direct relevance to studies of the Cid. It is that the two parts of the *PCG* which retell the Cid's story told by the *PMC* are found in two sections which were originally in independent and distinct manuscripts. The first part, mainly the first 'cantar', is in the 1289 text; from the siege of Valencia onwards is in the later interpolation. The juxtaposition is fortuitous, the act of an unsubtle compiler. Pidal's theory of a 'refundición' of the *PMC*, which had only affected the *PMC* from the siege of Valencia onwards (see *CMC*, pp. 126–30), fails on this point, for it depends on *PCG* for its evidence. It is not certain what was contained in the later part of the Cid's story in the 1289 text or in the earlier part of the interpolation, although other chronicles suggest the probable contents. What is certain is that the version of the *PMC* in the *PCG* should never be considered as one integrated product. It does not reflect the efforts of one 'juglar'.[27]

In short, it is clear that the *PCG* should be used more cautiously than it has been in the past. This is especially true with regard to its story of the Cid. This story must be examined in two separate parts, each one on its individual merits, and in the context of other chronicle versions of its content. Its account of the first 'cantar' can be dated with certainty to 1289 or shortly afterwards. Its account of the remainder of the hero's adventures, however, is far more difficult to date, more so when the poor quality and many errors of the manuscript reveal an original existence in chronicle form at least one step removed from that which survives.

(ii) The appearances of the Cid in the *PCG*

As in the other Alphonsine chronicles, in the *PCG* there is a great amount of space devoted to the life and exploits of Rodrigo Díaz. Much of the information is from sources known to us, but much of it is of unknown provenance, and new to prose histories. The *PCG* briefly mentions the hero early on, when it gives his lineage from the judge of Castile, Laín Calvo, as in the *Linaje del Cid*. The compilers added: 'et de la razon deste Roy Diaz contaremos adelante' (*PCG*, p. 387.b). This 'razon' does not start until the third year of the reign of Sancho II, when the Cid is Sancho's adviser (*PCG*, p. 497.b). In the other Alphonsine chronicles, Rodrigo plays quite a role in the preceding reign, that of Fernando I. He does not appear there in the *PCG*; but, between chapters 811 and 812 of the *PCG*, there is an unexplained jump of five years in the chronology, the succession of various popes is omitted, as is the succession of a king of France. All of these details the *PCG* in this section normally assiduously lists. Moreover, later in Sancho II's reign, the *PCG* has clear references to events in Fernando's reign which it has not included, but which are found in other chronicles. Examples are Fernando's commendation of the Cid (see *PCG*, p. 497.b.40–47), and Arias Gonzalo's prophecy (see *PCG*, p. 499.b.41–44). It is apparent there is an omission in the *PCG* of episodes involving the Cid in the 'partición de los reinos' by Fernando I.[28]

After his first intervention in Sancho's reign, the Cid continues to appear at frequent intervals in the highly dramatic, fictionalized account of the reign of Sancho 'el bravo' and the civil wars between the children of Fernando I. Once more, there is a new twist given to the rescuing of Sancho in a battle. In the *PCG*, as in the *Linaje*, Sancho is captured at Santarem; but in the *PCG* he is freed not by the Cid but by Alvar Fáñez. The *PCG* does add: 'Pero dize la estoria en otro lugar que el Çid fue aquel cavallero que alli acorrio et libro de la prision al rey don Sancho; pero mas se afirma que fue Alvar Fannez que non el Çid; mas muy bien acaescio en que el rey don Sancho fue alli librado de la prision' (*PCG*, p. 501.b.14–20). The chronicle then tells how the Cid arrived later at the·battle with three hundred men, and won the day for Sancho. The 'otro lugar' of the *PCG* must refer to the *Linaje*, a known, written source, but it is the other, probably poetic source which is given precedence. At Golpejera, it is the Cid who comes to Sancho's help, in an account reminiscent of the *Najerense* (*PCG*, pp. 502–03).[29] At the siege of Zamora, Rodrigo's role is expanded in new scenes, which involve a certain romantic interest in the relationship between the Cid and Urraca, new personages such as Arias Gonzalo and his sons, and an overall increase of detail and incident (*PCG*, pp. 506–12). The Cid chases Vellido Dolfos and fails to catch him, as before. The *PCG* quotes el Toledano at this point, but it is of interest that the words quoted do not exist in the *DRH* (*PCG*, p. 511.b.9–24).[30] The Cid is not involved in the new episode of the duels fought for the honour of Zamora, but he reappears to exact the oath of innocence from Alfonso VI, in a scene of much greater length than those found in el Tudense and el Toledano, and now set firmly in the church of Santa Gadea de Burgos (*PCG*, pp. 518–19). He fights two duels as champion of Castile and León as in the *Linaje*, and then the events leading to his exile are recounted, more or less as in the *HR* (*PCG*, pp. 522–23). These are not the only subjects in the *PCG* here, of course; after the Jura de Santa Gadea, for example, there are three chapters about the virtues of Alfonso VI, his wives, and a military expedition of his (*PCG*, pp. 519–22).

After the Cid's raid on Toledan lands (as in *HR*, 10), it soon becomes clear that the *PCG* is using the *PMC* as its principal source, indeed its only source for a long section, apart from the addition of chronological data and minor details (*PCG*, pp. 523–34). The events of the first 'cantar' are related until it is completed, when the *HR* reappears as a source (*PCG*, pp. 533–37). For the next twenty folios, the chroniclers turn to other affairs of great importance in Spanish history, such as the fall of Toledo to Alfonso, and the change in church offices from the Mozarabic to the French rite. They also recount the comings and goings over Valencia. The Cid steps back into the picture in the dealings over Valencia, and his involvement is the main theme until the 1289 text ends (*PCG*, pp. 559–65). Here, the sources are the *HR* for some details, but mainly the Moorish historian Ben Alcama, whose history of Valencia is now lost (see *EDC*, pp. 888–96). It is clear that only the first 'cantar' of the *PMC* is used in the *PCG* 1289 text. This is of value since it is of such an early date, and it uses the same poem that survives now (see note 27). But its tendency to rhetorical amplification must be remembered when comparing the two.

The second part of the story of the Cid in the *PCG* is not directly related to the earlier part, as said above. The interpolated text on folios 200–57 of the manuscript deals exclusively with Cidian affairs, yet it occupies nearly a fifth of the second volume of the *PCG* as printed. Its two sources seem to be Ben Alcama's history of Valencia for those events up to the capture of that city and events immediately afterwards (*PCG*, pp. 565–92), and a corpus of epic and legendary material about the Cid for the rest (*PCG*, pp. 592–643), although what form this took is uncertain. The latter section can be divided into two parts: a first part covering the same ground as *PMC*, lines 1212–3725, and a second part, involving the death and the miraculous post-mortem adventures of the Cid, a story generally known as the *Leyenda de Cardeña*, and assumed to be connected with the monastery of San Pedro de Cardeña. The equivalent section to the *PMC*, perhaps deriving from a 'cantar refundido' as Pidal calls it (e.g. *PCG*, 'Fuentes', pp. clxxxvi–xc), shows so many alterations from the text of the poem that it would be tedious to list them all. Pidal has described many of them (*CMC*, pp. 126–30). From these it can be seen how the whole character of the action and of the personages is fundamentally changed from the verisimilitude and sobriety of the *PMC* to a novelesque atmosphere of bravado and incident.[31] On the other hand, a close examination of the two accounts shows that now and again the *PCG* does seem to be using words and phrases direct from the *PMC*. This is especially so in the duels at the end of the *PMC*; compare, for example, *PMC*, lines 3623–45, and *PCG*, p. 626.a.45–b.25. Furthermore, in the court scenes in the *PCG* (pp. 620.b–21.a), it is Ordoño who is the first to challenge the Infantes, not Pero Bermúdez, as the *PCG* says later, agreeing with the *PMC*. There is another inconsistency in the *PCG*, in that, in his challenge, Ordoño accuses Diego González of fleeing from the Moor in the battle against Búcar, unfairly, for it is Fernán González who actually fled in poem and chronicle (*PCG*, p. 606.a; compare *PMC*, ll. 3313 ff.). Such inconsistencies suggest at least two sources poorly adjusted, and that one of the sources may have been the *PMC*.[32]

The *PCG* version of the later events of the *PMC* is of uncertain date. As noted earlier, its manuscript is a copy, more than once removed from its original, and the overall content of that original is, in any case, unknown. Compared to similar accounts in the *CRC*, it does not have the story of 'Martín Peláez el asturiano'; but it does have the inconsistencies mentioned above. These factors imply an early version or perhaps just a poor one. The *Leyenda de Cardeña* material has normally been assumed to have been joined to the 'cantar refundido' before their incorporation into any chronicle, although the separate previous existence of a 'poema refundido' would not be surprising, especially since it is not easy to see any parts of the 'cantar refundido' which are easily attributable to the author of the *Leyenda de Cardeña*. Russell suggests a mid-thirteenth-century date for the *Leyenda*, and Catalán a mid-fourteenth-century one. More recently, Smith suggests a date towards the latter part of the thirteenth century, while identifying possible inspiration for the authors of the *Leyenda* in Latin stories about Charlemagne (see note 31).[33] Whatever the answers to the problems raised by its sources, it is abundantly clear that the second volume of the *PCG* must now be considered a fragmented and devalued text. Its individual parts have their own points of interest, but they must be considered individually, especially where the story of the Cid is concerned. Both sections of this story in the *PCG* give versions which are different from others, and are of interest for that fact. However, each section by itself cannot be considered a vital text from which others descend; and, as a whole, they should no longer be used for theories of epic or chronicle development.

C. *Crónica de veinte reyes*

The *CVR* was given this name by Pidal, despite the manuscripts of the chronicle: 'Así la debemos llamar, aunque los manuscritos la denominen *Crónica de once reyes*, pues cometen en esto una impropiedad notoria' (*Catálogo* (1918), p. 107). An examination of one manuscript, which is divided into sections of chapters numbered separately for each monarch, reveals a total of fifteen in its pages, which only adds to the confusion. Whatever the correct title, the debt owed in studies of chronicles of this period to Pidal ensures that his title is the most widely known and accepted, and for the moment, it will continue to be used.[34] The chronicle contains the history of the period from the accession of Fruela II to the death of Fernando III; that is from the end of the ninth century to the middle of the thirteenth. It is within the period not covered by an accepted primary text of the *EE*, and, as will be seen, the *CVR* has strong claims for consideration as the earliest known version, at least for substantial parts of its content. The reason for beginning with Fruela II has nothing to do with that monarch, who seems quite undistinguished. Rather, he is the starting point for the *CVR* because it is with him that el Toledano begins book five of his *DRH*. Pidal noted also that it is in Fruela's reign that Castilian independence begins with the elected 'jueces'.[35]

The manuscripts of the *CVR* identify the chronicle as a definite 'de once reyes', showing it was conceived as a limited piece of history and was not simply an undefined section of the *EE*. On the other hand, some of the manuscripts at the accession of Fernando I in León speak of the beginning of the 'cuarta parte' of the chronicle of Spain, which is terminology associated with a full *EE* as conceived by Alfonso.[36] The importance of this chronicle has been accepted for some time, particularly in the field of *PMC* studies, but as a chronicle it has remained unedited and little studied. Its prosification of the *PMC* will be examined in detail in later chapters, but first the *CVR* will be placed in context in the tradition of Alphonsine chronicles

(i). The *CVR* in the Alphonsine series of chronicles

In Pidal's early studies of the chronicles, the scheme of relationships he created placed the *CVR* towards the end of the series of histories, and after the *Crónica de 1344* (*C1344*). According to Pidal, the *CVR*, like the *CRC* and the *TCG*, descended from an 'abreviación perdida' and a 'borrador' of the *EE*. It used the *PCG* when relating the first 'cantar' of the *PMC*, and then the poem itself when the *PCG* abandoned it. Much later, Lindley Cintra showed conclusively that the *C1344* came not second in the series after the *PCG* but towards the end of it. The *C1344* used both the *CVR* and the *CRC* as sources. In addition, he showed that the *CVR* was unusual in that it not only employed Alphonsine compilations as sources, but was also familiar with some of the original sources used for the compilations, including Latin texts and the *PMC*. For Cintra, however, this did not make the *CVR* text of primary importance, but rather it showed its author to be exceptional: 'transcritor e refundidor, mas também . . . crítico . . . posição originalíssima e, na sua constância, única na historiografia peninsular dos séculos XIII e XIV' (p. cclxxi). This was entirely accepted by Pidal, and the *CVR* was moved to 'poco posterior a la *de Castilla*' which is of the beginning of the fourteenth century (*Reliquias*, pp. lxiv–lxv). Diego Catalán, despite his devaluation of the *PCG*, seems to maintain the previous views on the *CVR*, while esteeming it highly: 'se eleva a un grado de "perfección" historiográfica . . . aunque posterior a la primera redacción alfonsí de la obra, no me parece ajena al taller historiográfico alfonsí' (*DAX*, p. 188). He does place the *CVR* in an important position for part of its account of the Cid's story, that part that falls after the break in *PCG* 1289 text: 'a partir del capítulo 896, la *EE* nunca llegó a escribirse: de lo que hubiera sido . . . nos lo deja entrever la *CVR* (no las otras crónicas generales)' ('Crónicas generales', pp. 214–15). For the previous part of the *PMC*, Catalán maintains that the *CVR* uses the *PCG* except when it uses the *PMC* itself. It is likely, in fact, that the *CVR* is using the *PMC* all the time. The *PCG* is not involved (see Chapter 3).[37]

Arguments for the consideration of the *CVR* as the earliest available text for its period have been raised from time to time. Babbitt pointed out that if *CVR* is closer to its vernacular and Latin sources, then it is logical to see it as the earliest text. Moreover, its style and language have been claimed to be less polished and more 'primitive' than those of other chronicles; and a detailed comparison of nine passages from various parts of the *CVR* with the nine equivalent passages of the *PCG* shows the *CVR* to be better organized, more consistent, and truer to source in all cases. The concept of an exceptional, antiquarian chronicler is rather hard to accept, while Gómez Pérez claims that the *CVR* is the 'texto más representativo de la *EE* alfonsí' for the whole of its extent.[38] It is difficult to disagree with arguments for the very early placing of the *CVR*. It has the most reliable text, the most primitive text, the text closest to its sources. Its authors obviously had access to the materials compiled for the *EE*, and have used them well. The only other text without later versions of the epic stories is the *PCG* 1289 text. This, however, has lacunae, a stylistically revamped content, and is in no way superior to the *CVR*. As has already been said, the high regard for it seems to stem mainly from its inclusion in the Escorial manuscripts which were accepted and published as the truest Alphonsine text. The second of these, of course, can now no longer be considered as such, and the authority of the *PCG* 1289 text thus disappears. The *CVR* is not the *EE*, since it is the 'crónica de once reyes'. Nevertheless, for the history of independent Castile, it should surely be given pride of place in the Alphonsine series of chronicles, as the nearest to what Alfonso's own *EE* might have been.

(ii)   The appearances of the Cid in the *CVR*

The *CVR* first refers to the Cid as a direct descendant of Laín Calvo, giving his family tree as in the *DRH* (Book 5, 1), in those manuscripts which start with Fruela II and in their very first folio more or less. The hero is called 'Rui Diaz . . . por sobrenombre el Cid Campeador' (B.N. MS 1501, Ll, fol. 1d).[39] His next mention is in the reign of Fernando I when the marriage of the Cid's daughter to Ramiro of Aragón is referred to, and he is 'mio Cid el Canpeador' (fol. 74a). He actually appears for the first time at the siege of Coimbra, when he is knighted by the king (fol. 75a), but he plays no part in the events of the reign until Fernando is on his death-bed. He then is an important figure in the extraordinary scenes surrounding Fernando's last days and his 'partición de los reinos' between his children. The *CVR* actually refers to its source for these scenes as 'el cantar que dizen del rey don Ferrando' (*Reliquias*, p. 243).[40] In these events, the Cid appears as a person respected and esteemed by Fernando, and as his closest confidant and adviser (implying previous services to Fernando not related in the *CVR*). But he is also rather wild when he causes a fight between his 'vando' and that of the 'condes de Carrión' while Fernando is dying in the next room. He is indebted to Urraca, but is given a 'condado' in Castile by Sancho. Fernando finally commends the Cid to his sons (*Reliquias*, pp. 242–55). Generally, the Cid is on the fringe of the main action, highly esteemed alongside the principal figures, but without a vital role. Ultimately, the story is of ambitions and dissensions amongst the royal personages, with Sancho II as the villain and Alfonso VI as the innocent who will triumph and survive. The highly unlikely nature of some of the goings-on eventually causes even the chroniclers to say: 'mas esto todo non semeja palabra de creer' (*Reliquias*, p. 254). As was noted above, the 1289 text of the *PCG* does refer to scenes found in the *CVR*, so these scenes do not show the *CVR* to be later than it. However, these novelesque episodes do cast doubt on the Pidalian picture of a conservative author of the *CVR*, who chose to use the *PMC* for its antiquity and sobriety.

During the next reign, that of Sancho II, the Cid plays broadly the same role in the *CVR* as has been outlined for the *PCG* above. The contents of the two chronicles, and indeed of later chronicles in the series, are very similar. Nevertheless, the *CVR* has some interesting differences from other texts. For example, it refers to its sources and the use of them in a passage which is long for its type, which mentions, amongst other things, 'el cantar del rey don Sancho' and 'la estoria del rey don Sancho, assi como la cuentan los joglares' (fol. 90c–d). It also has additional material on the Cid's family, with odd details (fols 88c–89a). On the other hand, the *CVR* does not have the passage referred to above (*PCG*, p. 501.b), where there is doubt over whether Alvar Fáñez or the Cid freed King Sancho from captivity. The *CVR* simply says Alvar Fáñez freed him, and that the Cid arrived after the rescue (fol. 93a–b).[41] After the death of Sancho II at Zamora, the *CVR* includes the quotation wrongly attributed to el Toledano (fol. 103c–d). It later includes a new episode, in which the Cid challenges fifteen Zamorans, to satisfy his honour after the murder of his lord (fol. 103c–d). He defeats his opponents single-handed in an account rather reminiscent of the *Historia Roderici*, 5, although it is at a different stage of the story from the *HR*, includes several more details, and has a precise motive. But variety and similarity in episodes in two separate texts dealing with the popular hero is worth noting once more. The duels between Diego Ordóñez and the sons of Arias Gonzalo are also in the *CVR*. The account of the Jura de Santa Gadea (fols 109d–10a) is unexceptional, as are the events leading up to the hero's exile (fols 112d–14a), except that *CVR* adds to the capture of García Ordóñez at Cabra, 'mesole una pieça de la barva' (fol. 113d). This episode and the *PMC* in the *CVR* are discussed in Chapter 3.

The *CVR* deserves a place of importance in the series of Alphonsine chronicles, especially as regards studies of the methods of composition and use of sources, and of the lost sources themselves. It is the best, if not the only, place in which an early prosification of a complete poem (*PMC*) can be studied in depth and in comparison with the original. Its identification and its discussion of sources is fascinating. It remains a mine of valuable information on early Castilian prose and on Castilian epic poetry, as will be seen in later chapters.

D. *Crónica de los reyes de Castilla*

(i) Its place in the Alphonsine tradition

The *Crónica de los reyes de Castilla* (*CRC*) often simply called *Crónica de Castilla*, takes its name from its own manuscripts.[42] It is a new version of the section of Spanish history from the accession of Fernando I in León to the death of Fernando III, notable mainly for its contributions to the stories of the life of the Cid. From the death of Alfonso VI, its text is virtually that of the *CVR*, so it is for the reigns of Fernando I, Sancho II, and Alfonso VI that the *CRC* is principally of value.[43] The *CRC* is found translated into Portuguese in a manuscript which can be dated to 1295–1312, and which seems to have been a basic source for the *C1344*. It was composed, therefore, before 1312.[44] From the time of its composition onwards, the *CRC* seems to have been the most popular of the Alphonsine chronicles to judge by its diffusion in many and varied manuscripts, which are difficult to relate closely one to another except in a few instances. Misleading statements have been made in the past simply because one manuscript has been taken as representative of the *CRC* and other readings discounted, when they are often merely variants within the scope of the *CRC*. There seem to be two main groups of manuscripts, representing two main versions of the *CRC*; one full version described sometimes as more 'poetic', and another comparatively abbreviated version, within which there is a sub-group of manuscripts of a very abbreviated version. The full version is considered the better. The *CRC* is generally more verbose than the *CVR*, and can be dated after it for the Fernando I–Alfonso VI section.

(ii) *Crónica particular del Cid*

The *Crónica particular del Cid* is the term used to refer to the history of the Cid published in 1512 by Fray Juan de Velorado, abbot of San Pedro de Cardeña, from an old manuscript in the monastery. The history turns out to be a section of the full version of the *CRC* from the accession of Fernando I to the death of Alfonso VI, including all the material pertaining only to the monarchs, as well as that referring to the Cid. Where the above section of the *CRC* ended, Velorado added genealogies of the Cid and his descendants plus information on San Pedro and its tombs.[45] Scholars in the past have seen special features in the *Particular*, but they prove to be merely features of one version of the *CRC* against another, or minor idiosyncrasies of the particular manuscript used by Velorado, which has now been identified.[46] The *Particular* is in fact a good and valid example of the text of the fuller version of the *CRC* for the three monarchs it includes.[47]

(iii) The Cid in the *CRC*

The contribution of the *CRC* to the story of the Cid known to the present day is mainly in its presentation of the early part of the Cid's life according to a lost poetic source, called the *Gesta de las mocedades de Rodrigo*. This introduces features which later survive in the popular and literary imaginations, such as the marriage of Rodrigo to Ximena Gómez whose father he had killed. Other episodes in the *CRC* had less success, such as those in which Rodrigo humiliates the Pope and the Emperor of France. In all, the *CRC* account shows a great increase in the importance of the role of the Cid in Fernando I's reign. It does help to explain elements of the partition scenes in the *CVR*, such as the relationship between Fernando and Rodrigo, and Fernando's bastard son, Cardinal Fernando. However, the partition scenes themselves are, surprisingly, not found in the *CRC*, although later, in the reign of Sancho II, the *CRC*, like the *PCG*, makes references only explicable in terms of the scenes found in the *CVR*.[48]

The reign of Sancho II in the *CRC* is basically the same as the account found in the *CVR*, and in the 1289 *PCG*, for that matter, within the limits of the minor variations found constantly in the Alphonsine series. The Cid's duel with, and defeat of, the Zamoran knights is not in the *CRC*. Its version of the Jura de Santa Gadea varies from manuscript to manuscript, but they are generally longer, more descriptive accounts and they concur in painting the Cid as a more aggressive character, prepared to challenge Alfonso in a minor way (see *Particular*, fol. xxv). There is nothing more of note until the 'destierro'. Here, for the first time, there are new, possibly poetic elements attaching to events around the opening of the *PMC*. Exile is ordered by Alfonso in a face-to-face confrontation on the road between Burgos and Bivar, and the Cid is almost impertinent, as during the 'Jura'. Preparations for exile are different in many details from the *PMC*. For example, Martín Antolínez is with the Cid at Bivar and goes to Burgos to see the Jews; on leaving Burgos, the Cid steals stray animals, returning them later. This variation continues until the arrival at Cardeña, whereafter, until the end of the first 'cantar', the *CRC* reverts to an account of the *PMC* similar to the poem (see *Particular*, fols xxviii–xxix).[49] The *CRC* version of the later adventures of the Cid is clearly related to that of the *PCG* interpolation rather than to the *CVR*. They are not the same, however. There are very many verbal differences and detailed variations. Furthermore, the *CRC* adds elements. One of these is the story of Martín Peláez el asturiano, a cowardly knight who runs away from the Moors at the siege of Valencia, but is turned into a brave man by the wisdom of the Cid. He later appears alongside Pero Sánchez at the head of the one hundred knights sent to accompany the Cid's daughters to Carrión. Other changes are in the court scenes, where, for example, the *CRC* adds a speech by Alfonso praising the lineage of the Cid's family against the insults of his enemies. In the *CRC*, Alfonso is rather less than neutral in the dispute, as in the above speech, and when he runs down the Infantes' family after their defeat in battle (see *Particular*, fols lxi–ii, lxvii–iii, lxxxiiii, lxxxix).[50] Finally the *Leyenda de Cardeña* section of the *CRC* is more or less the same as that of the *PCG*, with some verbal variations.

Overall, the *CRC* is an interesting and lively chronicle, whose poetic features of style and content offer various possibilities of interpretation. It is a later chronicle in style and content than the *CVR*, but was written not many years after the death of Alfonso X. It is evidence of the vitality and great activity of Castilian historiography of its era.

E. The Later Alphonsine Compilations

The remaining three texts of the Alphonsine series are all reorganizations of material found in the chronicles already examined. There is a little new material in the *C1344* on the 'mocedades', but the texts do not have the interest of the preceding ones. Two of the three, the *Tercera crónica general* (*TCG*) and the *C1344* are full chronicles, but the third is a summary, the *Crónica abreviada*.

(i)   *Tercera crónica general*

The designation *TCG* comes from Pidal's early view of chronicle relationships, in which the *PCG* was first, *C1344* the 'Segunda Crónica General', and thence the *TCG* (see *Leyenda, Catálogo*). The only example of the compilation *TCG* which is a complete version of the planned *EE*, and the text which led to the concept of the third general chronicle, is the edition published by Ocampo. Ocampo himself casts doubts on the validity of the 'cuarta parte' he presents as an Alphonsine product (pp. 279a, 426b), but prints it all the same.[51] His text proves to be a compilation of large sections closely related to those known in earlier chronicles. The details of the composition of Ocampo's edition seem to be the following. The section of the *PCG* completed under Alfonso X is used until it ends. The Ocampo text is then similar to the *CVR* from Fruela II until the death of Bermudo III, that is before the accession of Fernando I. Ocampo's text so far, the first three of the 'cuatro partes', is found in various manuscripts, and it is what Catalán calls the *Crónica general vulgata*. From the accession of Fernando I onwards, Ocampo's version is a careful compilation of the *CRC* and the *PCG*; up to the Jura de Santa Gadea, it seems to use the *CRC*, and thereafter the *PCG*, with added features from the *CRC*. One manuscript (Pal. 1877) seems to be a compilation like Ocampo's, but other manuscripts exist which seem to be different compilations of the *PCG* and the *CRC*. These manuscripts have all been called *TCG* in the past. Ocampo's 'cuarta parte' is what Catalán calls the *Crónica ocampiana*.[52] There seems no good reason to date the *TCG* to *c.*1390. Ocampo's sources are only later than the dates of the *CVR*, *CRC*, and *PCG*. The *TCG*, as a whole, can be dated to 1541.

(ii)   *Crónica general de 1344*

Pidal originally thought the *C1344* to be second in line to the *PCG* in the series of Alphonsine chronicles. Cintra, however, showed that the *C1344* was, in fact, the last of the line. He showed also that the chronicle was prepared for the Portuguese court, in Portuguese, and that Castilian manuscripts are based on translations. There are two versions: one of the year 1344, surviving in only one manuscript and that in Castilian; and one of *c.*1400. The differences between the two versions after Ramiro I (842–50) are only stylistic.[53] The story of the Cid in *C1344* is based on the *CRC*, with additions from the *CVR*, mainly in the partition scenes. The compilation is poorly done. For example, the *C1344* tells how Fernando divided his lands between all his offspring including his daughter Urraca, as in the *CRC*, and follows this by describing Urraca's complaints because she has been given nothing, as in the *CVR*. Later, the story of Martín Peláez is not included, but the character appears with Pero Sánchez after the Corpes scenes. There are deficiencies elsewhere in the *C1344* which, overall, provides a poor version of the *CRC*, with additions mainly from known sources, but with omissions too.[54]

(iii)   *Crónica abreviada*

The *Crónica abreviada* survives in just one manuscript. This, fortunately, has a prologue in which the reasons for the work are explained. It was written so that Alfonso el Sabio's history of Spain might become more easily accessible in a form that might be memorized. It was compiled by or for Alfonso's nephew the Infante don Juan Manuel (1282–1348), who reasoned thus: 'el su entendi-miento non abondaria a retener todas las estorias que son en las dichas cronicas, por ende fizo poner en este libro en pocas razones todos los grandes fechos que se y contienen' (fol. 25a–b).[55] Given the Infante's close proximity to Alfonso's libraries and schools, it might be hoped that he would provide a definite guide to the *EE*. However, his *Crónica abreviada* relies on a mixture of sources, which it abbreviates in the form of a summary of each chapter. He even adds a note of confusion by referring to the 'primer capitulo deste tercero libro' at the start of the traditional 'cuarta parte'. His bases for the story of the Cid seem to be the *PCG* 1289 text, until the break in it, followed by a manuscript of the *CRC* until the end of the hero's adventures. Since the 1289 text was not interpolated into MS X-i-4 until after the date of the *Abreviada*, the above explanation is not as straightforward as it may seem. In any case, Juan Manuel's work has so far proved of limited value in the classification of the other Alphonsine chronicles.[56]

F.   *Conclusion*

This ends the review of the Alphonsine cycle of chronicles. It can readily be seen that there are three principal texts for my purposes, the *CVR*, the *CRC*, and the *PCG* which should be considered in two separate parts. For the comparison with the *PMC*, the *CVR* is obviously the most important chronicle, and surely for all the epic stories it contains, it must be considered a primary text, given its proven proximity to its sources. The *PCG* is a mixture, and in some ways it is disappointing. Its 1289 text is of an early date, but it offers comparatively little of interest, especially when the rhetorical nature of its style casts suspicion on any 'poetic' features it may offer. The interpolated text, in contrast, is of a later date and of poor quality, although it does offer an apparently early stage of development of its part of the revised story of the Cid. The *CRC* provides the revised story in almost full splendour in a form in which the various parts at least fit together. In a way, it marks the climax of the development of the hero from modest beginnings to dominance over the histories of three famous monarchs, a development of which only a few stages are visible and whose processes are only superficially understood. For studies of the Cid, each of the three chronicles has its value. For studies of the *PMC*, the *CVR* is clearly the most important one.

CHAPTER 3

THE COMPOSITION OF THE
CRÓNICA DE VEINTE REYES
AND THE PLACE OF THE *POEMA DE MIO CID*
IN THE CHRONICLE

The remaining chapters of this study are the results of a detailed examination of that section of the *CVR* which contains the prosification of the *PMC*. This examination concentrates on how the chronicle used the poem, and on the effect of the use of a poetic source on the text of the chronicle itself. It reveals aspects of the attitudes of the chroniclers to history, to their sources, and to their work. It sheds light on the manuscript of the poem used for the prosification which must have been different from the one extant manuscript, which is of a later date than the chronicle. The present chapter begins by considering the value and originality of the *CVR*, expanding various points briefly raised in the previous discussion of the chronicle within the series of Alphonsine chronicles (see Chapter 2, II, *C*). It goes on to examine the structural bases and compositional techniques employed by the authors, and how the prosified poem has been fitted into the established framework, beside complementary information taken from prose sources.

I. THE ORIGINALITY OF THE *CVR*

It was stated in the preceding chapter that the *CVR* is closer to its sources than any of the other similar chronicles. It is the best example of what the original *Estoria de España* of Alfonso X might have been like, if the *EE* had been completed for the appropriate period of Spanish history. More importantly, it is the only chronicle to contain a prosification of the whole of the *PMC* more or less as it is known today, although, of course, the chronicle does not include every episode or every detail in the poem. The early version of the story of the Cid given by the *CVR* was quickly superseded in chronicles by more novel-esque accounts, particularly that of the *CRC*.[1] In fact, the *CVR* does not seem to have been well known in past centuries, for few references to it survive, and those that there are tend to be brief.[2] The work of Menéndez Pidal around the beginning of this century, however, showed clearly the importance of the *CVR*, particularly in the context of epic studies, but, even so, up to the present time, comparatively little work has been done on problems concerning the *CVR*, and the text remains unedited.[3]

A.   *'de veinte reyes'?*

Pidal seems to have been the first to call the chronicle 'de veinte reyes' (in *Leyenda*, p. 71). Examination of the chronicle itself, however, does not support this particular choice of title. The majority of known MSS refer to the work as including 'once reyes', although the actual contents include more than that number of monarchs.[4] The results of an examination of MS Esc. Y-i-12, N, of *CVR* were referred to above (Chapter 2, II, *C*). This particular manuscript marks each new reign it covers with a new numeration of chapters. It is thus comparatively simple to trace how many monarchs the chroniclers have covered. In N, the compilers distinguish fifteen monarchs up to and including Fernando III, with whom so many chronicles terminate. The reign of Alfonso VI, in which the prosification of the *PMC* falls, is the tenth, being followed by a number of chapters covering a period without anyone on the throne. This may not be the only possible division into reigns of the relevant period of Leonese–Castilian history, but it is the one made by this particular manuscript. Now, N is one of the minority of *CVR* manuscripts which begin with Ramiro II. The majority of the manuscripts begin with Fruela II and follow him with Alfonso IV, before they reach Ramiro. Therefore, in the larger group of manuscripts, there are seventeen monarchs, and Alfonso VI is the twelfth.[5]

At this point, it is appropriate to consider the theory put forward by Lang and Babbitt as to the original form in which the *CVR* was conceived. According to them, a 'Crónica de once reyes' was the original intention, a chronicle which would have ended (and did end, for Babbitt) with the death of Alfonso VI. The conclusions reached above, which make Alfonso the tenth or twelfth monarch, depending on the manuscript consulted, support, broadly if not precisely, such an idea. Further support of the theory of an original of reduced length is provided by the information that, after the death of Alfonso VI, the *CRC* and the *CVR* have almost the same text, while up to this point they are quite distinct.[6] In other words, it is fair to conclude that Babbitt may be correct in his suggestion that there was an original 'Crónica de once reyes' at least in conception, which would have ended with the death of the conqueror of Toledo. The prosification of the *PMC* is within this limit, as is all the material from presumed epic sources. Pidal's figure of twenty monarchs does not seem justified on any obvious basis. However, there seems to be little point in not using the name by which the chronicle has come to be known, and so it will continue to be called *Crónica de veinte reyes* in this study.[7]

Despite the preconceived unit of eleven kings which can be seen in the *CVR*, the chronicle should not be thought of as a totally independent compilation.

Rather it is a section of a longer work, of a larger history of Spain, and, even if there was an intention to extract a particular part of this history, the *CVR* remained inextricably tied to the *Estoria de España*. This is clear from the closeness of the text of the *CVR* to the text of other chronicles. It is also clear from within the *CVR*, when the transfer of power from Bermudo III to Fernando I earns a special mention: 'Acabasse la terçera parte deste libro que fabla de la estoria de España e comiençasse la quarta parte e fabla luego del ayuntamiento de los regnos de Castilla e de Leon' (fol. 71b; found in at least seven other *CVR* MSS; see Appendix A). The 'terçera' and 'quarta partes' are not divisions of the *CVR*, but of the full Alphonsine chronicle, and so the 'estoria de España' referred to by the *CVR* is also the full Alphonsine work (see Chapter 2, especially II, *A*, and note 36).[8] As pointed out in Chapter 2, the reason why the *CVR* begins with Fruela II is that book five of the *De Rebus Hispaniae* begins with him, and this work was a structural base for the composition of Alfonso's history. There is no obvious explanation for the fact that three of the *CVR* manuscripts, including the oldest and best, begin a little after the others with Ramiro II. Interestingly, four surviving manuscripts of the Alphonsine chronicle tradition all end where the *CVR* begins, confirming the idea of a division in the compilatory material between books four and five of el Toledano's history of Spain (MSS B, U, X, V: see Catalán, *De Alfonso X*, pp. 176–77, etc.).

To sum up: the *CVR* was extracted from the corpus of historical material gathered by Alfonso X, with the stated intention of creating a chronicle of eleven monarchs. The chronicle began with Fruela II (or Ramiro II) and was planned to end probably with Alfonso VI. However, no manuscript of this length survives, and there is no strong evidence to show that the chroniclers' original plan was carried out. Presumably, they did not stop at the originally intended point. For the period of Spanish history it covers, especially the period up to the death of Alfonso VI, the *CVR* is the best representative of what the *Estoria de España* might have been. It is the most complete text for this section, having no notable lacunae; it is the most accurate text, being closest to all its sources; and it is the most consistent text as far as the internal structure and composition of the chronicles are concerned.

B.   The 'CVR' and the 'PCG' of 1289

While the *CVR* is the only chronicle to contain a prosification of the whole of the extant *PMC*, there is one other chronicle which contains the prosification of part of the known poem. This chronicle is, of course, the 'Versión amplificada de la *PCG*', the *PCG* 1289 text, which prosifies the *PMC*'s first 'cantar', and alludes to parts of the second, before it abruptly breaks off in Chapter 896 of the *PCG*. It has already been shown that the *PCG* 1289 text is an unsatisfactory text, having defects in its make-up (Chapter 2, II, *B*). However, in its prosification of the *PMC* it is of value.[9] Its version of the first 'cantar' is generally longer than that of the *CVR*. This is due both to a slightly fuller use of the poem and to a more rhetorical and amplificatory style. Both chronicles include details from the poem which are not in the other, which obviously means that neither is dependent on the other. For example, in the *PCG*, the two Jews who lend money to the Cid are named, 'Rachel et Bipdas', while in the *CVR* they are merely called 'dos mercadores' (*PCG*, p. 523.b.44; *CVR*, fol. 114b; *PMC*, l. 89). Similarly, towards the end of the story of the first 'cantar', the *PCG* says: 'et peso ende a los de Monçon et a los de Huesca; mas plazie a los de Saragoça porque pechavan al Çid.' The *CVR* contains only the first half of the sentence, ending at 'Huesca' (*PCG*, p. 532.b.23–26; *CVR*, fol. 120c; *PMC*, ll. 940–41). On the other hand, when the *PCG* ends its account of Gabriel's appearance to the Cid, the *CVR* adds: 'El Çid quando desperto ovo grand plazer de la vision que viera e acomendose a Dios e rogole que le guiasse bien su fazienda' (*PCG*, p. 524.b.23; *CVR*, fol. 115a; *PMC*, ll. 409–12).[10]

Now, although neither chronicle is dependent on the other, they have great similarities. Their similarities are far more noticeable than their differences. The comparison of any section of the two prosifications of sufficient length makes this absolutely clear. One example will suffice here. It is taken from near the end of the first 'cantar', when the Count of Barcelona is a prisoner of the Cid (*PCG*, p. 533.b.36–46; *CVR*, fol. 121c; *PMC*, ll. 1024–27):

CVR	PCG
El Çid, quando sopo que no queria comer, fuele veer e como era omne mesurado dixole assi, 'Comed, conde, e beved ca esto en que vos agora veedes por varones pasa, e non vos dexedes morir por esto; que aun podredes cobrar e enderesçar vuestra fazienda. E ssi fizieredes como yo digo, saldredes ayna de la prision. E ssi lo non fizierdes, en todos vuestros dias non saldredes dende nin tornaredes a vuestra tierra'.	El Çid quando gelo dixieron fue a el, et como era omne mesurado, dixol assi: 'Conde, comet et bevet, ca esto en que vos sodes por varones passa, et non vos dexedes morir por ello, ca aun podredes cobrar vuestra fazienda et enderençar esto. Et si fizieredes como yo digo, fare yo como salgades de la prision; et si non fizieredes como yo digo, en toda vuestra vida non saldredes de la prision nin tornaredes a vuestra tierra'.

The structural and linguistic similarities of the two versions are obvious. They are far more noticeable than the minor variations between the two, although there are several of these. It was made clear above that the two chronicles are not interdependent. It is also clear that the similarities between them are too great for there to have been two separate and distinct prosifications of the poem. Therefore, there must have existed an intermediate form, presumably an original prosification, which contained all the information in the chronicles and which provided the basis for the virtual identity of structure and language of the greater part of the two prose accounts. This earlier prosification must have been part of the collection of historical material compiled by the scholarly teams of Alfonso X. It is interesting to note that neither the *CVR* nor the *PCG* can have copied the whole of the original version; rather they must have adapted it in order to produce the sort of differences that exist between them. Whether either or both teams of chroniclers had at their disposal the source text, the *PMC* itself, is a question which cannot be answered unless their intermediate source comes to light. It is worth noting, however, that in the year 1289 there seems to have been no sign of the later version of the story of the Cid found in the *CRC*.[11]

The calm consistency of style and method found in the *CVR* throughout the whole length of its prosification of the *PMC* surely shows that the original prosification which existed in the Alphonsine collection embraced the whole of the extant poem. Only the *CVR* can show us what this prosification was like in its version of the second and third 'cantares', while both the *PCG* and the *CVR* are useful when considering the first 'cantar'. The *CVR* is more important here, however, because it is less unreliable and more consistent overall. It also gives the impression of being closer to the poem, perhaps because of its more primitive and less rhetorical style. The *PCG* does, of course, remain a valuable point of comparison with the *CVR* for any study of the chronicle's version of the first 'cantar' of the *PMC*.

II. THE STRUCTURAL BASES OF THE *CVR*

One of the achievements of Alfonso X's historians was the creation of a compositional format, into which the material they had gathered could be fitted in order to produce a patterned history. This format had two basic and complementary ways of dividing historical information, into annals and into chapters. Although the reigns of monarchs were also seen as historical units, and could thus affect the annals and the chapters, it was these two features that lay at the heart of the structure of the chronicles. The structure of annals and chapters can be seen at its best in the *CVR*. Later chronicles are less disciplined and less interested in precision, to judge from their texts: in them, chapter-division becomes more frequent and more arbitrary, annalistic information becomes briefer and sporadic. The *CVR*'s prosification of the *PMC* furnishes good material for a study of the chronicle's structure, though it all falls within one reign, that of Alfonso VI. Such a study helps to show how the chroniclers used the poem and how they viewed it as history.

A. The Annalistic Structure

History is divided by the *CVR* into individual years. All available material is then placed precisely into one year, the events of each year are recounted together, and the years are placed chronologically one after the other. This means, for example, that the chronicle never recounts what the Cid did for, say, two or three years and then turns to Alfonso VI for the same two or three years. Its structure did not allow this type of historical perspective: each year must be dealt with and finished with in its turn. Moreover, for the chroniclers, it seems that each year had its principal story, and, if the Cid is featured in their account of any one year, then Alfonso is mentioned only briefly, if at all, and vice versa. This leads to some historical distortion, but it was how the chroniclers could best cope with their material at this stage in the development of historiography. Arrangement of information in annals as a basis for history was of course an old tradition, which imposed itself on the newer chronicles. However, the *CVR*, although strictly annalistic, appears less so than many earlier works because of the volume of material in it. The volume of material meant that annalistic information was often well spread out and not very obvious. It led to the subdivision of material into chapters, and the placing of chronological information sometimes many chapters apart. Nevertheless, the concern for accurate chronology is very strong: each and every year is carefully accounted for in the *CVR*.

Each year for which the chroniclers have sufficient information to fill at least one chapter is invariably introduced at the beginning of a chapter. The first item of chronological information is always the year of the reign which is followed by the year of the Caesarean 'era'. These two may then be followed by the year of the incarnation of Christ (that is A.D.) and that of the reign of the Holy Roman Emperor.[12] This chronological introduction is a formula which varies only in length. The order in which the details are given seems fixed, as is the wording, except for one small variation. Thus the chapter in which the prosified *PMC* begins starts with the following words: 'Andados quatro años del regnado del rey don Alfonso que fue en la era de mill e çiento e quatro años. Enbio el rey . . .' (fol. 112d). The death of the Cid, on the other hand, comes in a chapter which begins: 'Andados treynta e siete años del regnado del rey don Alfonso que fue en la era de mil e çiento e treynta e ssiete años. Quando andava el año de la encarnaçion en mill e noventa e nueve e el del inperio de Enrrique en uno. El Çid estando en Valençia . . .' (fol. 162c–d). The only possible variation in the wording is that the first part may take the form: 'En el veynte e segundo año del regnado' (fol. 135a).

The *CVR*, then, introduces a new year at the start of a chapter in a more or less fixed way. The events assigned to that year are then recounted, with most space usually given to one aspect of Leonese–Castilian history, normally the exploits of the monarch, but, in this particular section, more often the exploits of the Cid. The amount of material the compilers have for any one year varies, naturally. Thus, the amount of space required for one year varies too, from a line or two to one chapter, or to many. In the section containing the prosification of the *PMC* and other events in that period, the maximum number of chapters given to any one year is ten, there are ten years which have less than one chapter devoted to them, and there is one series of six chapters which each begin with a different year, all described with the typical annalistic formula. The total numbers involved are thirty-four years dealt with in a total of seventy-eight chapters.[13] When the chroniclers have less than enough information to fill a chapter on any year, they usually have virtually no information on that year. In this case, they mention the relevant year, or group of years, more often than not, at the end of the last chapter of the preceding year, before beginning the next substantial year at the start of the next chapter. They refer to the barren year in a way which is more or less formulaic in language and structure. Sometimes they have some minor items of information on the year in question, normally referring to events outside the Leonese–Castilian area. These items are always placed at the end of the reference to the year. An example is found at the end of the prosification of the third 'cantar' of the *PMC*:

Desde el treynta e quarto año fasta el treynta e sesto del regnado del rei don Alfonso non fallamos ninguna cosa que de contar sea que a la estoria de España pertenesca ca so estas cosas que avedes oydo pasaron. Pero en el treynta e sesto año murio el enperador Enrrique e regno en pos el su fijo don Enrrique el quinto quinze años (fol. 162c; see also fols 123a, 123d, 156b).

The type of information at the end of this quote is included by the chroniclers in reference to other years too. It is normally found at the end of the last chapter devoted to the year it refers to, and includes such information as papal succession, regal succession in Christian and Moorish kingdoms, and battles of lesser interest to the main history. In the last of seven chapters placed in the twenty-ninth year of Alfonso's reign, for example, after the description of the arrival of Jimena and her family in Valencia, the chronicle ends the chapter with the following: 'En el veynte e noveno año del renado del rey don Alfonso murio el papa Urban e fue puesto en su logar Pascual el segundo e fueron con el çiento e ssesenta e quatro apostoligos' (fol. 153c).

This type of annalistic structure is the one into which the prosification of the *PMC* had to be organized. The poem must have presented special problems of chronology to the compilers, because it is not in any annalistic pattern itself. Besides, the poem and the other sources for the life of the Cid during this period of his life add up to a large amount of material for the chroniclers to synthesize and to divide into years. The regal history of the time takes up comparatively little space, despite the fact that the king was a distinguished and active one, Alfonso VI, whose capture of Toledo was really a more important historical event than the Cid's capture of Valencia. The compilers of the *CVR* blended their sources well into a single coherent account of the adventures of the Cid from his exile onwards, and the resultant story is acceptable within the outlines of the *PMC* itself. However, from a chronological point of view, the bulk of available information has stretched the period of time from the start of the story in the *PMC* to the end, to a length greater than is really compatible with the *PMC*. The first 'cantar' of the poem is set in the fourth to sixth years of the reign, the major part of the second 'cantar' in the twenty-ninth and thirtieth years, and the third and final one in the thirty-third year, with the death of the hero put back to the thirty-seventh. This is an inclusive total of thirty-four years made up largely of the gap of twenty-three years between the end of the first 'cantar' and the capture of Valencia by the Cid. In terms of the *PMC* alone, this length of time is not acceptable. There is, however, no evidence to suggest that the chronicles had any qualms or doubts in this respect, except perhaps in their omission of references to the youth of the daughters of the hero when sought in marriage (*PMC*, l. 2083, for example). Pidal dates the Cid's exile to 1081 and his death to 1099 (*EDC*, pp. 270, 577), while the *CVR* also places his death in 1099 but has the exile in the year 1066.[14]

As is clear from the information given above, the *CVR* has its prosification of the first 'cantar' divided between three years, and that of the second 'cantar' after the capture of Valencia also divided into three. A large section of the earlier part of the second 'cantar' appears previously in the chronicle, and is placed earlier chronologically. Let us examine at which points the chronicle chose to divide the prosification. The first 'cantar' begins in the fourth year of Alfonso's reign, a year which began with the chapter containing the battle of Cabra. The change to the fifth year does not come until well on into the first 'cantar', at the point where Alvar Fáñez is in Castile, and the Cid is at his 'Poyo' (*PMC*, ll. 898–99; fol. 119d). The poem at this juncture mentions the passage of fifteen weeks, presumably wintering time for the Cid's men, a logical point at which to advance one year in dating. The change to the sixth year follows swiftly with the very next chapter, when the Cid has only just welcomed Alvar Fáñez back from Alfonso (*PMC*, ll. 934–35; fol. 120b). The *CVR* includes at this point information on the regal succession in Zaragoza, and the Cid's involvement there. Thus, the chronology of the chroniclers' other source, probably Arabic, may well have influenced their dating. The second 'cantar' is not prosified in one piece as are the others, because of the mass of information available to the *CVR* on the events leading up to the capture of Valencia. The first substantial piece of the 'cantar' used is the capture of Murviedro and the subsequent battle outside that city (*PMC*, ll. 1095–171; fol. 149b–d). This is placed in the twenty-eighth year of the reign, while the prose version of the 'cantar' from verse 1209 onward begins in the following year. This year is kept until the moment when the poem refers to the passing of winter, when the chronicle takes the opportunity to move on by one (l. 1619; fol. 153c). The thirtieth year lasts until the end of the 'cantar'. The next two years are dealt with briefly in the one chapter between the accounts of the two 'cantares'. The final 'cantar' thus begins in the thirty-third year of the reign. It is notable that

PMC itself says there is a gap of two years between the events of the two 'cantares'. The chroniclers seem to have heeded the poem. The whole of the third 'cantar' is set in the thirty-third year, except for the death of the Cid, which is, understandably, put back to four years later, although it occurs in the chapter following the end of the prosification of the 'cantar'.

It is clear, therefore, that the compilers of the *CVR* have made careful and sensible use of the opportunities offered by the poem for its division into the annalistic format. The second change in the first 'cantar' is rather odd in the context of the poem; but it is the twenty-year gap between the different parts of the prosified poem that stands out as more incongruous. Within the prose version of the poem, the chronological data are inserted in a way which does reveal a clear consciousness in the compilers of the detailed content of the work and of their task of fitting the work into an historically satisfactory pattern. Later chronicles than the *CVR* show less consistency, less concern, and less precision. Thus, the *CVR* is a chronicle composed on the basis of an annalistic structure which is consistent and well-ordered throughout. The prosification of the *PMC* is fitted neatly into this annalistic structure beside the other material available to the authors of the chronicle. There remains to be examined the subdivision of the organized material into the second of the structural bases, the chapter.

B. The Chapter

After dividing the information provided by their sources into annals, the compilers of the *CVR* (or of its source) must then have divided the material for each year into manageable chapters. As has been said above, one or more years are sometimes dealt with entirely within one chapter, but one year may also require several chapters to be completed. The chapters in the *CVR*, and in the other chronicles related to it, are normally numbered, and always begin with a heading which summarizes the content of each one. The first line of text of each chapter is usually marked by the use of capital letters in some way.[15] The numbering of the chapters of a chronicle may be done from the beginning of a manuscript through to the end, or each reign may have a separate numeration of chapters. This depends not on the chronicle involved but on the manuscript, and presumably on the preferences of the copyist. Thus, manuscript N of the *CVR* numbers the chapters of each reign separately, while manuscript Ll (B.N. 1501) numbers from beginning to end. In N, the prosification of the *PMC* begins in Chapter 9 of the reign of Alfonso VI, while the death of the Cid occurs in Chapter 84, giving an inclusive total of seventy-six chapters. In Ll, the corresponding numbers are Chapters 161 and 236, again adding up to seventy-six chapters.[16]

The chapter headings in the *CVR* are brief and accurate. Their wording is on the basis of a simple formula, 'Capitulo . . . de como . . .'; for example, 'Capitulo X de como el Çid se salio de la tierra e sse fue para tierra de moros' (fol. 114d). This type of chapter heading can be seen with the same form of wording in most later chronicle manuscripts. It might be expected that each chronicle would impose its own chapter division on the available information. However, a comparison of the *CVR* with the *PCG* 1289 text shows that both chronicles have the prosification of the first 'cantar' divided into exactly the same chapters. Interestingly, the two chronicles diverge later, before the 1289 text ends and only a little after the end of the prosified poem. This suggests that their source for the content of the poem was in a different state of preparation from the material that followed it (see I, *C*, above).[17] The beginnings and ends of chapters were the places at which the chroniclers added any minor information or comments of certain types. Previously, it has been pointed out that the beginning or the end of a chapter is where more or less all chronological information is found, and where details such as papal succession are included. In addition, the chroniclers sometimes announce a change of scene or of subject at the end of one chapter in preparation for the next.

We now turn to the chapter division of the actual prosification of the *PMC* in the *CVR*. The first 'cantar' occupies eleven chapters, the second takes up nine (one for the battle of Murviedro and, later, eight for the bulk of the 'cantar'), and the final one also takes up nine, excluding the death of the hero. Here is a list of the chapters in question, giving the folio and chapter number of manuscript N, the length of the chapter in lines of the chronicle, and the lines of the *PMC* which the chapter covers. It should be remembered that the division of the *PMC* in this way may be precise or it may be rather imprecise, depending on the way in which the poem has been used in the section concerned. It is sometimes impossible to say precisely at which line of the poem the division comes, although a specific line is chosen here for convenience. The number of lines of the chronicle refers to the number of lines which contain a prosification of part of the poem. This may not represent the total number of lines in the chapter, which may contain chronology or other extraneous information.

An examination of the information contained in this list of figures shows firstly that the length of a chapter in the *CVR* can vary considerably.[18] Thus the longest chapter, Chapter 81, which relates the challenges and counter-claims in the final court scenes, is four times as long as the shortest, Chapter 73, which rounds off the second 'cantar' after the return of the Cid and his prospective sons-in-law to Valencia. The average length is approximately halfway between these two extremes, being between ninety and one hundred lines. The chroniclers obviously wanted their chapters to be of manageable length, but they did not impose very strict limits on them. Rather, as well as length, they took into account the content of the story they were telling. Thus, an examination of the content of the chapters shows that the poem was divided sensibly into episodes.

| | CVR | | PMC | |
FOLIO	CHAPTER	LINES	LINES	VERSES
First 'cantar'				
114a	9	80	286	1–286
114d	10	51	138	287–424
115a	11	114	99	425–523
115d	12	113	100	524–623
116c	13	155	131	625–755
117d	14	123	81	756–836
118c	15	58	33	837–69
119a	16	95	28	871–98
119d	17	48	26	900–25
120b	18	117	81	936–1016
121b	19	109	68	1017–84
Second 'cantar'				
149a–c	61	54	77	1095–171
151d	66	83	86	1222–307
152b	67	72	63	1309–71
152d	68	46	77	1372–448
153a	69	65	62	1454–615
153c	70	77	118	1621–738
154b	71	63	76	1803–78
154c	72	164	290	1878–2167
155d	73	39	103	2175–277
Third 'cantar'				
156b	75	45	33	2278–310
156d	76	98	226	2311–536
157c	77	91	226	2537–762
158b	78	89	132	2763–894
158d	79	60	114	2898–3011
159b	80	83	187	3012–198
159d	81	168	193	3199–391
161a	82	119	141	3392–532
161d	83	80	191	3533–723

A logical episodic structure was more important than considerations of length in the division into chapters. Incidentally, the verse-divisions of the poem, the 'tiradas' or groups of lines of the same assonance, seem to have had no influence on the chroniclers. Even though the 'tiradas' tend to correspond to the episodic breaks in the poem, only twice can the chronicle's chapters be said to reflect a change of 'tirada' (Chapters 66–67, 75–76). This probably happens coincidentally, since there are many more examples of a change in chapter which is not equivalent to a change in assonance (Chapters 9–10, 10–11, 13–14, etc.).

The chapter is the second of the structural bases of the *CVR* and related chronicles. The annal was the primary and chronological base. On the foundation of annals the source material was broken up and each piece allotted to a particular place in history. After this stage came the imposition of the chapter on the compiled information. The chapter divided the information into complementary pieces, into sections of similar and logical content and of manageable length. The chapter became a basic unit of composition. The *CVR* is the best example, for its period of history, of what these methods of composition were able to produce; for it represents an early, careful, and disciplined stage in the development of this school of historiography. Fortunately, the methods and structures revealed by an examination of the prosification of the *PMC* are, in this context, the same as those found in other parts of this chronicle.

III.   THE INTERVENTIONS OF THE CHRONICLERS

The compilers and authors of the series of Alphonsine chronicles do not often make overt statements about themselves or about their view of what they are writing, nor do they normally embroider their accounts with rhetorical trimmings reflecting personal idiosyncrasies. Apart from Alfonso X himself, and Juan Manuel, author of the *Abreviada*, the composers of all the chronicles remain unknown. Moreover, the lack of individual, idiosyncratic features makes it impossible even to guess the identity of any of them. The anonymity also spreads to the copyists, for, despite the large number of extant manuscripts of the various chronicles, very few bear a name.[19] Now and again, however, the chroniclers do intervene in their texts to comment on the story they are telling, or to add a phrase warning the reader of a change of theme. There are occasional references back to information given earlier or forward to things to come. But the most interesting of the interventions are those in which the chroniclers express doubt about the veracity of their sources. Examples from the *CVR* are found in its account of the reign of Fernando I: 'Algunos dizen en sus cantares que avie el rey don Ferrando un fijo de ganançia . . .' (*Reliquias*, p. 242), 'Mas esto todo non semeja palabra de creer' (*Reliquias*, p. 254), and others. More common are references to el Toledano and el Tudense, usually expressing faith in their versions, although it has been noted that some references to el Toledano attribute to him things he does not say (see Chapter 2, note 30). More common still are phrases such as 'cuenta la estoria . . . como avemos dicho', which soon become familiar to readers of Alphonsine histories as part of the stock vocabulary of the chronicles. The section of the *CVR* containing the prosification of the *PMC* has comparatively few such interventions by the compilers. None of them makes reference to the poem in a direct way, but they do provide good illustrations of normal practice by the chroniclers as they composed. The different forms of reference will be considered separately.

A. *'Dizen'*

'Dizen' as a veiled form of attributing information to a source is used twice in the prosification of the poem. In both cases, there is no expressed subject for the verb: 'Dizen que cato por aguero' (fol. 114a; *PMC*, ll. 10–11); 'E dizen que a saliente del rio que ovo buenos agueros e señales de bien andança' (fols 118d–19a; *PMC*, l. 859). Both occurrences come in the prosification of the first 'cantar', and both are in reference to omens. The *PCG* has the same expression in the same two places (pp. 523.b.21, 530.b.29–31). Comparison can be made with a phrase quoted above: 'Algunos dizen en sus cantares . . .' (*Reliquias*, p. 242). Other comparable phrases in the story of Fernando I, are 'a como dizen' (*Reliquias*, p. 243), when the large number of important clergy accompanying Cardinal Fernando are listed; 'pero dizen' (*Reliquias*, p. 243), introducing a contradictory version; and 'algunos dizen que . . .' (*Reliquias*, p. 254), when Nuño Ferrández punches Prince Sancho. Examples from the story of Sancho when king are 'segund dizen', when Urraca threatens to murder Sancho (*PCG*, p. 507.b.17–18); and 'dizen en los cantares de las gestas', when the length of the siege of Zamora is discussed (*PCG*, p. 509.a.37–45).[20]

What these examples of the use of 'dizen' have in common is that they all refer to rather unlikely or controversial things. All the phrases seem to show a certain hesitation on the part of the chroniclers to accept what is said as true. By including 'dizen' they are showing that it is what an unspecified source says, and they are implying that the reader can decide whether to believe the information or not. All the above examples are from sections which appear to have poetic sources (but see note 20). The way in which 'dizen' is used implies that the *PMC* and the other sources were considered in the same light by the chroniclers, at least as far as their historical reliability was concerned. It is true, however, that no term such as 'cantar' or 'gesta' is found in reference to the *PMC*, whereas such terms are employed to identify other poetic sources.[21]

B. *'La estoria'*

The term 'estoria' is the word most widely used in the Alphonsine chronicles to designate the chronicle in which it is used, or 'history' in the abstract, or a source or sources. In the *CVR* prosification of the *PMC*, it occurs four times, but only in passages marginal to the content of the poem. It appears in a chronological aside in the chapter between the prose versions of the second and third parts of the poem: 'Del treynta e segundo año . . . non fallamos ninguna cosa que a la estoria de España pertenesca' (fol. 156b). It is found under virtually identical conditions at the end of the chapter in which the prosification of the third 'cantar' finishes (fol. 162c). Here it obviously means 'the history of Spain' either in the abstract sense or in the sense of 'this history of Spain which we are writing'. Later, it is used twice when the death of the Cid is recorded: 'E por que en la su estoria sse contiene de como murio . . . non lo pusimos aqui por non alongar esta estoria' (fol. 162b). Again, the meaning of 'estoria' is quite clear. First it refers to a source, probably the *HR*, and second to the *CVR* itself. Thus, in *CVR*, 'estoria' has a definite meaning and purpose.[22]

However, as the Alphonsine chronicles developed their style of writing, 'estoria' was used more and more frequently and more loosely, especially in the phrases 'cuenta la estoria . . . dize la estoria'. These became automatic phrases with which to begin a chapter, while other formulaic phrases incorporating 'estoria' appeared at the ends of chapters, for example 'agora dexa la estoria de fablar de . . . e torna a . . .'. The *PCG* 1289 prosification of part of the *PMC* uses 'estoria' seven times in places where the *CVR* never uses it; four of these come at the beginning or end of chapters (*PCG*, pp. 523.a–534.b). The *PCG* prosification of the 'refundición' of the second and third 'cantares' uses 'estoria' over thirty times (*PCG*, pp. 592.b–629.a). The *CRC* continues the progression by using the term on innumerable occasions; for example, over sixty of the eighty chapters containing events equivalent to those of the *PMC* begin with 'cuenta la estoria' or minor variants of the phrase. It is clear that 'estoria' became a virtually meaningless term, which was used as a cliché in certain situations. The freedom of the *CVR* from this automatic application of 'estoria' is evidence of its early composition and the directness of its descent from its sources.[23]

C. *'Nos' and 'vos'*

The remaining type of intervention by the chroniclers in the *CVR* is the most personal. It is when the chroniclers speak as 'nos' and refer to their intended audience as 'vos'. In the *CVR* prosification of the *PMC*, this form of comment is used by the chroniclers on some thirteen occasions, all except one involving the use of a first-person plural verb. The odd one uses a second-person plural verb. Four of the examples of the use of first-person plural verbs are comments by the authors which warn the audience of an imminent change of subject. All four occur at the ends of chapters, and all four have the same structure and basic wording: 'Mas agora dexaremos de fablar del Çid e diremos de Alvar Fanez' (fol. 119a; see also fols 119d, 154c, 156a). Changes are restricted to the names of the topics, obviously, and the possible insertion of 'vos' as object pronoun before the verbs. In six cases where 'nos' or 'vos' forms are found, the chroniclers are referring back to something previously mentioned, once to the year (fol. 156d), once to people (fol. 162b–c), once to a place (fol. 119d), once to 'esto todo' (fol. 151d) and twice to 'estas cosas' ('que avemos oydas', fol. 156b; 'que avedes oydo', fol. 162c). The last two examples occur in similar contexts, both following sentences which use first-person plural verbs: 'non fallamos ninguna cosa que de contar sea que a la estoria de España pertenesca' (fol. 162c; see fol. 156b quoted above in *B*). The last example of the use of such forms noted in the *CVR* occurs, like the preceding ones, in juxtaposition with the use of 'estoria' when the chronicle records the death of the Cid: 'non lo pusimos aqui por non alongar esta estoria' (fol. 162d).

In later chronicles, there seems to be an increase, if only a small one in the use of this form of expression. The *PCG* 1289 uses such phrases seven times, compared to the three in the equivalent part of the *CVR*. The 'refundición' in the *PCG*, on the other hand, appears to have only six examples. The *CRC* shows more adventurous use of the form, as well as the well-worn phrases. In the vocabulary of the *CRC*, 'contar' becomes common in various forms, as does 'tornar'. The use of first- and second-person plural forms in the chronicles is interesting because it is in these expressions that the historians who compiled the works show most clearly their consciousness of their intended audience. It is notable that the words used are those of oral and aural interchange: 'dezir', 'fablar', 'oir', 'contar'. Words such as 'leer', 'escribir', 'ver' are not found in any of the examples. Perhaps this selection of vocabulary shows that the authors expected the most common form of dissemination of their work to be that of reading aloud to a group of listeners. Perhaps, on the other hand, it is the result of the survival and co-existence of oral habits of phraseology beside learned, literary composition, which may help explain the easy acceptance of the epic as an accurate record of history, even when the learned men doubted some details in the version of the poets.[24]

IV. THE BLENDING OF THE PROSIFICATION OF THE *PMC* WITH INFORMATION FROM OTHER SOURCES

It is well known that the *CVR* includes material from other sources together with that taken from the *PMC*. These were alternative Christian sources in Latin and in the vernacular, the *Historia Roderici*, el Toledano's *De Rebus Hispaniae*, and the *Linaje del Cid*, and also substantial Arabic sources, particularly the lost history of Ben Alcama.[25] The task of integrating these sources was made less difficult than it might have been by the fact that the three principal sources dealt with the life of the Cid in different ways. The poem concentrates on the human story of a struggle to a peak of achievement, frequently dwelling on events not found elsewhere. The *HR*, although also concerned with personal achievement, is more historically and politically orientated, while Ben Alcama concentrated on the story of Valencia, writing from a Moslem point of view. The other sources named contribute only details. On the evidence of the *CVR*, it seems that the chroniclers were not looking for the historical 'truth' in the way that a modern historian might. There are examples of them specifically denying the truth of the events they chose to relate (see note 21). What they do seem to have been trying to achieve is the creation of a single unified narrative, which incorporated as much material as possible from the available sources without blatant contradictions in the resultant account. Details from any source might be altered or omitted or placed out of context, and no source was better than the others. A full, logical final story with value as entertainment and as historical material seems to have been the prime requirement.

The first occasion on which the *CVR* had to blend the *PMC* with its other sources is when the Cid is exiled by Alfonso. Unfortunately, the manuscript of the *PMC* is deficient at the start, and it is not known precisely where the poem first influences the chronicle. However, the account of events leading up to the exile is definitely based on the *HR*, 7–11, which does not seem to have needed any substantial alterations to satisfy the chroniclers. There are several minor additions which are possibly based on a poetic original, such as the pulling of García Ordóñez's beard (fol. 113b: 'Ordoñez e mesole una pieça de la barva'; see *PCG*, p. 522.b.38), but they all fit smoothly into the story provided by the *HR*. When the extant poem begins, the *CVR* is already using its version of the poem as its only source, as it does for most of the first 'cantar'. Towards the end of the prosification of the first 'cantar', the chroniclers were faced with the problem of reconciling the *PMC* version of events with that of the *HR*, particularly as both texts relate a battle against the Count of Barcelona. The first addition to the *PMC* occurs after Zaragoza becomes tributary to the Cid (*PMC*, l. 914). The mention of Zaragoza gives the chronicle a suitable opening, which it uses to insert a brief account of how the Cid joined an alliance with the king of that city, and was welcomed into it with his men (fol. 120a; *PCG*, p. 532.a.10–15; *HR*, 12). From now on in the *CVR*, Zaragoza is the site of the Cid's base camp, until he begins to set his sights on Valencia. In the poem, he never goes to the city; his base camp is Tévar for the rest of the 'cantar' (from *PMC*, l. 912). After these brief lines based on the *HR*, the *CVR* returns to the poem to relate Alvar Fáñez's return from Castile (ll. 915–34). At the start of the next chapter, the *HR* is again used, this time to recount the succession to the throne in Zaragoza, and the dissensions this caused (*HR*, 12). The appearance of the Count of Barcelona in these troubles, in the faction opposed to the Cid, is a useful introduction to his appearance at Tévar. After these political events, the *CVR* turns back to the *PMC* and concentrates on the story as told in the poem until the end of the first 'cantar'. There are minor adjustments to the poetic version of events in order to make it closer to the Latin one: instead of the *PMC*'s 'a la posada tornando se van' (l. 915), the *CVR* has 'tornosse luego para Çaragoça' (fol. 120c; *PCG*, p. 532.b.26); whenever the Count of Barcelona is named in his pursuit of the Cid, the *CVR* adds a companion 'Abenalhange, rey de Denia' (*PMC*, ll. 960–1010; *CVR*, fols 120d–121b; *PCG*, pp. 532.b–533.a; see *HR*, 14–16), who therefore has to be disposed of after the battle: 'E el rey Benalhange fuxo con aquellos que pudieron escapar' (fol. 121b, after *PMC*, l. 1010; *PCG* omits). Finally, after the prosified first 'cantar' is completed, the *CVR* finishes off its chapter with 'Desi tornosse el Çid para Çaragoça' (fol. 122a; *PCG*, p. 534.b.7–8). By these comparatively simple additions to the content of the poem the compilers of the chronicle were able, to a large extent, to reconcile their two sources. As much as possible of the poem is used, but at least one essential feature — the Cid's base camp — is completely altered.

For the section of the life of the Cid from the beginning of the second 'cantar' until the capture of Valencia, the *PMC* is brief, and the other sources known to the chroniclers were full and detailed. This is especially true of the Arabic histories, whose rather jaundiced view of the Cid did not prevent their use in the *CVR*. The poem was not ignored, however. Information taken from it appears now and again, when it can be logically included. The amount used at any one time varies from a detail or two to the whole of the capture of Murviedro and the following battle (*PMC*, ll. 1095–171). Approximately two-thirds of the total number of lines in this section of the poem seem to be utilized in some way by the *CVR* (fols 122, 147, 149–51).[26] In the first chapter after the end of the first 'cantar', the *CVR* uses several lines from near the beginning of the second 'cantar', fitting them into information presumably based on the *HR*, though the surviving text is defective at this point (*HR*, 13). Near the start of the chapter, the chronicle adds to the Cid's intention to attack Monzón (*HR*) the names 'de Xerica e de Onda e de Almenar' (fol. 122b; *PMC*, l. 1092; *PCG*, p. 534.b.22–23). Later in the same chapter, a larger section is based on the poem, incorporating the same line in a shortened form (*PMC*, ll. 1090–93, 1097–98; *CVR*, fol. 122b–c; *PCG*, pp. 534.b.44–535.a.4). The final two lines of the *PMC* used here relate the fear of the people of Valencia at news of the Cid's exploits. In the poem, they are the result of the capture of Murviedro, and lead directly to the Valencian army's attack on the Cid. However, the *CVR* happily uses them out of context to suit its own purposes. After the end of the chapter, which is where the *CVR* and the *PCG* begin to diverge, the *CVR* has no further information based on the *PMC* for many folios, although it does devote a lot of space to the story of the Cid. It is well on into the campaign for Valencia, after the rebellion led by Abeniaf and the murder of the king Alcadir, that the next items possibly attributable to the *PMC* appear. The two sentences are: 'El Çid fue luego sobre Cobolla e prisola e poblola de christianos. Desi corrio toda la tierra aderredor e gano Xerica e Honda e Almenar' (fol. 147b; see *PMC*, ll. 1150, 1092). The first of these two sentences is not repeated when the *CVR* later prosifies as a whole the section in which it is contained, but in any case its similarity with the poem is not very strong and it may not be taken from there. The second sentence, on the other hand, is very close to the words of the poem, the third time that this line seems to be used. Its appearance here, well away from any other references to the poem, except perhaps the sentence already discussed, is not easy to explain, although the Moslem history on which the bulk of the text is here based may hold the key.

A couple more folios of the *CVR* pass before the poem is next used, but then it is used clearly and substantially. After Abeniaf has presented the Cid with 'una huerta' outside Valencia, the *CVR* simply changes the subject: 'Desi a cabo de pocos dias sallio de ally e fue çercar Murviedro e tan de rezio lo conbatio que lo priso a pocos dias' (fol. 149b). The chronicle goes on to include the battle of Murviedro and its consequences, based on the *PMC*, ll. 1095–171 (fol. 149b–d). As soon as the poem becomes the source, the change in the tone of the *CVR* is clear. The overbearing Cid of the Arabic version is replaced by a livelier hero; Abeniaf and his cronies become 'los de Valencia', and two 'reyes' appear, only to be killed. The action is quick and eventful, the language is more vivid, brightened especially by the direct speech. In short, there is no attempt here to blend the *PMC*'s story into the Arabic one, as there had been with the *PMC* and the *HR* at the end of the first 'cantar'. The chroniclers have simply inserted the poetic episode into their dominant source, as if in parentheses. When they come to the end of what they want to use, they say: 'Despues que el Çid ovo todo esto fecho, tornosse a la huerta' (fol. 149d). The chronicle resumes its previous, duller tone. Shortly afterwards, when the leader of the Almoravids finally fails to come to the aid of the citizens of Valencia, the *CVR* finds its explanation in the *PMC*, ll. 1181–82. This opportunity to use the poem is seized by the chroniclers, and a series of details is included from the poem about preparations for the final siege of the city (*PMC*, ll. 1187–90, 1199, 1201–94; fol. 150b–c). Later still in the chronicle, at the very end of the siege, the poem seems to have been used once more for precise details of the length of time taken to reduce the city: 'fue en nueve meses e entrante el dezeno entregaronle la çibdad' (ll. 1209–10; fol. 151d). The preceding few lines in the chronicle on the riches won by the Cid and his men may also owe something to the poem (ll. 1214–15; fol. 151c–d). This final series of references to the poem seems to show that the chroniclers had its contents at hand and were looking for opportunities to use them. What they do use are frequently precise details, especially the names of places. The value attached to the poetic text is clear.

After the capture of Valencia, the *CVR* returns to the *PMC* as its principal source and as its only source until the preamble to the battle with Yuçef begins

(*PMC*, l. 1620; fol. 152d). The chroniclers chose to relate this battle in the poem to one in the *HR*, which also mentions Yuçef but which is placed immediately after the capture of Valencia (*HR*, 62). As before, the poem gives the *CVR* its basic account, but alterations are made to reconcile that account with the *HR*. The final version is complicated by a few additional details without a known source. In this episode the features of the *CVR* story taken from the *HR* are as follows:

1. Mohammed, Yuçef's nephew, left in command in Morocco, though in the *HR* he leads the army against the Cid
2. the composition of the army 'de almoravides, de alaraves e de andaluzes'
3. the site of the battle: 'Quarte que es a quatro migeros de Valençia'
4. the supplies and assistance received from Spanish Moors
5. the size of the army; one hundred and fifty thousand men on horse and on foot (see *HR*, 62: *CVR*, fol. 153d).

All this fits easily into a framework based on the *PMC*, except that the army has only fifty thousand men in the poem. After the battle, the fate of the defeated perhaps owes something to the *HR*: 'los unos presos e los otros muertos' (fol. 154a; compare *HR*, p. 960, ll. 9–11). Details not known in any source are the presence of 'el rey Bucar e el rey Soro de Lerida' (fol. 153d), the death of 'siete reyes moros' and of 'Pero Salvadorez' (fol. 154a).[27]

After this battle, the *CVR* returns to the *PMC* alone until the end of the second 'cantar', except for a reference to the conversion of all the mosques of Valencia into churches (fol. 154c). Between the second and third 'cantares' one short chapter is included on conquests in Portugal by Alfonso VI, and battles in Spain outside the spheres of influence of both Alfonso and the Cid (fol. 156a–b). Once the *CVR* begins the third part of the *PMC*, it prosifies virtually all of it to line 3723 without interruption, and with just one detail probably from another source. This is found when Búcar and his army come to attack the Cid (ll. 2312 ff.; *CVR*, fol. 156d). The chronicle says that Búcar camped 'en un lugar que dizen Quarte', a contamination, presumably from *HR*, echoing the battle with Yuçef where Búcar also appears in the *CVR*. Otherwise, the prosification seems unaffected by other sources. Of course, the third 'cantar' does concentrate on episodes for which no other sources are known. As already stated, the death of the hero is placed a little after the main part of the prosification ends: 'El Çid estando en Valençia enfermo e murio en el mes de mayo' (fol. 162d). The illness referred to is new to the chronicle, and can be attributed to the compilers as a rhetorical expansion preferable to a simple 'murio'.[28] The time of year agrees with the *Linaje del Cid*, and with the *PMC*, if the *CVR* is interpreting the date of 'Cinquaesma' named there (l. 3726), against the 'mense iulio' of the *HR*, 75 (see *EDC*, p. 577). The *CVR* goes on to say that the hero's body was taken to Cardeña by Jimena and Alvar Fáñez, adding the name of the latter in place of 'cum militibus' of the *HR*, the source. The chronicle's final reference to the 'estoria' of the Cid, previously discussed (see III, *B*), must surely refer to the *HR*. The present survey shows that, outside the campaign for Valencia, the *HR* frequently provides material for the chronicler, who therefore had it at hand and in mind. The *HR* fits the requirements for the 'estoria' since it does contain an account of events surrounding the death of Rodrigo, and it can certainly be called 'la su estoria', as the *CVR* says. Finally, the *HR* material on his death is limited in length and content, so that the *CVR* does not omit anything of importance or of substance about the man to whom they have previously devoted so much space.[29]

There are certain conclusions to be drawn from this study of the blending of sources in the *CVR*. The most basic is that at any one time the *CVR* uses one text as its basic source. It does not divide its sources into small parts and produce a complex version. Rather, it chooses one source for one section of some length and concentrates on it. Thus, the whole of the first 'cantar' of the *PMC* is included as one piece, with only minor amendments. Similarly, the bulk of the second 'cantar' and virtually all the third are included in two long sections with only a small break between them. At other times in the story of the Cid, the *HR* or the history of Ben Alcama become the basic source to which minor additions or minor amendments are made. In all parts, the changes to the main narrative are comparatively small, though they may be in conflict with it as in the replacement of Tévar by Zaragoza in the *CVR* version of the first 'cantar'. There is compilation without commitment to any one source as absolutely accurate. The chroniclers seem to prefer a full version of events, though not the fullest available to them, where perhaps this would involve too many complications for them. Thus, the capture of Murviedro (*PMC*) is incorporated into the siege of Valencia (Ben Alcama), but the other version of the capture is not included (see *HR*, 68–72). The chronicle even states that it has not included all possible information on the death of Rodrigo. None of the sources seems to have been given precedence over another. Much space is given to Ben Alcama; the *PMC* is preferred to the *HR* as much as the latter is preferred to the former. The longer version in general seems to have been preferred to a shorter one. The happy acceptance of the poetic life of the hero and the apparent equality of status given to all sources reveal much about the philosophy of history lying behind the composition of the Alphonsine chronicles, especially the *Estoria de España* and the *CVR*.

V. CONCLUSION

It is hoped that the material in this chapter has shed some light on the methods of chronicle composition that were developed from the compilatory work that was done in the schools of Alfonso X. The *CVR*, I am sure, represents the best surviving example of these methods for the period of history it covers, since it reveals a stage before successive chroniclers developed their formulae to a point at which they become meaningless and automatic. Thus, the *CVR* shows the annalistic structure at its most precise, with each year carefully accounted for, and interventions by the chroniclers which, although distinctly formulaic, are used sparingly, appropriately, and with deliberate intent. The way in which the chronicle blends its account of the *PMC* with the other sources at its disposal tells us a great deal about the attitudes of the chroniclers towards their task as historians, which they seem to have seen mainly as that of organizers and transmitters of information rather than that of interpreters of the information for their audience, although there is a small element of the latter in some of the things they do. It is true, of course, that the *PMC* and probably other sources had been prepared for use before incorporation into the *CVR*, but my comments are equally applicable to those of Alfonso's scholars who prosified the *PMC* and prepared the other sources, even if they did not compile the *CVR*. As for the other chronicles, the *PCG* 1289 text is similar to the *CVR*, but even it has some features which seem to be developments of those found in *CVR*, while the *CRC* shows such developments taken to extremes of erraticness in the case of annalistic information, and automatism in the division of chapters and in the use of phrases such as 'cuenta la estoria'. Once again, the *CVR* displays the earliest stage of development amongst these chronicles. Once again, it stands out as the chronicle closest to what Alfonso's *EE* would have been like for this section of history, had it ever been completed.[30]

CHAPTER 4

THE STYLE AND LANGUAGE OF THE
POEMA DE MIO CID
IN ITS PROSIFICATION IN THE
CRÓNICA DE VEINTE REYES

Critical studies of the relationship between the *PMC* and the vernacular chronicles have concentrated on the poem. The chronicles have been used to illuminate the poem, to emend and improve its text, and to fill its lacunae. Pidal's critical edition of the *PMC* (*CMC*, III, 1022–164), for example, used the chronicles to provide numerous 'corrections' to the manuscript readings. In these studies, comments on the chronicles are much less full than those on the poem. They tend to be generalizations about the style or about the overall use made of the *PMC*.[1] The style and language of the Alphonsine chronicles as such have been studied comparatively little. Most of the articles that have been published take the *PCG* as their subject, as it is the most widely known text. Badía Margarit, in particular, has studied the use of sources by the *PCG* and the Castilian prose of the chronicle resulting from a variety of sources. He has shown that, whatever the source and however detailed the translation, the resultant prose in the *PCG* is always stylistically the same. After comparing a section of the *PMC* with its prosification in the *PCG*, he lists five features of the syntax of the chronicle, which he calls 'sintaxis trabada', and five contrasting features of the syntax of the poem, 'sintaxis suelta'. The features of the chronicle are: the constant grammatical linking of clauses, the strong tendency to subordination of clauses, logical, correct tenses of verbs, the introduction of direct speech by a verb, and frequent expansions and explanations.[2]

Such elements of the style of the *PCG* are also found in the *CVR*, which is, after all, an almost contemporaneous product of the same historiographical tradition, although the expansions and explanations are less extensive in the *CVR*. The *CVR* has series of linked clauses, often simply joined by 'e'; it has frequent subordinate clauses which often cause clumsy, laboured forms of expression; it uses tenses perfectly; and it consistently introduces direct speech with a verb.[3] The style of the *CVR* tends to be inflexible and repetitive, with only a limited number of ways of relieving the monotonous pattern of recurrent prepositions and conjunctions. The reader soon comes to expect sequences of time clause or phrase, one or more main clauses, and other subordinate clauses in attendance. The prose may strike the modern reader as stilted, but it is well controlled by the chroniclers, so that it is at least comprehensible and correct, if not elegant. The following quotation is an example of the frequent subordination in the chronicle:

Bien sepades que todos los omnes que por armas han de guarir, assi como nos, que, ssy en un lugar quieren sienpre morar, que non puede estar que non menoscaben y mucho (*CVR*, fol. 120c–d; *PMC*, ll. 947–48).

The sentence is clumsily expressed, but it is not difficult to follow. Compare the brevity of the more accomplished style of the poem, which compresses the essentials of the quotation into one line.

The comparison mentioned above provides a good illustration of the problems faced by the prosifiers of the *PMC*. They were dealing with a vernacular text which handled the Castilian language with much greater fluency than they were able to achieve in their prose. They seem to have set themselves the task of disguising the poetry of the original to produce a version which would be stylistically indistinguishable from other sections of their chronicle. As stated earlier, studies have shown that chronicle prose based on different sources is normally the same, although a source such as the *PMC* was bound to have some effect on the prosification of it. The extent of this effect will, I hope, become clear, as various aspects of the style and language of the prose version of the *PMC* in the *CVR* are considered in detail.[4]

I. THE STYLE OF THE *PMC* IN THE *CVR*

A. *The Use of Direct Speech*

An obvious feature of the *PMC* is the amount of direct speech used by the poet. Speech is especially useful in defining characters by what they say in ways which no amount of straightforward description could achieve. The personages of the poem are illustrated by their words, which can contain subtle changes of tone, as in the discussions of each other by Alfonso and the Cid and in their face to face exchanges. It is likely, too, that speech was a valuable dramatic device in any performance of the *PMC*, for the poet could present the protagonists more vividly by variations in his voice (see Smith, *PMC*, pp. lii–liii). An examination of the lines of the *PMC* shows that over forty per cent of them in each 'cantar' are in direct speech. The exact figures are forty-one per cent in the first 'cantar', forty-four per cent in the second (after line 1222), and forty-six per cent in the third. It will be seen that such a high proportion of speech has directly affected the *CVR*. This is clear from the amount of direct speech in the prosification of the *PMC* in comparison with non-epic parts of the chronicle. To obtain a statistical figure for the *CVR*, the number of lines of the chronicle text were counted and the number of lines of direct speech were noted. The results were: in the prosification of the first 'cantar' thirty-seven per cent of the text represented direct speech, in the second 'cantar' (after line 1222) forty-two per cent, and in the third thirty-nine per cent. In comparison, the chapters from the description of Alfonso VI's marriages to the exile of the Cid (*CVR*, fols 111–13) have less than four per cent of direct speech, and the first five folios after the end of the first 'cantar' (122–26) have less than two per cent direct speech. Similar contrasting figures can be found elsewhere.[5]

The amount of direct speech in the *CVR*'s prosification of the *PMC* is obviously a direct borrowing from its source. The direct speech of the chronicle normally seems to be taken from direct speech in the poem, although the speech of the poem is not always reproduced as direct speech in the *CVR*. Sometimes, when not omitted, it is transmitted as reported speech, particularly when the chroniclers are summarizing. Occasionally, there is a mixture of direct and indirect speech, as in the following examples:

E Martin Antolinez dixole . . . que les diria que eran llenos de oro e de plata e de piedras presçiosas, 'E que les rogades vos que vos den paños e dineros . . .' (fol. 114b).

dixoles como los infantes de Carrion avien sabor de casar con fijas del Çid, 'E pues que assi est, tengo por bien . . .' (fol. 154d; ll. 1900–04).

The first of these two examples has no precise equivalent in the *PMC*, since the chronicle changed the roles of the characters in this episode (see Chapter 5). Another interesting mixture found in the *CVR* is where a speech in the poem becomes narrative and speech in the prose:

fizole obispo porque le semejo buen christiano. El Çid dixo estonçes a Alvar Fanez, 'Graçias a Dios, agora podredes levar . . .' (fol. 152b; ll. 1297–301).

There is not as much reported speech in the *CVR* as there is direct speech, but its presence in addition to such large quantities of the latter underlines the contribution made by this aspect of the poem to its prosification. It is obviously an important contribution in quantity alone, but it will be seen as this chapter progresses that it is also important because speech is the part of the poem best preserved linguistically and stylistically in the chronicle.

One characteristic of the style of the *PMC* in its treatment of speech is the frequent omission of a verb of speaking or saying before a speech begins. The poem often describes an action by a person and then immediately begins the speech of that person without an introductory verb (see ll. 13–14, 40–41, 102–03, 105–06, 191–92, etc.). In dialogue the poem often demands that the reader or listener identify alternate speakers by their words, because it does not say who is speaking or replying. In practice, the speakers are normally obvious (see ll. 492–93, 1909–10, 2194–96, etc.).[6] This feature of the poem's style has not survived into the prose redaction. The chroniclers are careful to identify each speaker, and to introduce each speech with an appropriate verb in their version, frequently 'dixo' or 'dixo assi'. Compare, for example, the *PMC*'s introduction of a speech with an action, 'levantos', with the *CVR*'s 'levantosse e dixo' (fol. 161a; ll. 3402–03). In a conversation of three separate parts (fol. 122a; ll. 1059–76), the *PMC* has no verb of speaking whilst the *CVR* has 'dixo el conde al Çid . . . , el Çid . . . dixole assi . . . , el conde le dixo'. Further examples could be adduced to show that the *CVR* is always precise in introducing its speakers. Just one case has been noted in which the *CVR* introduces reported speech in an elliptic way reminiscent of the poem. This is found when the message to Tamin, King of Valencia, is recounted: 'enbiaron sus mandaderos al rey de Valençia que les viniesse a acorrer; ca supiese que el Çid . . .' (fol. 116d; ll. 627–29). The *CVR* in this solitary example has omitted any introductory word, passing directly from 'mandaderos' into the reported speech.[7] However, its usual practice is to eliminate such 'poetic' constructions, although cases of mixed reported and direct speech (see above) have an elliptical element.

In short, the prosification of the *PMC* strongly reflects its source in the quantity of direct speech to be found in it, especially since speech is a minor feature of non-poetic parts of the chronicle. As will be seen, direct speech is also notable in the prosification for the way in which it preserves the language and syntax of the poem better than narrative sections do, although the elliptical syntax often found in the poem when introducing speech has not been preserved in the prose.

B. Word Order

The order of words permissible in poetry is always more flexible than that of prose. In the *PMC* there is much inversion of what may be called normal word order to create poetic rhythms, to emphasize particular words, and to fit phrases into the bipartite assonanced lines of the poem (see ll. 1, 14, 15, 17, 19, 23, etc.). My intention here is to examine the extent to which this characteristic of the *PMC* has affected the prose redaction in the *CVR*.[8]

First, it must be noted that there are inversions of word order present in the chronicle and in the poem which were normal and acceptable in prose composition at this early stage of its development, but which are not normal in modern Castilian. The most important are:

1. Object pronouns may follow the verb in a main clause. See many examples; e.g. fol. 114a; ll. 12, 154. (Cases are found in recent Castilian prose, particularly with the reflexive pronoun).
2. The subject of a subordinate adverbial clause may precede the conjunction at the beginning of a sentence. See many examples, particularly with clauses whose conjunction is 'cuando'; e.g. fol. 116a–d; ll. 588, 2648.

3. In subordinate clauses, subject pronoun, object pronoun, and negative particle have no fixed order, except that they precede the verb. Object words or short phrases may also precede the verb in such clauses. See fols 117b, 119b, 119c, 120c; ll. 305, 466, 1252, etc.

4. An object word or phrase dependent on an infinitive may precede the infinitive. See fols 117d, 118c; ll. 712, etc.

5. 'Tanto', 'tan', 'tal' precede the verb when referring to its object, and may attract the object to them. See fols 116c, 162a, 162b; ll. 480, 2678, etc.

6. 'Mucho' may follow its noun, particularly when accompanied by 'además'. See fols 152a, 154a, 155c, 156a.

Many apparent inversions of word order in the prosfication of the poem are, therefore, normal in the written language of the day, and cannot be attributed to poetic influence.[9]

There are, however, a number of inversions which do reveal the influence of the poem. Some of these fit into categories listed above, but show direct parallels with the *PMC*. We find in adverbial subordinate clauses, 'pues que vuestros yernos son' (fol. 155c; l. 2123), 'pues que de casar he mis fijas' (fol. 155d; l. 2220), 'ssi con los moros non lidiaremos' (fol. 117a; l. 673); in relative clauses, 'que menos de lid non se podia librar' (fol. 121a; l. 984), 'que todas las armas le falso' (fol. 118a; l. 766).[10] Other examples are more 'poetic' in that they do not fit into the listed groups. These are very often in direct speech. Here are some examples: 'firmes veo estar aun los moros' (fol. 117d; l. 755), 'nos por armas avemos a guarir' (fol. 118c; l. 834), 'grandes tuertos tiene el Çid de Bivar fechos' (fol. 120d; l. 961). There is a concentration of examples in the speeches at Alfonso's 'cortes' in the final 'cantar', for example:

'Derecho demanda el Çid; ca destos tres mill marcos los dozientos tengo yo . . .', Ferrand Gonçalez dixo, 'Aver monedado non tenemos nos onde le entreguemos'. El conde don Remondo dixo, 'El oro e la plata despendisteslo vos . . .' (fol. 160a; ll. 3230–38).

There are four inversions here, all in speech.[11]

Finally, there are a small number of cases in the *CVR* verbally close to the poem, but which neither respond to the word order of the *PMC* nor fit into the usual categories. They mostly have a colloquial tone, unlike the normally dull chronicle prose, but without the fluency of the poem. It may be that the change of wording has been made by the prosifiers to make the chronicle just a little different from the poem. Examples include: 'nunca me lo despues emendo' (fol. 120d; l. 963), 'ca esta vida avremos a fazer' (fol. 121d; l. 1047), 'nos aviltados somos' (fol. 154c; l. 1862), (see also fol. 119c; l. 886; fol. 119b; l. 874; fol. 158c; l. 2814). Almost all are found in direct speech. The *CVR* contains very few 'poetic' inversions when it is not using the poem in detail. In one addition to the poem we find 'ca el vuestro vasallo es' (fol. 152c; compare ll. 1325–26), but no other example as striking as this one has been noted. Overall, most inversions of modern word order in the *CVR* are due to the different word order acceptable at this stage of development of the language. There are a number of inversions directly repeating inversions of the *PMC*, although there are also a few misleading examples where unexpected inversion is due to the chroniclers. The amount and variety of inverted word order present in the poem is rarely noticeable in the chronicle.[12]

C. Pairs

By 'pairs', here, is meant combinations of two words or short phrases in which the 'pair' exists as one unit of meaning. English expressions such as 'by hook or by crook', 'ups and downs' are 'pairs' in this sense.[13] Pairs are found in both the *PMC* and the *CVR*. In the poem, they tend to be formed of non-abstract elements, so that the poet can express an idea in a concrete way. In place of the concept 'all the people' in the first 'cantar' of the poem, for example, the following pairs appear, in appropriate contexts: 'mugieres e varones', 'burgeses e burgesas', 'moros e christianos', 'moros e moras', 'cativos e cativas', 'grandes e chicos', 'cavalleros e peones'. Noun pairs are most frequent in the *PMC*, but a number of adjectival and adverbial pairs and a few verbal ones are also found. The pairs which appear in the *CVR* and are not related to the *PMC* are normally more abstract than those of the poem. Their purpose seems to be one of rhetorical amplification and adornment rather than anything else. They are generally single creations of the chronicle, rather than part of the accepted vocabulary of the language of the day as many of the poetic expressions probably were. Studies of the style of Alphonsine texts have cited pairs in examples of the amplification of Latin texts.[14]

Like other aspects of the style of the *PMC*, its use of pairs is only partially reflected in the prosification in the *CVR*. The majority of the pairs in the prosification are pairs created by the chroniclers and not in the poem, but the more concrete and vivid ones are often taken direct from the poem. The most frequent pairs to appear in the *PMC* are: 'oro e plata', 'noche e dia', 'moros e christianos'. This has influenced the *CVR* to some extent. Amongst the examples of the *CVR*'s pairs borrowed directly from the *PMC* are the following basic pairs, which are subject to minor verbal variations: 'oro e plata' (fols 115c, 118c, 154a, 160a (twice); compare ll. 473, 821, 1737, 3204, 3238), 'moros e christianos' (fols 121a (twice), 157c; compare ll. 968, 988, 2498), 'dia e noche' (fols 116a, 158c; compare ll. 562, 2810), 'pies e manos' (fols 119b, 152b, 159a; compare ll. 879, 1323, 2937), 'malo e traydor' (fols 160c, 161b; compare ll. 3343, 3442), 'de reyes e de enperadores' (fols 157d, 160b; compare ll. 2553, 3297), 'moros e moras' (fol. 115b; compare l. 465), 'mis manos e mis hordenes' (fol. 157b; compare l. 2373). Despite accepting these and other pairs from the poem into their prose version, the chroniclers saw to it that the pairs often do not have the same stylistic effect in the chronicle. They did this by amplifying a pair with a third element or by placing it in an otherwise longer expression: e.g. 'mucho oro e mucha plata e otras muchas donas buenas' (fol. 115c); or they changed the order of the two parts: e.g. 'traydores e malos' (161b). Many of the well-preserved pairs appear in direct speech.

Besides these parallel pairs in poem and chronicle, the *PMC*'s pairs perhaps influenced the *CVR* elsewhere in the prosification. Some poetic pairs are found in parts of the prose redaction which do not correspond to their use in the poem. The examples noted are: 'oro e plata' (fols 114b, 114c, 116c, increased by a third element in two of the three cases), 'moros e moras' (fols 115c, 116c; though compare l. 619), 'cavalleros e peones' (fols 114d, 115d, 150b; see ll. 848, 395, 512–14, 1199. Note the rhetorical amplification of the poem in two of the three examples), 'de pie e de cavallo' (fol. 116c; see l. 1291), 'a rey e a señor' (fol. 155a; see l. 2109). In other cases, the *CVR* has altered the *PMC* pairs by changing or omitting one or both parts, often leaving no pair at all. For example, 'çient moros e çient moras' (l. 534) becomes 'çient moros con sus mugeres' (fol. 116a); 'a los unos firiendo e a los otros derocando' (l. 1007) becomes 'derribando los unos e matando los otros' (fol. 121b); 'Calla alevoso, malo e traydor' (l. 3383) becomes 'Calla, alevoso traydor' (fol. 160d), despite the original including a poetic pair, in direct speech, and used elsewhere by the chroniclers. Many of the other pairs of the poem, and they are numerous, have, of course, left no trace in the *CVR* text. There seems to be no particular pattern common to those pairs omitted or included by the chroniclers.

As mentioned previously, there are quite a few pairs in the *CVR* which are not found in the poem. A few of these are worthy of being poetic pairs, while the majority are more prosaic, and include some which are hardly pairs at all. Pairs not in the *PMC* but which seem worthy of a poetic origin are: 'parientes e vasallos' (fol. 114a; before the *PMC* begins), 'ensellados e enfrenados' (fol. 118b, 152a; see quote in Pidal, *CMC*, p. 640), 'la su graçia e el su amor' (fol. 118c), 'fuero nin costunbre' (fol. 121d), 'alueñe e açerca' (fol. 151d). More prosaic pairs in the *CVR* include: 'paños e dyneros' (fol. 114b), 'graçias e merçedes' (fol. 162b), 'mucho bien e mucha merçed' (fol. 118d), 'mucho bien e mucha honrra' (fol. 157c), 'en la su pro e en la su honrra' (fol. 155b), 'del mal e de la desonrra' (fol. 159a), 'ricos e honrrados' (fols 114b, 151d, 154b), 'ricos e abondados' (fol. 157c), 'suelto e quito' (fol. 152d), 'sueltos e benditos' (fol. 119c), 'quebranto e robo' (fol. 149c), 'levando e sacando' (fol. 117d). As can be seen, most of these examples occur only once, although elements may occur in more than one pair. Like the pairs based on the *PMC*, these pairs may be diffused in effectiveness by inclusion in more amplificatory expressions (e.g. 'ricos e honrrados e con grand honrra' (fol. 114b)). It is clear that the habit of creating pairs existed alongside other methods of rhetorical amplification in the compositional technique of the prosifiers of the poem. The fact that the prosaic pairs are mainly found once only, while poetic pairs are often found repeatedly, suggests that the former were individual creations, while the latter were probably part of the common usage of the period.[15]

In the use of pairs in the *CVR*, therefore, we can see the influences of the poetic, the popular, and the rhetorical traditions. The majority of pairs in the chronicle are the result of the third of these, but the popular and poetic have left their mark. Their pairs are the more concrete and vivid, although they too can become the basis for rhetorical amplification. It is they that make the prosification of the poem different in this stylistic aspect from parts of the chronicle not based on a poetic source.[16]

D. *Other Stylistic Features*

(i)   Absolute phrases

Absolute phrases are those phrases which have no active verb and no grammatical link with the sentence in which they stand. Traditionally, the most famous type of absolute phrase is the Latin ablative absolute, based on the past participle of the verb. It has been observed that the *PMC* has some notable absolute phrases based on past participles, and a learned Latin origin has been suggested for them. Absolute phrases which use the gerund have also been noted in the poem.[17] In the *CVR*, such absolute phrases are found, but there seems to be no traceable influence of the poem in their use. In the prosification, two absolute phrases of noun and past participle appear, but they are the rather uninteresting 'esto fecho, esto dicho' (fols 152b, 155a; compare ll. 54, 320, 366, 1703, 3678). Although the *PMC* uses both 'fecho' and 'dicho' in absolute phrases, these phrases have a more concrete noun in them than 'esto', which is, however, used elsewhere with the same verbs as in the *CVR* (see ll. 188, 915, 1473, 2686). Expressions with the gerund are more common in both texts. In one example, the *CVR* has copied the *PMC*: 'faziendome el mucho serviçio' (fol. 154d; l. 1891), but in other examples, the two texts are independent. The *CVR* has a majority of cases in which the gerundial expression is equivalent to an adverbial clause, usually of time: e.g. 'El Çid diziendo esto, vieron . . .' (fol. 121b; compare l. 1000), 'Ellos en esto fablando, enbio . . .' (fol. 157a). The poem has a few examples of this (e.g. ll. 1926, 2311), but most of its absolute expressions in this category are caused by elliptical omissions of an active verb: e.g. 'por el cobdo ayuso la sangre destellando' (ll. 501, 781, 1724, 2453). On the whole, therefore, the use of absolute expressions with the past participle is a stylistic feature of the poem which is not frequent in the chronicle, whereas the use of gerundial expressions is more developed in the *CVR* than in the *PMC*.[18]

(ii)   *Admiratio*

The rhetorical topic of *admiratio*, that is the use of special phrases for the description of superlative amounts, is present in both the *PMC* and the *CVR*. It is typically used in the poem for numbers of men in battle and for amounts of booty. The few examples of this type of expression found in the *CVR* tend to reflect, but not to copy, the poem. In two cases, the *CVR* uses the phrase: 'tantos . . . que non avian cuenta' (fols 117b, 157b). Although there are several lines of this nature in the poem (see ll. 918, 1983, 2257, 2491, 2529), neither case in the *CVR* reflects such a line. Instead, the first one in the *CVR* replaces a different *admiratio* phrase: '¿qui los podrie contar?' (l. 699; see also ll. 1214, 1218), while the second conveys the effect of a long description (ll. 2403–06).[19] The other two examples in the *CVR* replace two further ways of expressing *admiratio* in the *PMC*. A metaphor in the poem (l. 696) is replaced by the more prosaic, 'tantos eran los roydos . . . que se non podien oyr los omnes' (fol. 117b), and a similar phrase in the *CVR*, 'las mas ricas tiendas que omne nunca vio' (fol. 154a), seems to replace a simple exclamation, '¡Tanta tienda preçiada!' (l. 1783; but compare l. 1996). The *PMC* does not seem to use *admiratio* expressions based on 'omne', as the *CVR* does.[20] Therefore, the *admiratio* phrases of the poem are poorly represented in the chronicle. There are no cases of direct verbal parallels. For the most part, to describe great amounts, the *CVR* sticks to 'mucho' and its variants, sometimes reinforced or replaced by 'ademas' (e.g. fols 118a, 155c, 156a, 157b).

(iii)   *Oppositum*

Oppositum is a rhetorical device which consists of emphasizing a positive statement with an immediately subsequent negative one. The bipartite line of the *PMC* lends itself to this type of expression, and there are many examples in the poem, ranging from simple contrast of words to that of more complex ideas. The second hemistich in the negative can have strong dramatic resonance. Examples are:

mas nos preçiamos, sabet, que menos no (l. 3300; see ll. 2038, 2320, etc.)
passo gelo todo, que nada nol valio (l. 3632; see ll. 1193, 2011, etc.)
por muertas las dexaron, sabet, que non por bivas (l. 2748).

In the *CVR*, the use of the device is infrequent, but it does seem to respond to its use in the *PMC*, on some of the occasions when it appears. There is one clear example taken from the *PMC*, 'muertos, que non vençidos' (fol. 161d; l. 3529), and one less clear, 'que el casara sus fijos con ellos, ca el non' (fol. 159a; l. 2908). One other example possibly had a poetic origin, but it falls in the lacuna near the start of the third 'cantar': 'fuxo, que solamente non lo quiso esperar' (fol. 157a). Other cases of this device in the *CVR* are diffused by the wording of the chronicle, so that the two parts are not simply expressed nor obviously contrasted. Some are hardly examples of *oppositum* at all; for example, 'que sse callassen de aquella razon, e que non fablasen y mas' (fol. 161b; ll. 3563–64; see fols 120a, 157a). In other words, the *CVR* rarely employs the device of *oppositum*, and only once does it clearly use it as the poem does.[21].

(iv) *Sententiae*

The final stylistic feature to be noted here is the use of *sententiae*, or proverbial pieces of wisdom. The poet of the *PMC* uses these occasionally, and it is interesting to note that two of them have been very carefully preserved in the *CVR*. With the first of them, the chroniclers even mention the 'palabra del proverbio'. The two are: 'quien buen señor sirve, esse bive en bienandança' (fol. 118d; l. 850), and 'quien buen mandadero enbia, buen mandado espera' (fol. 153b; l. 1457). The proverbial nature of these two sentences, which is visible even in their language, must have helped ensure their preservation, but they seem to be the only such examples preserved in the prosified *PMC*.[22]

II.   THE LANGUAGE OF THE *PMC* IN THE *CVR*

A.   *Assonance Words in the 'CVR'*

The assonance words at the end of the lines of the *PMC* are obviously important points in the poem, for they are the rhythmic points around which the rest revolves. In critical studies which aim to correct the manuscript of the poem (see note 1 above), the key to many emendations is the establishment of an assonance word, since other parts of a line are more flexible in the metre of the *PMC*. The chronicles, and particularly the *CVR*, have often been used to emend or to provide assonances in the critical editions of the poem. It is of interest, therefore, to examine the number of assonance words from the manuscript of the poem which demonstrably survive in the prosification in the *CVR*. Many assonance words in the poem are names, such as 'Sol', 'Carrión', 'Alfonso', which the chronicle was bound to use. Many others are verbs in tenses which provide assonance, but which are not strictly logical, and which are therefore changed in the *CVR* (e.g. ll. 458–72). The comparison of the two texts can, then, give only a rough guide to the presence of assonance words in the *CVR*, but it can place in perspective the possibility of rescuing lost poetic assonances from the prose.

In the prosification of the first 'cantar' of the *PMC* in the *CVR*, just over one hundred assonance words are preserved, approximately ten per cent of the total.[23] The longest series of assonances preserved in the prose is four. This occurs once in the prosification of the roll-call of heroes at Alcocer (fol. 117c;

ll. 737–40). Three of the four words are names of people or places, and so unavoidable in the *CVR*. The fourth, 'criado', does not fit into the stressed 'o' assonance sequence of the 'tirada' anyway.[24] A second series of four is kept, from near the end of the 'cantar', none of which are proper names. The four assonance words form part of a nine-line section of the poem which is unusually well-preserved in the *CVR*, in direct speech, of course (fol. 122a; ll. 1068–76, particularly ll. 1072–75). In the rest of the 'cantar' no more than two successive assonances seem to have survived in the prose, although such pairs are quite frequent. Beside the assonance words from the poem, however, there are often misleading words in the chronicle text, words of the same assonance as the poem is using in the section where they appear, but not taken directly from the poem. A good example from the first 'cantar' is Alfonso VI's speech in reply to the presentation of the Cid's first gift to him (fol. 119c; ll. 881–93). In direct speech, and beginning in á–a assonance in the poem, the speech in the chronicle contains thirteen words which could end a poetic line of that assonance. Only six of them are, in fact, from the *PMC*, and seven are new to the chronicle.[25]

In the prosification of the second 'cantar' in the *CVR*, less than six per cent of the poem's assonance words are kept. No more than two successive assonance words are preserved. It may be instructive, at this point, to cite an example of the preservation of two such words, which shows how much the chronicle can change the poem even while preserving assonances:

e fizole obispo de Valençia, porque le semejo buen christiano. El Çid dixo estonçes a Alvar Fanez, 'Graçias a Dios, agora podredes levar buenos mandados a Castilla' (fol. 152b; ll. 1300–01).

The two assonance words are 'christiano' and 'mandado'. The poetic rhythm which joins them in the poem is destroyed by the prose, so that to recreate the lines accurately would be very difficult. An example of the presence of misleading words in the *CVR* of the same assonance as the parallel poetic section can be given from the second 'cantar'. In a speech by the Cid to his family on the arrival of a Moorish army at Valencia (fol. 154a; ll. 1647–56), there are six words appropriate to the á(–e) assonance of the poem. Not one of these is, in fact, in the poem.[26] In the prose version of the third and final 'cantar' of the poem, a little under ten per cent of the assonance words could be traced. A large number of pairs of assonances are preserved. There are two series of three, and two series of four, which are all found in the court scenes towards the end of the 'cantar' (fols 159c–d, 160a, 160b–c, 161a; ll. 3145–48, 3266–68, 3302–04, 3394–97). The concentration of names and of direct speech in the court scenes seems to lie behind the comparatively high number of assonances kept in the prosification of that section of the *PMC*. Of the series cited above, the first of the four-word groups has three lines of direct speech and includes one name; the second such group is made up of four names, in what is admittedly a section of the poem which invites emendation. The two three-line series are in direct speech, and one line of one of them ends in a name.[27]

In the whole prosification of the *PMC* in the *CVR*, then, just over three hundred of the assonance words are preserved directly from the poem, from more than three thousand seven hundred lines of the original. No more than four successive words seem to have been kept at any time. Many of the words that are preserved are names, and therefore unavoidable for the chroniclers. Otherwise, the chroniclers seem to have avoided assonance words on many occasions, when they could easily have used them. Obviously, therefore, the creation of lines, for an edition of the poem, based on the text of the *CVR* must be a speculative process, which is complicated by the presence of misleading words in the prose. Examples quoted above clearly show that the mere presence of words of the same assonance is no assurance of their origin in lines of the poem. Even where possible assonance words exist, it does not seem sensible to see new poetic lines in the *CVR*, unless there is definite extra information to that found in all known sources, which could not have been deduced or added by the compilers of the chronicle.[28]

B. *Personal Epithets*

Personal epithets, epic epithets, are a very prominent feature of the language of the *PMC*. They are used very frequently, particularly in reference to the Cid himself (see Smith, *PMC*, p. lv). They are found as a whole line or in the second hemistich of a line, thus providing the assonance. They are formulaic in that they are often used more than once with or without minor variations to the basic epithet, but they are still used with conscious artistry to fit the context in which they appear.[29] The prosifiers of the *PMC* must have regarded the epic epithet as a distinctly poetic element, for, in the *CVR*, very few have survived. Apart from names applied to the Cid, which are considered below, the only clearly poetic epithets preserved in the chronicle all appear in one group. This group is the roll-call of heroes at the battle of Alcocer, the only roll-call in the *CVR* (fol. 117c; ll. 734–41; compare ll. 1991–96, 3063–71). The six epithets applied to the Cid's knights are all kept in some form in the prose, but none of them is preserved exactly as in the poem. The poetic words and wording are changed so that rhythm and emotional effect are lost. For example, 'el burgales de pro' becomes 'de Burgos', 'el bueno de Aragon' becomes 'un buen cavallero de Aragon'. The poem is descriptive, the chronicle is factual. Outside this list, scarcely any personal epithets are found. Perhaps the following qualify: 'don Garçia, que era enemigo del Çid' (fol. 154b; l. 1836), 'Bucar, aquel fi de henemiga' (fol. 157a; lacuna ll. 2337–38). Otherwise, the prosifiers have simply ignored epithets of the type used so well in the poem.[30]

The names attached to the Cid himself are of interest as a separate group. Most of them can hardly be called epic epithets; but they show distinct preferences on the part of the chroniclers. Of the true epithets, few survive. 'Campeador' is only found three times in the whole prosification, although it is the most frequent epithet apart from 'el Çid' in the poem (and it is used in Latin texts, particularly the *HR*). In its three appearances in the prosification in the *CVR*, it twice replaces more poetic epithets, 'el buen lidiador' (fol. 117c; l. 734), and 'que en buen ora çinxo espada' (fol. 119b; l. 875). It once corresponds to the same form in the poem (fol. 152d; l. 1369). The *CVR* seems to have deliberately not used 'Campeador' very much, and to have thus avoided copying the poem.[31] The epithet 'de Bivar' is found twice in the *CVR*, on both occasions taken directly from the *PMC* (fol. 116d, l. 628; fol. 120d, l. 961). The most poetic epithet preserved in the chronicle is found in direct speech, said by the Cid about himself, when he shouts to Búcar: 'Veerte as con el Çid de la barva luenga' (fol. 157b; l. 2410). The prose redaction has changed the poetic adjective, but the substance of the epithet remains.[32] As regards the straightforward names used for the Cid, 'el Çid' is by far the most common in the *CVR* whatever the source being used, with 'Ruy Diaz' the next most popular form. In the prosification of the *PMC*, 'don Rodrigo' is found proportionately more often than in the poem. It is clearly considered a polite form, since it is used to the Cid by the Count of Barcelona, Bishop Jerónimo, and King Alfonso. Only once do poem and chronicle coincide in its employment (see fol. 121c; l. 1028; and fols 121d, 122a, 155b, 157b, 161c–d). The familiar 'mio Çid' appears only three times in the prosification, all in the first 'cantar', and all taken directly from the *PMC* (fol. 119b, l. 875; fol. 119c, l. 892; fol. 120a, l. 902).[33]

Overall, the highly developed system of epic epithets which we find in the *PMC* has almost completely vanished from the *CVR*. The role of the personal epithet in the poem is in no way reproduced in the chronicle. This is particularly clear in the names applied to the Cid in the chronicle. Except for rare instances, the dullest and most obvious forms are used. The only mild exception is that the chroniclers' sense of propriety has led them to use the polite 'don Rodrigo' more often than any more poetic form.

C. 'Physical' Phrases

The appearance of phrases which include references to parts of the body in a symbolical or metaphorical way is a feature of epic language that has received some critical attention. While such phrases are probably a universal element of language, there is a concentration of them in the *PMC* not to be found elsewhere. In presentation of the *PMC* or similar works by a performer to an audience, it is probable that at least some of the references to parts of the body were accompanied by apt mime and gestures from the 'juglar'.[34] In the *CVR*, the complexity and variety apparent in the *PMC*'s use of such phrases is drastically reduced, but not entirely lost. Although many of the phrases in the *CVR* were probably in general usage, others seem certain to be examples of the influence of the poem. The parts of the body referred to by the chronicle are mainly 'corazón', 'mano', 'barba', with, in addition, a few miscellaneous ones.

(i) *Corazón*

In western civilization, the heart has commonly been associated with the emotions. This holds true for its use in the *PMC* and the *CVR*. In both texts, it is used frequently with verbs of pleasure and pain. Seven cases have been noted where 'corazón' appears in the *CVR* directly from the *PMC*. In all seven, the verbs in both texts are the same: three times 'plazer' (fol. 152c, l. 1355; fol. 155a, l. 1947; fol. 158a, l. 2623), three times 'pesar' (fol. 116d, l. 636; fol. 158c, l. 2815; fol. 158c–d, l. 2825) and once 'doler' (fol. 158b; l. 2767). The frequency of the word 'corazón' in the language as a whole at the time of *CVR* seems to be indicated by the fact that the prosification has a further seven cases of the word in places where it is not in the *PMC*. Three cases are in additions to the poetic text probably due to the compilers, although their wording is reminiscent of the examples referred to above: 'le plazie el coraçon' (fols 153b, 157d), 'le dolie el coraçon' (fol. 158c). The other four cases show the *CVR* following the poem, but introducing the physical reference where the poem has none. Two represent emotion and excitement: 'pesole mucho de coraçon' (fol. 120d; see l. 959), 'non gelo pudo sofrir el coraçon' (fol. 117b; see l. 704). The other two refer to thoughts: 'si vos viniere a coraçon, . . . non tengo agora en coraçon' (fol. 122a; ll. 1070, 1076). The acceptance by the *CVR* of phrases involving 'corazón' suggests that the use of the word was very common in the language, and that certain phrases were clichés typical of the rather staid, repetitive vocabulary of the chronicle. However, it seems possible too that the general use of physical phrases in the *PMC* may have encouraged the chronicle.[35]

(ii) *Mano*

Reference to the hand or hands is the most frequent type of physical reference in both the *PMC* and in the prose redaction of it in the *CVR*. The act of humility, allegiance, or petition, represented by the kissing of the hand of a social superior, is particularly well accepted by the chroniclers. They use it on more than a dozen occasions, directly copying the poem, except that twice the poem has stronger expressions of humility, which the *CVR* has watered down (fol. 154b, l. 1844; fol 159a, l. 2935). Several times feet are mentioned as well as hands (e.g. fol. 119b, l. 879; fol. 152b, ll. 1322–23; fol. 155b, l. 2028; fol. 159a, l. 2937). The *CVR* never uses such an expression where the poem does not, and it seems fair to suggest that frequent reference to this type of action elsewhere in the chronicle would denote a probable poetic source. Other sections of the *CVR*, and other chronicles tend to support this suggestion.[36]

Other references in the *CVR* to the hand range from the purely physical, such as the washing of hands (fol. 122a; l. 1049), to the symbolic. More symbolic instances taken from the poem include the giving of the Cid's daughters (fol. 155c–d; ll. 2134, 2228), the promise of freedom to the Count of Barcelona (fol. 121d; l. 1035), and the desire for honour of Jerónimo (fol. 157b; l. 2373). The grasping of the beard is mentioned too (see below). A couple of examples have no direct poetic equivalent: on leaving Castejón the Cid, in the *CVR*, 'dexolos [moros] de su mano en el castillo' (fol. 116a); for the raid on Alcañiz, the Cid took, 'dozientos cavalleros . . . escogidos a mano' (fol. 120c; possibly of poetic origin, see *CMC*, III, 1061). These two examples are not very surprising, except that they have a slightly colloquial tone in the *CVR*. They were, and are, common expressions. It did not need their appearance in the poem for the chroniclers to use them, although the frequency of phrases with 'mano' in the *PMC* perhaps suggested their employment to the prosifiers of the poem.[37]

(iii) *Barba*

The Cid's beard is a sign of his virility and authority in the *PMC*, and it is a symbol of traditional significance of this kind outside the *PMC*, in texts from Spain and elsewhere.[38] The power and life of the symbol is shown by the fact that it has survived into the *CVR* in several contexts. It was noted above that the most poetic epithet preserved in the *CVR* is a reference to the Cid's beard (fol. 157b; l. 2410; see II, *B*). In addition, the chronicle includes the Cid's original decision to let it grow, the clutching of the beard and the swearing by it, and the exchange of insults concerning beards between the Cid and García Ordóñez.[39] The Cid's beard is the strongest poetic symbol accepted by the *CVR*. It is mentioned quite consistently in the chronicle, if not as often or with as much variety as in the *PMC*. The reason may have been that the image of the Cid and his beard had established itself in the general Cidian tradition outside the *PMC*, by the time of the prosification.[40]

(iv) Other 'physical' phrases

The majority of 'physical' phrases used in the *CVR* prosification fall into the categories already discussed. There are other purely physical references, especially in battles and in the duels. Of greater interest here are the more symbolic ones. 'Cuerpo' is found twice taken from the poem (fol. 121d, l. 1035; fol. 152d, l. 1365), and twice when not in the poem: 'fue el Çid por su cuerpo ferir en los moros' (fol. 117c), and the euphemistic 'el cuerpo que estarie a su merçed' (fol. 152a; see l. 1254). Some of the metaphors of the *PMC* have been adopted: 'mi diestro braço' (fol. 117c; l. 753), 'lengua ssyn manos' (fol. 160c;

l. 3328), 'boca ssin verdad' (fol. 160d; l. 3362). These all occur in direct speech. Finally, the use of a superfluous physical reference to reinforce a verb is found only as 'dezir de la boca', which occurs twice in quick succession, once when the poem only has the verb (fol. 160d, ll. 3370–71; fols 160d–61a, l. 3389).[41]

The practice of using 'physical' references as an integral part of the linguistic system of the *PMC* has undoubtedly had an influence on the *CVR*. The majority of 'physical' phrases in the prose are taken directly from the poem. However, the existence of a number of examples in the *CVR* where 'physical' references have been added to the poem shows that the said system extended beyond poetic usage (as Smith and Morris show), although the richness of the language of the poem is unchallenged.

D. References to the 'Divine'

The *PMC* contains frequent references to God, Christ and the Saints. They are invoked almost in passing, or their help is sought, or thanks are given to them (see, for example, ll. 8, 20, 48, 94, 457, 675, 792, etc.). Such expressions were useful to the poet, for they can fill out lines, and provide half-lines or full lines with appropriate assonances. They take a great variety of forms including periphrases, although the simple 'Dios' or 'el Criador' are most frequent (see, for example, ll. 1047, 1651, 3714). Occasionally, their use in the poem seems almost ironical (see ll. 8, 2830), and God's name particularly is included almost casually (see ll. 243, 806, 1052, etc.). In the *CVR*, 'divine' references get much less space than in the poem, despite the concern shown elsewhere for ecclesiastical affairs (see fols 128, 131–35). The more casual references to God are entirely omitted, except for a single 'Por Dios', uttered by Feliz Muñoz (fol. 158c; ll. 2781–82). All periphrases are also removed by *CVR*. In the prosification, 'Dios' is invoked over thirty times, and help is sought or thanks given in simple repeated phrases such as 'graçias a Dios', 'mande Dios que', 'si Dios quisier' (e.g. fols 118c, 119d, 152c, 158c). Once, the name of 'Santiago' is added, and twice that of 'Santa Maria' (fol. 149c, l. 1138; fol. 152a, l. 1267; fol. 153d, l. 1637). The use of 'Dios' in the *CVR* is paralleled directly in the poem by 'Dios' on eight occasions (e.g. fol. 154a, l. 1656; fol. 157c, l. 2412), by 'el Criador' on seven (e.g. fol. 117b, l. 706; fol. 152c, l. 1334), and twice by longer names (fol. 121d, l. 1047; fol. 162b, l. 3714). In the other half of the examples, the *CVR* names the deity without there being a direct equivalent in the *PMC*. Christ is named proportionately more often in the *CVR* than in the *PMC*, but still only in three cases. Just one of these corresponds to this name in the *PMC*, although the other two correspond to different divine references (see fol. 116c, l. 614; fol. 117a, l. 675; fol. 157c, l. 2477).

In other words, the *CVR* responds to the 'divine' references in the *PMC* only to a limited extent. It in no way reflects the frequency with which such phrases occur in the poem, nor the variety of language found there. It used its conventional phraseology when responding to references in the *PMC*, and when adding divine references of its own, where the chroniclers felt they were appropriate.[42]

III. CONCLUSION

The intention of this chapter has been to study the influence of the very distinctive style and language of the epic poem, the *PMC*, on the prose of the chronicle, the *CVR*. The theme is of fundamental interest, particularly because of its implications for the study of other sections of the chronicle which have lost sources thought to have been epic poems. The detailed examination and comparison of the two texts for the purposes of this chapter yielded evidence of varying degrees of usefulness, and this evidence I have dealt with in categories which reflect both the internal nature of the evidence itself and relevant previous studies of style and language, particularly of the poem. The categories are by no means comprehensive, but they provide a good range of material, which, I believe, does not omit any substantial area of poetic influence on the prose of the chronicle. As I have said, the results of the study are of varying degrees of value. On the positive side, there is, first and foremost, the emergence of direct speech as the most prominent linguistic pointer to the presence of a poetic source. The contrasting amounts of speech recorded in sections of the chronicle dependent or not dependent on the *PMC* are very striking. The prosification of speech is mentioned as the place where the most notable poetic expressions are revealed in the studies of word-order, pairs, assonance words, epithets, and physical phrases. There is no doubt that it is in their treatment of speech that the chroniclers reveal most obviously that there is a poetic original behind their prose. On the positive side, too, although of less profound resonance, is the effect of the repeated action of kissing the hand, which seems a small detail, as it perhaps did to the chroniclers, but which copies the poem more consistently than any other single phrase or expression (although it reflects content as well as language, for which see Chapter 5). The remainder of the results of my study tend to be on the negative side. There are inevitably reflections of the *PMC*'s use of certain categories of expression or modes of expression in the prose of the *CVR*, but these are relatively few, and tend to be the more conventional ones. There is no doubt in my mind that the prosifiers of the poem had the general intention to conceal the poetic nature of their source, to omit or replace its assonance words whenever they could, to change its poetic phraseology to the prosaic, and to transfer the poem to prose as similar as possible to the prose of the rest of their chronicle. With the exception of the large amounts of speech, and even in the transcription of most of that speech, they have carried out their intention very successfully. Stylistically, despite the poetic source, the *CVR* remains very much the prose chronicle written in rather dull, repetitive style and language. So efficient were the prosifiers, that the idea of reconstructing parts of the poem from the text of the chronicle is not a practical one. To recreate more than a very few lines of the *PMC* on the basis of the *CVR* would obviously be impossible.[43]

CHAPTER 5

THE REPRESENTATION OF THE *POEMA DE MIO CID* IN THE *CRÓNICA DE VEINTE REYES*

The purpose of this chapter is to study the accuracy of the representation of the extant *PMC* in the *CVR*; to examine how far the exact information in the *CVR* agrees with that in the *PMC*, and the extent to which the chroniclers introduced distortions of the poetic content into their prose redaction. It will be seen that the composers of the account found in the *CVR* were selective in what they chose to include from the *PMC*. Their approach and their methods involved a systematic overall reduction of the poem's content for the prose version. The chroniclers had less interest in certain categories of topics, such as descriptions of clothing and the Cid with his family, than in others, such as battles and the Cid and Alfonso VI. Every episode that was included went through a process of pruning, in which half-lines, whole lines, or groups of lines were omitted by the chronicle, while others were prosified closely; or whole episodes were reduced to summaries of their poetic content, in which individual lines are hard to identify. The result of all this is that some sections of the *PMC* are well reproduced in the *CVR*, while others are severely curtailed.[1] On the other side of the coin, when they did prosify the *PMC* closely, the chroniclers were often obliged to expand colloquial, elliptical, or densely expressed parts of the poem in order to convey their meaning in prose. In addition, they added comments or information on their own accounts, to clarify events, to explain the motivations of the personages, or to add rhetorical adornment, and they introduced changes to the exact content of the poem, by, for example, altering the roles of some of the persons, and reordering series of lines to improve the logic of the narrative flow. In the past, many of these additions and changes to the content of the *PMC* have been used to emend the *PMC*, on the basis that they have their origin in a more perfect form of the *PMC* which was known to the *CVR* (or to the *PCG* in most studies). I shall argue, however, that the vast majority of them are explicable in terms of the chroniclers' own methods. They are the result of interference with the poem's content during the prosification. Admittedly, there are a small number of cases, where differences of factual detail are involved, for which the chroniclers are unlikely to be responsible. These cases will be discussed, of course, in this chapter.[2]

I. THE ACCURACY OF THE *CVR*

A.   *The Personages and their Names*

The names of the personages who appear in the *PMC* are recorded in the *CVR* with notable accuracy. There are often minor variations of one or two letters in the spelling of the names between the two texts (as there are between MSS of the *CVR*). For example, the *CVR* normally has 'Miñaya' compared to the *PMC*'s 'Minaya', and 'Bermudez' for the *PMC*'s 'Vermuez'. But there are also such variations in spelling within the texts themselves (e.g. *PMC*, l. 1211; *CVR*, fol. 162b). Thus, in the *CVR*, besides the most prominent characters, we find the names of knights of the Cid such as 'Muño Gustioz', 'Feliz Muñoz', 'Alvar Alvarez', of Moors such as 'Abengabon', 'Fariz', 'Galve', 'Tamin', and of Christians such as 'Asur Gonçalez', 'Gomez Pelaez', 'Ojarra', 'Yñigo Ximenez'. The similarity of these forms to those of the *PMC* is striking.[3] In two cases, the chronicle seems to have reacted warily to more unusual Christian names, and turned them into common ones: 'Guillen' for 'Galin', 'Enrrique' for 'Anrrich' or 'Anrric' (fol. 117c, l. 740; fol. 159b, l. 3002; fol. 159c, l. 3135). In both cases, the name preferred by the chroniclers is a familiar one which has obvious similarities with the unusual poetic one. There seems to be no example where the chronicle has distorted a person's name in the poem to any serious extent.

Five personages not in the relevant section of the *PMC* are mentioned in the prosification. Three of them appear around the events of the battle between the Cid and Yuçef, where the *HR* is being used to add details to the *PMC* (see Chapter 3, IV). Two kings are named as allies of Yuçef, 'el rey Bucar e el rey Soro de Lerida', and, after the battle, 'Pero Salvadorez' dies in the pursuit (fols 153d–54a; ll. 1625–728). Although 'Bucar' appears elsewhere in the poem and 'Pero Salvadorez' is reminiscent of 'Alvar Salvadorez' (l. 1681), who is not mentioned in the *CVR*, these details do not seem likely to have come from the poetic source of the *CVR*.[4] The two other extra names in the *CVR* both appear in the list of nobles who go to Alfonso VI's court to hear the complaints against the Infantes de Carrión (fol. 159b; ll. 3001–08). The list of nobles in the *CVR* is the same as that in the *PMC* except that 'Alvar Diaz' is named after Count García and 'Pero Ançurez' after 'Gonçalo Ançurez'. Despite Pidal's emendations (*CMC*, III, 1137–38), it seems best to regard these additions as the initiative of the chroniclers. Alvar Díaz is mentioned elsewhere in the poem amongst the enemies of the Cid (fol. 155b; l. 2042). Pedro Ansúrez was perhaps the most illustrious member of that family, since he was a close adviser of Alfonso VI, and figured in events of the reign of Sancho II (see *PCG*, pp. 503, 513–15; *CVR*, fols 95r, 105). There are precedents for such an initiative by the chroniclers within the prosification of the *PMC*. The daughters of the Cid are named in the *CVR* long before they are named in the poem (fol. 153a). The Abbot of Cardeña is identified by his name where the *PMC* omits it (fol. 153a; l. 1422). Certainly, there is no need for Alvar Díaz and Pedro Ansúrez to have been in the original source of the *CVR* to explain their appearance here.[5]

The chronicle does not mention the personages of the poem by name every time that its source does. Omissions of special interest are the names of the money-lenders, Rachel and Vidas (l. 89, etc.), and that of the angel Gabriel, who appeared to the Cid (fol. 114d; l. 407). Perhaps the chroniclers found this particular name hard to accept. There are many other omissions, too, of people referred to in some places in the chronicle but not in others, as well as of those personages only named once in the poem and never in the prose.[6] However, the *CVR* transmits those names it mentions with notable accuracy, consistency, and closeness to the extant manuscript of the poem.

B.   Place Names

There is a great amount of geographical information contained in the lines of the *PMC*. It ranges from the names of great cities through towns and villages to topographical features such as rivers, woods and mountains. Attempts have been made to identify all the locations named in the poem, in order to ascertain the areas best known to the poet, in the belief that this will reveal the homeland of the poet or the district in which the poem was composed. The chronicles have been used to 'correct' or to support the geographical details in the *PMC* (and, in one edition, the reverse has been done). Different studies have come to different conclusions, because of varying identifications of places named in the poem and varying methods of deduction.[7] The general comparability of the *CVR* and the *PMC* from this point of view has not been fully considered previously.

The *CVR* transmits most place names it includes in forms which are close to those of the extant *PMC*. Place names presented a different problem from names of characters, for the latter were normally easily recognizable for the chroniclers, at least in the case of the Christian characters. Two first names they did not recognize the chroniclers changed (see above). With geographical references, however, they must have been faced frequently with names they had not come across before. Thus, there are more variations in spelling geographical names than names of people, both between the *PMC* and the *CVR* and between manuscripts of the *CVR*, but most places are still clearly identifiable as the same ones being referred to in both poem and prose. Of course, some names of important features are transmitted without any problems. Thus, many names such as Valencia, Burgos, Duero, Bivar and the frequently repeated Castejón, Alcocer, Corpes, are accurately conveyed.[8] So are those of smaller places such as 'La Figueruela', 'Ssierra de Miedes',

'Çetina', while others have small differences in spelling between the poem and the chronicle. Compare, for example: *CVR* Espinazo de Can, *PMC* Spinaz de Can; una Nava de Palos, Navas de Palos; Anguita, Anquita; Çelfa la del Cañal, Çelfa la de Canal. Both texts are not entirely consistent in their orthography of such names, in any case. Greater divergence between chronicle and poem exists in the names of a few places: *CVR* Çuhera or Cullera, *PMC* Gujera (fols 154a, 149c; ll. 1727, 1160); Fronchales, Frontael (fol. 153b; l. 1475); Deça, Teca (fol. 116d; ll. 625, 632). In the first and second cases, Pidal maintained that the *CVR* is closer to the name of the place referred to than the *PMC* (*CMC*, II, 696, 713).[9]

Real differences between the *CVR* and the *PMC* in the matter of places and their names are also found. They are found both with single words, and with longer examples which involve more than simply a name. The single words imply either a difference in the manuscript source of the *CVR* from the extant manuscript, or that the manuscript was barely legible. Legibility seems the likely reason in the case of *PMC* Alucad (l. 1108) and *CVR* Calatayud (fol. 149c) (but with wildly different versions in manuscripts J, Ll). *CVR* N seems to have chosen a safe name. 'Alucat' is transmitted accurately elsewhere (fol. 120d; l. 951). The reason is less obvious in the case of *PMC* Molina and *CVR* Medina (fols 119a, 158a; ll. 867, 2647). There is no doubt that Molina is the place referred to (see especially fol. 158a). However, the *CVR* does not normally copy badly; other manuscripts of the *CVR* agree with N (as does *PCG*, p. 530.b), and the copyist of the extant *PMC* corrected the same error elsewhere (see CMC, III, 955, note to 1545). Probably the *PMC* has the name corrected from an earlier manuscript, but the *CVR* derives from an uncorrected manuscript. A copyist's error seems unlikely, too, in the case of the wide variation between *PMC* Anssarera (l. 2657) and *CVR* Alxaria (fol. 158a), although Pidal suggests such an explanation (*CMC*, I, 62) and there is no more satisfactory alternative one. More substantial differences between the extant manuscript of the *PMC* and the one used for the *CVR* seem to lie behind three other variations between the *PMC* and the *CVR*, which include place names. Two of these include reference to Atienza. In the first, the *CVR* is closely following the *PMC*, when there is an addition between lines 415 and 416 of the extant poem: 'e yaziale de siniestro Atiença, que era estonçes de moros' (fol. 115a; *PMC*, p. 524.b). In the second, an itinerary, which is the same as in the *PMC* up to line 551, is changed by the replacement of line 552 by 'tornaronsse esa noche a Huerta e dende tomo camino de Atiença' (fol. 116a; *PCG*, p. 526.b, notes). The third example of a sharp variation between the *CVR* and the *PMC* occurs much later in the story, in the second 'cantar'. When Alvar Fáñez travels to see King Alfonso to ask for the release of the Cid's family, he finds Alfonso attending Mass in Carrión, after passing through Sahagún according to the *PMC* (ll. 1311–17); but the *CVR* reads 'sopo como el rey don

Alfonso era en Sand Fagund e fazie y sus cortes, fuesse para el' (fol. 152b). The appearance of Sahagún in both texts is a similarity, but the rest of the information differs so much that it implies a real difference between the *PMC* and the *CVR*'s source.[10] In all these three cases, there is different factual information in the *CVR* from what is in the *PMC*, and in all of them it is hard to see how the *CVR* could have created the information itself. Therefore, it has to be accepted that the source of the *CVR* must have been responsible, and that the manuscripts of the poem varied at these points.

Apart from the above examples, two other place names are added to information in the *PMC*, but it is not difficult to deduce that their source is the initiative of the chroniclers themselves. Both names are towns added to the list of the Cid's conquests given by Alvar Fáñez to Alfonso VI (fol. 152c; ll. 1327–31). The eight names in the poem are in the *CVR* and in the same order, but after 'Çebolla' appears 'Juballa' and after 'Peña Cadilla' appears 'Denia'. The first of these, 'Juballa', is historically the same as 'Çebolla', but the former is the name used when the *CVR* has an Arabic source. The *CVR* relates the capture of 'Juballa' by the Cid on folio 147d, without realizing it is the same place as 'Çebolla' whose capture was recounted on folio 147b, based on the *PMC*, line 1150. The inclusion of Denia is more surprising. Nowhere except here is the Cid credited with its capture, although the city is mentioned in poem and chronicle (fol. 149c; l. 1161). It seems a lapse by the chroniclers. The initiative of the chroniclers here, in including two extra places, is reminiscent of their initiative in the addition of names of people to a list from the *PMC* (see I, *A*, above).

Finally, it must be observed that the *CVR* does not, of course, include in its prosification all the places named in the *PMC*. Itineraries in the poem are often abbreviated in the chronicle, and sometimes omitted. The *CVR* may only give the resting-places for the night, as in the journeys of Muño Gustioz (fol. 153b; ll. 1475–76, 1491–94) and the Infantes de Carrión (fol. 158b; ll. 2689–97). However, when the *CVR* does name those places, mountains, rivers, etc., referred to in the *PMC*, it has very accurate forms of the names in the great majority of cases, as we have seen. This suggests that the manuscript of the *PMC* used by the *CVR* and the extant one were verbally very close, although there are a few examples of variations which show that they had some differences, too.

C. Numbers

A comparison of the precise numbers cited in the poem with their counterparts in the prose redaction in the *CVR* provides another test of the accuracy of the content of the chronicle. The *CVR* quotes numbers taken from the *PMC* on over fifty occasions. On only three of these do the texts disagree. Thus, the

CVR transmits accurately such numbers as the 115 knights who join the Cid at Cardeña (fol. 114d; l. 291), the 510 horses left by the Moors at the battle of Alcocer (fol. 118a; l. 796), the five battles alleged by Alvar Fáñez, to have been won by the Cid, although not all have been related in the *PMC* (fol. 152c; l. 1333), the three blows dealt to Yuçef (fol. 154a; l. 1725), the 200 marks given to Alfonso VI by the Infantes de Carrión (fol. 160a; l. 3231).[11]

The occasions on which the two versions disagree concern three quite different numbers. When a census is taken after the defeat of the King of Seville, the Cid's men total 3,600 in the poem, but only 3,200 in the chronicle (fol. 152a; l. 1265). There seems no obvious aesthetic reason for the difference; Pidal accepts the *PMC* (see *CMC*, III, 1074), but it is interesting that this variation, like the other two examples, involves a difference of only one Roman numeral, between the numbers in the poem and in the chronicle. The poem uses Roman numerals for its numbers, although manuscript N of the *CVR* uses words, outside its chapter headings. The second case occurs after the agreement on the marriage of the Cid's daughters between Alfonso and the Cid; the Cid presents Alfonso with horses: 'xx palafres . . . e xxx cavallos' (*PMC*, ll. 2144–45), or 'treynta cavallos e treynta palafrenes' (fol. 155c). The *CVR* number is more logical and more symmetrical, so that, here, the copyist of the *PMC* is probably at fault (see Pidal, *CMC*, III, 1106). Finally, after the battle with Búcar, the Cid's pursuit lasts seven miles in the *PMC*, but eight in the *CVR* (fol. 157b; l. 2407). As with the first of the three examples, neither text is obviously wrong.[12] In only one place in the prosification of the poem has the *CVR* a number where there is none in the equivalent part of the *PMC*. When the Cid sets off on his raid on 'Alcamiz' he takes with him 200 picked men. The *PMC* does not mention this detail (fol. 120c; ll. 935–36). The manuscript of the poetic source behind the *CVR* seems the obvious source for the addition (see Pidal, *CMC*, III, 1061; *PCG*, p. 532.b.18, and Chapter 4, II, *C*, ii). In other examples, the *CVR* does not include the numbers that appear in the *PMC*. It may just ignore them (e.g. fols 115c, 153c; ll. 472, 1564, 3101), or it may express the information more vaguely, as when Fariz and Galve's army of 3,000 Moors is called simply 'muy gran hueste' (fol. 116d; l. 639).[13]

Overall, the comparison of precise numbers in the two texts shows how close the version in the *CVR* generally is to the extant *PMC*. It is worth underlining that there seem to be only three clear disagreements in the whole range of more than fifty examples. One of these at least is probably an error in the manuscript of the *PMC*, which leaves only two possible errors in manuscript transmission from its poetic source to the *CVR*.

II. THE ROLES OF THE PERSONAGES

An examination of the roles played by the personages of the *PMC* and of the space afforded to them in the *CVR* shows that the compilers of the chronicle seem to have had definite intentions about what they wanted to emphasize from the poem, and the way in which they wanted to present the characters to their readers. This helps to illustrate how well the content of the *PMC* is represented in the *CVR*, but it also reveals differences of approach between epic poet and prose chronicler.

A. The Role of the Cid

The Cid is obviously the most important personage in the *PMC*. It is his story that is told, and the other characters in the work are mainly defined in their relationship to him. His military prowess, his absolute loyalty to Alfonso VI, his love for his family, and his sense of honour are the dominant themes of the work, but the Cid also shows comradeship with his men, mercy to the Moors, a sense of humour, and other admirable qualities.[14]

The variations in the presentation of the Cid in the *PMC* and in the *CVR* are several. At first sight, it is tempting to assign some of them to the *CVR*'s sources, but they do fit into a pattern which suggests that the reason is a consistent policy on the part of the chroniclers rather than a variant source. They reduce the individuality and the heroic persona of the Cid, and make his behaviour duller and more predictable. The process begins with the hero's response to the bad omen seen between Bivar and Burgos. In the *PMC*, the Cid is grimly ironical, in the *CVR* he is happy (fol. 114a–b; ll. 13–14).[15] Irony and despondency are moods the Cid is not allowed in the chronicle. Shortly afterwards, the Cid's role is radically altered in the episode with the chests of sand. In the *PMC*, the Cid concocts the plan of deceit, orders Martín Antolínez to carry it out, and concludes the deal himself at a meeting with the money-lenders (ll. 80–207). In the *CVR*, in a very abbreviated account, it is Martín Antolínez who suggests the plan, and who agrees the loan with the 'merca-dores' in Burgos (fol. 114b–c). The compilers of the *CVR* seem to have disliked this particular episode, and probably considered unworthy of a hero trans-actions of this nature. The reappearance of the money-lenders in the *PMC* is omitted in the *CVR* (fol. 153a; ll. 1431–38).[16] The enhancement of the import-ance of the Cid seems to be the purpose behind three small changes elsewhere in the prosification. In two cases, the Cid is given the credit for successful plans of action which are suggested by Alvar Fáñez in the *PMC*. The first is the plan for the raid on Hita and Guadalajara (fol. 115b; ll. 438–41; same in the *PCG*). The second is the idea of attacking the Moors on the very next day, at the siege of Alcocer (fol. 117b; l. 676; not *PCG*). The third comes in the second 'cantar', in the pursuit after the battle of Murviedro. The poem reads: 'Dos reyes de moros mataron' (l. 1147); the chronicle has: 'El Çid fue . . . e mato y dos reyes moros' (fol. 149c). These are small changes, but have the same purpose and effect.

More subtle differences in the characterization of the Cid are revealed by an examination of the scenes between him and the Count of Barcelona (fols 121b–22a; ll. 1017–82). The situation after the battle of Tévar and the capture of the Count is cleverly exploited in the *PMC* to draw sharp distinctions between the two men. The humiliated Count tries hard to keep his dignity under a stream of mocking words from the Cid. The Cid tries to force the Count to recognize his authority over him, by insisting that the Count accepts his food with good grace. The scenes are full of humour. The Cid is harsh, but playful. In the *CVR*, on the other hand, the dominant tones of the poem are dissipated. The chronicle imposes an atmosphere of politeness and urbane behaviour which is, at times, ridiculous, given the situation of captive and captor that is portrayed. The Cid and the Count become two gentlemen indulging in pleasantries. Food is prepared by order of the Cid, 'por fazer plazer al conde'. When the Cid goes to encourage the Count to eat, he goes as an 'omne mesurado', although 'mesura' is hardly the quality the Cid is revealing here in the *PMC*. The Count's reply to the Cid is polite and flattering: 'sodes omne de buena ventura e lo meresçedes, e folgad en paz e salud' (compare ll. 1028–29). Later, the Cid visits the Count again, 'con el grand duelo que ovo del', and asks him to eat, 'por que podades vivir' (compare l. 1034). When the Cid has agreed to release the Count and has explained the conditions to him, the chroniclers, misinterpreting the poem, produce a patently absurd statement: 'El conde ovo gran plazer de aquello que el Çid dezia, que le non daria nada de lo que le tomara' (fols 121d–22a; compare l. 1049). Finally, the *CVR* discreetly ignores the Cid's gloating over the Count, and the latter's ignoble and nervous departure (ll. 1053–55, 1077–79). Thus, the two distinct personalities of the *PMC* are much more similar to one another in the *CVR*: they are two polite gentlemen, without excesses of words, emotions, or actions. The chroniclers try to make the Cid's intentions pure and his motives kind. The humour is gone, except perhaps in the play of sounds in 'Comed, conde' (fol. 121c; l. 1025) and in the pun on 'franco' (fol. 121d; l. 1068).[17] The imposition of moderation in words and behaviour is a policy of the chronicle which can be exemplified from elsewhere in the text. According to the *CVR*, the Cid lets his beard grow because of his unjust exile, and not for love of Alfonso as in the poem (fol. 152a; ll. 1240–42). At the first meeting of the Cid and Alfonso, the Cid of the chronicle kneels to kiss the king's feet, but the abasement and weeping of the poem are not described (fol. 155b; ll. 2021–25). After the return of his daughters to Valencia following the disgrace of Corpes, the Cid asks God for vengeance on the Infantes in the *PMC*, but in the *CVR* he requests only 'buen derecho' (fol. 158d; l. 1594).

The prosifiers of the *PMC* or the compilers of the *CVR* probably thought that by these and other changes they were enhancing the figure of the Cid. In fact, for the modern reader, they have reduced the heroic but human person portrayed in the poem into someone who is dull and predictable. The Cid's absolute loyalty to Alfonso, his deceit of the Jews, his treatment of the Count of Barcelona, and so on, do not detract from his image as a hero for us, since they are parts of a fictional reality we find acceptable; but it seems that the chroniclers of the thirteenth century took a different view, and it is this that lies behind the changes that they made in the Cid's role in their version of the story. [18]

B.   The Role of the Family

The family of the Cid plays an important part in the *PMC*. The Cid is more of a family man than possibly any other epic hero. His family is constantly of concern to him: he sees that they are cared for while he is in exile; he summons them to him once he has a home for them. His personal honour is dependent on that of his daughters (see note 14). Besides the broader role for the family, they appear in smaller scenes of delicacy and emotion; for example, the departure (ll. 368–75), the reunion (ll. 1577–617), and before the battle with Yuçef (ll. 1644–56). The chroniclers of the *CVR*, however, do not seem to have appreciated the beauty of this aspect of the poem, or, at least, they did not value it as material for their history. They carried out a systematic reduction of the part played in the poem by the family, as far as they were able. They were bound to refer often to Ximena and her daughters because of their prominence in the story, but they did so as briefly as they could.

In the first 'cantar' in the chronicle and in the poem, the family only appears in the scenes at San Pedro de Cardeña, which are long and detailed in the *PMC*. In the *CVR*, the women's intervention is reduced to: 'E su muger, doña Ximena, e sus fijas besaronle las manos', when the Cid arrives, and 'espidiosse de su muger e sus fijas', when he departs; although details of the financial arrangements for the family are also given (fol.. 114c–d; ll. 235–390). In the second 'cantar', the journey of the family from Cardeña to Valencia is given some space in the *CVR*, but it is abbreviated; speeches to the women are summarized, and speeches by Ximena are ignored (fol. 153a–c; ll. 1392–569). The arrival in Valencia is again given a little space, but is hardly comparable to the *PMC* (fol. 153c; ll. 1570–617). Before the battle with Yuçef, the *CVR* gives Ximena her only piece of direct speech to survive in the chronicle out of all the speeches she makes in the poem. It consists of five words, 'Señor, ¿que tiendas son aquellas?' (fol. 154a; ll. 1646–47). The polite, formal tone shows the chroniclers at work. The scenes of the Cid with his family after the defeat of Yuçef are omitted (fol. 154a–b; ll. 1743–48). The conversation between them before the wedding to the Infantes is reduced to one subordinate clause (fol. 155d; ll. 2183–205). The details of the marriage itself and the celebrations that follow, at the end of the second 'cantar' of the poem, are almost all left out (fols

155d–56a; ll. 2205–70). In the third 'cantar', the emotional preparations for the departure of the daughters for Carrión with the Infantes are omitted, and the scenes of departure themselves are reduced to, 'se despidieron los unos de los otros' (fols 157d–58a; ll. 2584–608, 2624–43). The scenes at Corpes are brief, omitting the lovemaking and most of the violence, and the rescue by Feliz Muñoz is similarly reduced, especially the part played by the girls (fol. 158b–c; ll. 2697–823). Finally, the description of the daughters' return to Valencia in the *CVR* makes no mention of the girls' mother, unlike the poem (fol. 158d; ll. 2285–97).[19]

The attitude of the compilers of the prosification is apparent. While the *CVR* is forced to give some prominence to Ximena, Elvira, and Sol because of the importance of their roles in the *PMC*, it has reduced their participation to a minimum. As noted above, of Ximena's many speeches in the *PMC*, which include her long prayer for the safety of her husband, all that is left, apart from some reported speech, is one short sentence, which is not even taken from the poem. None of the girls' speeches is to be found in the chronicle either, except as brief reported speech. The individuality of the characters, their dignity and feminine bearing is entirely lost in the prose redaction. It can be inferred that the chroniclers considered that family affairs were not the concern of their history, and perhaps they considered them not a particularly heroic aspect of the figure of the Cid.

C.   The Cid's Friends and the Cid's Enemies

The majority of the Cid's entourage in the *PMC* are named at one point or another in the *CVR*, and the active roles they play in the story are often recorded in the prose. Thus, the Cid's messengers are recorded by name, the speech-makers at the court scenes are identified, and so are the people to whom the Cid grants the honour of the first blows in battle. Likewise, all the opponents of the hero are named in the *CVR* from García Ordóñez to Gómez Peláez, and the name of Alvar Díaz is even added by the chroniclers at one point (see I, *A*, above). However, in the presentation of these personages, the approach of the chroniclers to the distinctive characters of the poem is seen at work once again, transforming the well-defined individuals of the poem into blander figures. Impolite behaviour and apparent exaggerations are changed or suppressed. The hero's men become less like comrades; the enemies become less villainous. Examples of the type of change introduced in the *CVR* include the following: Martín Antolínez's carefree attitude to Alfonso VI, and his devotion to his wife are omitted (fol. 114b–c; ll. 71–77, 228–31); Alvar Fáñez's cool reply to the Infantes de Carrión in the *PMC* becomes a polite 'dixoles que lo farie de grado' (fol. 153a; l. 1390); Pero Bermúdez's refusal to take care of the Infantes during the battle with Búcar is omitted (fol. 157b; ll. 2350–60); the dishonour pertaining to Alfonso VI after the outrage at Corpes, which the Cid and his men insist on, is completely suppressed (fol. 159a; ll. 2950–51; fol. 159d; ll. 3049–50, etc.); the delight taken by the Infantes de Carrión in their riches is omitted (fol. 157d; ll. 2540–56); the refusal of the Infantes and others to rise for the Cid is omitted (fol. 159c; ll. 3112–13); the unseemly entrance by Ansur González is played down (fol. 160d; ll. 3373–81); and the evil intentions of the Infantes' side before the duels are suppressed (fol. 162a; ll. 3540–41).

Of course, the differences that such changes make should not be exaggerated. The Infantes de Carrión are still villains in the *CVR*; the Cid's men are still brave and admirable. The court scenes, especially, preserve many of the words of the poem, thus lending some subtlety to the characterization. Some of the Cid's men stand up comparatively well in the *CVR*. Pero Bermúdez, particularly, retains parts of his poetic personality, perhaps because his actions are as important as what he says.[20] As with the Cid himself, the chroniclers tried to ensure that the other personages conformed as much as possible to standards of behaviour which they imposed themselves, rather than to those of the poem. This, of course, makes them much less individual and much less fascinating in the *CVR* than in the *PMC*.

D. The Role of the Moors

The role of Moorish characters in the *PMC* is not very extensive, although they do appear regularly. Abengalbón, lord of Molina, is the one Moor who is prominent as an individual in the poem, but, besides him, Tamín, Fáriz and Galve, Yuçef, and Búcar are all named as enemies of the Cid, and the Moorish inhabitants of various captured towns are also mentioned. Although their scope for intervention was limited, the compilers of the *CVR* seem to have reduced references to the Moors to a marked extent, sufficiently so to suggest it was a deliberate policy on their part.[21] In the prose redaction of the first 'cantar', the journey to Alcocer by Fáriz and Galve is only briefly given, as are the first moves to besiege the Cid (fols 116d–17a; ll. 643–60). The expulsion of Alcocer's inhabitants is omitted (fol. 117b; ll. 679–80). When the Cid abandons Alcocer, the weeping of its inhabitants and the fear of the other Moorish towns are omitted (fols 118d–19a; ll. 856, 860–61).[22] In the second 'cantar', Abengalbón's greetings and his generosity with food and men are not recorded, whereas they are referred to more than once in the *PMC* (fol. 153b; ll. 1477–90, 1517–32, 1545–54). The complaint of Yuçef against the Cid is also omitted (fol. 153d; ll. 1623–24). In the third 'cantar', the meeting between Abengalbón and the Infantes is abbreviated. The gifts to the daughters and the threats and insults to the Infantes are suppressed (fol. 158b; ll. 2647–88). Abengalbón's final brief appearance in the *PMC* is also omitted (fol. 158d; ll. 2880–83).[23] The evidence suggests that the *CVR* was not very interested in the Moorish personages in the poem. The names are transmitted, as well as the fate of the vanquished, the numbers killed, and the numbers of horses they abandoned. Otherwise, the chronicle seems to have taken every chance it had to reduce their participation in events, and to minimize the description of that participation which was unavoidable.

Overall, the roles of the personages of the *PMC* are the same in the poem as in the chronicle. The poem clearly devotes much of its available space to aspects of characterization which the chroniclers reduce systematically, but the motives of the chroniclers in doing so are apparent. The only real differences in the parts the characters play are found in the role of the Cid himself. It seems likely that the differences there are again due to the chroniclers, who attempted to enhance the figure of the Cid by amending the story in the poem. There is no need to suppose that differences stem from differences in the poetic source used for the *CVR* from the text of the extant poem.

III. OTHER ASPECTS OF THE COMPARISON BETWEEN THE *PMC* AND THE *CVR*

A. *The Additions in the Prosification in the 'CVR'*

Although the prose redaction of the *PMC* abbreviates the content overall, there is material in the *CVR* which is additional to the extant poem. This material has three possible origins: sources other than the *PMC* (for which, see Chapter 3), additions compared to the extant manuscript in the manuscript used for the prosification, and initiatives of the chroniclers themselves. The additions which come from the source manuscript of the prosifiers fill gaps at the beginning of the poem and in the third cantar (ll. 2337–38, 3507–08; but see Smith, *PMC*, p. 106, note), and supply other details, some of which have been discussed earlier in this chapter. The additions by the chroniclers themselves add details from other parts of the story, fill out the narrative where the poem is brief, or expand the poem for the sake of clarity or rhetorical adornment.

(i) Additions from the other manuscript of the *PMC*

The missing folio or folios at the very beginning of the extant *PMC* is, in some ways, the most unfortunate gap in the manuscript. What was related there is uncertain. From the *CVR*, it seems safe to say only that the chronicle is using the poetic source from the beginning of the chapter in which it begins to use the extant story. There, we find a short passage full of direct or reported speech typical of a poetic source, which leads into the extant poetic content (fol. 114a). The nine-days grace given to the Cid is specified, 'Miñaya Alvar Fañez' is named. Otherwise, there is nothing worthy of special attention. In the remainder of the first 'cantar', there are three other places where the *CVR* has positive factual information, which the chroniclers could not have deduced, and which is not from another source. The first is the addition of Atienza; the second the addition of Atienza and Huerta (fols 115a, 116a; see I, *B*, above); and the third the detail of the 200 men who raid 'Alcamiz' with the Cid (fol. 120c; see I, *C*, above). All other additions to the first 'cantar' of the *PMC* could have been, and probably were, creations of the prosifiers or chroniclers, and, as such, are discussed below. In the second 'cantar', the only factual details not in the *PMC* and not from a known source are Alfonso's 'cortes' in Sahagún (fol. 152b; see I, *B*, above), and the mysterious 'Soro de Lerida' and 'Pero Salvadorez', named along with the less mysterious but equally inexplicable 'Bucar', and the seven Moorish kings who were killed in battle (fols 153d–54a; see I, *A*, above, and Chapter 3, IV).

In the third 'cantar', apart from the two lacunae in the *PMC*, there is one item of positive information new to the *CVR*. When the Cid and García Ordóñez exchange insults at the court in Toledo, the Cid in poem and chronicle reminds García Ordóñez of the time he pulled his beard at Cabra. He then says, in the *CVR*, of the piece of beard he pulled out: 'yo la trayo aqui en mi bolsa' (fol. 160b; ll. 3290–91). Up to this point, the *CVR* is following the Cid's speech (ll. 3281–90) virtually line by line, and the quote is clearly an addition to the *PMC*. It is difficult to see how the chroniclers could have deduced the information, or why they should have wanted to invent it. The most likely explanation is that it comes from their poetic source (see *CMC*, II, 812).[24]

The first of the two lacunae in the third 'cantar' contains events prior to the battle with Búcar (fol. 157a; ll. 2337–38). According to the *CVR*, the missing section of the poem consisted of the following: after the Cid's speech to the Infantes, a messenger arrives from Búcar to demand the surrender of Valencia, and the Cid sends him packing in no uncertain terms. The Infantes ask the Cid for the honour of the first blows, and Fernando, in cowardly fashion, flees from Aladraf, the first Moor he meets. He is saved by Pero Bermúdez, the only person to see his cowardice. Pero Bermúdez gives Fernando the Moor's horse, and promises to keep Fernando's behaviour secret. Now, this account in the chronicle has some definite peculiarities. The messenger from Búcar is the only pre-battle messenger in the story, although messages do pass between the Count of Barcelona and the Cid. The Cid's reply to him is worded strangely, and includes the epithet 'fi de henemiga', which does not have an epic ring to it. The name of the minor Moorish character is given, whereas elsewhere only kings are identified individually. In short, it seems that the account that fills the lacuna would not sit completely happily in the extant *PMC*. The features which the lacuna must have contained are those mentioned elsewhere in the *PMC* (ll. 3316–25), but the others may not have had a poetic origin. Given that fact, it seems that the lacuna existed in the manuscript used for the prosification in the first place, and has been filled in by an imaginative mind with more details than the poem justifies.[25] The second lacuna must have described how, on the way out of Toledo, Alfonso VI asked the Cid to display the prowess of Bavieca, his horse, and how the Cid did so (fol. 161c–d; ll. 3507–08). In the *CVR*, there is direct speech, in which the two men are very polite to each other, but the additional material is brief. It seems likely to have had a poetic origin.[26]

The sum total of factual information which seems to have come from the manuscript of the *PMC* used for the prose redaction in the *CVR*, and which is not in the extant *PMC*, has been listed above. It does not amount to a great deal, only a few details, apart from the missing parts of the extant manuscript. This suggests that the two manuscripts were not very different from each other, as other evidence has suggested above.

(ii) Additions by the chroniclers

There are literally dozens of additions to the content of the *PMC* which can be ascribed to the prosifiers or chroniclers. Apart from those additions of details taken from elsewhere in the *PMC* or *CVR* already discussed (see I, *A* and *B*, above), there are many others which contain no real new information, but are deductions from what is in the *PMC*. The *PMC* is notoriously elliptical in its forms of expression. The *CVR* is definitely not. There are far too many examples to list here, but typical ones will be cited. They occur frequently when the *CVR* is following the *PMC* closely, when the prose has to be more explanatory to take account of the implications of the poem, or when the chroniclers simply choose to explain. For example, when the Cid pretends to flee from Alcocer, the *PMC* briefly refers to the joy of the inhabitants: 'Dios, commo se alabavan' (l. 580). Obviously based on this and using the same verb, the *CVR* expresses the same sentiments: 'començaronsse de alabar como fueran esforçados e que sse tovieran bien' (fol. 116b). Similarly, a half-line of the poem, 'no lo fare, señor', becomes the full and explanatory, 'señor, no fare yo al sy non lo que vos mandaredes, e esto en vos lo dexo yo de oy mas' (fol. 161c; l. 3472). This type of expansion is fairly frequent, and the reason for it, clearly, is that the chroniclers want to interpret fully for their readers what the *PMC* means.[27] This type of explanation can be taken further, so that the *CVR* virtually introduces its own reasons, reasons which the poem hardly implies: compare, for example, 'son estos a escarmentar' and 'escarmentemos a los de Valençia, en guisa que nunca osen despues venir a nos' (l. 1121; fol. 149c). One of the best examples is when Feliz Muñoz is hiding from the Infantes de Carrión. Not only does the *CVR* explain what Feliz Muñoz overheard, it explains his heartache (fol. 158b–c; ll. 2772–75; see l. 2767). Other additions are found when the *CVR* completes narrative which the *PMC* leaves incomplete: compare *PMC*, lines 759–60 with the *CVR*'s logical, but laboured, 'vio el Çid al rey Fariz, e dexosse yr para el a mas poder del cavallo, e diole . . .' (fol. 117d). Even in reference to the Cid's daughters, where the *PMC* seems too brief, the *CVR* introduces a logical progression of actions additional to those described in the *PMC* (fol. 158c; ll. 2817–18). The poem leaves much to the imagination of the reader; the chronicle spells things out.[28]

Less obviously due to the chroniclers are small items of information, which they have deduced from other parts of the poem. Thus, in the *CVR*, the money the Cid gives to San Pedro de Cardeña is 'de plata', and what he leaves for his family 'de oro' (fol. 114c; ll. 250–53), based, no doubt, on what the Cid had earlier received from the money-lenders, which was both silver and gold. Babieca is said by the *CVR* to have been won from the King of Seville, because of what the *PMC* says, 'poco avie quel ganara', related to the Cid's previous battle, against the King of Seville (fol. 153c; l. 1573; but see *CMC*, III, 1084). After shutting away the escaped lion, the Cid in the *CVR* returns, and sits on his 'escaño', a detail not in the *PMC* (fol. 156c; l. 2303–04; see l. 2280). There are other examples, too.[29] More rhetorical additions in *CVR* have been referred to in the previous chapter, where 'pairs' of the poem were expanded in the chronicle, for example (see Chapter 4, I, *C*, and elsewhere). Some of the expansions already referred to here are as rhetorical, in that they scarcely add anything to what the poem says. The repetition of the meaning of a word in other ways is a typical device: *PMC*'s 'quebranta', for example, is glossed as, 'fizo . . . muy grandes daños e quebranto e robo quanto fallo' (fol. 149c; l. 1162).

In all, therefore, the basic material visible in the extant *PMC* has additions to it in the *CVR* which can be explained in a number of ways. But when these additions are examined in detail, it is clear that very few of them need to be, or should be, explained by the supposition of a more perfect or fuller manuscript of the *PMC* than the extant one. Rather, the positive intervention of the chroniclers or prosifiers is sufficient explanation, in the great majority of cases, for the additions that are found.[30]

B. Changes from the 'PMC' in the Prosification in the 'CVR'

Differences between the two versions of the story of the Cid in the *PMC* and the *CVR* have been pointed out earlier in this chapter. A few of them can be put down to differences between the two manuscripts of the poem; namely, variations of places named (see I, *B*, above), and of numbers (see I, *C*, above). Others are due to the chroniclers, who change the roles and characterization of the personages of the poem, particularly the Cid (see II, above). There remain other differences in narrative content between the two texts, in descriptions of events which they both recount. A few of them seem to be the result of misunderstandings or misreadings by the prosifiers. At Alcocer, when the Cid and Alvar Fáñez charge back towards the town, the *PMC* says that they went between the inhabitants and the town: 'entrellos y el castiello' (l. 603; and

PCG, p. 526.b.45). *CVR* MS N seems to have misread this, for it has 'entre los del castillo' (fol. 116c), which paints a different picture of the skirmish although *CVR* MS J describes what happens in the poem. In the speeches of challenge in the third 'cantar', when Martín Antolínez reminds an Infante of his cowardice, the *PMC*'s logical, 'Saliste por la puerta, metiste al corral' (l. 3364) comes out in the *CVR* as 'te saliste del corral' (fol. 160d). Considering the length of the *PMC* and the difficulties of comprehension and interpretation posed by parts of it, the number of apparent 'errors' of this nature in the *CVR* is very small.[31]

A number of changes made in the prosification affect the sequence of narrative events. These seem to have been made by the prosifiers to make their narrative progress more logically than the poem does, and perhaps more 'sensibly' in their eyes, in both the order and timing of events. Thus, in the first 'cantar', while abbreviating the Cid's arrival and discussions at Cardeña to a very simple account, the *CVR* (and the *PCG*) change the narrative so that Sancho and Ximena greet the Cid on his arrival, and the negotiations with the abbot are postponed to the following day. The *PMC*'s version is less logical (fol. 114c; ll. 245–62). In the second 'cantar', Alvar Fáñez's farewells are postponed in the *CVR* until after his words with the Infantes de Carrión (fols 152d–53a; ll. 1377–91). An example from the third 'cantar' is when, before the duels, the Cid's men go out to the battlefield before they speak to King Alfonso (fol. 162a; ll. 3573–76). More detailed changes seem to have been made by the chroniclers in other cases, where it is possible to follow the sequence of the lines of the poem in the prosification. The prosification can present the lines in a different order from the *PMC*. Examples include: the Cid's speech before the battle between Fariz and Galve, where the changes make little practical difference (fol. 117b; ll. 667–69–68–71–70); the departure from the 'Poyo de mio Çid', where the *PMC* describes the sequence illogically (fol. 120a; ll. 910–09); in the second 'cantar', García Ordóñez's speech is reordered, logically (fol. 154c: 1861–63–62–65); in the third 'cantar', some of the speeches are rearranged with varying degrees of accuracy (fol. 159a; ll. 2937–38–48–51–49; fol. 159d; ll. 3156–58–53–55; fol. 160a–b; ll. 3271–76–73–79).[32]

This is by no means an exhaustive list of the differences between the *PMC* and the version in the *CVR*. However, these examples are sufficient to show that here, too, the prosifiers were active in altering the details of the story in the poetic version, in order to adapt it to suit their own preferences. Very few of these differences need any explanation other than the intervention of chroniclers, who were out to ensure that their account was clear, logical and reasonable, even when the poem, in their view, was not.

IV. CONCLUSION

The evidence adduced in this chapter seems to me to show conclusively that the version of the *PMC* prosified in the thirteenth century and included in the *CVR*, and the version known to us today in the extant fourteenth-century copy, were very similar to one another. They were so similar that they must have been related via a manuscript tradition, which means, incidentally, that they were not two distinct representatives of an oral tradition. When they are comparable in matters of factual detail, they correspond very closely. In both, the names of the characters are the same and almost all are spelled the same; the names of places, too, show virtual identity in almost all cases; the numerical figures for people, animals, and objects are in agreement in all but three examples, and all three of these differ by one numeral only. In fact, there tends to be more variation between manuscripts of the *CVR*, where copyists have made errors, than there is between the *PMC* and the best manuscript of the chronicle. The body of evidence represented by all these points of factual detail is an impressive one, and it argues strongly that the two poetic manuscripts were not only related, but closely related in a manuscript tradition. Of course, there is no denying that there are, too, many differences between the *PMC* and the account of its contents given by the *CVR*. What I have shown in the course of this chapter is that almost all such differences can be ascribed to what happened to the poetic text during the processes of, firstly, prosification, and secondly, incorporation into the chronicle. They were introduced as a result of the attitudes and methods of the prosifiers and chroniclers themselves. These anonymous scholars omitted a great deal of what is in the *PMC*, systematically shortening narratives, descriptions, and speeches, reducing drastically facets of the work, such as the role of the family, which did not interest them, or, at least, which they did not regard as relevant or appropriate to their history. They expanded or added to the original, when they wished to clarify its content or to embroider it with rhetorical emphases (in other words, to prosify it). They made changes in the sequence of the narrative to make it more logical, and they altered the characters in ways which seem designed to ensure that these behave according to standards of gentlemanly conduct which the chroniclers found more to their liking, and more convincing, than those of the poem. In other words, we need to think of prosification and compilation as active processes of narrative creation, and not as mechanical ones in which a source is respected absolutely. As in their treatment of stylistic and linguistic matters (see Chapter 4), in their treatment of the content of the poem, the chroniclers were undoubtedly conscious of what they were trying to do, and had certain approaches to their task which consistently affect the resultant prose. It is the practical and systematic application of these approaches that results in the great majority of variations between the extant *PMC* and the *CVR*. As I said earlier in the chapter, it is only when the chronicle contains new information, which the chroniclers could not have got from elsewhere or deduced for themselves, that it is reasonable and necessary to seek to explain this new information by supposing that it comes from a more 'perfect' version of the *PMC*. Such information appears in the *CVR* when the extant poem has folios missing, that is at the beginning and at two points within the text, and in only five other places, where, each time, the amount of new information is very small. This paucity of new information attributable to the other version of the poem is not really surprising, if, as I have argued, the two manuscripts of the poem were very closely related in a manuscript tradition. From all this, the extant manuscript of the poem emerges with credit. There is no justification for seeing it as defective and dotted with omissions, in comparison with the poem behind the *CVR*. Apart from the lost beginning, the two lacunae, one of which possibly existed in the other manuscript, and the few minor details, there is nothing to say that the extant manuscript was much worse or much better than the other one; in fact, as I have said, the evidence points to their being very similar to each other. What else emerges with credit from this chapter is the *CVR*, particularly in MS N. It transmits the poem, as far as it wanted to transmit it, with factual accuracy, and following criteria which we may not like, but which, we must admit, are applied with logic and with consistency.

CHAPTER 6

FINAL CONCLUSION

Most of the chapters of this study, with the exception of the first, have their own conclusions. Consequently, this final conclusion will be relatively brief. Its purpose is to bring together the threads of what has been said in each of the preceding chapters, so that the juxtaposition of this material may shed more light on all aspects of it.

The *PMC* was composed in the early years of the thirteenth century, possibly in the year 1207 and possibly by a poet named Per Abbat. Both this name and this date are found on the only extant manuscript of the poem, which is, however, a copy made in the fourteenth century. The story told in the *PMC* presupposes a well developed legendary tradition dealing with this period of the Cid's life. The way in which the tale is told assumes that the audience for which the poem was intended were familiar with such a tradition. Both these facts show that stories about the Cid existed, and that such stories circulated widely in the period around one hundred years after his death, and before the poem was composed. Such wide circulation means that these stories were found principally in the vernacular. Moreover, the skilful and varied linguistic, stylistic, and artistic techniques which are employed in the *PMC* demonstrate that there was an existing tradition of vernacular narrative poetry within which such techniques had been developed and refined to the point at which the poet of the *PMC* could use them with familiar ease, and probably adapt them and refine them further for the purposes of his own poetic art.

The stories about the life of the Cid other than the *PMC* that circulated during the century or so after the hero's death are known to us, imperfectly, in texts of the twelfth and early thirteenth centuries. Although most of these texts are Latin chronicles, they record a varied tradition of stories rather than one fixed legend passed on from one to another. A number of these stories must have been transmitted in poems belonging to the vernacular epic tradition, a tradition which included oral works, and which possibly spawned a written genre too. The *PMC*, unless it is unique, would obviously belong to the latter, whilst it certainly bears marks of the influence of the former. As far as the content of the poem is concerned, the evidence of the other texts suggests that elements of the story it tells are adopted from general Cidian tradition, but that dominant themes of the poem which have a more personal than military emphasis, were not important elements previously, and consequently that their importance in the *PMC* reflects the contribution of the poet of the *PMC* to the tradition.

In the second half of the thirteenth century, the *PMC* was turned into prose by scholars who were working under the auspices of Alfonso X, el Sabio. The prose version of the poem was required for inclusion as historical material in Alfonso's national history, the *EE*. But the *EE* was never completed, and the *PMC* was never included in a definitive historical text approved by Alfonso. The prosification of the *PMC* was included, however, in the text of the *CVR*. The *CVR* was compiled from materials collected for the projected *EE*, and, for the period after the year 900, it is representative of what Alfonso's *EE* would most probably have been like, had it been completed. It contains the whole of the Alphonsine prosification of the *PMC*. Elsewhere, only that part of the prosification equivalent to the first 'cantar' and the beginning of the second has survived. This is found in the manuscript dated 1289 which now forms part of the fourteenth-century compilation, published as the second volume of the *PCG*. Later in the *PCG*, in a manuscript of a later date, the prosification of the remainder of the *PMC* appears, but it appears in a changed version. This revision of the story known in the *PMC* and in the *CVR* is present in the *CRC*, also, where it can be seen to have been a full revision of the story, affecting the first 'cantar' too. The revision is quite substantial in places, involving, as it does, new incidents and new characters, as well as alterations to the content of the previous version. Such a 'refundición' must have required a determined and imaginative mind intent on carrying it out, but whether it derives from a poetic 'refundición' is by no means certain. The revised version of the story, first found in the *CRC*, is the one which continues to be reproduced, with minor variations, in later chronicles such as the *C1344*.

All the Alphonsine chronicles recount the participation of the Cid in events set in the reigns and in the years preceding those in which the *PMC* and its prosification take place. These stories are not the same as those found in the earlier texts mentioned above, although they relate to the same historical period and sometimes to similar incidents. They are longer and more detailed, and, in most cases, they show clear evidence of derivation from poetic originals, in the same way as, or, occasionally, even more explicitly than, the *PMC* shows evidence of its origins. They underline the vitality of the legendary tradition of the Cid, and they emphasize the importance of vernacular narrative poetry in the transmission of that tradition.

Amongst the several chronicles, and amongst the several epic legends, the *CVR* is the only place where one can study the complete prosification of an extant poetic text, the *PMC*. The detailed examination of the chronicle text in comparison with the poem, then, should provide valuable evidence. It shows that the chroniclers, amongst whom I include those who first prosified the *PMC* as well as those who incorporated it into the *CVR*, approached their tasks with specific and positive intentions. They wished to conserve from their source those parts of the story which were mainly of military and political interest, while reducing or removing material from the original which was irrelevant to or unsuitable for their purposes. This means, for example, a much smaller role for Jimena and her daughters in the *CVR* than in the *PMC*. At the same time as they edited the poem in this way, they examined each episode that they included, and, whenever the content was not precisely to their liking, they felt free to alter it. The more ungentlemanly behaviour of characters was a particular target for the attentions of the chroniclers, although there are other targets, too. Some of these omissions and amendments are found in both the *CVR* and in the 1289 text of the *PCG*, while others are found only in the *CVR*. This means that such tampering with the material from the original poem seems to have been carried out both by the prosifiers of the poem and by the chroniclers who later used the prosification in their own chronicles. It was not only whole episodes that were subject to omissions and amendments in this way. The process was applied, also, to groups of lines or even single lines. On occasions, one can follow the poem in the prosification, line by line, and one can observe the chroniclers discarding unnecessary lines or half-lines within such closely transcribed passages. There is no need to seek to explain such omissions of lines by supposing another version of the *PMC* in which such lines did not exist. Indeed, there is no evidence in favour of such a supposition. There is instead a coherent pattern, which is that deliberately established by the chroniclers, with the purpose of reducing the poetic material to a more essential core of content. Many of the lines that are omitted are what would be called 'poetic' in tone. It was the chroniclers' general intention to disguise the poetic nature of their source, so it is no surprise that such lines should vanish. Moreover, in their pursuit of a prose version which would not reflect the poetry of the source, the chroniclers attempted to prosify it in such a way that its style is not evident in their prose. Poetic vocabulary, turns of phrase, word order, epithets, and so on are changed. Assonance words are disguised or replaced, so that only a small proportion remain. Even of this small proportion, many are names, which the chroniclers could not replace. The chroniclers carried out this prosification very efficiently, on the whole, so that the poetic stylistic features of the *PMC* are not present in the *CVR*. The principal exception to this is that they use direct speech far more when prosifying the poem than when using other sources, reflecting the high proportion of speech in the *PMC* itself. In sections of comparable length, there is at least ten times as much direct speech in the chronicle prose when there is a poetic source, compared to when there is not such a source. This is due both to the difficulty there would be in rendering the content of the *PMC* without recourse to speech, and also perhaps, to the higher status that would be granted to the spoken word compared to words of description or narrative.

The chroniclers set out, then, positively to create their own version of the *PMC*, by being true to its basic story of the Cid, Alfonso, and the Infantes de Carrión, but not being tied to all the details of that story; by following the text where necessary, but by changing it linguistically to make it comply with the stylistic and linguistic patterns of their chronicle prose; by positively discriminating against what did not suit them both in content and in language; and by intervening directly to amend and adapt, until there was a prose redaction which was to their liking. The resultant text was fitted neatly into the compositional structure of the *CVR*, which, with its annalistic format, and division into chapters, proved capable of accepting it with little difficulty.

Finally, the detailed study of the prosification of the *PMC* provides the opportunity to re-examine the extant manuscript of the poem in the light of another version of its content. The extant manuscript is of a later date than the *CVR*, which means that there must be two manuscripts involved in the two versions. What the examination demonstrates is that the two manuscripts were, in fact, very similar to each other. It has been observed above, that the chroniclers were an active force in altering their original poetic version and in creating a version more suitable for their purposes. Consequently, differences between the *PMC* and its prosification must not simply be attributed to different poetic versions. On the contrary, great care should be taken before attributing any differences to different poems. When it is possible to compare objective facts in the *PMC* and *CVR*, facts which the chroniclers would not change, such as the names of people, names of places, precise numbers and quantities, the comparison shows two versions that are almost identical. It is noteworthy that there are more variations between manuscript N of the *CVR* and other manuscripts of the chronicle, which are obviously attributable to copyists' errors, than there are differences between N and the *PMC*, despite the potential errors that might have been made in the original prosification or in the incorporation of that into the *CVR*. When such 'facts' are concerned, one could attribute differences between the texts to variations between the two poetic manuscripts. There are, in fact, a small number of these, but they are very few in the whole mass of material that the prosification of the poem represents. All other differences, it seems to me, can be reasonably explained in other ways which have been outlined above. Indeed, the demonstrable closeness of the two versions in factual details argues strongly against the idea that there should be many other differences between them. The *PMC* and the poetic original of the prosification were very similar, so similar that I believe they were closely related in the same manuscript family.

In conclusion, I would underline two points that derive from the examination of the two texts. The first of these is that the value of the manuscript of the *PMC* is reinforced. It is obviously defective in places, but it is not as defective as had been thought. The *CVR* does not show evidence of an alternative version of the poem to which deference should be paid. As modern authoritative editions of the poem have shown, the *PMC* stands up very well in its own right, and emendation of the manuscript on the basis of the *CVR* is generally unreliable and unwise. Secondly, in future analyses of poetic legends in chronicle texts, the active participation of the chroniclers in shaping the stories they tell will have to be taken into account more fully than it normally has been in the past. As Catalán and Pattison have tentatively suggested, variations in stories cannot simply be attributed to variable poetic texts which came to the notice of different chroniclers at different times. In most cases, variations from one chronicle to another are due to the chroniclers, who intervened more in the transmission of their sources than has been thought. This does not mean that there was not more than one poetic version of a particular legend, but it does mean that more positive evidence than that of simple variations between chronicle texts must be adduced in any argument for the existence of more than one such version.

This study of the prose redaction of the *PMC* in the *CVR*, then, does not tell us a great deal more about the *PMC* than we knew already. It does, however, shed some light on the attitudes and methods of those who adapted the epic legend, and created the prose version for inclusion in chronicles. If, in doing this, it can help towards a better understanding of how the epic legends of Spain were adapted for use in chronicles, and, thence, towards a more satisfactory view of the epic legends themselves, then it will have been of some value.

APPENDIX A

THE MANUSCRIPTS OF THE
CRÓNICA DE VEINTE REYES

At the present time, twelve manuscripts are known which contain all or part of the *CVR*. They vary considerably in length and in importance, but not so much in the details of the actual text of the chronicle. The manuscripts of the *CVR* were first identified, described, and classified into two main families by Pidal in *Leyenda*, pp. 406–08, 411–12. There, Pidal listed eight manuscripts and gave them their corresponding letters. They are N, J, X, N', Ll, K, L, Ñ in the list below. To these he later added a ninth, B, when studying the *PMC* (see *CMC*, II, 504). Lang used three of the manuscripts in his study 'Contributions', but Babbitt was the next to consider all nine (see *La CVR*, pp. 164–66). Later, three more manuscripts of the chronicle came to light, and all twelve are described by Gómez Pérez in 'La Estoria de España alfonsí', pp. 515–20. One of these, M, is discussed briefly by Pidal in the additions to *Leyenda*, p. 572, and has recently been claimed as a new discovery and shown to be related to J, in a laborious if convincing study by Larry Collins, 'An Unknown Manuscript of the *CVR*'. Finally, there is a detailed description of the manuscripts, and a discussion of their relationships in Dyer, '*El PMC* in the *CVR*', pp. 2–26.

I. THE MANUSCRIPTS

1. Escorial Y-i-12, N.
   Paper, 260 folios, numbered 1–245 in the original script. It begins:

   En el nonbre de Dios. Aqui comiença la coronica de los nobles reyes de España e los sus notables fechos que fizieron, en la qual dicha coronica se contienen honze reyes de España e eso mesmo sse contienen los fechos muy famosos que fizieron el conde Ferrand Gonçalez e el Çid Ruy Diaz de Bivar (fol. 1r).

   A fourteenth-century date, earlier rather than later, would seem right for the script. J. Zarco Cuevas, *Catálogo*, III, 18, describes it as 'letra gótica del siglo XIV'. The first folio is of vellum with a very richly decorated initial and surround on the recto, the predominant colour being gold. The reign of Fernando I begins on fol. 71, and the prosification of the *PMC* is in fols 114–62. The quality of the manuscript is excellent, with a clear, consistent script, comparatively few abbreviations, and very few copyist's errors. It seems to be the oldest known manuscript of the *CVR*. It would be the best basis for a critical edition of the chronicle, and has been transcribed in Appendix B.

2. Escorial X-i-6, J.
Paper, 165 folios. It begins oddly: 'Aqui comiença la segunda e terçera parte de los reyes que ovo en Castilla e en Leon en la qual fabla de sus muy grandes fechos que fizieron' (fol. 1r). It is in a fourteenth-century script (see Zarco Cuevas, II, 453–54). There is a minor change of hand in the middle of a chapter early on (fol. 16v), but the script then remains consistent. It makes much greater use of abbreviations than N, and it contains many more errors. However, its text is still good. The reign of Fernando I begins on fol. 48, and the prosification of *PMC* is within fols 72–102. This manuscript has been used, in Appendix B, for variants from N.

3. Salamanca 1824 (previously Palacio 2-C-2, later II-180), X.
Paper, 222 folios in a rather confused state towards the end. Of probable fifteenth-century date, it is incomplete at the beginning and at the end. However, the old numeration of the folios suggests that only two folios are lost at the start. The 'cuarta parte' begins with Fernando I on fol. 64c; the prosification of *PMC* is within fols 98–143. Of the same family as N and J, it does not seem to be directly descended from either. A comparison of the small number of variants shows X to have a version between those of the other two generally, although the evidence is not substantial.

4. Palacio 2437 (previously 2-K-8), N'.
Paper, 321 folios. It begins as N above, and is a copy of that manuscript, as suggested by Pidal. It is in various hands of the sixteenth century, and the *CVR* is found in non-consecutive sections separated by other works. The reign of Fernando I is missing. What there is of the story of the Cid under Alfonso VI is found in fols 149–80, but this ends well before the surrender of Valencia.

5. B.N. 1501 (previously F-32), Ll.
Paper, 419 folios. It begins: 'Comiença la coronica de los onze reyes de España.' In more than one hand of the fifteenth and perhaps early sixteenth centuries, it has a few misplaced or odd folios of no direct importance here. Fernando I's reign in León begins on fol. 107, and the prosification of *PMC* is within fols 166–243. It is the best known manuscript of the *CVR* because it was the basis for Pidal's examination of the *CVR*'s prosification of the *PMC*. However, Pidal nowhere claims that it is the best manuscript of the chronicle.

He seems to have used it for convenience. It is a representative of the second family of *CVR* manuscripts identified by Pidal, and, as such, it is used for variants in Appendix B. The value of its text is discussed further below. Dyer calls this manuscript F.

6.   B.N. 18416 (previously 1079), P.

Paper, 169 folios. It begins as Ll above. In a neat sixteenth-century hand, it is complete from the accession of Fruela II to the death of Fernando III. The 'cuarta parte' begins on fol. 53, and the prosification of the *PMC* is in fols 80–109. An examination of the text reveals that it is of the same family as Ll, to which it is closely related, although manuscripts of the *CVR* are close in any case. This is one of the manuscripts first identified as containing the *CVR* by Gómez Pérez. Here the letter P is introduced to refer to this manuscript in the discussion below. Dyer calls the manuscript G.

7.   B.N. 1507 (previously F-124), Q.

Paper, 399 folios. It begins as Ll above. It is precisely dated at the end of the text: 'Se acavo de trasladar oy domingo a Primero de hebrero del año de mil y quinientos y ochenta y siete a las diez antes de medio dia' (fol. 388v). The 'cuarta parte' begins on fol. 106, and the prosification of the *PMC* is in fols 159–229. This is another manuscript identified as being of *CVR* by Gómez Pérez. It is of the same family as Ll, but is not as close to Ll as P. Here the letter Q is introduced to refer to this manuscript. Dyer calls it C, and argues that it is probably a copy of B.

8.   Salamanca 2211 (previously Palacio 2-M-1, later II-1782), K.

Paper, 227 folios. It begins: 'Aqui comiença la coronica de los onze rreys de España que es la segunda parte que hizo copilar el rrey don Alfonso' (fol. 4r). The old numeration on fol. 4 is xcvi. In a difficult sixteenth-century hand, this manuscript begins the 'cuarta parte' on fol. 57, and has the prosification of the *PMC* within fols 90–130. Its variants agree at times with those of either family of *CVR* manuscripts, but overall it seems somewhat closer to the Ll group.

9.   Escorial X-ii-24, L.

Paper, 202 folios. It begins: 'Chronica de algunos reyes de Castilla desdel rey don Fruela segundo deste nonbre y ansi suçesivamente hasta otros diez sus suçesores.' It is in two sixteenth-century hands (fols 1–20, 21–202), and the prosification of the *PMC* is in fols 98–142. The text is of the Ll group, but the copyist has intervened quite frequently to modernize the text or otherwise alter it to his satisfaction.

10.　Pelayo 319 (previously R-I-5-6), Ñ.

Paper, 393 folios. Dating from the fifteenth century, it begins as does Ll above, and, overall, has a text similar to that of L. It would seem to be perhaps the oldest manuscript of its family, but its readings are not particularly good. The 'cuarta parte' begins on fol. 109, and the *PMC* is in fols 163–246.

11.　Pelayo 320 (previously R-II-II-8), B.

Paper, 264 folios. Of sixteenth-century date, it is in poor condition owing to the spreading of its ink, according to Babbitt and Dyer. According to Gómez Pérez, it derives from Ll; Dyer merely classifies it as related to Ll, but as the source of Q, above. I have not seen this manuscript.

12.　University of Minnesota MS Z 946. 02-f.C881, M.

This manuscript, which I have not seen, was first mentioned as containing the *CVR* by Gómez Pérez. In fact, it is a mixed manuscript, and the part containing *CVR* (fols 498r–547v) only has the early part of the chronicle, ending well before the start of the 'cuarta parte'. Of fifteenth-century date, it seems to have a text similar to that of J, and both are perhaps copied from a common ancestor (see Pidal, *Leyenda*, Adiciones, p. 572; Collins, 'An Unknown Manuscript of the *CVR*').

II.　CLASSIFICATION OF THE MANUSCRIPTS

In general, manuscripts of the *CVR* have very similar texts and variations between them are small. They are much closer than manuscripts of the *CRC*, for example, which diverge so much at times as to be consistently different versions of the sources, suggesting differing compositional criteria (see Chapter 2, II, *D*). However, the manuscripts of the *CVR* have sufficient minor differences for Pidal to have established two families amongst them, as has already been said (see *Leyenda*, pp. 411–12). In one group he placed N, J, X, N', and in the other Ll, K, L, Ñ. Pidal was, of course, interested in the section of the *CVR* containing the story of the Infantes de Lara, but my examination of ten of the manuscripts, concentrating on the story of the Cid, has not suggested any alteration of the broad relationships established by Pidal. The four manuscripts not known to Pidal when he wrote *Leyenda* can be attributed without difficulty to his two groups. To the first of the two M should be added, as it seems to be derived from the same source as J. B, P, Q belong to the other family, and are, apparently, close to Ll, with Dyer arguing that Q is copied from B. Thus Pidal's diagram of the relationships of the manuscripts of the *CVR* may be amended in the following way (see *Leyenda*, pp. 414, 572):

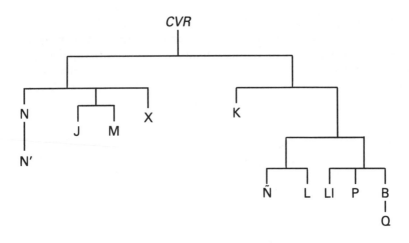

III. THE CHOICE OF MANUSCRIPT IN THIS STUDY

In *Leyenda*, Pidal used mainly Ll as his text of the *CVR* apparently out of convenience. Later, in *Reliquias* (see p. 240), he used J with variants from N and L, the other Escorial manuscripts, in the account of the death of Fernando I. Babbitt quite strongly recommended J as the basis for an edition of *CVR*: 'In addition to its accuracy and completeness, we find in 'J' that brevity of expression which is the salient characteristic of the chronicle' (*La CVR*, p. 116). He therefore used J for most of his quotations. The superiority of both J and N over Ll had already been pointed out by Lang ('Contributions', p. 46). Dyer, in her critical edition, uses J as her basic manuscript, although she does not seem to explain why.

Given the preference for J shown by Babbitt, Pidal (in *Reliquias*), and Dyer, the use of N as the text of the *CVR* in this study requires some justification. Let it be said, first of all, that N is an impressive manuscript in its presentation. It has a strikingly decorated first folio of vellum, with an extremely large first initial and a coat of arms. It uses few abbreviations, has a pleasant consistent script, an extremely small number of errors, and even a respectable punctuation of its own. Overall it is a most pleasing manuscript to use, although this does not, of course, make its text superior. J and N are the oldest manuscripts of the *CVR* known at present, both of fourteenth-century date. Of the two, N has what seems to me to be the older script, and a comparison of the language of the two shows N to have forms which are more archaic than those of J. In the following list, both forms may be found in both manuscripts, but the predominant form in each is one attributed to it here:

N	J
desi	despues
o, ho	donde
estonçes	entonçes
toller	tomar
bisquiesse	beviese
priso	prendio

Furthermore, the imperfect ending in -*ie* is more frequent in N than in J. There are more examples of the older forms in J than there are of the modern ones in N, suggesting that J's text has been modernized, though not consistently, by a copyist.

In addition to these linguistic considerations, the comparative accuracy of the texts supports the preference of N. There are a number of examples where N provides a correct version of a corrupt J. The following ones are taken only from the prosification of the first 'cantar' of the *PMC*:

N	J
fue posar en la glera de Burgos (fol. 114b)	fue posar en la vega de Burgos (fol. 72c)

(Compare *PMC*, l. 56; Ll and associated texts have 'en la iglesia de Burgos')

N	J
e avia y dos señas cabdales de los dos reyes moros e de pendones de los otros pueblos tantos que non avian cuenta (fol. 117b)	e avia y dos reyes moros e de pendones de los otros pueblos tantos que non avian cuenta (fol. 74b–c)

(Compare *PMC*, ll. 698–99)

N	J
llamaron a aquel logar fasta el dia de oy el Poyo de mio Çid. E de aquel logar fizo el (fol. 120a)	llamaron a aquell lugar fasta fizo el (fol. 75d)
mando . . . que los fuesen ferir derranchada mente (fol. 121b)	mando . . . que los fuesen ferir derecha mente (fol. 76c)

These comparisons show clearly that J is inferior to N, and is subject to copyists' errors of some importance. There are not a great number of differences like these considering the total length of the prosification of the poem, although others can be found in the second and third 'cantares', but there are sufficient to make N preferable on grounds of accuracy and faithfulness to source. N has hardly any readings which are not satisfactory in themselves, and seems to have none which are nonsensical owing to scribal error. In fact, J may well be derived, although not copied, from N, since its weaknesses can normally be explained by reference to N, and both manuscripts share the same erroneous numeration of chapters in the section before the fall of Valencia (a series 47, 48, 47, 48, 49; later 55, 57; later 63, 65; see N, fols 141b–150c; J, fols 86d–94d; and Chapter 3, II, *B*).

To sum up: N's impressive standards of composition, its antiquity of script and language, its correctness, and its accuracy all make it preferable as a basis for the text of the *CVR* to J, the only other manuscript seriously suggested for this role. Coincidentally, Diego Catalán has chosen to use N for quotations from the *CVR*, without giving reasons, in his most recent study involving the *CVR* (see 'Crónicas generales y cantares de gesta'). For what it contains, N offers a better text, of greater antiquity, than that offered elsewhere. In this study, therefore, N has been used for quotations and as the text of the *CVR* in Appendix B. J and Ll, as the two manuscripts mainly used in previous studies of *CVR*, have also been consulted, and significant variants have been noted in the notes to Appendix B.

APPENDIX B

A TRANSCRIPTION OF THE PROSIFICATION
OF THE *PMC*
FOUND IN MANUSCRIPT N OF THE *CVR*

There follows a transcription of the prosification of the *PMC* found in N, the oldest and best of the manuscripts of the *CVR*. The text of N has been transcribed in full without editorial interference, except in the instances mentioned below. Thus, the minor inconsistencies of spelling and language of the type found in most chronicle manuscripts are faithfully conveyed here, although this particular manuscript is well composed. It contains very few poor readings, and it is never nonsensical. References to the folios of N are given at the side of the text; a and b refer to the columns of the recto, c and d to the columns of the verso.

In the transcription capital letters and lower case letters and punctuation are according to modern practice, except that the written stress accent is not used. Otherwise, the precise spelling of the manuscript has been respected, except for the following cases:

1. Consonantal u has been changed to v.

2. Final s and z can be difficult to differentiate in the script. Therefore, modern practice has been followed. In particular, surnames have been standardized to end in z, where it is uncertain whether s or z was originally intended.

3. The abbreviations of N have been expanded, and the letters added are italicized in the text. The additions follow the spelling of the particular word when this is found in full elsewhere in the manuscript. There are just a few exceptions to this, cited immediately below.

4. Oṁe, oṁs are never found except in shortened form. They have been expanded to om*n*e, om*ne*s.

5. Ihū Xpō, xp̄ianos (or minor variations) are also never found in expanded form in the manuscript. They have been transcribed as Ih*esu Christo, christia*nos.

6.   Some diacritic marks require no expansion, and they have been omitted without comment. They occur in the following instances: -cħ (which is always written thus), cõmo, alguñd, ninguñd, grañd, grañt, Sañd, Faguñd, Ferrañd, Remõnt, cieñt, mĩll, villã.

7.   Word-division can be difficult to be certain of in the manuscript, especially with combinations of pronouns, verbs and pronouns, and prepositions and pronouns. Generally, modern usage has been introduced, although necessarily adapted to the linguistic circumstances of the text; thus, for example: tenerlos ha, gelo, me lo, con el, con *ellos* (<coñllos), por que (purpose), porque (cause).

In the notes, variants to the text of N are given, taken from manuscripts J and Ll, the two other manuscripts of the *CVR* widely used in the past for quotations. The notes are intended to show important variations between the manuscripts, underline the value of N, or give possibly valid other readings. Therefore, not all differences between the manuscripts are given. Variations in spelling are not shown, unless they concern names of people, places, or things identified in the *PMC*, or are particularly poetic or unusual words or phrases. Differences in the selection of virtual synonyms are not given, unless they seem of special interest. Minor variations in word order are not normally mentioned, neither are grammatical differences in such things as tenses or the inclusion or omission of pronouns and other small words, unless they are noteworthy. Finally, clear scribal errors in J or Ll are not shown, unless they are extensive or otherwise of interest. N, of course, is given in full. The abbreviations of J and Ll are expanded without comment. Where J and Ll coincide in a variant, the precise text given in the note is that of J. Square brackets in the footnotes enclose words omitted by J or Ll. Parentheses contain comments by the transcriber.

THE FIRST 'CANTAR'

The transcription of the first 'cantar' begins here with the chapter in which the *CVR* starts its version of the surviving text of the *PMC*. The two preceding chapters of the chronicle cán be seen in Pidal, *CMC*, III, 1022–24. The folios of J and Ll containing the transcription of the first 'cantar' are as follows: J, fols 72v–77r; Ll, fols 166r–178r.

114a   Capitulo noveno de como el Çid sallio con todos sus parientes e sus
vasallos de la tierra al rey don Alfonso.

Enbio por sus parientes e sus vasallos, e dixoles[1] como el rey le
mandava sallir de toda su tierra, e que le non dava de plazo mas de

nueve dias; e que queria saber dellos quales querian yr con el o quales fincar. Miñaya Alvar Fanez[2] le dixo, 'Çid, todos yremos convusco e seervos hemos leales vasallos'. Todos los otros dixeron, otrossi, que yrien con el ondequier[3] que el fuesse, e que se non quitarian nin le desenpararian por ninguna cosa.[4] El Çid gradesçiogelo estonçes mucho, e dixoles que, ssi les Dios bien fiziesse, que gelo gualardonaria muy bien. Otro dia, sallio el Çid de Bivar con toda su conpaña; e dizen que cato por aguero e que tomo[5] corneja diestra, e a entrante de Burgos

114b ovola siniestra; e dixo a sus | cavalleros, 'Amigos bien sepades que tornaremos[6] nos a Castilla ricos e honrrados e con grand honrra'. E despues que llego a Burgos, fue posar en la glera[7] de Burgos. Ca[8] el rey avia ya defendido que non le acogiessen en la çibdad. E Martin Antolynez diole esse dia de comer, e aun todas las otras cosas que ovo menester. E el Çid apartosse con ese Martin Antolynez, e dixole como non tenia ninguna cosa de que guisase su conpaña,[9] e que le manlevasse alguna cosa. E Martin Antolinez dixole como non le podie el manlevar todo quanto el avia menester. Mas que mandasse fenchir dos arcas de arena e çerrarlas muy bien, e el que las levaria de su parte a dos mercadores muy ricos que avia y en la çibdad, e que les diria que eran llenas de oro e de plata e de piedras presçiosas; 'E que les rogades vos que vos den paños e dyneros sobre ellas, fasta un plazo sseñalado, e vos que les daredes su aver e aun demas ganançia. E si al plazo non les quitaredes las arcas, que las abran ellos e que sse entreguen de su aver; e

114c lo que fincar de mas que vos lo guarden, fasta que en-| biedes vos por ello. E esto les dire yo por mayor segurança'. E el Çid, quando aquello oyo, tovo que era buen consejo, e mando fenchir las arcas de la arena, e diolas a Martin Antolinez que las levasse.[10] E Martin Antolinez puso estonçes con los mercaderos que le diessen sobre aquellas arcas sseys-çientos marcos de oro e de plata, para el Çid. E los mercadores dieronle el aver e el troxolo al Çid. Otro dia, sallio[11] el Çid de Burgos e fuesse para Sand Pedro, o tenia la muger e las fijas. E el abad del logar, que avia nonbre don Sancho, resçibiolo muy bien. E su muger, doña Ximena e sus fijas besaronle las manos. E otro dia, fablo el Çid con el abad toda su fazienda, e dixole que queria dexarle la muger e las fijas en encomienda, e que le rogava, como amigo, que pensasse bien dellas. Desi dio a el e a los monjes çinquenta marcos de plata, e a doña Ximena e a sus fijas çient marcos[12] de oro; e rogo al abad que, ssi aquello les fallesçiesse, que les diesse el quanto oviessen menester, ca el gelo daria

114d todo. E el abad dixole que lo | farie muy de grado.

Capitulo Xº de como el Çid se salio de la tierra e sse fue para tierra de moros.

Quando sopieron por Castilla que el rey don Alfonso echava al Çid de la tierra, vinieronsse para el Çid alli a Sand Pedro çiento e quinze cavalleros, e Martin Antolinez con ellos, e aun otras conpañas muchas de omnes a pie. El Çid, quando los vio, plogole mucho con ellos, e resçibiolos muy bien; e partio luego con ellos todo el aver que tenia. E, desque fue la noche, espidiosse de su muger e de sus fijas e fuesse su via; e andudo toda esa noche e otro dia llego a Espinazo de Can e, alli estando, llegole otra conpaña muy grande de cavalleros e de peones. Sallio el Çid de alli, e paso Duero sobre una[13] Nava de Palos e fue yazer a la Figueruela. E quando fue ya la noche e se echo a dormir, veno a el

115a en vision uno, como en figura de angel, que le dixo a-| ssi; 'Ve, Çid, aosadas e non temas; ca sienpre te yra bien mientra bivas e seras rico e bien andante e honrrado'. El Çid, quando desperto, ovo grand plazer[14] de la vision que viera, e acomendose a Dios; e rogole que le guiasse bien su fazienda. E otro dia, sallio de alli con su conpaña muy grande e fue posar[15] a la Ssierra de Miedes, e yaziale de siniestro Atiença que era estonçes de moros. E antes que se pusiesse el sol, mando el Çid fazer alarde a todos quantos yvan con el, e fallo mas de trezientos cavalleros e muchos omnes a pie. E dixoles, 'Amigos, vayamosnos luego e passemos de dia esta ssierra[16] e salgamos de la tierra del rey; ca oy sse cunple el dia del plazo. E despues quien nos quisier,[17] fallarnos ha'.

Capitulo XI° de como el Çid priso el castillo de Castejon.

Cavalgaron luego todos, e pasaron luego todos aquella sierra ya de noche. E al pie de la sierra, avia una montaña muy grande e mandolos el

115b Çid posar alli, por tal que non fuessen | descubiertos. E mando a todos que diessen çevada con dia, ca queria el trasnochar. Desy movieron de alli e andudieron toda la noche. E quando fueron açerca de un castillo que dizen Castejon,[18] que yaze sobre Henares, echosse el Çid alli en çelada. E mando a Alvar Fanez que fuesse con dozientos cavalleros correr toda la tierra bien fasta Guadalfajara, e que llegassen las algaras a Alcala; e que acogiesse quanto fallase, tan bien omnes como ganados, e que lo non dexasse por miedo de los moros; 'E yo fincare aqui', dixo[19] el, 'con estos çient cavalleros çerca este castillo de Castejon. E ssi yo menester fuere en[20] alguna cosa, enbiadme mandado; ca yo vos acorrere'. Quando fue la mañana, fue Alvar Fanez correr toda aquella tierra, assi como le mandara el Çid. E los moros de Castejon, non sabiendo parte del Çid, abrieron las puertas del castillo e sallieron a sus lavores, assi como solien. E el Çid sallio de la çelada e corrio todo el castillo aderredor, e priso los moros e las moras e el ganado que fallo. E fuesse luego derechamente para la puerta del castillo. E el apellido e el

roydo seyendo muy grande en el castillo, acogieronsse los moros que
115c andavan fue-| ra, quando lo oyeron a la puerta. E con el grand miedo que
ovieron metieronsse adentro, e finco la puerta desenparada. E el Çid
entro luego en pos ellos, su[21] espada en la mano, matando en los moros
que fallava ante ssi. E tanto fizo y que gano el castillo, e fallo y mucho
oro e mucha plata e otras muchas donas buenas, e tomolo todo. En todo
esto, Alvar Fanez e los otros, que con el fueran, corrieron fasta Alcala,
e tomaron y grand plea[22] de moros e de moras e de ganados e de otras
cosas muchas. Desi acogieronsse, otrossi, Fenares arriba, robando
otrossi quanto ffallavan, e llegaron al Çid alli a aquel castillo de
Castejon que avie y el ganado. El Çid, quando sopo que vinie Alvar
Fanez, dexo el castillo en guarda, e salliole resçebir. E quando le vio tan
bien venir,[23] plogole mucho, e dixole, 'Alvar Fanez, tengo por bien que
lo que yo he ganado aca e lo que vos traedes, que se ayunte todo en uno e
que levedes vos ende el quinto'. Mucho gradesçio Alvar Fanez al Çid
esto que le dava, mas non gelo quiso tomar, por que cunpliesse el Çid
con ello a sus conpañas en aquello que les oviese a dar. E dixole assi,
115d 'Çid, fasta | que vos yo non vea en canpo aver grand fazienda con moros,
e que lidie[24] yo del mi cabo, faziendo grand mortandad en los moros, e
que entendades vos que lo meresco, non vos quiero tomar nada'. El Çid,
quando sse vio tan bien andante en su comienço, fue muy alegre, e
gradesçiolo a Dios. E mando luego ayuntar quanto el ganara en
Castejon e todo lo al que Alvar Fanez traxiera de su cavalgada, e tomo
el ende su quinto e lo al partio a sus cavalleros e a los peones por sus
suertes[25] derechas, como convinie a cada uno. E el Çid non fallo alli a
quien vender el su quinto, e enbio mandado a los moros de Fita e de
Guadalajara que gelo quisiesen[26] conprar. E ellos vinieron sobre tre-
gua. E quando vieron el aver, apreçiaronle en tres mill marcos de plata;
e dieronle por el estos tress mill marcos, e fue pagado de todo al terçer
dia.

Capitulo XII° de como dexo el Çid el castillo de Castejon e gano a
Alcoçer.

116a Otro | dia, sallio el Çid de Castejon e fuesse Henares arriba; ca non
quiso fincar alli por non fazer pesar al rey don Alfonso, su sseñor. Pero
non quiso dexar el castillo assi desenparado, mas aforro çient moros con
sus mugeres, e dexolos de su mano en el castillo. El Çid con sus
conpañas llegaron[27] aquel dia que sallieron de Castejon a las Cuevas de
Anguita; e pasaron luego el rio e entraron al Campo de Tarançio,[28] e
fueron albergar entre Hariza e Çetina. Otro dia, pasaron Alfama, e
tornaronsse[29] esa noche a Huerta. E dende tomo camino de Atiença, e

124

fueron posar sobre Alcoçer, en un otero muy fuerte çerca el rio Xalon,[30] por que les non pudiessen vedar el agua. Otro dia, mando el Çid posar los unos contra el rio e los otros contra la sierra, e fizo fazer una carcava aderredor de ssi, por guardarsse de rebate de dia e de noche. Despues que el Çid ovo fecho alli su bastida, cavalgo e fue veer si podria prender a Alcoçer. E los moros de la villa, con el miedo que ovieron del, dixieron le que le pecharian quanto el quisiesse, e que los dexase en paz. E el Çid

116b non lo quiso | fazer, e acogiose a su bastida. Quando esto supieron los de Calatayud e de las otras villas de aderredor, pesoles mucho con el. E duro alli el Çid quinze ssemanas. E quando vio que non podia aver el castillo, fizo enfinta que se yva, e mando coger todas las tiendas sy non una sola que dexo en esa bastida. E fizo cargar e cavalgaron todos, e pensaron de andar a mas poder Xalon ayuso, faziendo muestra como que sse yvan. Los moros, quando los vieron yr, començaronsse de alabar como fueran esforçados, e que se tovieran bien. E dixieron que non levava el Çid vianda ninguna nin aun las tiendas, pues que aquella dexava alli. E ovieron su acuerdo de yr en pos el e de le desbaratar, antes que le prisiessen los de Tiruel. 'Ca, si lo ellos prendien',[31] dixieron ellos, 'non nos daran nada de la ganançia. E ssy lo nos desbaratamos, tornarnos ha las prendas,[32] que de nos levo, dobladas'. E sallieron a grand priesa, e fueron en pos el; e, desque se fueron alongando de la villa, cato el Çid en pos ssi.[33] E quando los vio, plogole mucho. E por los alongar bien del castillo, fizo aun[34] ademan que se yva

116c a mas poder. Los de Alcoçer, quando los asi | vieron yr a grand priesa, dixeron, 'Vassenos la ganançia que cuydaramos aver, e andemos[35] en guisa que los alcançemos'. E començaron todos a correr de pie e de cavallo, e tanto ovieron grand sabor de yr en pos el Çid, que dexaron las puertas del castillo abiertas. E el Çid, quando vio que eran bien alongados del castillo, torno contra ellos; e lidiando todos de buelta, entro[36] el Çid e Alvar Fanez entre los del castillo, e mataron alli mas de trezientos moros. El Çid e Alvar Fanez, demientra que la otra cavalleria lidiava con los moros, fueronsse quanto mas pudieron para el castillo, e entraronle luego. E Pero Bermudez, que traye la seña del Çid, fuesse luego quanto mas pudo para el castillo, e puso la seña en el mas alto logar que y avie. El Çid, con el grand plazer que avia, dixo, 'Amigos, graçias al Nuestro Señor Ihesu Christo, ya mejoraremos las posadas'. Estonçes el Çid mando escudriñar toda la villa, e fallaron y muchos moros e muchas moras que yazian escondidos, e mucho oro e mucha plata e otro aver muy grande.

Capitulo XIII° de la batalla que ovo el Çid en Alçocer con el rey Fariz e
116d con Galve. |

Los moros de Deça[37] e de Calatayud e de Tiruel, quando supieron que el Çid avia preso Alcoçer, pesoles mucho; ca tenian que les avernia[38] algund daño eso mismo a ellos. E enbiaron luego sus mandaderos al rey de Valençia que les viniesse a acorrer; ca supiesse que el Çid Ruy Diaz de Bivar, que lo avia echado el rey don Alfonso, su sseñor, de su tierra, e que entrara por aquella su tierra, e que avia preso el castillo de Alcoçer. E que, ssi el a esto non diesse consejo, que contasse que Deça e Tiruel e Calatayud, que las avia perdidas, e aun amas partes de riberas de Xalon. Aquel rey de Valençia avia nonbre Tamin, e, pesandole muy de coraçon con estas nuevas, guiso de muy grand hueste de moros a dos reyes de moros que eran y con el, que avian[39] nonbre Fariz e Galve. E dixoles que sse fuesen para Alcoçer, e que tomassen todas las gentes que y eran aderredor e las levassen consigo, e que punassen en aver derecho del Çid. Ffueronse | aquellos dos reyes para Alcoçer, e enbiaron por todos los conçejos de las fronteras, e fizieronsse muy grand hueste. E començaron de guerrear al Çid e de le conbatir cada dia, e vedaronle el agua luego a pocos de dias; e tovieronle alli çercado de aquella guisa tres semanas. E los del Çid querian sallir lidiar con ellos,[40] mas vedavagelo el Çid. Pero, quando vio que sse yva prolongando aquella çerca, dixoles, 'Amigos, ¿que tenedes por bien que fagamos? Ya nos tollieron los moros el agua e, ssi otro consejo non tomamos, fallesçernos ha el pan. E ssi quisieremos lidiar con los moros, ellos son muy grandes poderes e nos pocos. Otrossi, que nos queramos yr de noche a furto, non podremos, ca nos tienen çercados de[41] todas partes'. Alvar Fanez respondio estonçes e dixo contra los cavalleros, 'Amigos, ¿como[42] queredes fazer, o que responderemos al Çid sobre esto que nos ha dicho? Nos somos sallidos de Castilla, assy como sabedes, e, ssi con los moros non lidiaremos, non fallaremos quien nos quiera governar. Nos[43] somos mas de seysçientos omnes de armas, e pues, en el nonbre de Nuestro[44] Señor Ihesu Christo vayamos a | los moros e lidiemos con ellos; ca los vençeremos a[45] grand ganançia'. El Çid gradesçio mucho este esfuerço que Alvar Fanez dio a la gente, e dixole, 'Alvar Fanez, fablastes como yo queria e honrrastesvos en ello. E pues que asi es, aguisemosnos oy como cras salgamos a ellos'. Otro dia por la mañana, salio el Çid con todos los suyos del castillo, e paro sus azes. E Pero Bermudez mudava la seña del Çid, e defendio el Çid que non derranchase con ella, fasta que gelo el mandasse. Los moros estavan otrossi ya sus azes paradas; e tantos eran los roydos que ffazian con los atanbores,[46] que se non podian oyr los omnes. E avia y dos[47] señas cabdales de los dos reyes moros, e de pendones de los otros pueblos tantos que non avian cuenta. Pero Bermudez, que tenia la seña, quando vio el grand poder de los moros, non gelo pudo sofrir el coraçon, e dixo contra el Çid, 'Dios ayude oy a la vuestra lealtad; ca yo non puedo aqui mas estar'. E aguijo el cavallo, e fue meter la seña en la mayor espesura que vio de los moros. Los moros çercaronle alli, e començaronle a dar

117c grandes golpes | en el de las lanças, por levar la seña del. Mas, como traye[48] buenas armas, non le pudieron enpeesçer. Estonçes, el Çid mando a sus conpañas que le acorriessen, e fue el Çid por su cuerpo con todos los suyos ferir en las azes de los moros. E tan grande fue la mortandad que en ellos fizieron, que mataron mas de mill e trezientos dellos. Los cabdillos de los christianos, que[49] acabdellavan las conpañas, fueron estos: Ruy Diaz, el Çid Canpeador, Miñaya[50] Alvar Fanez que tovo Çorita, Martin Antolinez de Burgos, Muño Gustioz criado del Çid, Marti Muñoz que tovo Monte Mayor, Alvar Alvarez, Alvar Salvadorez, Guillen Garçia un buen cavallero de Aragon, Feliz Muñoz sobrino del Çid. Estos[51] e todos los otros lidiaron tan bien que moro ninguno non se les osava parar delante. E andando todos bueltos en la priesa, mataron los moros el cavallo a Alvar Fanez. El Çid, quando lo vio, fuele acorrer; e mato y de su[52] yda un moro alguazil, e tomole el cavallo e diolo a Alvar Fanez; e dixole, 'Cavalgad, Alvar Fanez; ca vos

117d sodes el mi diestro braço, e, ssi Dios quisier, assi se mos-| trara en esta batalla. Ca firmes veo estar aun los moros, e non nos quieren dexar el canpo, onde ha menester que los cometamos de cabo. E ssy de la primera los cometimos de rezio, non ssea menos desta vez.

Capitulo XIIII° de como el Çid vençio al rey Fariz e al rey Galve.

Despues que cavalgo Alvar Fanez, fueron ferir en los moros. E porque los moros estavan ya mal[53] escarmentados de la otra vegada, non sse atrevieron a lidiar con los christianos nin de los atender en[54] el canpo, e aun fueronsse vençiendo. E los christianos yendolos ya levando[55] e sacando del canpo, vio el Çid al rey Fariz. E dexosse yr para el a mas poder del cavallo, e diole un golpe con la espada tan grande que a pocas le oviera muerto. El moro, quando sse sintio mal ferido, non quiso y mas atender, e bolvio la rienda al cavallo, e fuxo del canpo. Las

118a otras conpañas de los moros, quando vieron assi fuyr al rey Ffa-| riz, desenpararon otrossi el canpo e fuxeron. Martin Antolinez fallosse otrossy con el otro rey moro, que dizian Galve, e diole tan grand golpe con la espada por somo del yelmo que todas las armas le falso,[56] e llegole fasta la carne. Galve, quando sse vio tan mal ferido, penso de foyr con[57] todas sus conpañas, e dexaron el canpo a los christianos. El rey Fariz fuxo para Tiruel[58] e Galve para Calatayud. E el Çid e Alvar Fanez con sus conpañas fueron en pos ellos en alcançe bien fasta las puertas de cada una de las villas, matando e faziendo grand estragamiento en ellos.

Desi tornaronsse el Çid e sus conpañas al logar, o fuera la batalla, e cogieron el canpo e fallaron y en[59] el canpo muy grande aver ademas. E de los cavallos de los moros que fincavan, que andavan esparzidos, quando los llegaron,[60] fallaron y quinientos e diez. E de los suyos non fallaron menos mas de quinze cavallos. Despues que ovieron cogido el canpo, fueronse para su castillo de Alcoçer. Desi, mando el Çid partir la
118b ganançia que ganaran,[61] e cayo a cada uno muy grand | algo en su parte. E al Çid cayeron en el su quinto çient cavallos. E fueron todas las conpañas muy pagados, porque tan bien les fuera[62] partido e dado su derecho a cada uno en la su guisa. Despues desto, mando el Çid que los moros naturales de alli de aquel castillo, que los acogiessen dentro para servirsse dellos; ca el los mandara echar fuera del castillo, quando yva[63] a lidiar. E aun sobre esto, fizoles el algo de aquello que ganara[64] de los otros moros. Desi, llamo el Çid a Alvar Fanez, e dixole, 'Miñaya Alvar Fanez, todo algo que vos omne fiziesse, meresçedeslo vos muy bien. E quiero que tomedes vos deste mi quinto, lo que vos ovieredes menester. E desi, porque vos sabedes como me echo de su tierra mi señor, el rey don Alfonso, querria, ssi pudiese,[65] trabajarme de ganar la su graçia. E por ende, quiero que escojades treynta cavallos muy buenos,[66] destos que cayeron a mi en suerte, e que me los levedes, ensellados e enfrenados con sendas espadas a los arzones, a mi señor, el rey don
118c Alfonso, e que gelos presentedes por mi. E, | en quanto vos pudieredes ganarme[67] la su graçia e el su amor, en tanto vos trabajad. E levad, otrossy, tanto de oro e de plata, por que me fagades cantar mill misas en Santa[68] Maria de Burgos; e lo que fincare de mas, darlo hedes a mi muger e a mis fijas, e dezirles hedes que rueguen a Dios por nos, e que nos va muy bien, merçed a Dios. Otrossi vos digo, Alvar Fanez, que esta tierra es muy angosta, e non podremos en ella fincar, e nos por armas avemos a guarir. E si por aventura non nos fallaredes aqui, quando tornaredes, ydvos para nos, oquier que supieredes que somos'. E Alvar Fanez dixo que assy lo faria. Desy, guiso sus cosas que avie de levar, e despidiosse del Çid e fuesse para Castilla.

Capitulo XV° de como el Çid se fue de Alcoçer e poso sobre Monte Real.

118d   El Çid finco en aquel castillo con sus conpañas. E los moros | de las fronteras aderredor metien mientes cada dia que faria el. E ovieron su acuerdo con el rey Fariz, ca ya era sano, en como se guardassen del Çid. E el Çid, aviendo sabor de sallir de alli para yr buscar mejor loga[69] e mayor conssejo, enpeño este castillo de Alcoçer[70] a los moros desse mismo logar, por tres mill marcos de plata. Desi, quito todas las[71] cosas que tenia enpeñadas con aquel aver, e pago el sueldo a todas sus conpañas, e mandoles que sse guisasen bien. E ellos tovieronsse por muy pagados e mucho amados del, porque tan granadame*n*te les fazie algo. E dixeron la palabra del proverbio que,[72] 'quien buen señor sirve esse bive en bienandan*ç*a'. Desi, quando sse ovo de yr el Çid, comença-ronse a q*u*exar mucho los moros q*u*e y moravan porque les fazia el mucho bien e mucha merçed, e rogavan a Dios que le guiasse, e la su[73] bienandan*ç*a q*u*e sienpre fuesse adelante. Pero, antes que se dende fuesse, quito el castillo e dexolo en recabdo. Desi, salliose de Alcoçer e

119a fuesse, e paso el rio Xalon. E dizen q*u*e a sa-| liente[74] del rio que ovo buenos agueros e señales de bienandança. El Çid, despues q*u*e llego a un poyo[75] que es sobre Mont*e* Real, finco y sus tiendas. E aquel logar es ta*n* alto e tan fuerte, que se non temie alli el Çid de guerra de ninguna parte. E de aq*u*el logar, fizo el mucho mal a Medina[76] e a Teruel e a las otras villas que eran aderredor, fasta que le oviero*n* a pechar. E metiosse so su poder a Çelfa[77] la del Cañal. Mas agora dexaremos de fablar del Çid e diremos de Alvar Fanez.

Capitulo XVI° de como fue Alvar Fan*e*z con el rey don Alfonso.

Qua*n*do Alvar Fanez llego desta vez al rey don Alfonso, presentole luego aq*u*ellos treynta cavallos que el Çid le enbiava. El rey don Alfonso, qua*n*do los vio con el,[78] sus espadas a los arzones, con el plazer que ende ovo, começo de so*n*reyrsse. E antes q*u*e Alvar Fan*e*z le

119b dixiesse ninguna co-| sa, preguntole[79] el rey, 'Miñaya, estos cavallos ¿quien me los enbia?' Alvar Fan*e*z le dixo, 'Señor, sepades que mio[80] Çid el Canpeador que, despues q*u*e le vos echastes de la tierra, que gano de moros el castillo de Alcoçer. E teniendole el, sopolo el rey de Valençia. E enbio y sus poderes con dos reyes moros contra el, e çercaronle alli e tollieronle el agua, assi q*u*e lo non podiemos ya sofrir. E el Çid tovo por bien de sallir a ellos, ho morir o bevir antes por buenos lidiando con *e*llos que por malos yaziendo ençerrados. E sallimos e lidiamos con ellos en canpo, e vençiolos el Çid; e fueron y mal feridos amos los reyes moros, e morieron e fueron y presos muchos de los otros. E fue muy grande la ganançia que y fezimos, de los despojos que dellos levamos. E de los cavallos q*u*e cayero*n* de alli al Çid en el su quinto, enbia ende,[81] Señor, estos treynta cavallos con sus espadas, como a su señor natural, cuya graçia querria el mas que otra cosa. E Sseñor, mandome que vos besasse los pies e las manos por el, e yo, Señor,

119c fagolo; e pidovos por mesura que lo perdonedes e que aya el la vu-| estra graçia'. Dixo el rei, 'Miñaya,[82] mucho es ayna de om*n*e ayrado e echado de ti*e*rra e ssin la graçia de su sseñor, de acogerle[83] a tres semanas. E esto non pertenesçe a rei; ca ningund señor non sse deve ensañar por tan poco tienpo, ssi non ssi vier que le cunple mucho. Pero, porque los cavallos son de ganançia que el fizo de moros, tomarlos he por ende, e plazeme mucho por esta cavalgada que fizo el Çid e por la batalla que vençio. Mas a vos, Miñaya, perdono yo; e otorgovos la tierra que[84] teniades, que la ayades, e dovos mi graçia que vayades o quisieredes, o dovos mi graçia que vengades cada quisieredes. Mas del Çid non vos digo agora nada, sy non que le fago esta graçia a el e a vos, que todos los omnes de mi reno, que son para armas e sse quisieren yr[85] para mio Çit, que vayan sueltos e benditos, e franquoles los cuerpos e los[86] averes e las heredades'. Besole estonçes Alvar Fanez las manos, e dixole assi, 'Señor, devos Dios vida por muchos años e buenos, e graçias muchas

119d por lo que vos dezides; ca, pues[87] | que esta merçed nos fazedes agora, ssi Dios quisier, mas e mejor nos la faredes adelante. E ssi Dios quisiere, nos guisaremos por do la ayamos'. En este quarto año, que es de suso dicho, murio Albet[88] Almucamiz, rey de Sevilla, e reno en pos el su fijo, Abenhabed, en Sevilla e en Cordova, veynte años. Este fue sseñor de toda el Andalozia, e mantuvo muy bien su tierra fasta el tienpo que pasaron a aquen mar los Amoravides, que le tollieron el señorio. Mas agora dexaremos aqui de fablar desto e de[89] Alvar Fanez, e diremos del Çid.[90]

Capitulo XVIIº de como el Çid corrio Çaragoça e le dieron los moros parias.

En el quinto año del regnado del rey don Alfonso, que fue en la era de mill e çiento e çinco años, quando andava el año de la encarnaçion en mill e sessenta e ssiete, e el del inperio de Enrrique en diez e nueve. En aquel poyo que dixiemos que es sobre Monte Real, mantovo el Çid

120a posada | quinze selmanas. E de alli adelante, llamaron a aquel logar, fasta el[91] dia de oy, el Poyo de Mio Çid. E de aquel logar fizo el muchas buenas cavalgadas de grandes ganançias, e apremio e quebranto muchas tierras; e gano ribera de rio Martin e tovola toda por suya. Estas nuevas de aquellos sus grandes fechos llegaron a Çaragoça, e pesoles mucho con ellas a todos los moros. El Çid, quando vio que Alvar Fanez tanto tardava, pesol mucho de estar en aquel logar tanto e de non yr a otra[92] parte. E dexo el poyo desenparado e fizo una trasnochada; e paso Teruel e fue posar al pinar de Tovar. E corrio Çaragoça, e fizoles tanto de mal que por fuerça le ovieron a pechar e darle parias. E desi a pocos de dias, puso el Çid su amor muy grande con Almondafar, que era rey de Çaragoça. E el rey resçibiole en la villa mucho honrradamente, e fizole mucha honrra. Despues desto, a cabo de pocos de dias, llego de Castilla

Minaya Alvar Fanez con dozientos cavalleros de linaje e con escuderos
120b   a pie, e, de otros omnes, tan grandes con-| pañas que eran ademas. El
Çid, quando sopo que venia, salliole resçebir, e Alvar Fanez començole
luego a contar todas las nuevas de como le fuera con el rey don Alfonso,
e de lo que le dixiera. El Çid, quando oyo de parte del rey aquellas[93]
nuevas tan buenas, plogole mucho con ellas, e sonrriosse[94] con el gran
plazer que ende ovo, e gradesçio mucho a Miñaya, porque fuera tan
buen mandadero.

Capitulo XVIIIº de como el Çid corrio tierras d'Alcamiz[95] e lidio con el
conde don Remondo e lo priso.

Andados sseys años del regnado del rey don Alfonso, que fue en la era
de mill e çiento e sseys años,[96] quando andava el año de la encarnaçion
en mill e sesenta e ocho, e el del inperio de Enrrique en veynte. El Çid
estando en Çaragoça, avino assi que enfermo muy mal Almondafar,[97] el
rey desse logar, e morio. E dexo dos fijos; al uno dixeron Çulema e al
120c   otro Benalhange. E partieron el reno en-| tre ssi.[98] Çulema ovo el regno
de Çaragoça, e Benalhange el de Denia. Çulema rey de Çaragoça amo
mucho al Çid e metiole todo el reno en poder, e que fiziessen todo lo que
el mandasse. Desy, començosse grand enemistad entre Çulema e
Benalhange amos hermanos, e guerrearonsse el uno al otro. E el rey
don Pedro de Aragon e el conde Remont Bereguel[99] de Barçelona
ayudavan a Benalhange, e desamavan mucho al Çid, porque sse atenia
con Çulema e le guardava la tierra. En todo esto, tomo el Çid dozientos
cavalleros de sus conpañas todos escogidos a mano, e trasnocho con
ellos; a fue correr tierras de Alcamiz, e duro alla tres dias e troxo muy
grand prea.[100] E sono aquella cavalgada mucho por tierra de moros, e
peso ende a los de Monçon e de Huesca. El Çid tornosse luego para
Çaragoça, e partio su cavalgada con todos los suyos, e dio a cada uno su
derecho. Desi, dixoles, 'Amigos, bien sabedes que todos los omnes que
120d   por armas han de guarir, assi como nos, que, ssy en un lugar quieren si-|
enpre morar, que non puede estar que non menoscaben mucho y. E por
ende, guisadevos todos para cras[101] mañana, e saldremos de aqui e
yremos buscar otras posadas'. Otro dia, sallieron dalli, e fueron e
assentaronsse en un logar[102] que dizen el Puerto de Alocat. E de alli,
corrio el Çid Huesca e Montalvan, e duro alla diez dias. E llego el
mandado desto que el Çid fazia a don Remont Berenguel, conde de
Barçelona, e a Benalhange, rey de Denia. El conde, quando lo oyo,
pesole mucho de coraçon, porque tenia el aquellas tierras de los moros
en guarda. E con la grand saña que ovo contra el Çid, dixo sus palabras
grandes en esta guisa, 'Grandes tuertos me tiene el Çid de Bivar

fechos.[103] Ffiriome ya mi sobrino dentro en mi corte, e nunca me lo despues emendo. Agora, correme las tierras que yo tenia en mi guarda, e yo nin[104] le desafie nunca nin le torne amistad. Mas, quando me lo el busca tantas vezes, yo non puedo estar que gelo non demande'. El

121a conde e Benalhan-| ge ayuntaron estonçe grandes poderes de moros[105] e de christianos, e fueron en pos el Çid e alcançaronle en Tovar del[106] Pinar. E assi yvan esforçados contra el, que le cuydaron tomar a manos. El Çid traye estonçes muy grand presa, e desçendia de una ssierra, e llegava ayuso a un valle. E llegole alli mandado como el conde don Remon[107] e Benalhange vinien en pos el, por le toller lo que levava, e matar a el o prenderlo. El Çid quando lo oyo, enbio luego dezir al conde que non toviesse el por mal por[108] fazer aquello que el fazia, e, demas, que non levava nada de lo suyo, e que le dexasse yr en paz. El conde enbiole dezir que aquello non sseria, mas que le pecharia agora lo que le fiziera antes e lo de agora, e assi entenderia a quien ffazia desonrra. El mandadero tornosse apriesa con este mandado al Çid. El Çid, quando vio que menos de lid non se podia librar, dixo a sus conpañas, 'Fazed aparte la presa que traemos, e armadvos quanto pudieredes; ca vienen alli el conde don Remondo e el rey Benalhange con grandes gentes de christianos e de moros. E bien cuydo que nos quieren toller lo que

121b levamos. | Menos de batalla non sse querra partir de nos. E ssi nos de aqui fueremos, tras nos yran, fasta que nos alcançen. E pues que de su entençion[109] non nos podemos partir, mejor sera que lo ayamos aqui con ellos que yr fuyendo. E bien fio en Dios que çient cavalleros de nos que vençeran a todos ellos. E antes que ellos[110] lleguen al llano, firamos en ellos, e por algunos que derribemos, desmayaran[111] los otros, e fuyran'. El Çid diziendo esto, vieron venir la cuesta ayuso los poderes de los françeses. El Çid, quando los vio, mando a los suyos que los fuessen ferir derranchadamente,[112] e ellos fizieronlo muy de grado, e enplearon sus lanças e sus espadas muy bien;[113] e derribando los unos e matando los otros,[114] vençio el Çid aquel torneo; e priso y al conde, e gano y la espada que dizian Colada. E el rey Benalhange fuxo con aquellos que pudieron escapar. E el Çid levo al conde preso para su tienda,[115] e mandole guardar muy bien. E partio luego la ganançia que avie fecha con todos los suyos.

Capitulo diez e nueve de como el Çid solto al conde don Remondo de la prision e lo enbio para su tierra.

121c Despues desto, mando ffazer[116] de | comer muy bien, por fazer[117] plazer al conde don Remondo. Mas el conde non lo presçio nada, nin quiso comer ninguna cosa, maguer que gelo trayen delante. E quando lo

aq*ue*xaron mucho que comiesse, dixo que por qua*n*to avie en España
que non comerie un bocado; antes pre*n*deria muerte. El Çid, qua*n*do
sopo[118] que non queria comer, fuele veer, e, como era om*n*e mesurado,
dixole assi, 'Comed, co*n*de, e beved, ca esto en q*ue* vos agora veedes por
varones pasa. E non vos dexedes morir por esto, que aun podredes
cobrar e endereçar vuestra fazienda.[119] E ssi fizieredes como yo digo,
saldredes ayna de la p*ri*sion. E ssi lo no*n* fizierdes, en todos vuestros dias
non saldredes dende nin tornaredes a vuestra tierra'. El conde[120] le
dixo, 'Don Rodrigo, comed vos q*ue* sodes om*n*e de buena ventura[121] e
lo meresçedes, e folgad en paz e en salud;[122] ca yo non comere, mas
dexarme he morir'. Tres dias contendieron con el, rogandole, assi el
Çid[123] como los suyos, que comiese, mas non pudieron con el. El Çid,

121d quando esto vio,[124] con el grand duelo que ovo | del, dixole, 'Conde,
bien vos digo que, ssi non comedes algund poco, que nu*n*ca tornedes a la
tierra onde venistes. E ssi comedes por que podades bivir, darvos e yo
dos cavalleros de los vuestros, destos que aqui tengo presos, que vos
guarden, e quitarvos he a vos e a ellos los cuerpos, e darvos he de mano
que vos vayades'. Quando esto oyo el conde, fuesse[125] mas alegra*n*do, e
dixo al Çid, 'Don Rodrigo, ssi vos fiziessedes esto q*ue* agora avedes
dicho, yo me maravillaria dello en qua*n*tos dias visquiesse'. El Çid le
dixo, 'Pues, comed agora q*ue* lo vea yo, e luego vos soltare e vos
enbiare. Pero digovos que, de quanto vos tome, que vos non dare ende
nada; ca non es fuero nin costu*n*bre, ssy non lo quisiere fazer por mesura
aquel que lo gana. Demas, helo yo men*e*ster para estos que lo han
lazdrado[126] comigo; ca, tomando de vos e de los otros, yremos nos
guaresçiendo; ca esta vida avremos a fazer, fasta que Dios quiera, asi
como om*n*es que son echados de tierra, e han yra de su señor'. El conde

122a ovo grand plazer de aquello que el Çid dezia, q*ue* le non daria nada de |
lo que le tomara. E demando agua para las manos e comieron[127]
aquellos dos cavalleros que el Çid le dio. Despues que ovieron[128]
comido, dixo el conde al Çid, 'Don Rodrigo, mandad nos dar las bestias,
ssi vos ploguier, e yrnos hemos'. El Çid dioles estonçes muy bien[129] de
vestir, e fue con ellos fasta el p*ri*mer albergue.[130] E en espidiendosse el
Çid d*e*l conde, dixole assi, 'Yde vos, conde, a guisa de muy franco, e
gradescovos yo mucho q*ua*nto me dexades. Pero, ssi vos viniere a
coraçon de vos ve*n*gar de mi, fazedmelo ante saber. E ssi vinieredes, o
me dexaredes de lo vuestro, o levaredes algo de lo mio'. El co*n*de le
dixo, 'Çid, vos en vuestro salvo estades; e yo pagado vos he por todo
este año. E non te*n*go agora en coraçon de vos venir buscar tan ayna'.
Fuesse el conde, e tornosse el Çid para sus conpañas, gradesçiendo
mucho a Dios la merçed que le fazia en todos sus fechos. Desi, tornosse
el Çid para Çaragoça.

II.   THE SECOND 'CANTAR'

In the context of its use in the *CVR*, the second 'cantar' of the *PMC* can be considered in two parts. First, for events before the capture of Valencia by the Cid (*PMC*, l. 1210), there were long and detailed sources other than the poem available to the *CVR*, and thus references to the material in the poem occur only occasionally, when they can conveniently be fitted into the principal narrative in the chronicle. These references vary greatly in length. Second, after the capture of Valencia, the *PMC* becomes once again the principal source used by the chronicle, which follows the remainder of the 'cantar' until its conclusion. (For a detailed consideration of the use of the second 'cantar', see Chapter 3, IV.)

In the following transcription, for the section between the end of the prose version of the first 'cantar' and the account of the capture of Valencia, those parts of the *CVR* which seem to depend on information taken from the *PMC* are given in full, with any additions needed to make the context clear. In addition all the headings to the chapters of the *CVR* are given, so that the general content of this part of the chronicle can be followed, and thus broad comparisons with chronicles such as the *PCG* and *CRC* are made possible. From the beginning of the chapter after the capture of Valencia, the whole of the text of the *CVR* appears once more.

Variants are provided from J and Ll only for the parts based on the *PMC* and not for the chapter headings. The relevant folios of J and Ll for the second 'cantar' are as follows: J, 77r–95r (capture of Valencia), 95r–97v; Ll, 178v–226v (capture of Valencia), 226v–32v.

122a   Capitulo XX de como el Çid desatara todos los cavalleros del rey don Pedro de Aragon e gano tierras de Burriana.

122b   En el seteno | año del regnado del rey don Alfonso, que fue en la era de mill e çiento e ssiete años. El Çid, estando en Çaragoça, guiso su hueste muy grande por yr sobre Monçon e[1] correr tierra de Xerica e de Onda e de Almenar . . . Despues desto, a pocos de dias sallio el Çid de alli, e fue desçendiendo contra la mar de medio de la tierra, por fazer y
122c   sus cavalgadas e guerrear alla. E | gano desa yda Onda e todas[2] las tierras que dizen de Burriana. E tanto eran grandes las conquistas del Çid e fechas ayna, que llegaron las sus nuevas a Valençia, e sonaron por toda la villa e por todos sus terminos[3] aderredor. E fueron ende todos espantados, e temieronsse mucho del. El Çid tornosse entonçes a Tamarid, ho era el rey de Çaragoça.

Capitulo XXI de como el Çid lidio con Benalhange e con los condes.

147b   . . . El Çid enbio luego su carta a Abeniahaf, en que le enbiava dezir que le diese su pan que dexara en Valençia, e que fiziera muy mal, otrossy, en matar a su señor, e que le reptava por ende. Abeniahaf, quando ovo leyda la carta, enbio su respuesta al Çid tal de que se non pago el Çid. El Çid fue, luego, sobre Cobolla,[4] e conbatiola e prisola, e poblola de christianos. Desi, corrio toda la tierra aderredor, e gano Xerica e Honda[5] e Almenar.[6] Despues, tornosse a Valençia. . . .

Desy, demando Abeniahaf que le diesse una huerta que era açerca de Valençia . . . Abeniahaf tovo por bien de gela dar . . . Despues que el Çid entro en la huerta, apoderosse de todo el arraval que era en derredor della. Desi, a cabo de pocos dias, sallio de ally e fue çercar Murviedro;[7] e tan de rezio lo conbatio que lo priso a pocos dias. Los de Valençia, quando lo oyeron, temieronsse mucho del Çid, e ovieron su acuerdo de

149c lo yr çercar; e trasnocharon e fueron | con el a la mañana. El Çid, quando los vio, plogole ende mucho, e enbio sus mandaderos a Xerica e a Calatayud[8] e a Onda e Almenar e a tierra de Burriana, que fuessen luego todos con el. Desi, dixo a sus conpañas,[9] 'Amigos, ssi nos queremos morar en esta tierra, menester faz que escarmentemos a los de Valençia, en guisa que nunca osen despues venir a nos. E por ende, cras de grand mañana seed todos[10] guisados e yrlos hemos veer a sus tiendas'. Alvar Fanez e todos los otros le dixeron, 'Çid, mucho nos plaze de lo que vos dezides, e faremos[11] de buena voluntad quanto nos mandades'. Otro dia mañana, armaronsse, e fueron ferir en los de Valençia, llamando, 'Dios, ayuda e Santiago', e mataron y muchos dellos. Los otros que escaparon desenpararon el canpo e fuxeron. El Çid fue en pos ellos en alcançe, bien fasta Valençia. E mato y dos reyes moros, e gano grandes averes dellos. Desi, tornosse para Murviedro con su conpaña muy rico e mucho honrrado. Despues desto, sallio el Çid de Murviedro, e fue correr Cullera[12] e Xativa e tierra de Denia e fizo y a los

149d moros muy grandes daños, e quebranto e robo quanto fallo. Los de Va-| lençia, quando lo oyeron, ovieron ende muy grand pesar. E tan grande fue el miedo que en ellos entro de aquel dia adelante, que solamente non osavan sallir fuera de la çibdad.[13] Despues que el Çid ovo todo esto fecho, tornosse a la huerta que le diera Abeniahaf. . . .

150a Capitulo LXII° de como el Çid çerco Valençia.

150b . . . Despues desto, quando llego el tienpo del plazo que el Çid diera a los de Valençia, e non vino el rey de los almoravides a acorrerlos, porque avie guerra con el señor de los Montes Claros,[14] allegoseles mas a la çibdad. E mando pregonar por todo Aragon e Navarra e Castilla, que todos los que quisiesen sallir de cuyta e venir a grand riqueza que se viniessen para el.[15] Las gentes, quando aquello oyeron, vinieronsse para el muy grandes conpañas de cavalleros e de peones.[16] El Çid,

150c quando vio que tenie gente asaz, çerco la | çibdad[17] toda aderredor, e conbatiola cada dia.[18] En todo esto, era ya la carestia muy grande en Valençia.

Capitulo LXIII° de la desabenençia que ovo el Çid con Abeniahaf.

151b Capitulo LXV° de como el Çid priso Valençia e a Abeniahaf por el aver que oviera de Alcadir.

138

151c   . . . Deste aver e de otro mucho que fallo el Çid en Valençia, fue el
151d   ta*n* rico e toda su conpaña, que | mas non podrien seer om*n*es.[19] Esto
todo, que aqui avemos dicho, fue en nueve meses e, e*n*trante el dezeno,
entregaro*n*le la çibdad,[20] assy como avemos dicho.

Capitulo LXVI° de como el Çid lidio con el rey de Sevilla e fizo obispo
en Valençia e enbio a Alvar Fanez a Castilla al rey don Alfon*so*.

Qua*n*do[21] el rey de Sevilla sopo que el Çid avie presa Valençia, allego
muy grand hueste, e veno sobre el. E fueron por cue*n*ta treynta mill
om*n*es de armas. El Çid, quando los vio, sallio a ellos, e ovo con ellos su
batalla; e vençiolos e mato muchos dellos. E los que ende escaparon
fuxeron, e fue el Çid en pos ellos en[22] alcançe, bien fasta Xativa. E
pasando por Xucar, ovo y con ellos un torneo, e murieron y muchos, e
fuxo el rey de Sevilla con tres golpes. Despues que el Çid los ovo
desbaratados, tornosse para Valençia rico e honrrado de grant aver, que
gano de los moros. Las nuevas del Çid eran ya sabidas alueñe e açerca.
152a   En | todo esto, yva ya creçiendo mucho la barva al Çid e alongandossele
el cabello. Ca el Çid avie jurado que nunca rayese la barva nin tajasse
della nada, porque el rey don Alfonso lo avie echado de la tierra, syn
cosa que el meresçiesse. El Çid heredo estonçes en Valençia muy bien a
todos los suyos. E defendioles que se no*n* partiessen del, a menos de su
mandado; que el que lo osase fazer, que le tomarie quanto oviesse, e el
cuerpo q*ue* estarie a su merçed. E fizolos ayu*n*tar todos en un logar, e
mandolos contar; e fallaron y tres mill e dozientos om*n*es de armas. El
Çid dixo contra Alvar Fanez 'Graçias a Dios e a Santa Maria. Pero que
co*n* pocos salimos de Castilla, muchos nos cresçieron despues. E por
ende, vos ruego, Alvar Fanez, que me vayades al rey don Alfonso, mi
señor, e que le levedes çient[23] cavallos destos que gane, ensellados e
enfrenados; e que le besedes las manos por mi, e le roguedes que me
dexe traer para aca a mi muger e a mis fijas'. Alvar Fanez le dixo, 'Çid,
mucho me plaze, e fare de buena mente lo que vos ma*n*dades'. El Çid
152b   diole estonçes los cavallos, e mill marcos de plata que diese al abad do*n* |
Sancho de Sand Pedro. Ellos en esto estando, veno de partes de oriente
un om*n*e mucho honrrado que avie nonbre don Geronimo, que era
clerigo muy letrado e sabio e mucho esforçado en todo fecho, porq*ue*
oyera dezir[24] del Çid mucho bien, e porque avie muy grand sabor de se
veer con moros en canpo e lidiar con ellos. El Çid, q*ua*ndo sopo la razon
por q*ue* viniera, plogole mucho con el, e fizole obispo de Valençia,
porque le semejo buen *christ*iano. El Çid dixo estonçes a Alvar Fanez,
'Graçias a Dios, agora podredes levar buenos[25] mandados a Castilla'.
Esto fecho, despidiosse Alvar Fanez del Çid, e fuesse para Castilla.

Capitulo LXVII° de como el rey don Alfonso perdono al Çid e a todos los que con el eran.

Despues que Alvar Fanez llego a Castilla e sopo como el rey don Alfonso era en Sand Fagund e fazie y sus cortes, fuesse para el. E luego que entro, finco los ynojos ante el, e besole la mano, e dixole,[26] 'Señor, Ruy Diaz[27] vos manda besar los pies e las manos, como | a sseñor natural. E ruegavos[28] que le ayades merçed, e que le perdonedes, sy alguna querella avedes del, e lo resçibades en vuestra tierra, ssi el y vinier; ca el vuestro vasallo es, e a vos cata por señor. E enbiavos dezir el bien que Dios le fizo, despues que sallio de Castilla. E este es el que gano Xerica, Onda, Almenar, Murviedro, Çebolla, Juballa, Castrejon, Peña Cadilla,[29] Denia e Valençia, e es sseñor de todo e aun de otros logares muchos. E fizo y obispo a uno que ha nonbre don Geronimo. E vençio çinco lides canpales, e gano muy grandes riquezas, graçias a Dios. E por que creades que esto es verdad, enbiavos estos çient cavallos[30] en sserviçio, que le cayeron en el su quinto'. El rey don Alfonso, quando lo oyo, plogole mucho, e dixo que el querie tomar los cavallos que le enbiava en presente. El conde don Garçia Ordoñez, quando esto vio, pesole mucho, e dixo contra el rey, 'Señor, por grand maravilla lo ternia yo, ssy assi es como Alvar Ffanez dize'. El rey le dixo, 'Conde, callade vos, ca mucho[31] mejor me ssirve el Çid que vos, en todas guisas'. Alvar Fanez dixo al rey,[32] 'Señor, el Çid vos enbia pedir merçed que le dexedes levar para Valençia su muger, doña Ximena, e sus fijas amas'. El rey dixo que le plazie de coraçon, e que les darie to-| das las cosas que oviessen menester, e quien las levasse fasta el Çid bien[33] honrradamente. 'E demas, non quiero que pierda el Çid, nin ninguno de quantos le sirven, ninguna cosa de quantas han en Castilla, asi en heredades e donadios como en todo lo al. E lo que les yo tome, quiero gelo entregar, que lo ayan suelto e quito e se sirvan dello. E atregoles los cuerpos, que nunca sse teman[34] de prender mal ninguno de mi por esta razon'. Alvar Fanez besole estonçes la mano. El rey, estando muy alegre, dixo, 'Todos los que quisieren yr servir al Çid Canpedor, vayan con la graçia de Dios, ca mas ganaremos en esto que en aver y otro desamor'.

Capitulo LXVIII° de como Alvar Fanez levo a doña Ximena, la muger del Çid, para Valençia.

Los infantes de Carrion, quando vieron que tan bien yva al Çid, ovieron su conssejo de casar con sus fijas, cuydando que les vernie ende[35] pro. E non sse atreviendo de lo dezir a ninguno que les anduviesse el casamiento,[36] porque non era casamiento para ellos, e que

153a sse raheçarien mucho por y, ovieron su acuerdo de sallir con Alvar Fanez, quando sse fuesse, e de le[37] rogar que los encomen-| dasse mucho al Çid. E assi lo fizieron. Alvar Fanez dixoles que lo farie de grado. E estonçes, se despidieron los unos de los otros, e fuesse Alvar Fanez para Sand Pedro. Doña Ximena, la muger del Çid, e sus fijas, doña Elvira e doña Sol, quando lo vieron, fueron muy alegres. Alvar Fanez, quando las vio, saludolas de parte del Çid, e contoles como ganara Valençia e era señor della, e como el rey don Alfonso le avie perdonado a el e a todos los que con el andavan; e que guisassen ellas todas sus cosas e yrsse yan para el Çid. Alvar Fanez enbio estonçes[38] tres cavalleros al Çid, que le dixiesen como lo avie perdonado el rey don Alfonso e le enbiava la muger e las fijas. Minaya Alvar Fanez dio estonçes al abad don Sancho quinientos marcos de plata. E los otros quinientos retovo para ssy, para dar a doña Ximena todo lo que oviesse menester. Estonçes, sse despidieron del abad don Sancho, e fueron su carrera.[39] E allegaron alli a Alvar Fanez muchos cavalleros, que se fueron con el para el Çid.

Capitulo LXIXº de como el Çid resçibio a su muger doña Ximena.

153b Quando | el Çid sopo que doña Ximena venie e sus fijas, dixo contra sus cavalleros, 'Amigos, quien buen mandadero enbia, buen mandado espera. E por ende, quiero que vos armedes vos, Pero Bermudez, Muño[40] Gustioz,[41] Martin Antolinez e el obispo don Geronimo, e çient cavalleros otros, como para lidiar, e yde vos a Albarrezin[42] e dende a Molina. E yra convusco Abengabon, que es señor de esa tierra, con otros çient cavalleros. Desi, yde vos para Medina, ca y fallaredes a mi muger e a mis fijas, e traedmelas mucho honrradamente'. Ellos fueronsse estonçes, e posaron[43] esse dia en Fronchales. Otro dia, llegaron a Molina. Abengabon, quando lo sopo, sallioles resçebir. Muño Gustioz[44] le dixo, 'Abengabon, saludavos el Çid e enbiavos dezir que vayades conusco fasta Medina con çient cavalleros; ca es y su muger e sus fijas, e manda que gelas levemos a Valençia'. Abengabon dixo que le plazie muy de coraçon. Otro dia, sallieron de alli, e fueron a Medina. Alvar Fanez, quando los vio venir armados, temiosse, e enbio a ellos dos cavalleros a saber quien eran, o como venien. Los cavalleros, quando sopieron la razon, enbiaronlo dezir a Alvar Fanez. Minaya salio estonçes contra ellos, e fuelos resçebir. Otro dia, sallieron de alli, e fueronsse

153c para Molina, desy para Valençia. | El Çid, quando sopo que vinien, mando a dozientos cavalleros que los fuessen a resçebir bien a tres leguas.[45] E quando fueron llegados a la çibdad,[46] dexo el Çid quien guardasse el alcaçar, e cavalgo en un cavallo a que dizien Bavieca, que

ganara el del rey de Sevilla, e salio a resçebir a doña Ximena. El obispo
don Geronimo, que venie con la dueña, adelantosse, e fuese a la çibdad;
e llamo a toda la clerezia, e sallieron resçebir a doña Ximena con grand
proçesion. Despues que el Çid e doña Ximena fueron en la çibdad,
contole el Çid todo el bien que Dios le fiziera. E demonstrole a ella e a
las fijas toda la çibdad e la huerta e la mar, e todas las otras cosas que
eran de solaz. En este veynte e noveno[47] año del renado del rey don
Alfonso, murio el papa Urban, e fue puesto en su lugar Pascual el
segundo; e fueron con el çiento e ssesenta e quatro apostoligos.

Capitulo LXX de como el Çid lidio con Yuçef[48] que era rey de
Marruecos e con el rey Bucar e el rey Ssero e los vençio en Quarte.[49]

153d   Andados treynta años del renado | del rey don Alfonso, que fue en la
era de mill e çiento e treynta años, quando andava el año de la
encarnaçion en mill e noventa e dos, e el del inperio de Enrrique en
quarenta e quatro. Quando Yuçef, el rey de Marruecos, sopo que el Çid
avie presa Valençia, pesole mucho; e alço rey a Mahomad, que era fijo
de su hermana, e dexolo en la tierra que la guardasse. E el allego muy
grand hueste de almoravides e de alaraves e de andaluzes, e fueron por
cuenta çient mill omnes de armas. E paso la mar, e fue çercar Valençia.
E vinieron[50] y en su ayuda el rey Bucar e el rey Soro de Lerida. E
fincaron[51] todos sus tiendas en Quarte, que es a quatro migeros de
Valençia. E trayenles todos los moros de España grandes conduchos, e
todo lo al que les fazie menester. E fueron alli por todos çiento e
çinquenta mill, entre cavalleros e omnes a pie, todos bien guisados. El
Çid quando los vio, plogole mucho con ellos, e dixo, 'Graçias a Dios e a
Santa Maria su madre, todas las cosas que yo mas amava aqui las tengo
comigo. E pues que atan grand riqueza me viene de allen mar e de todas
partes, faznos menester que nos armemos todos e salgamos a lidiar con
154a   ellos. E vera mi muger, doña Xi-| mena,[52] e mis fijas como se gana el
pan en la tierra agena'. Luego que esto dixo, fizolas sobir en la torre mas
alta, onde pudiessen veer la batalla. Doña Ximena, quando vio las
tiendas de los moros muchas ademas, fue toda espantada, e dixo al Çid,
'Señor, ¿que tiendas son aquellas?'. El Çid le dixo, 'Aquello que vos
veedes es riqueza que nos viene de allen mar. E porque ha poco que
llegastes aqui, quieren vos lo presentar para casamiento de vuestras
fijas. E vos estad aqui pagada, e non ayades miedo ninguno. E yo yre e
lidiare[53] con ellos; ca fio en Dios que los vençere, e ganare dellos quanto
traen'. Otro dia, armaronsse los moros, e fueron conbatir la çibdad, e
destruxeron las huertas. El Çid, quando vio que le farien mal, sallio a
ellos, e ovo su batalla con ellos, en aquel lugar que dizen el Quarte, e

vençiolos. E morieron y siete reyes, e todos los otros fueron los unos presos e los otros muertos. E el rey Yuçef fuxo del canpo con tres lançadas, e acogiosse al castillo que dizen Çuhera,[54] e fue el Çid en pos el en alcançe bien fasta alli. En aquel alcançe murio Pero Salvadorez. El Çid tornosse estonçes, e cogieron sus conpañas el canpo; e ffallaron y muy grand aver en oro e en plata, e en otras cosas muchas, e las mas ricas tiendas que omne nunca vio. Despues | que todo lo ovieron cogido, tornaronsse para Valençia ricos e honrrados.

154b

Capitulo LXXI° de como el Çid enbio al rey don Alfonso dozientos cavallos e una tienda.

El Çid, seyendo muy alegre de quanto bien le fazie Dios, dixo a Alvar Fanez que querie enbiar al rey don Alfonso dozientos cavallos, de aquellos que le cayeran a el en la su parte, e la tienda que fuera del rey Yuçef. Alvar Fanez loogelo, e tovolo por bien. El Çid le dixo, 'Pues, quiero que los levedes vos e Pero Vermudez, e que me encomendedes en la graçia del rey'. E ellos dixeron que les plazie. E cavalgaron luego otro dia, e fueronsse. E fallaron al rey don Alfonso en Valladolid. El rey don[55] Alfonso, quando sopo que venien, sallio los resçebir con toda su cavalleria. E fueron y con el los infantes de Carrion e el conde don Garçia, que era enemigo del Çid. Alvar Fanez e Pero Vermudez besaron estonçes la mano al rey, e dixeronle, 'Señor, el Çid se vos enbia encomendar, e enbiavos dezir que poco ha que vençio una batalla[56] con el rey de Marruecos, e fueron los mo-| ros por todos çiento e çinquenta vezes mill. E gano y muy grandes riquezas, assi que todos sus vasallos son ricos e salidos de lazeria. E de lo que a el cayo en la su parte, enbiavos estos dozientos cavallos, con sillas e con frenos e con sus espadas a los arzones, e esta tienda que fue de Yuçef, rei de Marruecos'. El rey don Alfonso dixo estonçes a Alvar Fanez e a Pero Vermudez, 'Gradesco yo mucho al Çid los cavallos e la tienda que me el enbia, e a vos que me lo traedes'. El rey fizoles, estonçes, mucha de honrra, e dioles de sus dones muchos. El conde don Garçia, con grand pesar que ovo desto, apartosse con sus parientes, e dixoles, 'Grand cosa es esta de tanta honrra cresçer[57] al Çid, e de vençer assi reyes en canpo. E pues que a el[58] tanto bien viene, nos aviltados somos, e venirnos ha del algun[59] mal'. Demientre que Alvar Fanez e Pero Vermudez eran con el rey don Alfonso, desfizo el Çid todas las mezquitas que avie en Valençia, e fizo dellas yglesias a honrra de Dios e de Santa Maria. Mas agora vos dexaremos aqui de fabler desto, e dezirvos emos de los infantes de Carrion.

154c

Capitulo LXXII° de como el rey don Alfon*so* caso los infantes de
154d Carrion con las ffijas | del Çid

Los infantes de Carrio*n*, qua*n*do viero*n* que tanto bien fazie Dios al
Çid, ovieron su acuerdo de demandarle las fijas para casamie*n*to, e
dixeron!o al rey don Alfonso, que gelas demandase. El rey les dixo, 'Yo
eche[60] al Çid de la tierra, e fizele mucho mal, faziendome el mucho
serviçio. E agora, non ssey ssi se pagara de tal pleytesia como esta. Mas,
pues q*ue* vos sabor avedes del casamie*n*to, digamoslo a Alvar Fanez e a
Pero Vermudez'. El rey llamo estonçes a Alvar Fan*e*z e a Pero Vermudez, e dixoles como los infantes de Carrion avien sabor de casar con
fijas del Çid. 'E pues[61] que assi es, te*n*go por bien que sse venga veer el
Çid comigo'. Alvar Fan*e*z le dixo, 'Señor, nos diremos esto al Çid; e el
faga y despues lo que toviere por bien'. Estonçes sse despidieron del rey
e fueronsse para Valençia. El Çid resçibiolos muy bien, e preguntoles
por nuevas d*e*l rey. Alvar Fanez le dixo, 'Çid, sepades q*ue* el rey resçibio
de grado lo que[62] le enbiastes, e gradesçiovoslo mucho. E enbiavos
155a dezir que le pidieron | los infantes de Carrion v*uest*ras fijas para
casamiento, e vos q*ue* vos vayades veer con el a Toledo sobre esto. E
quiere poner luego convusco[63] su amor, e acordaredes de so uno lo que
mejor tovieredes'. El Çid le dixo q*ue* le plazie muy de coraçon. Desi,
preguntoles que le consejava*n* en tal fecho como aq*ue*l. Ellos dixeron
que non le consejarien ninguna cosa, sy non q*ue* fiziesse lo que por bien
toviesse. El Çid les dixo, 'Los infantes de Carrion son om*ne*s muy
fidalgos e muy loçanos, e han muchos parientes. E por ende, me non[64]
plazera deste casamiento. Mas, pues que el rey quiere, vayamos a el, e
demosle honrra, como a rey e a señor; ca eso quiero yo, lo que el toviere
por bien'. Esto dicho, enbio sus cartas al rey don Alfonso por dos
cavalleros. El rey, despues que las cartas ovo leydas, dixo a los cavalleros q*ue* se tornassen al Çid, e que le dixiessen que fuesse a Toledo a
cabo de tres semanas. Qua*n*do los cavalleros fueron en Valençia e
dixeron al Çid lo que el rey les dixera, plogo mucho al Çid; e guiso muy
bien a si e a toda su conpaña, e, quando fue tienpo de se yr, allego muy
grand gente, e fuese para Toledo. El rey saliole resçebir estonçes, e
155b fizole mucha honrra. El Çid desçendio de | la bestia, e finco los ynojos en
tierra por le besar los pies. El rei le dixo, 'Levantadvos,[65] Çid, ca no*n*
qui*e*ro que me besedes los pies mas las manos, e, ssy lo assy no*n* fazedes,
non avredes mi amor'. El Çid le dixo, 'Señor, pidovos por merçed que
me otorguedes vuestro amor, en guisa que lo ayan[66] todos quantos aqui
estan'. El rey le dixo que le plazie, e perdonolo a*n*te todos e otorgole su
amor. El Çid besole estonçes la mano. A muchos de los que alli estavan
plogo mucho. Mas peso a Alvar Diaz e al conde don Garçia Hordoñez.[67]

Aquel dia, fue el Çid huesped del rey don Alfonso. Los infantes de Carrion fueron estonçes al Çid, e dixieronle como andavan ellos en la su pro e en la su honrra quanto mas podien. El Çid les dixo, 'Assy lo mande Dios'. Otro dia mañana, entraron el rey e el Çid en su fabla. E dixole el rey, 'Don Rodrigo, los infantes de Carrion me pidieron vuestras fijas para casamiento, e tengo que seran bien casadas[68] e que gelas dedes, sy vos ploguier'. El Çid le dixo, 'Señor, vos criastes mis fijas, e ellas e yo somos a la vuestra merçed. E vos fazed como por bien tovieredes, ca yo pagado so de quanto vos y fizieredes'. El rey gradesçiogelo. Los infantes de Carrion besaron[69] estonçes las manos al Çid, e camiaron con el las

155c   espadas. | El rey mando estonçes al Çid, para bodas de sus fijas, trezientos marcos de plata en ayuda. Otrossi el Çid, con el plazer que ende ovo, dio alli mucho de su aver e de otros dones muchos. El rey tomo estonçes a los infantes, e metiolos en poder del Çid, diziendole assy, 'Çid, ahe aqui vuestros fijos, ca tanto es, pues que vuestros yernos son. E de aqui adelante, fazed dellos como tovieredes por bien. E mando que vos sirvan como a padre e vos aguarden como a señor'. El Çid le dixo, 'Sseñor, muchas graçias por lo que me fazedes, e Dios vos de por ende buen gualardon. Mas, Señor, ruegovos que, pues que mis fijas son casadas, asi como vos tovistes por bien, que las dedes vos con vuestra mano a quien vos tovieredes por bien, que las entregue a los infantes de Carrion; ca yo non gelas dare en otra guisa'. El rey dixo, 'Ahe aqui Alvar Fanez, a que mando que las tome e las de a los infantes'. Alvar Fanez dixo que lo farie. El Çid dixo estonçes al rey don Alfonso, 'Señor, traygovos aqui treynta cavallos e treynta palafrenes muy[70] buenos e bien guisados de frenos e de sillas. Ruegovos que los mandedes resçebir'. El rey le dixo, 'Çid, mucho sserviçio me avedes ya fecho; mas, pues que vos assy queredes, resçebirlos he de vos'. El Çid dixo estonçes,

155d   'Amigos, todos los que quisieredes yr a las bodas, e prender | algo de mi, de aqui vos yd luego comigo'. Despidiose estonçes el Çid del rey, e fuesse para Valençia. E fueron con el muy grandes cavallerias de las del rey, para fazerle honrra en bodas de sus fijas.

Capitulo LXXIII° de las bodas que fizieron los infantes de Carrion con las fijas del Çid.[71]

Despues que el Çid llego a Valençia, e mando dar posadas a los infantes de Carrion, e ovo contado todo su fecho a su muger doña Ximena e a sus fijas, enbio por los infantes e por Alvar Fanez, e dixoles, 'Pues que de casar he mis fijas convusco, non lo quiero detardar. E por ende, digo a Alvar Fanez que las resçiba, assi como mando el rey don Alfonso, e que vos las entregue, assi como es ya dicho e puesto'. Alvar

Fane*z* resçibio estonçes las donzellas[72] de mano del Çid, e dixo a los
infa*n*tes de Carrion, 'Infantes, dovos[73] yo estas donzellas por mugeres,
e que las resçibades vos a bendiçion, assy como manda santa[74] iglesia, e
les fagades honrra e todos los conplimie*n*tos que buenos maridos fazen a
156a dueñas[75] fijasdalgo'. | Los infantes resçibieron estonçes las dueñas,[75] e
fueron con ellas para la iglesia. El obispo don Geronimo canto la misa, e
dioles las bendiçio*n*es. E duraron las bodas quinze dias, faziendo cada
dia muchas alegrias. E dio el Çid muy grand aver con ellas, e cavallos e
paños de preçio muchos[76] ademas. E fincaron los infantes con el Çid en
Valençia dos años, mucho en paz[77] e alegres e pagados. Mas agora
dexaremos aqui de fablar desto, e dezirvos hemos del rey don Alfonso.

III. THE THIRD 'CANTAR'

Between its versions of the second and third 'cantares', the *CVR* has one
chapter which tells of conquests by Alfonso VI in Portugal (repeating in
different words much of Chapter XXXVII above), and, briefly, of events in
Aragón. Only its heading is given here. Variants continue to be given from J
and Ll. The folios of these manuscripts containing the third 'cantar' are as
follows: J, 98r–102r; Ll 233r–43r.

156a Capitulo LXXIIII° de las conqu*i*stas q*ue* fizo el rey don Alfonso.

156b Capitulo LXXV° de como los infantes de Carrion se ascondieron con
miedo del leon.

156c   Anda-| dos treynta e tres años del regnado del rey don Alfonso que
fue en la era de mill e çiento e treynta e tres años, qua*n*do andava el año
de la encarnaçion en mill e noventa e çinco, e el del inperio de Enrriq*ue*
en quarenta e ssiete. El Çid estando en Valençia de so uno con sus yernos,
avino asi un dia que sse solto un leon, q*ue* tenie preso en una red. E el
Çid durmie estonçes. Los infantes, quando lo vieron, ovieron grand
miedo. E el uno dellos, a quien dizien Ferrand[1] Gonçalez, fuesse meter
tras u*n* escaño[2] mucho espantado. E su hermano, Diego Gonçalez, salio
fuera por la puerta, da*n*do bozes que nunca verie Carrion, e ascondiosse
con *e*l gra*n*t miedo so una viga de lagar.[3] E tan feo[4] se paro y que,
quando dende salio, non eran de veer los paños que vistie. Los cavalleros del Çid, quando esto vieron, punaron de guardar su sseñor. El Çid,
quando desperto e se vio çercado de los cavalleros, preguntoles por que
lo fizieran. Ellos le dixeron, 'Señor, soltosse el leon, e metionos a todos
en gra*n* rebato'.[5] El Çid fue estonçes al leon, e prisolo e metiolo en la

red. El Çid asentosse estonçes en un escaño, e demando por sus yernos.
156d Enpero,[6] | aunque ellos veyen que los buscavan e los llamavan, tan
grande era el miedo que avien que non osavan responder. E assi avian la
color perdida como ssy fuessen enfermos. E quando los fallaron e
sopieron que por el miedo del leon sse ascondieran assi, començaron a
profaçar[7] dellos e a fazer escarnio. Mas defendiolo el Çid. Los infantes
teniensse por muy maltrechos e muy envergonçados desto que les
acaesçiera.

Capitulo LXXVI° de como el Çid lidio con el rey Bucar e lo vençio.

En este año sobre dicho, que vos agora dixiemos, paso de allen mar el
rey Bucar con muy grand hueste. E fue çercar Valençia, e poso en un
lugar que dizen Quarte.[8] El Çid, quando los vio, plogole mucho con
ellos. Mas a los infantes de Carrion pesoles mucho, e dixeron, 'Nos
catavamos a la ganançia que averiemos con las[9] fijas del Çid, mas non a
la perdida que nos ende vernie. Ca non podremos estar que non
vayamos con el Çid a lidiar con estos moros'. Esto que ellos dizien,
157a oyolo Muño[10] Gustioz, | e dixolo al Çid. El Çid, quando lo oyo,
sonrriosse un poco, e dixo a los infantes, 'Esforçad, infantes de Carrion,
e non temades nada; e estad en Valençia a vuestro sabor'. Ellos en esto
fablando, enbio el rey Bucar dezir al Çid que le dexasse Valençia e se
fuesse en paz; ssy non, que le pecharie quanto y avie fecho. El Çid dixo a
aquel que troxiera el mensaje, 'Yd dezir a Bucar, a aquel fi de henemiga,[11] que ante destos tres dias le dare yo lo que el demanda'. Otro dia,
mando el Çid armar todos los suyos, e sallio a los moros. Los infantes de
Carrion pidieronle estonçes la delantera. E despues que el Çid ovo
paradas sus azes, don Ferrando,[12] el uno de los infantes, adelantosse
por ynferir[13] a un moro, a que dizian Aladraf. El moro, quando lo vio,
fue contra el otrossi. E el infante, con el grand miedo que ovo del, bolvio
la rienda e fuxo, que solamente non lo oso esperar. Pero Vermudez, que
yva açerca del, quando aquello vio, fue ferir en el moro, e lidio con el e
matolo. Desi, tomo el cavallo del moro, e fue en pos el infante, que yva
fuyendo, e dixole, 'Don Ferrando, tomad este cavallo, e dezid a todos
que vos matastes al moro cuyo era, e yo otorgarlo he convusco'. El
157b infante le dixo, 'Don Pero Vermudez, | mucho vos gradesco lo que
dezides'. El obispo veno estonçes al Çid, e dixole, 'Don Rodrigo,
porque yo oy dezir que ssienpre guerreavades con moros, por eso me
vine yo de mi tierra para vos, cobdiçiando lidiar con ellos. E por ende,
por honrrar mis manos e mis hordenes, pidovos por merçed que me
dedes la delantera desta batalla; ssy non, bien vos digo que luego me
quite de vos'. El Çid le dixo, 'Obispo, mucho me plaz de lo que

demandades, e otorgovoslo'. El obispo fue luego ferir en los moros, e mato y dos moros[14] de su entrada. Los moros, como eran muchos, çercaronle todos en derredor, mas acorriole luego el Çid. Alli[15] se bolvio la batalla, e fue muy fuerte e muy ferida ademas. Mas enpero, vençio el Çid, e saco los moros del canpo, e levolos fasta las tiendas mal de su grado. E tanto los cuyto, que los saco de las tiendas e fizoles fuyr. E fue en pos ellos en alcançe bien ocho migeros, e mato tantos dellos que non avien cuenta. El, matando en ellos, ovo de veer al rey Bucar, e diole bozes, e dixole, 'Atiende, Bucar, e veerte as con el Çid de la barva luenga. E pornemos entre nos amistad'. Bucar le dixo, | 'Guardeme Dios de te[16] tu veer ya mas comigo. E ssi el cavallo non entropeçar que me derribe, bien creo que me non alcançes fasta la mar'. En todo esto, yvasse quanto mas podie a poder[17] del cavallo. E el Çid yva en pos el con Bavieca, su cavallo. E alcançolo a entrante de la mar, e diole una ferida con la espada que le corto todo, e cayo en tierra muerto. Despues[18] que Bucar fue muerto e la batalla vençida, tornosse el Çid con todos los suyos para las tiendas, e mando[19] coger el canpo. Desi, fuesse para Valençia, e partio la ganançia con todos muy bien. Desi, puso la mano en la barva, e dixo, 'Ssenor Ihesu Christo, a ti do loor e graçias[20] por quanto bien me as fecho; ca me dexaste veer todas las cosas que yo cobdiçiava, e so temido de moros como de christianos. Loado sea el tu nombre e honrrado e servido de todos assy'. Los infantes de Carrion le dixeron, 'Don Rodrigo, vos nos avedes fecho mucho bien e mucha honrra, e somos ya por vos ricos e abondados de quanto avemos menester. E demostrastesnos ya bien a lidiar'. Desto[21] que ellos dixieron, fazien muy grand escarnio los del Çid, e profacavan[22] dellos. E duro aquel escarnio unos dias, fasta que lo entendieron ellos.

157d Capi-| tulo LXXVII° de como los infantes de Carrion açotaron las fijas del Çid e las dexaron por muertas en el monte de Corpes.[23]

Los infantes de Carrion, quando entendieron que dellos profacavan e fazien escarnio, ovieron ende muy grand pesar. E ovieron su conssejo de sse yr para Carrion, e levar sus mugeres conssigo, e fazerles toda aquella desonrra que quisiessen, en el camino. Ca dizien que tales como ellas non eran para sseer sus mugeres, sy non fijas de reyes e de enperadores. 'E demas, faz menester', dixieron ellos, 'que nos vayamos, ante que nos retrayan lo que nos acaesçio del leon'. Despues desto, fueron al Çid e dixeronle como sse querien yr para Carrion e levar consigo sus mugeres, e demostrarles todas las riquezas que y avien. El Çid les dixo que le plazie de coraçon, e que les darie de su aver e dos espadas muy preçiadas; a la una dizien Colada[24] e a la otra Tizon. E ellos

148

que honrassen a sus fijas, assi como a dueñas fijasdalgo. E ellos
158a otorgaron que assi lo farien. Otro dia, cavalgaron por se yr, e | el Çid
sallio con ellos con toda su cavalleria[25] por los honrrar. E yendo aun por
entre las huertas, cato el Çid por aguero, e vio[26] que non avien mucho de
durar aquellos casamientos. Mas enpero, non pudo y al fazer. E llamo
estonçes a Feliz Muñoz, e dixole que fuesse con sus fijas fasta Carrion, e
verie la honrra que les fazien los infantes. Ffeliz Muñoz le dixo que le
plazie de coraçon. Estonçes, se despidieron los unos de los otros. Los
infantes fueron por Santa Maria de Alvarrezin[27] e por Medina, e
resçibiolos muy bien Abengabon que era ende señor, e fue con ellos
fasta Xalon. E posaron[28] en un lugar que dizen el Alxaria. Abengabon
dio alli a los infantes mucho de su aver, e cavallos e otras donas muchas.
Los infantes, quando vieron las grandes riquezas de aquel moro,
ovieron su acuerdo[29] de lo matar. Lo que ellos dizien, estando en aquel
conssejo, oyolo un moro que era latinado, e dixolo a Abengabon.
Abengabon, quando lo oyo, cavalgo con dozientos cavalleros que
traxiera consigo, e dixo a los infantes, 'Amigos, ¿que vos fiz yo, por que
vos mi muerte conssejades?'. Estonçes, sse despidio de doña Elvira e de
doña Sol, e paso Xalon[30] e fuesse para Molina, denostando a los
158b infantes, e diziendo dellos que eran falsos e ma-| los. Los infantes
sallieron otrossi de alli, e dexaron a Atiença a su ssiniestro e a Sand
Estevan a su diestro. E entraron en el robredo de Corpes,[31] que era
mucho grande e mucho espeso e lleno de muchas bestias bravas, e
albergaron y. Otro dia mañana, mandaron yr adelante toda su conpaña,
e ellos fincaron alli, solos con sus mugeres. Desi, desnudaronlas e
açotaronlas muy mal.[32] E tanto las firieron fasta que las dexaron por
muertas. Estonçes, cavalgaron, e fueronsse en pos su conpaña, e
dexaron alli a las dueñas desanparadas.

Capitulo LXXVIII° de como el Çid enbio por sus fijas a Sand Estevan.

Avino assy que, demientre que los infantes firien a las fijas del Çid,
que començo a doler muy fuertemente el coraçon a Feliz Muñoz, que
yva con[33] la conpaña a adelante. E tanto le aquexo aquel dolor, que sse
aparto de los otros e metiosse en el monte, que era mucho espeso, por
atender alli a las fijas del Çid, que eran sus primas. E el estando alli, oyo
lo que vinien diziendo los infantes; ca yvansse alabando de la desonrra
158c que fizieron a las fijas del Çid. Fe-| liz Muñoz, quando aquello oyo, ovo
muy grand pesar, e entendio que por aquel grand mal le dolie el
coraçon. E tornosse por el rastro fasta la posada onde salieran, e fallo las
dueñas como por muertas. El allegose estonçes a ellas e llamolas; e dixo,
'Por Dios, muy mal fecho ensayaron los infantes de Carrion. E mande

Dios que sse fallen ende mal'. Estonçes, les dixo que se esforçassen, e yrsse yen de alli, 'Ca mucho ayna tornaran aca los infantes, quando me fallaren menos, e matarnos yen'. Ellas dixeron que esforçadas estavan, pues que a el veyen. Estonçes, las cavalgo en su cavallo, e fuesse con ellas. E andudieron todo el dia e toda la noche. Otro dia, llegaron a una torre, que era de doña Urraca, que estava sobre Duero, e estudieron alli, demientre que el fue a Sant Estevan. E quando y llego, fallo[34] y a Diego Tellez, vasallo que fue de Alvar Fanez, e contole todo lo que le aviniera[35] a las fijas del Çid. El, quando lo oyo, pesole mucho de coraçon, e tomo luego paños e bestias, a fuesse para ellas. E vistiolas muy bien, e sacolas de la torre, e traxolas a Sand Estevan. Los de Sand Estevan sallieron las resçebir, e fizieronles mucha honrra, e dieronles quanto ovieron menester. Estas nuevas fueron sabidas por toda la
158d tierra. El rey don Alfonso, quando lo | oyo, pesole mucho de coraçon. E non tardo mucho que lo ovo otrossy de saber el Çid. E con el grand pesar que ende ovo, tornose a la barva, e dixo,[36] 'Para esta mi barva, que nunca meso ninguno, non me escaparan assi los infantes que los non desonrre yo mucho peor[37] desto'. Estonçes, mando a Alvar Fanez e a Martin[38] Antolinez e a Pero Vermudez, que le fuessen por las fijas. E dioles dozientos cavalleros que fuesen con ellos. Quando llegaron a Sant Estevan, dixo Alvar Fanez a los del logar, 'Amigos, mucho vos gradesçe el Çid, e nos[39] con el, la honrra que vos fezistes a sus fijas'. Estonçes, sse fueron para el palaçio, ho las dueñas estavan. Las dueñas, quando los[40] vieron, fueron muy alegres ademas, e dixeron que eran sanas e guaridas, pues que a ellos veyen. Otro dia, sallieron de alli con las fijas del Çid, e fueronse para Valençia. El Çid, quando sopo que vinien,[41] saliolas resçebir, e fue muy alegre con ellas. E dixo, 'Ruego a Dios que me de buen derecho de los infantes de Carrion'.

Capitulo LXXIX de como el Çid se enbio querellar al rey don Alfonso por la desonrra que le fizieran los infantes de Carrion.

159a   Despues | desto, enbio querellar el Çid al rey don Alfonso de la desonrra que le fizieran los infantes de Carrion. E enbio a el a Muño Gustioz,[42] que le demostrasse el fecho en como fuera e que le dixiesse que el casara sus fijas con ellos, ca el non; e, ssy honrra o desonrra y avie, que mas era suya que non del; e que le rogava que gelos fiziesse venir a vistas o a su corte, por que pudiesse aver derecho dellos. Muño Gustioz[43] fue estonçes para Castilla, e fallo el rey en Sand Fagun. El rey, quando lo vio entrar por el palaçio, fuelo resçebir. Muño Gustioz, luego que le ovo besada la mano, dixole, 'Señor, el Çit vos manda besar los pies e las manos, como a su señor natural. E pidevos por merçed que vos pese del mal e de la deso*n*rra que le fizieron los infantes de Carrion, e que gelos fagades venir a vistas o a corte'. El rey dixo, 'Muño Gustioz, mucho me pesa de lo que y es fecho. Mas, pues que assy es, yo fare mis cortes en Toledo, e vos tornadvos para el Çid e dezilde q*ue* sea y, de oy a ssiete semanas'. Muño Gustioz despidiosse estonçes del rey, e fuesse para Valençia. El rey mando luego *p*regonar las cortes por todo su regno, e enbio dezir a los infantes de Carrion que viniessen a ellas. Los

159b infantes, temiendosse que vernie el Çid a las | cortes, enbiaron rogar al rey que los escusasse de non venir y. El rey mandoles dezir q*ue* lo non farie, ca el Çid avie querella dellos, e que querie que gela emendassen. Quando llego el plazo de las siete semanas, fuesse el rey para Toledo, e fueron y con el muchos altos omnes. E fueron estos: el conde don Enrriq*ue*, e el conde don Remondo,[44] e el conde don Fruela, e el conde don Beltran,[45] e el conde don Garçia Ordoñez, e don Alvar Diaz, los infantes de Carrion, Ansuer[46] Gonçal*e*z, Gonçalo Ançurez, don Pero[47] Ançurez, e otros muchos altos om*n*es.

Capitulo LXXX de como el Çid veno a cortes que el rey don Alfon*s*o fazie en Toledo.

El Çid, quando sopo por Muño Gustioz que el rey don Alfonso le enbiava dezir que fuesse con el en Toledo a sus cortes, guiso muy bien a ssi e a toda su conpaña, e fuesse para el. El rey, quando sopo que venie, fuelo resçebir con grand cavalleria. El Çid descavalgo estonçes de la bestia, e fue de pie contra el, por honrrar su señor. El rey le dixo,

159c 'Cavalgad, Çid, si me q*ue*redes fazer plazer; ca bie*n* | sse que mas honrrada[48] sera agora mi corte por vos, que antes era'. El rey tornosse estonçes para Toledo. E el Çid albergo esa noche en Sand Sservan, e tovo y vigilia. Otro dia, despues que oyeron misa, ma*n*do el Çid armar a todos los suyos, e vestir de suso[49] las armas sus vestiduras, e que levassen sus espadas so los mantos. Desi, cavalgaron estonçes, e fuer-onsse para la corte. El rey don Alfonso resçibiolo muy bie*n* co*n* todos los altos om*n*es que con el estavan. El rey tomo estonçes al Çid por la mano, e quisole assentar conssigo en el escaño, diziendole assi, 'Çid, e*n* este escaño que me vos distes, quiero q*ue* vos assentedes comigo'. El Çid le dixo, 'Señor, muchas graçias, mas aca posare con *e*stos que vienen comigo'. El rey don Alfonso levantose estonçes e dixo, 'Yo desde q*ue* fuy rey, nunca fiz mas de dos cortes, la una en Burgos, la otra en Carrion; e esta es la terçera que agora fago aqui en Toledo, por amor del Çid, que le fagan derecho los infantes de Carrion de la querella que dellos ha. E quiero que sean alcaldes desto el conde don Enrriq*ue* e el conde don Remo*n*t.[50] E agora demande el Çid lo q*ue* quiere, e respon-

danle los infant*e*s'. El Çid levantosse estonçes, e dixo, 'Señor, mucho
159d vos gra-| desco, porque[51] vos esta corte fezistes por mi amor. E digo a
los infantes de Carrion que, pues q*ue* assi me desenpararon las fijas en el
robredo de Corpes,[52] q*ue* me de*n* dos espadas q*ue* les di, Colada e
Tizona, con que vos fiziessen serviçio'. El conde do*n* Garçia, que era
enemigo del Çid, dixo que sse fablarien sobre aquello, e ovieron su
acuerdo de dar al Çid sus espadas; ca tenien que les fazie gra*n*t amor
pues que otra desonrra non les demandava. Estonçes vinieron al rey, e
entregaronle las espadas. E el rey diolas al Çid. El Çid beso luego la
mano al rey, e puso la mano en su barva, e dixo, 'Por aq*ue*sta mi barva,
que nunca meso ninguno, aun sse vengaran doña Elvira e doña Sol'. El
Çid dio estonçes a su sobrino, Pero Vermudez, la espada Tizona, e a
Martin Antolinez la espada Colada.

Capitulo LXXXI° de como reptaron los del Çid a los infantes de
Carrion.

Desp*ue*s desto, dixo el Çid a el rey, 'Señor, pues que yo[53] so
entregado de las espadas, q*ue*rria q*ue* me salliesen los infantes de otra
160a querella que he aun de-| llos. Quando sse ovieron de venir de Valençia,
diles en oro e en plata tres mill marcos, e agora querria que me los
diessen'. Los infantes, quando esto oyeron, pesoles mucho. Pero
ovieron su conssejo, e acordaro*n* de entregar al Çid en heredades en
tierra de Carrion, ca non podrien en otra guisa pagar aquel aver. El rey
don Alfo*n*so dixo estonçes a los infantes, 'Derecho demanda el Çid; ca
destos tres mill marcos los dozientos tengo yo, que me distes vos, e yo
darlos he al Çid, e vos entregalde de todo lo al'. Ferrand Gonçalez dixo,
'Aver monedado non tenemos nos onde le entreguemos'. El conde don
Remondo dixo, 'El oro e la plata despendisteslo vos. E pues que assi es,
pagalde en apreçiadura, e el resçibalo'. Estonçes, le dieron en preçio
muchos cavallos e muchas mulas. Despues q*ue* el Çid fue entregado de
todo, dixo, 'Los infantes de Carrion me desonrraron mal, e quierolos
reptar por ende'. Estonçes le[54] dixo, 'Infantes, ¿que vos meresçi yo por
que vos assi me desonrrastes mis fijas, e las açotastes e desenparastes en
el robredo de Corpes? Ca mucho valedes menos por lo que y feziestes'.
El conde don Garçia dixo, 'Señor rey don Alfonso, en lo q*ue* fizieron los
160b infantes a las | fijas del Çid non erraron y nada; ca non las devien[55]
querer solamente para seer sus barraganas. E el Çid es avezado de venir
a cortes pregonadas, e por eso trae la barva luenga. E por quanto el diz,
non damos[56] por ello nada'. El Çid, quando esto oyo, levantosse en pie,
e puso la mano en su barva, e dixo, 'Conde, graçias a Dios porq*ue* la mi
barva es luenga; ca fue sienpre criada en viçio e a sabor de ssy. E pues,

¿que avedes vos en me retraer della? Ca nunca della me priso om*n*e del mundo ni*n* me la meso, como yo la messe a vos, conde, en el castillo de Cabra; e vos saq*ue* della mas q*ue* una polgada grande. E bien cuydo que la non tenedes aun bien cunplida, que yo la trayo[57] aqui en mi bolsa'. Fferrant Gonçalez dixo estonçes, 'Çid, vos sodes bien pagado de quanto vos aviemos a dar, e non q*ue*remos aver convusco otra entençion. Vos sabedes que nos somos de los condes de Carrion; e non nos convenie de estar casados[58] con vuestras fijas, sy non ssi fuesen fijas de reyes o de enperador*e*s. E por vos las dexar, feziemos en ello derecho'. El Çid cato estonçes contra Pero Vermudez, e dixole, 'Fabla, Pero mudo. ¿Como te

160c callas? ¿Non sabes que tus p*r*imas corma-| nas son mis fijas? E comoquier que ellos a mi digan esto, a ti dan las orejadas'. Pero Vermudez le dixo, 'Çid, nu*n*ca tal costunbre vi qual vos avedes. Nunca me llamades en las cortes ssy non Pero mudo'. Estonçe, sse torno contra Fferrand Gonçalez e dixole, 'Mentiste en quanto dexiste. Ca sie*n*pre valiste tu mas por el Çid. E todas las tus mañas yo te las dire agora.[59] Sabes que venie un moro por lidiar contigo, e con el grand miedo que oviste, fuxiste ante[60] el. E ovierate muerto ssy non por mi, que lidie con el e matelo, e tome el cavallo del e ditelo; e alabastete tu a*n*te el Çid que tu mataras al moro cuyo era. Tu eres fermoso, mas mal barragan. Pues, ¿como osas fablar, lengua ssyn manos? Otrossy, ¿no*n* te acuerdas de lo que te contesçio en Valençia, quando se solto el leon? Que te metiste tras[61] el escaño con grand miedo que oviste del. Por quanto alli feziste, vales oy menos. E por ende, por lo que feziste a las fijas del Çid, rieptote por malo e traydor, e lidiartelo he aqui delante el rey don Alfon*s*o, nuestro señor'. Despues desto, dixo Diego Gonçalez, 'Nos somos de natura de co*n*des, e non nos pertenesçie de estar casados con fijas del

160d Çid. E por-| que las assy desanparamos, tenemos que fiziemos y gra*n* derecho, e que nos honrramos en ello. E ssi alguno quisier dezir por ende alguna cosa, yo gelo lidiare en canpo'. Martin Antolinez le dixo estonçes, 'Calla, alevoso, boca ssin verdad. ¿Non te acuerdas de lo q*ue* te co*n*tesçio quando viste el leon suelto? Que te saliste del corral[62] e fustete meter con miedo del tras la viga del lagar, ho pareste[63] tales los paños que nu*n*ca despues vestiste. E por lo q*ue* feziste a las fijas del Çid, vales oy menos, e lidiartelo he, e fazerte dezir por tu boca q*ue* eres traydor'. E Martin[64] Antoline*z* acabando de dezir esto, levantose Ansur[65] Gonçalez, e dixo pocas palabras e ssyn recabdo, en *e*sta guisa, 'Varones, ¿quien vio nu*n*ca tan grand mal como este, que avemos nos de veer con Ruy Diaz Çid? Librarie[66] el mejor de yr picar los molinos a rio d'Ovierna, e tomar sus maquilas, como solie fazer, que non de conten-der[67] conusco. Ca no*n* conviene a los de nuestro linaje de estar casados con sus fijas'. Muño Gustioz sse levanto estonçes e dixo, 'Calla, alevoso traydor. Que antes almuerzas que vayas oraçion fazer,[68] e nunca dizes verdad a sseñor nin a amigo que ayas. Ca eres falso a Dios e a todos los omnes. E esto te fare yo dezir por tu boca, que assy | es como yo digo'. El rey don Alfonso dixo estonçes que tenie por bien que lidiasen aquellos que avien reptado.

161a

Capitulo LXXXIIº de como enbiaron pedir por mugeres a las fijas del Çid los infantes el de Navarra e el de Aragon, e repto Alvar Fanez a los infantes.

Ellos en esto fablando, entraron por el palaçio dos cavalleros que eran mandaderos el uno del infante de Navarra[69] e el otro del infante de Aragon. E avien nonbre estos mandaderos el uno Ojarra[70] e el otro Yñigo Ximenez. E luego que entraron, besaron las manos al rey don Alfonso, e pidieronle las fijas del Çid para casamiento de sus señores. El Çid, quando lo oyo, levantosse e dixo, 'Señor rey don Alfonso, mis fijas son en vuestro poder, e vos las casastes la primera vez. E por ende, ssy las vos quisieredes dar a estos infantes que las enbian pedir, a mi mucho me plaz'. El rey dixo que tenie aquel casamiento por bueno, e que le plazie, e assi fiziesse a el. E el Çid otorgolo. El rey dixo estonçes a los cavalleros que vinieran con el mensaje, 'Cavalleros, yo vos otorgo este
161b casamiento que me venistes demandar para vuestros | señores, a pleyto que las tomen a bendiçiones,[71] assi como es derecho'. Los cavalleros besaron estonçes las manos al rey e al Çid, e fizieron pleyto e omenaje que todo cunplimiento que menester faz para bodas, que todo lo cunpliessen los infantes sus señores. Deste casamiento peso mucho a los infantes de Carrion. Alvar Fanez sse levanto estonçes, e dixo, 'Sseñor rey don Alfonso, yo he muy grand querella de los infantes de Carrion por la desonrra que fizieron a las fijas del Çid; lo uno, porque gelas di yo por vuestro mandado, lo al, porque las desanpararon en el robredo de Corpes, e las firieron malamente. E por esto que les fizieron, rieptolos yo, e digo que son traydores e malos. E[72] ssy ay alguno que responda a esto e diga que non es assi, yo gelo fare desdezir, e que otorgue que tales son[73] como yo digo'. Gomez[74] Pelaez le dixo, 'Alvar Fanez, asaz avedes dicho. E ssi Dios quisier, vos vos fallaredes mal dello; ca muchos ha en esta corte que vos lo lidiaran, e estonçes veredes lo que dexistes'. El rey don Alfonso mando que sse callassen de aquella razon, e que non fablasen y mas; ca luego otro dia querie que lidiassen tres por tres los omnes que se reptaron. Los infantes de Carrion dixeron estonçes al rey
161c don Alfonso, 'Se-| ñor, dadnos plazo fasta que vayamos a Carrion; ca non podriemos lidiar cras[75] por los cavallos e las armas que dimos al Çid'. El rey[76] dixo estonçes al Çid, 'Don Rodrigo, ssea esta lid o[77] vos

tovieredes por bien'. El Çid le dixo, 'Señor, non fare yo al, sy non lo que vos mandaredes. E esto en vos lo dexo de oy mas; ca mas quiero yo yrme para Valençia que para Carrion'. El rey le dixo, 'Pues, dexadme vos vuestros cavalleros, que vayan comigo a la lid. E yo las guardare de guisa que non prendan ningund pesar. E quiero que ssea la lid de oy a tres semanas en las vegas de Carrion. E el que non viniere aquel plazo, que pierda la razon e escape por traydor'. El Çid le dixo, 'Señor, ruegovos que estos cavalleros, que vos yo aqui dexo, que me los enbiedes honrradamente para Valençia. E pues que vos tenedes por bien que esta lid sea en Carrion, quierome yo yr para Valençia'. Estonçes, mando dar el Çid a los mandaderos de los infantes de Navarra e de Aragon bestias e todo lo al que menester ovieron, e enbiolos. El rey don Alfonso cavalgo estonçes con todos los altos omnes de su corte, para salir con el Çid que se yva fuera de la çibdad. E quando fueron quanto[78] dos leguas de la çibdad, yendo el Çid en su cavallo que dizien
161d Bavieca, dixo-| le el rey, 'Don Rodrigo, ruegovos[79] que remetades agora esse cavallo, que tanto bien oy dezir'. El Çid començosse[80] a sonrreyr, e dixo, 'Señor aqui en vuestra corte a muchos altos omnes[81] e guisados para fazer esto, e a esos mandat que trebejen[82] con sus cavallos'. El rey le dixo, 'Çid, pagome yo de lo que vos dezides, mas quiero todavia que corrades ese cavallo por mi amor'. El Çid remetio estonçes el cavallo, e tan de rezio lo corrio que todos sse maravillaron del correr que fizo. Estonçes, veno el Çid al rey e dixole que tomasse aquel cavallo. E el rey dixo que lo non farie; ca mas valie para el que non para otro omne. Alli se despidieron, los unos de los otros. E el Çid fue castigando a Martin[83] Antolinez e a Pero Vermudez e a Muño Gustioz, que fuessen muy firmes en la lid, e que non desmayassen por ninguna cosa. Ellos le dixeron que, pues que en ellos fincava la cosa, que antes oyrie nuevas que eran muertos, que non vençidos. Estonçes, se despidio el Çid dellos, e fuesse para Valençia. E ellos tornaronse para el rey don Alfonso.

Capitulo LXXXIII de como lidiaron los del Çid con los infantes de
162a Carrion, e los vençieron. |

Despues que fueron conplidas las tres semanas del plazo, fueron a Carrion el rey don Alfonso e los cavalleros del Çid, para conplir lo que les mandara su señor. Los infantes, otrossi, vinieron y con muchos de sus parientes. Otro dia mañana,[84] armaronse los unos e los otros, e sallieron al canpo. Los del Çid dixeron al rey que los guardasse de tuerto e de fuerça, que gela non fiziesse ninguno. E el rey assegurolos. Estonçes, demostraron, asi a los unos como a los otros, el rey e los fieles las señales del çerco. Alli sse dexaron yr los unos a los otros, tres por tres, e tan grandes golpes sse dieron que bien cuydaron quantos y estavan que muertos eran. Pero Vermudez e Ferrand Gonçalez lidiaron uno por otro, e dieronse grandes golpes. Mas al cabo vençiolo Pero Vermudez, e dio con el en tierra por muerto. Desi saco la espada Tizona por descabeçarlo. Ferrand Gonçalez, quando aquello vio, dio bozes, e

162b dixo que non le matasse, ca sse dava por su vençido. Los fieles dixeron, | estonces, que lo non matase, pues que por vençido sse dava. Martin[85] Antolinez e Diego Gonçalez lidiaron, otrossi, de so uno, e tan grandes golpes sse dieron que luego quebrantaron las lanças en ssy. Desi, metieron mano a las espadas. E diole Martin[85] Antolinez un golpe que le tajo la meatad del almofar e la cofia, e aun una pieça de los cabellos. Diego Gonçalez ovo, estonçes, miedo que lo matarie, e bolvio la rienda al cavallo e parossele[86] de cara. Martin Antolinez alço estonçes otra vegada la espada, e diole otro golpe muy grande asi que Diego Gonçalez ovo de fuyr, e sallio fuera del çerco. Muño Gustioz[87] lidio con Ansur Gonçalez, e dieronsse muy grandes feridas; mas, al cabo, vençiolo Muño Gustioz,[87] e derribolo del cavallo con una grand lançada que le dio. Quando esto vieron el rey e los fieles, dieron a los infantes por vençidos, e mandaron librar el canpo. El rey don Alfonso enbio, luego, los del Çid para Valençia. El Çid, quando sopo que vençieran a los infantes de Carrion, alço las manos al çielo, e dixo, 'Señor Dios, a ti graçias e merçedes porque mis fijas son oy assy vengadas'. Despues

162c desto, caso el Çid sus fijas con los infantes | de Navarra e de Aragon, de que vos diximos ya. E fueron estos casamientos mucho mejores que los primeros, ca fueron ellas sseñoras la una de Navarra e la otra de Aragon. En esta treynta e terçero año del renado del rey don Alfonso, el infante de Aragon de so uno con . . .[88]

Capitulo LXXXIII° de la muerte de Ruy Diaz Çid e de como sse perdio Valençia.

Andados treynta e siete años del regnado del rey don Alfonso, que fue en la era de mil e çiento e treynta e ssiete años, quando andava el

162d año de la encarnaçion en mill e noventa | e nueve, e el del inperio de Enrrique en uno. El Çid, estando en Valençia, enfermo e murio en el mes de mayo deste[89] dicho año. E dio el alma a Dios. Doña Ximena, su muger, e don Alvar Fanez Minaya levaron el su cuerpo a Sand Pedro de Cardeña. E porque en la su estoria sse contiene de como murio, e lo que acaesçio a la su muerte, por eso non lo pusimos aqui por non alongar[90] esta estoria. E agora torna a fablar del rey don Alfonso de Castilla. . . .[91]

NOTES AND REFERENCES

CHAPTER 1

1. The most important corpus of work on the *PMC* is that of Ramón Menéndez Pidal, whose publications on this field stretch from the beginning of this century to the middle sixties. The major work on the *PMC* is Pidal, *Cantar de mio Cid: texto, gramática y vocabulario*, fourth edition, 3 vols (Madrid, 1964–69), the first edition of which was published in 1908–11, and the second, with additions, in 1944–46. References to Pidal's many other works will appear throughout the footnotes, but some of his more significant articles for his view of the *PMC* are collected in Pidal, *En torno al Poema del Cid* (Barcelona, 1963). For a detailed historical account of scholarship on the *PMC*, although its conclusions tend to agree too automatically with those of Pidal, see Miguel Magnotta, *Historia y bibliografía de la crítica sobre el PMC (1750–1971)* (Chapel Hill, 1976). For a more perceptive survey of the modern period, see A. D. Deyermond, 'Tendencies in "Mio Cid" Scholarship, 1943–73', in *'Mio Cid' Studies*, edited by A. D. Deyermond (London, 1977), pp. 13–47.
2. The manuscript is in the Biblioteca Nacional (hereafter BN), Madrid, BN Va. 7–17. For a description of the manuscript, see Pidal, *CMC*, I, 1–18. For the current condition of the manuscript, see Ian Michael, *PMC* (M., 1976), pp. 52–56. It is probable that one folio is missing at each of the three points where the manuscript is deficient.
3. *PMC*, l. 3373. Quotations from the poem are based on the palaeographic edition by Pidal, *CMC*, III, 909–1016. Future references will be given in the text where possible, and will cite the line numbers of the edition only. Pidal's critical edition, *CMC*, III, 1017–164, is still widely used, but has been superseded by those of Colin Smith, *PMC* (Oxford, 1972), translated by Abel Martínez-Loza (M., 1977), and Ian Michael, *PMC*.
4. In the last century, for example, José Amador de los Ríos described the Cid as representing 'el carácter nacional personificado . . . y reconcentrado', *Historia crítica de la literatura española*, 4 vols (M., 1861–65; reprinted M., 1969), III, 203. Pidal, too, saw symbolic significance in the person of the Cid, as he made clear in his historical study *La España del Cid*, 2 vols, seventh edition (M., 1969; first edition M., 1929), especially I, vii–x.
5. For the stories of the Cid before the composition of the *PMC*, see section II of this chapter. For the developments in the chronicles of the thirteenth and fourteenth centuries, see Chapter 2. Later uses of the legends of the Cid are described in: Pidal, *La epopeya castellana a través de la literatura española* (Buenos Aires, 1945), pp. 209–39; Smith, *PMC*, pp. lxxvii–lxxxi; Michael, *PMC*, pp. 15–17.
6. Jules Horrent, 'Tradition poétique du *CMC* au XIIᵉ siècle', *Cahiers de Civilisation Médiévale*, 7 (1964), 451–77 (p. 464); Smith, *PMC*, pp. xix–xxii. Other studies which doubt the historical accuracy of the *PMC* include: W. Kienast, 'Zur Geschichte des Cid', *Deutsches Archiv für Geschichte des Mittelalters*, 3 (1939), 57–114; E. Lévi-Provençal, 'Le Cid de l'histoire', *Revue Historique*, 180 (1937), 58–74, and 'La toma de Valencia por el Cid', *Al-Andalus*, 13 (1948), 97–156; Leo Spitzer, 'Sobre el carácter histórico del *CMC*', *NRFH*, 2 (1948), 105–17; and, more recently, in Spain, A. Ubieto Arteta, *El 'CMC' y algunos problemas históricos* (Valencia, 1973). It should not be inferred that Pidal was not aware of the artistic nature of the *PMC*: he was aware of it, but argued that art and history went hand in hand in the poem. See, for example, Pidal's reply to Spitzer: 'Poesía e historia en el *Mio Cid*', *NRFH*, 3 (1949), 113–29.
7. The two texts whose historical value has inevitably to be considered are the *Carmen Campidoctoris* and the *Historia Roderici*. Both have the Cid as their protagonist, and both were considered to be historically reliable by Pidal. See sections II, *A* and II, *B*, below.
8. Andrés Bello, *Obras completas*, Volume II, *Poema del Cid* (Santiago de Chile, 1881), p. 15; D. G. Pattison, 'The Date of the *CMC*: a Linguistic Approach', *MLR*, 62 (1967), 443–50. It has also been argued that old linguistic forms in the poem may occur because of the nature of the poetry itself, which may have resulted in the preservation of archaisms; see Michael, *PMC*, pp. 23, 56. The deductions which Pidal made from textual references are not difficult to refute; see A. Ubieto Arteta, 'Observaciones al *CMC*', *Arbor*, 37 (1957), 145–70;

answered by Pidal in 'La fecha del *CMC*', in *Studia Philologica: Homenaje ofrecido a Dámaso Alonso*, III (M., 1963), 7–11.

9.　P. E. Russell, 'Some Problems of Diplomatic in the *CMC* and their Implications', *MLR*, 47 (1952), 340–49. Russell's conclusions have been modified by R. Fletcher, 'Diplomatic and the Cid Revisited: the Seals and Mandates of Alfonso VII', *Journal of Medieval History*, 2 (1976), 305–38, but Fletcher still shows 1140 to be too early a date for the poem. Ubieto, 'Observaciones', and *El 'CMC' y algunos problemas*; Pattison, 'The Date of the *CMC*'; B. Gicovate, 'La fecha de composición del *PMC*', *HBalt*, 39 (1956), 419–22; Colin Smith, 'The Personages of the *PMC* and the Date of the Poem', *MLR*, 66 (1971), 580–93 (compare Bello, *PMC*, pp. 15–16); D. W. Lomax, 'The Date of the *PMC*', in *'Mio Cid' Studies*, pp. 73–81. Lomax does not propose 1207 as the date of composition, but says (p. 81): 'perhaps it would be safest to conclude that the poem was written in the reign . . . of Alfonso VIII' (1158–1214). One study in support of Pidal's dating is F. Mateu Llopis, 'La moneda en el *Poema de Cid*: un ensayo de interpretación numismática del *CMC*', *BRABLB*, 20 (1947), 43–56, where it is shown that the coins referred to in the poem reflect an early system of coinage. As with old linguistic forms, however, it is probable that this can be explained by the nature of the work involved, a story set in the past, in which one would expect some archaism.

10.　Pidal, 'Los cantores épicos yugoeslavos y los occidentales. El *Mio Cid* y dos refundidores primitivos', *BRABLB*, 31 (1965–66), 195–225 (p. 222). Pidal's grandson had already written 'el *Mio Cid* conservado bien pudiera ser medio siglo mas tardío de lo supuesto por Menéndez Pidal, pero faltan argumentos probatorios': Diego Catalán, 'Crónicas generales y cantares de gesta. El *Mio Cid* de Alfonso X y el del pseudo Ben-Alfaray', *HR*, 31 (1963), 195–205, 291–306 (p. 291).

11.　Miguel Magnotta, *Historia y bibliografía*, p. 37, lists fifteen scholars who have argued for a date later than Pidal's, but concludes that 'la fecha de hacia 1140 . . . parece ser hoy la más generalmente aceptada'. Some Spanish scholars have argued against Pidal for a later date, notably Ubieto, but also J. Fradejas Lebrero, *Estudios épicos: el Cid* (Ceuta, 1962); T. Riaño Rodríguez, 'Del autor y fecha del *PMC*', *Prohemio*, 2 (1971), 467–500; M. Criado de Val, 'Geografía, toponimia e itinerarios del *CMC*', *ZRP*, 86 (1970), 83–107.

12.　See Pidal, *CMC*, I, 5–7, 12–18. He followed earlier critics in supposing a missing C. Ubieto, 'Observaciones', and *El 'CMC' y algunos problemas*, Horrent, 'Tradition poétique', Criado de Val, 'Geografía', Riaño, 'Del autor', Smith, *PMC*, and Michael, *PMC*, all accept 1207 as the date referred to in the manuscript. Attempts have been made to identify the Per Abbat of the *explicit*, both by Riaño, 'Del autor', and, more convincingly, by Colin Smith, 'Per Abbat and the *PMC*', *Medium Aevum*, 42 (1973), 1–17. Pidal, *CMC*, I, 17–18, showed that the name was frequent.

13.　The *CAI*, *Najerense*, and the *LR* and *Linaje* are dealt with in section II, below. The *CAI* was used by Pidal as evidence for the existence of the *PMC* at the time of the composition of the chronicle; see *CMC*, I, 23–25, III, 1169–70.

14.　I prefer to use these rather simple terms instead of the more usual ones of Neo-Traditionalism and Individualism, although there are clear links between Pidalian Neo-Traditionalism and the oral approach and between Bédieriste Individualism and the learned one. Criticism has, of course, moved on from the more rigid theories that were held. For a good discussion of the current questions facing the Neo-Traditionalist, see Charles B. Faulhaber, 'Neo-Traditionalism, Formulism, Individualism, and Recent Studies on the Spanish Epic', *RPh*, 30 (1976–77), 83–101.

15.　For discussion of this, see Faulhaber, 'Neo-Traditionalism', and Deyermond, '"Mio Cid" Scholarship'. For a trenchant restatement of the case for a tradition of oral epic in Spain, see S. G. Armistead, 'The *Mocedades de Rodrigo* and Neo-Individualist Theory', *HR*, 46 (1978), 313–27. For references to singers of stories, see Pidal, *Poesía juglaresca y orígenes de las literaturas románicas* (M., 1957), sixth, expanded edition of *Poesía juglaresca y juglares* (M., 1924). For possible epic survivals in chronicles, see Pidal, *Reliquias de la poesía épica española* (M., 1951), and for the *PMC* in the chronicles, see the remaining chapters of this study.

16.　On oral poetry, see Ruth H. Finnegan, *Oral Poetry* (Cambridge, 1977), and references in Faulhaber, 'Neo-Traditionalism'. On epic poetry, see C. M. Bowra, *Heroic Poetry* (London, 1952). On the Spanish ballads, see, for example, Pidal, A. Galmés, and D. Catalán, *Como vive un romance, dos ensayos sobre la tradicionalidad* (M., 1954).

17.　Albert B. Lord, *The Singer of Tales* (Cambridge, Mass., 1960). Pidal made a considered response to Lord's findings in 'Los cantores épicos', where he argued that evidence from modern Yugoslavia is only partially relevant to medieval Spain, and that medieval singers preserved their poems more accurately than the modern ones.

18.   L. P. Harvey, 'The Metrical Irregularity of the *PMC*', *BHS*, 40 (1963), 137–43; A. D. Deyermond, '*The Singer of Tales* and Mediaeval Spanish Epic', *BHS*, 42 (1965), 1–8; Kenneth Adams, 'The Yugoslav Model and the Text of the *PMC*', in *Medieval Hispanic Studies Presented to Rita Hamilton*, edited by A. D. Deyermond (London, 1976), pp. 1–10. Other studies cited below are also dependent on Lord's findings, of course.

19.   In favour of oral composition are: E. de Chasca, *El arte juglaresco en el 'CMC'* (M., 1967); J. M. Aguirre, 'Epica oral y épica castellana: tradición creadora y creación repetitiva', *Romanische Forschungen*, 80 (1968), 13–43; J. J. Duggan, 'Formulaic Diction in the *CMC* and Old French Epic', *FMLS*, 10 (1974), 260–69. Agreed on the presence of typically oral material, but arguing the insufficiency of the total amount are Margaret Chaplin, 'Oral-Formulaic Style in the Epic: a Progress Report', in *Medieval Studies . . . Hamilton*, pp. 11–20, and John S. Miletich, 'Medieval Spanish Epic and European Narrative Traditions', *La Corónica*, 6 (1977–78), 90–96.

20.   Armistead himself points out that 'the very act of copying an epic poem presupposes a profound learned intervention, and a profound distortion of the epic's natural mode of existence as a traditional oral form ('Neo-Individualist Theory', p. 324).

21.   Russell, 'Some Problems of Diplomatic', suggested that the author of the *PMC* had a legal background, and, in 'San Pedro de Cardeña and the Heroic History of the Cid', *Medium Aevum*, 27 (1958), 57–79, he argued that the poet might have had links with a Cidian tomb-cult at San Pedro. Colin Smith's ideas are set out in the Introduction to *PMC*; in a series of articles from 1967 onwards, now collected with three new items in *Estudios cidianos* (M., 1977); in 'On the Distinctiveness of the *PMC*', in *'Mio Cid' Studies*, pp. 161–94; and in 'Further French Analogues and Sources for the *PMC*', *La Corónica*, 6 (1977–78), 14–21.

22.   Smith, *Estudios cidianos*, p. 144. Roger M. Walker, 'A Possible Source for the "Afrenta de Corpes" Episode in the *PMC*', *MLR*, 72 (1977), 335–47. Walker's study has produced the most convincing parallels between the *PMC* and a proposed source, but the proposition faces severe chronological difficulties, since the source was composed very shortly before the *PMC*.

23.   John K. Walsh, 'Religious Motifs in the Early Spanish Epic', *Revista Hispánica Moderna*, 36 (1970–71), 165–72; Kenneth Adams, '*Pensar de*: Another Old French Influence on the *PMC* and Other Medieval Spanish Poems', *La Corónica*, 7 (1978–79), 8–12; A. D. Deyermond and Margaret Chaplin, 'Folk-Motifs in the Medieval Spanish Epic', *Philological Quarterly*, 51 (1972), 36–53. Jules Horrent, *Historia y poesía en torno al CMC* (Barcelona, 1973), pp. 341–74, reviews the question of parallels between the *PMC* and the *Chanson de Roland*, and concludes that there is no evidence of direct influence either way.

24.   For Serbo-Croatian poems, see Milman Parry and A. B. Lord, *Serbo-Croatian Heroic Songs* (Belgrade and Cambridge, Mass., 1954). It would, however, be dangerous to declare that oral poetry is not capable of creating highly artistic works. On the epithets in the *PMC*, see Rita Hamilton, 'Epic Epithets in the *PMC*', *RLC*, 36 (1962), 161–78; de Chasca, *El arte juglaresco*, Chapter 9; R. L. Hathaway, 'The Art of the Epic Epithets in the *PMC*', *HR*, 42 (1974), 311–21.

25.   On the metre of the *PMC*, see: Pidal, *CMC*, I, 76–124, III, 1173–85; Harvey, 'Metrical Irregularity'; Kenneth Adams, 'The Metrical Irregularity of the *CMC*: a Restatement Based on the Evidence of Names, Epithets and some Other Aspects of Formulaic Diction', *BHS*, 49 (1972), 109–19. On tenses, see: Stephen Gilman, *Tiempo y formas temporales en el 'PMC'* (M., 1961); Oliver T. Myers, 'Assonance and Tense in the *PMC*', *PMLA*, 81 (1966), 493–98; Thomas Montgomery, 'Narrative Tense Preference in the *CMC*', *RPh*, 21 (1967–68), 253–74; de Chasca, *El arte juglaresco*, Chapter 13.

26.   The existence of oral heroic poetry is not really in dispute. Smith himself, *Estudios cidianos*, p. 128, refers to 'una tradición indígena de épica oral de la cual sabemos muy poco'. What is in dispute is the importance of this tradition as an influence on the *PMC*, and the extent to which the poem resembles a typical product of that tradition. I would argue that the tradition is the most important influence on the poem, and that the poem would have been recognizable as associated with it. I would further argue that similarities between the *PMC* and the *chansons de geste* are probably the result of features of the tradition, and not from the direct influence on the *PMC* or its author of the French compositions. As for a tradition of written epics like the *PMC*, we have: the *Roncesvalles* fragment, edited by Pidal, '*Roncesvalles*. Un nuevo cantar de gesta español del siglo XIII', *RFE*, 4 (1917), 105–204; the *Mocedades de Rodrigo* (*MR*), edited by Pidal, *Reliquias*, pp. 257–89; and the *Poema de Fernán González* (*PFG*), edited by A. Zamora Vicente, *PFG* (M., 1946); but none of these is very similar to the *PMC*.

27.   See note 12, above. Michael, *PMC*, pp. 48–49, 310, argues that the verb 'escrivio' in the

explicit means 'copied'. Deyermond, '"Mio Cid" Scholarship', pp. 21–22, agrees, but points out that Smith's evidence is possibly identifying the right man, even if he is only the copyist. I would like to mention a couple of uses of 'escrivir', in this context, one by Berceo, *Milagros de Nuestra Señora*, edited by Brian Dutton, in *Obras completas de Berceo*, II (London, 1961), stanza 45b, 'e de los sos miraclos algunos escrivir', and the other in the *Primera crónica general* of 1289 (see below, Chapter 2), p. 489.b.15–17, 'este sancto apostoligo Leon compuso canto de muchos sanctos, et fizo et escrivio muchas buenas cosas'. If it is still argued that 'escrivio' must mean 'wrote down', not 'composed', it seems to me that in the same way as Berceo might have thought of himself as 'writing down' past events, the Per Abbat of the *PMC* could well have thought of himself as 'writing down' past events, even if no one had written them down previously in the same way. In other words, the use of 'escrivio' does not mean that Per Abbat had to be a copyist.

28. For his study of the *MR*, in which he demonstrated clearly its learned authorship and elaborated his theory of transmission, see A. D. Deyermond, *Epic Poetry and the Clergy: Studies on the 'MR'* (London, 1969); see also, 'The *MR* as a Test Case: Problems of Methodology', *La Corónica*, 6 (1977–78), 108–12. For the metre of the *PMC*, see note 25, above. For an introduction to the chronicles and the *PMC*, see Pidal, *CMC*, I, 124–36. I am speaking of the chronicles that use the *PMC* story as in the poem, the *Crónica de veinte reyes* and part of the *Primera crónica general*.

29. The *Carmen* survives in the Bibliothèque Nationale, Paris, Latin MS 5132, fols 79v–80v. It was edited by Pidal in *EDC*, II, 882–86, and references are to that edition. Pidal discusses the poem in *EDC*, II, 878–82. Jules Horrent, 'Sur le *Carmen Campidoctoris*', in *Studi in onore di Angelo Monteverdi*, I (Modena, 1959), 334–52. The erasure is covered by eighteen lines of prose; Pidal estimated that ten or eleven stanzas of the poem would have fitted into that amount of space.

30. Pidal dates the *Carmen* to before 1093, Horrent to 1093–94, and W. Kienast, 'Zur Geschichte', to 1098–99. More recently, Miguel Barceló, 'Algunas observaciones al *Carmen Campidoctoris*', *Saitabi*, 16 (1965), 37–58, proposed 1082–84, and Roger Wright, 'The First Poem on the Cid: the *Carmen Campidoctoris*', in *Papers of the Liverpool Latin Seminar*, edited by Francis Cairns, II (Liverpool, 1979), 213–48, suggests *c.*1083. One scholar has argued for a date in the second half of the twelfth century: E. R. Curtius, 'Zur Literarästhetik des Mittelalters', *ZRP*, 58 (1938), 1–50, 129–232, 433–79, in '5. Der Cid Rhythmus', pp. 162–73; this was answered by Pidal in 'La épica española y la "Literarästhetik des Mittelalters"', *ZRP*, 59 (1939), 1–9.

31. The most convincing argument for a very early date for the *Carmen* is the complete absence in the poem of any overt reference to the Cid's later and greater exploits, particularly the capture of Valencia. This is difficult to account for, although lines 9–12 suggest great things and the poem could conceivably have gone on to relate them. Wright, 'The First Poem', makes out the best case for an early date, but he also points out the poor historical accuracy of the poem. For further consideration of the account of the *Carmen* in an historical context and in relationship to other texts, see: Barceló, 'Algunas observaciones', 'En torno a la primera lid singular del Campeador', *Príncipe de Viana*, 102–03 (1966), 109–26, and 'Una nota en torno al destierro del Cid', *Ligarzas*, 1 (1968), 127–40; Ubieto, *El 'CMC' y algunos problemas*, pp. 163–70; Geoffrey West, 'King and Vassal in History and Poetry: a Contrast between the *Historia Roderici* and the *PMC*', in *'Mio Cid' Studies*, pp. 195–208.

32. Although reflecting a 'popular', that is a widely-held, view of the Cid, one would assume, the *Carmen* itself is in no way a 'popular' work, but is, rather, an eminently learned work, dependent on Latin traditions. It would not have been intelligible to the 'people', as Wright points out, simply because it is in Latin. The learned nature of the poem is stressed in G. Cirot, 'Le *Carmen Campidoctoris*', *BH*, 33 (1931), 144–49, and 'Le Rhythme du *Carmen Campidoctoris*', *BH*, 33 (1931), 247–52; Curtius, 'Der Cid Rhythmus'; Wright, 'The First Poem'.

33. The *HR* is in two manuscripts in the collection of the Real Academia de la Historia, Madrid, MS 23-7-A-189, fols 75–96, and MS 3-4-G-1, fols 69–86. It is edited by Pidal in *EDC*, II, 921–71; references are to that edition and to its numbered divisions. Pidal's study of the *HR* is in *EDC*, I, 906–20, where he refers to earlier editions of the work.

34. For the dates proposed by earlier critics, see Pidal, *EDC*, II, 917–18. H. R. Lang, 'Contributions to the Restoration of the *PMC*', *RH*, 66 (1926), 1–509; A. Ubieto Arteta, 'La *HR* y su fecha de redacción', *Saitabi*, 11 (1961), 241–46, reprinted in *El 'CMC' y algunos problemas*, pp. 170–76. J. Horrent, *Historia y poesía*, pp. 123–43, reviews Ubieto's arguments and proposes 1145–60, while Louis Chalon, *L'Histoire et l'épopée castillane du moyen âge* (Paris, 1976), pp. 4–6, agrees with Ubieto.

35. See Smith, *PMC*, p. xxxii; John Morris, 'Medieval Spanish Epic Style: its Character and

160

Development and its Influence on Other Forms of Literature' (unpublished Ph.D. dissertation, University of Leeds, 1961).

36.	Ubieto Arteta, *El 'CMC' y algunos problemas*, pp. 176–78, argues that most of *HR*, 1–5, is legendary, promising a book on the subject. Barceló, 'En torno a la primera lid', shows that the *HR* cannot be accepted at face value, in respect of the supposed duel with 'Eximino Garcez'.

37.	Barceló, 'Una nota', points out the unlikely nature of the account of events given by the *HR*, and attempts to reorder the chronology in order to explain a possible historical origin, which the *HR* could have distorted.

38.	Michael, *PMC*, p. 146, notes this link between the *PMC* and the *HR*. He suggests (p. 38) that the author of the *PMC* knew the *HR*; but the evidence for this possibility is not strong.

39.	Ubieto and Barceló (see notes 36, 37, above) have expressed serious historical objections to parts of the *HR*. In addition, West, 'King and Vassal', and Horrent, *Historia y poesía*, pp. 123–43, have voiced certain doubts about its trustworthiness.

40.	References are to the edition of L. Sánchez Belda, *Chronica Adefonsi Imperatoris* (M., 1950). Sánchez Belda in his Introduction to the edition and H. Salvador Martínez, *El 'Poema de Almería' y la épica románica* (M., 1975), Chapter 3, show that Arnaldo was the author. For the date of the work, see Sánchez Belda, Martínez, and Ubieto Arteta, 'Sugerencias sobre la *CAI*', *CHE*, 25–26 (1957), 317–27. The influence of biblical language is studied by Sánchez Belda. Martínez discusses at length possible influences between the *Poema de Almería*, vernacular epic, and a possible tradition of Latin epic, which he somehow sees as 'popular', despite the fact that the 'people' would not have been able to understand it. The principal similarities that he establishes between the *Poema* and the *PMC* seem to me to be that they are both in verse, both about military affairs, and both 'historical'. The possibility of Latin epic is also mentioned in J. Gibbs, 'Quelques observations sur le *Poema de Almería*', in *Actes et Mémoires. Société Rencesvals. Quatrième congrès international* (Heidelberg, 1969), pp. 76–81. Vernacular epic language is re-examined in the light of the *CAI*, and other texts, in Colin Smith, 'Latin Histories and Vernacular Epic in Twelfth-Century Spain: Similarities of Spirit and Style', *BHS*, 48 (1971), 1–19, reprinted in *Estudios cidianos*, pp. 87–106.

41.	Martínez, *El Poema*, pp. 351–55, argues that 'Meo Cidi' is not necessarily evidence of a vernacular source, since the title is known in Latin documents of the period. Even if the title does appear on the odd document, it is still very much a vernacular form, of course. In fact, Martínez goes on to argue (pp. 355–95) that the association of the Cid and Alvar Fáñez does imply the existence of a vernacular poem or poems, or, at least, he suggests that as one explanation of the quotation.

42.	The *Najerense* is found in MS A-189, fols 1–64, and MS G-1, fols 1–57 (see note 33, above). See G. Cirot, 'Une Chronique léonaise inédite', *BH*, 11 (1909), 259–82, 'La Chronique léonaise', *BH*, 13 (1911), 133–56, 382–439, and 'La Chronique léonaise et la chronque dite de Silos', *BH*, 16 (1914), 15–34; Pidal, 'Relatos poéticos en las crónicas medievales', *RFE*, 10 (1923), 329–72. Pidal suggests a date for the chronicle of *c*.1160. Ubieto Arteta, *Crónica najerense* (Valencia, 1966), has edited the chronicle, and references are to this edition. In the Introduction to the edition, Ubieto (pp. 21–30) says that the work was composed after 1152, by a French monk in Nájera. He lists the sources used on pp. 14–20. For early Spanish chronicles, including the Asturo-Leonese series, see B. Sánchez Alonso, *Historia de la historiografía española*, second edition, I (M., 1947).

43.	The fullest study of the tradition of the *CSZ* is Carola Reig, *El CSZ* (M., 1947); see also J. Puyol y Alonso, *Cantar de gesta de don Sancho de Castilla* (M., 1911). Both Latin and vernacular poems have been proposed as sources of this part of the *Najerense*. For the seminal article on a Latin poetic source, see W. J. Entwistle, 'On the *Carmen de morte Sanctii regis*', *BH*, 30 (1928), 204–19, in which hexameters are extracted from the chronicle prose. See also Reig, *El CSZ*, pp. 31–42; Pidal, *Reliquias*, pp. xli–xlii; F. Rico, 'Las letras latinas del siglo XII en Galicia, León y Castilla', *Abaco*, 2 (1969), 9–91 (pp. 83–85); H. S. Martínez, 'Tres leyendas heroicas de la *Najerense* y sus relaciones con la épica castellana', *Anuario de Letras*, 9 (1971), 115–77 (pp. 143–77); Charles F. Fraker, 'Sancho II: Epic and Chronicle', *Romania*, 95 (1974), 467–507; A. D. Deyermond, 'Medieval Spanish Epic Cycles: Observations on their Formation and Development', *KRQ*, 23 (1976), 281–303 (pp. 293–94).

44.	Reig, *El CSZ*, pp. 24–27, notes the growing importance of the Cid in the accounts of that period in history; see also Martínez, 'Tres leyendas', pp. 166–74. Ubieto, *El 'CMC' y algunos problemas*, pp. 176–78, doubts that the historical Cid had any important role under Sancho II.

45.	See P. Henrique Flórez, *Memorias de las reynas catholicas*, second edition, 2 vols, (M.,

1770; first edition, M., 1761), pp. 193, 492–505, where a date of before 1234 is proposed; M. Serrano y Sanz, '*Cronicón villarense (Liber regum)*', *BRAE*, 6 (1919), 193–220, and *BRAE*, 8 (1921), 367–82, suggests *c*.1200; Ubieto Arteta, *Corónicas navarras* (Valencia, 1964), p. 12, dates the genealogy of the Kings of Aragón to 1205–09 and the *Linaje* to before 1194, and edits them in pp. 25–29, 30–35.

46. Diego Catalán, *Crónica general de España de 1344*, I (M., 1971), liii–lxii, shows that the original Navarrese version of the *LR* was brought up to date in Toledo in 1217, in a version which must have been the forerunner of Flórez's text. Catalán (pp. 219–337), edits a Navarrese version of the *LR* brought up to 1260–70, based on the Navarrese original, but adding extraneous material such as the histories of Troy and of Britain, the whole being entitled the *Libro de las generaciones*, after the title of its fifteenth-century manuscript. He dates the earliest version of the *LR* to 1196–1209, and points out that it must have used the *Linaje* as one of its sources.

47. References are to the edition of the *Linaje* by Ubieto, *Corónicas*, pp. 30–35. Where Flórez's text fills an obvious lacuna in Ubieto's, the relevant words are added in square brackets.

48. The two references are in the genealogies of Castile and of Navarre, neither of which is in the manuscript used by Ubieto. See Serrano, '*Cronicón*', p. 209: 'De el lignage de Nunno Rasuera vino l'emperador de Castiella. E del lignage de Lain Calbo vino mio Cith el campiador'; p. 212: 'Est Remir Sanchez priso muller la filla del mio Cith el Campiador, e ovo fillo en ella al rei don Garcia de Navarra.' On the *Linaje*, see also M. Barceló, 'Sobre dos textos cidianos', *BRABLB*, 32 (1967–68), 15–25 (pp. 19–25).

49. See Pidal, *EDC*, pp. 536, 819–24. On Diego Ruiz, see also A. Huici Miranda, 'Las luchas del Cid Campeador con los almorávides y el enigma de su hijo, Diego', *Hesperis Tamuda*, 6 (1965), 79–114; Martínez, *El Poema*, p. 366, note. On the daughters, see Pidal, *CMC*, II, 636, 722, 856–57; Ubieto, 'Observaciones', 155–57; Louis Chalon, 'A propos des filles du Cid', *MA*, 73 (1967), 217–37.

50. In the genealogy of the house of Castile in *LR* (Serrano, p. 209), the descendants of Nuño Rasura are given in detail. They include 'el comte Fernand Goncalbez', 'el comte Garcia Fernandez', and 'ifant Garcia, el que matoron en Leon', all of whom are thought to have been characters in epic poems.

51. On the beginning of the *PMC*, see, Pidal, *CMC*, III, 1019–21, Horrent, 'La Jura de Santa Gadea. Historia y poesía', in *Studia Philologica: Homenaje ofrecido a Dámaso Alonso*, II (M., 1961), 241–65; Smith, *PMC*, pp. 1–2; Michael, *PMC*, p. 75.

52. Of course, it is true that most of the works that provide evidence of the twelfth-century tradition are historical in intent. They would inevitably be more interested in the civil wars, particularly with their strong regal connections, than in more personal affairs. One would expect them to underline the Cid's participation in the wars, while perhaps ignoring other stories about him. It is also true that the *CAI* refers to what is a personal relationship, that between the Cid and Alvar Fáñez, because of its interest in the latter. This personal relationship is illustrated with some fine touches in the *PMC* (e.g., ll. 378–81, 744–58). It seems possible, therefore, that the poet of the *PMC* is indebted to the heroic tradition for more of the human side of his poem than I have suggested, but positive evidence to this effect is limited.

CHAPTER 2

1. References are to Lucae Tudensis, *Chronicon Mundi ab Origine Mundi ad Eram MCCLXXIV*, edited by Andreas Schottus, in *Hispaniae Illustratae seu Rerum Urbiumque Hispaniae, Lusitaniae, Aethiopiae et Indiae Scriptores Varii*, 4 vols (Frankfurt, 1603–08), IV, 1–116.

2. The 'laus Hispaniae', found here and in other medieval works, seems to have its origins in the beginning of St Isidore of Seville's *Historia Gothorum*; see Sánchez Alonso, *Historia*, pp. 72–73.

3. Quotation from Andreas Schottus, *Hispaniae Bibliotheca seu de Academis ac Bibliothecis . . .* , three vols in one (Frankfurt, 1608), p. 346. Aspects of Lucas's work are studied in: Pidal, 'Relatos poéticos', pp. 352–63, *Reliquias*, pp. xliii–xlvii, *Primera crónica general de España que mandó componer Alfonso el sabio y se continuaba bajo Sancho IV en 1289* (hereafter *PCG*), 2 vols (M., 1955; text first published M., 1906), pp. xxxvii–xxxix; P. Hogberg, 'La Chronique de Lucas de Tuy', *RH*, 81 (1933), 404–20; J. Gómez Pérez, 'Manuscritos del Toledano I', *RABM*, 60 (1954), 189–213; B. F. Reilly, 'Sources of the Fourth Book of Lucas of Tuy's *Chronicon Mundi*', *Classical Folia*, 30 (1976), 127–37. On Bernardo del Carpio, see: W. J. Entwistle, 'The *Cantar de gesta* of Bernardo del Carpio',

MLR, 23 (1928), 307–22, 432–52; A. B. Franklin, 'A Study of the Origins of the Legend of Bernardo del Carpio', *HR*, 5 (1937), 286–303.

4. See Pidal, *EDC*, pp. 711–13; compare Horrent, 'La Jura de Santa Gadea'.
5. On Pedro de Aragón, see Ubieto, *Colección diplomática de Pedro I de Aragón y Navarra* (Zaragoza, 1951); Pidal, *EDC*, passim. On Búcar, see: Pidal, *CMC*, II, 515–16, *EDC*, II, 812; E. García Gómez, 'El rey Búcar del *CMC*', in *Studi orientalistici in onore di Giorgio Levi Della Vida*, I (Rome, 1956), 371–77; L. Chalon, 'Le Roi Bucar du Maroc dans l'histoire et dans la poésie épique espagnole', *MA*, 75 (1969), 39–49.
6. See Chapter 1, III.
7. See Schottus, *Hispaniae Bibliotheca*, p. 346. References to the *DRH* are to the edition in Schottus, *Hispaniae Illustratae*, II, 26–148. Editions of el Toledano's works include that by F. de Lorenzana, *SS. PP. Toletanorum quotquot extant opera*, 4 vols (M., 1782–97), III (M., 1793), reprinted in Rodrigo Ximénez de Rada, el Toledano, *Opera* (Valencia, 1968).
8. On el Toledano, see Pidal, 'Relatos poéticos', pp. 359–63, *Reliquias*, pp. xlvii–xlix, *PCG*, pp. xxxvii–xxxix; J. Gómez Pérez, Manuscritos del Toledano I', 'Manuscritos del Toledano II', *RABM*, 63 (1957), 157–74; and more generally on the man, J. Gorosterratzu, *Don Rodrigo Jiménez de Rada* (Pamplona, 1925), with another perspective in P. Linehan, *The Spanish Church and the Papacy in the Thirteenth Century* (Cambridge, 1971).
9. Gómez Pérez, 'Manuscritos I', and Smith, *PMC*, p. lxxv, suggest that el Toledano and el Tudense knew the *PMC*. Búcar appears alive and well in ballads, of course; see, for example, G. di Stefano, *Sincronia e diacronia nel Romanzero* (Pisa, 1967), p. 28.
10. The *DRH* seems to have been translated into the vernacular at an early stage, although Alfonso el Sabio's compilers probably had access to the Latin original. See: B. Sánchez Alonso, 'Versiones en romance de las crónicas del Toledano', in *Homenaje ofrecido a Menéndez Pidal*, I (M., 1925), 341–54; J. Gómez Pérez, 'Noticia sobre la traducción ampliada del Toledano', in *PCG*, I, lxix–lxxii, 'La más antigua traducción del Toledano', *Hispania*, 22 (1962), 357–71, 'Jiménez de Rada y su traductor, Domingo Pascual', *Celtiberia*, 23 (1962), 119–29; Diego Catalán, 'El Toledano romanzado y las estorias del fecho de los godos del siglo XV', in *Estudios dedicados a J. Homer Herriot* (Madison and Valencia, 1966), pp. 9–101.
11. On Alfonso X, see A. Ballesteros Beretta, *Alfonso X el Sabio* (Barcelona and Murcia, 1963). On his teams of scholars, see: Evelyn S. Procter, 'The Scientific Works of the Court of Alfonso X of Castile', *MLR*, 40 (1945), 12–29, *Alfonso X of Castile, Patron of Literature and Learning* (Oxford, 1951); A. G. Solalinde, 'Intervención de Alfonso X en la redacción de sus obras', *RFE*, 2 (1915), 283–88; Gonzalo Menéndez Pidal, 'Como trabajaron las escuelas alfonsíes', *NRFH*, 5 (1951), 362–79; Américo Castro, 'Acerca del castellano escrito en torno de Alfonso el sabio', *Filologia Romanza*, 1, no. 4 (1954), 1–11.
12. The fundamental studies of the relationships between these chronicles are: Pidal, *La leyenda de los Infantes de Lara*, third edition (M., 1971; first published M., 1896); Pidal, *Crónicas generales de España: Catálogo de la Real Biblioteca*, I (M., 1898), third edition published as *Catálogo*, V (M., 1918); L. F. Lindley Cintra, *Crónica geral de Espanha de 1344*, 3 vols (Lisbon, 1951–61), I, 'Introdução', with the important review article by Pidal, 'Tradicionalidad de las crónicas generales de España', *BRAH*, 136 (1955), 131–97; Diego Catalán, *De Alfonso X al Conde de Barcelos* (M., 1962).
13. On the quotations from the *GE*, see *PCG*, pp. xviii–xxi. Of the text of the *GE*, five and a bit 'partes' survive in varying stages of completeness, of which only the first two have been published: *GE: primera parte*, edited by A. G. Solalinde (M., 1930); *GE: segunda parte*, edited by A. G. Solalinde, L. A. Kasten, and V. R. B. Oelschlager, 2 vols (M., 1957–62).
14. The two volumes are the basis of volume one and volume two, respectively, of the edition of the *PCG* by Pidal. The truly Alphonsine manuscript is volume one plus the first seventeen folios of volume two, *PCG*, pp. 1–350.a.10. See: Pidal, *PCG*, pp. xv–xxv; Catalán, *De Alfonso X*, studies A and B, passim, and section *B*, below.
15. On dating, see Pidal, *PCG*, pp. xx–xxv; on Bamba, Catalán, 'El Toledano romanzado', p. 53; on the aqueduct of Segovia, Francisco Rico, *Alfonso el sabio y la 'GE'* (Barcelona, 1972), p. 44, note.
16. See Rico, *Alfonso el sabio*, pp. 36–44. Alfonso's imperial ambitions and frustrations also played a part, no doubt, in stimulating his interest in history on a wider scale; see A. D. Deyermond, *A Literary History of Spain. I. The Middle Ages* (London and New York, 1971), p. 90; A. Ballesteros Beretta, *Alfonso X*. For evidence of Alfonso's imperial ambitions in the *PCG*, see Charles F. Fraker, 'Alfonso X, the Empire and the *Primera crónica*', *BHS*, 55 (1978), 95–102.
17. Pidal first expounded his theory of the 'borrador' of the chronicle in *La Crónica General de España que mandó componer el rey Alfonso el sabio. Discursos leídos ante la Real Academia*

de la Historia el día 21 de mayo de 1916 (M., 1916), pp. 10–58. It is then present in all his later studies of the chronicles. The concept of 'tradicionalidad' in chronicle-writing is present from Pidal's earliest work on the chronicles, although not called by that name; see *Leyenda*, pp. 53–54. It is developed most fully at a later stage, and particularly in 'Tradicionalidad de las crónicas', passim, from where the quotation is taken.

18.   See J. Gómez Pérez, 'La elaboración de la *PCG* de España y su trasmisión manuscrita', *Sc*, 17 (1963), 233–76. Cintra, *A Crónica Geral*, suggests that there was a 'rascunho original', which was prepared under Alfonso X as far as the death of Alfonso VI. Catalán, 'El taller historiográfico alfonsí. Métodos y problemas en el trabajo compilatorio', *Romania*, 84 (1963), 354–75, argues that, in Alfonso's time, the whole of el Toledano's *DRH* was reorganized in preparation for the writing of the *EE* and that certain other preparatory work was also done.

19.   The Marqués de Pidal, Gayangos, and Caveda planned to publish the text of the two manuscripts, but the edition never materialized. As noted above (note 14), part of Pidal's edition can be accepted as the true representative of Alfonso's *EE*. However, more than half of the edition cannot be so regarded.

20.   Henceforth, in references to manuscripts, manuscript collections are referred to by the abbreviations listed on p. xii, above. When letters are used in reference to manuscripts, they are those in current critical usage, unless otherwise stated. For manuscripts used in the edition of the *PCG*, see *PCG*, pp. lvii–lxii.

21.   M. Milá y Fontanals, *De la poesía heroico-popular castellana* (Barcelona, 1874), reprinted in Milá, *Obras*, edited M. de Riquer and J. Molas, I (Barcelona, 1959), p. 52, note 2; Catalán, *De Alfonso X*, especially pp. 88–93.

22.   On MSS C and I, respectively, see *PCG*, pp. lvii, lix, and *De Alfonso X*, pp. 38, 42. Both studies identify MS I as B.N. 10314 bis. This, however, is the reference number of a chronicle of Aragonese origin. The correct reference for I is B.N. 10314 ter.

23.   Catalán bases his argument for the date of 1344–50 on the following quotation from the prologue to Alfonso XI's *Crónica de tres reyes*; see BAE, LXVI, p. 3: 'Mando catar las coronicas e estorias antiguas e fallo scripto en los libros de su camara los fechos de los reyes que fueron en tiempos pasados, reyes godos fasta el rey Rodrigo e desde el rey don Pelayo que fue el primero rey de Leon fasta que fino el rey don Fernando.' But this quotation does not necessarily refer to two separate volumes, merely to two separate periods of history which may well have been dealt with in one volume. Even if the quotation is speaking of two volumes, there is no hard evidence that the two Escorial volumes are those referred to.

24.   At times, Catalán seems to discount entirely the second part of the 1289 text, X-i-4, fols 257–320, which ends in mid-sentence, as when he talks of a radical change in the nature of the *PCG* from fol. 198 onwards; see, for example, 'Crónicas generales', passim. However, Catalán is talking of the structure underlying the composition of the chronicle, not about the dates of its various parts. The second part of the 1289 text is undoubtedly of the same date as the first, but it does not have the same quality in its compilation of sources, because, Pidal and Catalán would argue, of the inferior state of compilation of this section of Spanish history reached in the period of Alfonso's scholarly activity. For further consideration of the prosification of the first 'cantar' of the *PMC* in this text, found in X-i-4, fols 164r–173r, see below, and Chapter 3.

25.   On all these matters, see Catalán, *De Alfonso X*, studies A and B, passim. On the 'versiones regia y vulgar', see Pidal, *PCG*, pp. xxix–xxx. On F, see Catalán, *De Alfonso X*, pp. 65–68, where he compares it with the Cidian interpolation. Basically, the interpolation and F are copies of the same chronicle version, and F has fewer errors than the interpolation. All the differences between them are not shown in the footnotes to the edition in *PCG*.

26.   *PCG*, having been printed by Pidal, has enjoyed a status which its second half does not deserve. Even Catalán, in 'El taller historiográfico', after detailing the weaknesses of X-i-4, still tends to talk of the *CVR* as dependent on it, which it cannot be. Chalon, in *L'Histoire et l'épopée*, pp. 7, 214–15 fundamentally misunderstands Catalán's conclusions about *PCG*, II, believing that the interpolation dates from the time of Sancho IV, and that the whole of the *PCG* was completed in his reign. This makes his whole study of the relationship of the *PCG* to the other Alphonsine chronicles unsound.

27.   On the *PMC* and the *PCG*, see: Pidal, 'El *Poema del Cid* y las crónicas generales', *RH*, 5 (1898), 435–65, of which pp. 435–41 are rewritten in *CMC*, I, 124–26, with further comments in *CMC*, III, 1185–91; Lang, 'Contributions'; G. Cirot, 'La Chronique générale et le Poème du Cid', *BH*, 40 (1938), 306–09; Catalán, 'Crónicas generales'. The text of the *CVR* suggests that the missing part of the 1289 text would have included a prosification of later parts of the *PMC*, while the *CRC* suggests that the earlier part of the interpolation may well have had a revised version of the first 'cantar'.

28.   The inclusion in the *PCG* of references to events it has not related was first noted by
        Theodore Babbitt, *La Crónica de Veinte Reyes.: a Comparison with the PCG and a Study of
        the Principal Latin Sources* (New Haven, 1936), pp. 57–63. The gap in the contents of the
        chronicle was pointed out by Catalán, 'El taller historiográfico', p. 367. For the 'partición de
        los reinos', see section *C*, below.
29.   For the *Linaje* and the *Najerense*, see Chapter 1, II, *D* and *E*. On the *CSZ* in the *PCG*, see
        Charles F. Fraker, 'Sancho II: Epic and Chronicle', *Romania*, 95 (1974), 467–507, where,
        however, Fraker does not seem familiar with the most comprehensive study of the *CSZ*,
        that of Reig, *El CSZ*.
30.   Babbitt, *La CVR*, p. 79, observed that both the *PCG* and *CVR* attribute passages to el
        Toledano which do not exist in the Latin original. The passages are perhaps from a
        translation of the *DRH* amplified by the translator; see *PCG*, I, lxxii, where such
        attributions are listed, and note 10, above.
31.   The *Leyenda de Cardeña* is so called in *PCG*, II, 'Fuentes', pp. cxc–cci. It has been
        suggested that the whole of the revised version of this part of the Cid's life on which the
        Cidian interpolation and other chronicles such as the *CRC* and *TCG* are based was compiled
        at Cardeña. See: W. J. Entwistle, 'La estoria del noble varon el Cid Ruy Diaz el Campeador
        sennor que fue de Valencia', *HR*, 15 (1947), 206–11; P. E. Russell, 'San Pedro de Cardeña
        and the Heroic History of the Cid', *Medium Aevum*, 27 (1958), 57–79; Catalán, 'Crónicas
        generales', 'La Estoria de los Reyes del Señorio de Africa del maestro Gilberto o
        Sujulberto: una obra del siglo XIII perdida', *RPh*, 17 (1963–64) 346–53, and 'Poesía y
        novela en la historiografía castellana de los siglos XIII y XIV', in *Mélanges offerts à Rita
        Lejeune*, I (Gembloux, 1969), 423–41; Colin Smith, 'The Cid as Charlemagne in the
        **Leyenda de Cardeña*', *Romania*, 97 (1976), 509–31. A detailed examination of one episode
        of this section in the successive chronicles has been published: D. G. Pattison, 'The
        "Afrenta de Corpes" in Fourteenth-Century Historiography', in *'Mio Cid' Studies*,
        pp. 129–40, shows that the *PMC* and *CVR* have one version of this episode, while the *PCG*,
        CRC, *TCG*, and *C1344* contain another. The differences between the first version and the
        second are so numerous that they seem to me to require the supposition of a detailed
        revision or 'refundición' behind them, whereas the minor differences between the different
        chronicles in the second group can easily be accounted for by the tinkerings of chroniclers.
        Whether this 'refundición' was a poetic 'refundición' of the text of the *PMC* is a different
        and problematical question, which would demand a separate study.
32.   Lang, 'Contributions', noted the closeness of the *PMC* and parts of the expanded *PCG*
        account, including the final duels. Such textual similarity may be attributable, of course, to
        the 'refundición' mentioned above.
33.   It is interesting to note that there is no surviving documentary evidence of generosity to
        Cardeña by the Cid; see Luciano Serrano, *El obispado de Burgos*, 3 vols (M., 1935–36), II,
        249, and that two 'Cronicones de Cardeña', which end in 1312 and 1327, do not mention the
        death of the Cid, or any link between him and the monastery; see Henrique Flórez, *España
        Sagrada*, 29 vols (M., 1745–75), XXIII, 370–80.
34.   The manuscript examined is Esc. Y-i-12, N, which is the main manuscript used and quoted
        in this study. The *CVR* remains unedited, although I am preparing an edition. The
        prosification of the *PMC* is edited in Appendix B. The manuscripts of the chronicle are
        described in Appendix A. The majority of manuscripts state on their title pages that the
        chronicle will contain eleven kings.
35.   See *Catálogo* (1918), p. 107. Three of the MSS of the *CVR*, including the two best ones,
        begin two kings later than Fruela II, thus omitting the story of the 'jueces'.
36.   Many manuscripts of Alphonsine chronicles mention the start of the 'cuarta parte' of the
        history, when Fernando I takes over the throne of León; see Cintra, *A Crónica Geral*, I,
        ccix, ccxxx, and Catalán, *De Alfonso X*, pp. 97–98. The first published text of a full
        Alphonsine chronicle is entitled *Las quatro partes enteras de la crónica de España*, edited by
        Florián d'Ocampo (Zamora, 1541).
37.   Chalon, *L'Histoire et l'épopée*, pp. 256–57, also doubts whether the *CVR* relies on the *PCG*
        in the early part of the prosification of the *PMC*.
38.   See Babbitt, *La CVR*; Lang, 'Contributions'; Jose Gómez Pérez, 'La *Estoria de España*
        alfonsí de Fruela II a Fernando III', *Hispania*, 25 (1965), 481–520.
39.   References to manuscripts are to the folio and either to the recto and verso, or to a and b,
        columns one and two of the recto, or c and d, columns one and two of the verso. In
        references to the *CVR* where only the folio is given, the reference is to MS N.
40.   For the 'Cantar de Fernando el Magno', see Pidal, *Reliquias*, pp. 240–56, where the relevant
        part of the *CVR* is printed. Whenever possible, I shall cite the printed text rather than the
        unpublished manuscript. See also, Rosa M. Garrido, 'El Cantar del rey don Fernando el
        Magno', *BRABLB*, 22 (1967–68), 67–95.

41. The material on the Cid's family includes lists of places belonging to his great-uncle and to his maternal grandfather, and of places captured by his father from the Navarrese. It discusses whether it was Fernando I or Sancho II who knighted him, concluding that it was the former, and it goes on to say that Sancho II married him to Jimena, and that their daughters married 'condes de Carrión'.

42. The manuscripts of the *CRC* are described most fully in S. G. Armistead, '*La Gesta de la mocedades de Rodrigo*: Reflections of a Lost Epic Poem in the *Crónica de los reyes de Castilla* and the *Crónica general de 1344*' (unpublished doctoral dissertation, Princeton University, 1955), pp. 228–66. See also Catalán, *De Alfonso X*, pp. 323–42; Armistead, 'New Perspectives in Alfonsine Historiography', *RPh*, 20 (1966–67), 204–17 (a review of *De Alfonso X*), and 'MS Z of the *Crónica de Castilla*: Lost and Found', *La Corónica*, 6 (1977–78), 118–22. Both Catalán and Armistead mention Ac.Hist. 12-26-4 (previously D-82) as a MS of the *CRC* which neither was able to consult. On my investigating this in the Academia de la Historia, it turned out that there was no chronicle MS of that number. MS 9-24-4-D-82 is a novelesque *Chronicón de siete reyes de Castilla y León*, copied in the year 1654, which begins with the reign of Alfonso VI, and mentions the Cid; but its contents are unlike those of the Alphonsine chronicles. MS 9-11-2-51, not mentioned by Catalán or Armistead, does contain an Alphonsine text, but in the form of a late seventeenth-century hand-written copy of the printed *Crónica Particular*, discussed below.

43. See Cintra, *A Crónica Geral*, pp. ccxxxvi–ccxlv, and Catalán, *De Alfonso X*, pp. 323–49, where he argues that the *CRC* ended originally with the death of Alfonso XI. Its uniqueness, however, is for the three reigns in which the Cid appears.

44. The MS is B.N. 8817, A. See Cintra, *A Crónica Geral*, p. ccxxx; Diego Catalán and María Soledad de Andrés, *Crónica general de España de 1344*, I (M., 1971), xlv. The text of the MS is edited in full in Ramón Lorenzo, *La traducción gallega de la Crónica General y de la Crónica de Castilla*, 2 vols (Orense, 1975–77).

45. See *Crónica del famoso cavallero Cid Ruy Diez Campeador* (Burgos, 1512); two copies of the second edition (Medina del Campo, 1552) by different printers are in the British Library; the third edition (Burgos, 1593) was reprinted without the genealogical and monastic additions by D. V. A. Huber (Marburg, 1844; reprinted Stuttgart, 1853). Velorado's original edition has been reproduced in facsimile by Archer M. Huntington (New York, 1903; reprinted New York, 1967).

46. The MS used by Velorado is Paris 326, B, identified by Catalán, *De Alfonso X*, p. 326, notes. Both Reig and Cintra tried to distinguish between the *CRC* and the *Particular*, but were identifying variants between MSS only. Since the *Particular* offers a good text of the relevant part of the *CRC*, and it is available in a printed edition, it has been used for references to the *CRC*, whenever possible (facsimile edition, New York, 1967). Virtual identity between the *CRC* and the printed text was also noted by J. Zarco Cuevas, *Catálogo de los manuscritos castellanos de la Biblioteca del Escorial*, 3 vols (M., 1924–26, San Lorenzo, 1929), II, description of X-i-11, which is MS G of the *CRC*.

47. The *Particular* should not be confused with the *Crónica popular del Cid* (Seville, [14]98), reprinted by R. Foulché-Delbosc, 'La corónica del Cid Ruy Díaz', *RH*, 20 (1909), 316–428. This chronicle certainly was 'popular'. Foulché-Delbosc lists no less than 15 editions by 1627, one of which (Toledo, 1526) has been reproduced in facsimile by Huntington (New York, 1903; reprinted New York, 1967). Its text contains a very novelesque account of the life of the Cid, which J. Puyol y Alonso, *La crónica popular del Cid* (M., 1911), has shown to be based on the *Crónica de España abreviada* of Diego de Valera, which dates from 1481, and which in turn is based loosely on the *C1344*, at least for the life of the Cid.

48. For the text of the *CRC*, see *Particular*, fols i–xi. The lost poem is studied in Armistead, '*La Gesta*'; compare the clerical version, the *MR*, in *Reliquias*, pp. 257–87. See Deyermond, *Epic Poetry and the Clergy*, passim.

49. The poetic language and proliferation of detail around the exile of the Cid enabled Pidal to construct lines for the opening of his critical edition of the *PMC* (*CMC*, III, 1025). It must be remembered, however, that these cannot have been the opening lines of the *PMC*, since they precede a part of the *CRC* which has many differences from the corresponding extant part of the poem.

50. Pidal saw poetic 'refundiciones' behind changes in the story of the Cid in the *CRC* and other chronicles. Many, however, are due to the successive chroniclers, and some, probably, to new prose sources. See Catalán, 'Poesía y novela'; Pattison, 'The "Afrenta de Corpes"'; and note 31, above. For a proposed prose source, see Catalán, 'La Estoria de los Reyes'.

51. Ocampo, *Las quatro partes enteras*, p. 279a; Ocampo was 'Cronista imperial' to Charles V. His chronicle was widely read in its time, and its contents were used as the basis for the composition of ballads, by Timoneda, for example. A second edition was published (Valladolid, 1604).

52. See Pidal, *Catálogo* (1918), pp. 125–32; Cintra, *A Crónica Geral*, pp. ccix–ccxxx, ccciii; Catalán, *De Alfonso X*, pp. 188–93, 323–35. To Catalán's list of MSS should be added British Library MS Egerton 289, which is also a mixture of the *PCG* and *CRC*, although it has some peculiarities of its own. The relationships between these mixed MSS, and between them and other texts, are extremely complex.

53. See Cintra, *A Crónica Geral*, passim. Catalán, *De Alfonso X*, studies C and D, shows the importance as a motive force behind the chronicle of Count don Pedro de Barcelos. Before the accession of Ramiro I, the *C1344* is not based on Alphonsine materials, and it is with Ramiro I that MS A of the *CRC* begins (see note 44, above).

54. The content of the *C1344* was examined for this study in MSS Pal. 1069, and B.N. 10815. No complete edition exists. Cintra's two volumes of text end at the point of the first reconciliation of the Cid and Alfonso VI (see *PCG*, Chapters 864–65). Catalán and Andrés, *La C1344*, do not reach the Alphonsine section, and there seem to be no plans at present to publish a second volume of the text.

55. The *Abreviada* survives only in MS B.N. 1356, which is edited by R. L. and M. B. Grismer, Juan Manuel, *Crónica Abreviada* (Minneapolis, 1958). It is one of Juan Manuel's earliest works, and possibly his least original. See Pidal, *Leyenda*, pp. 52–54; Germán Orduna, 'Los prólogos a la *Crónica abreviada* y al *Libro de la caza*: la tradición alfonsí y la primera época en la obra literaria de don Juan Manuel', *Cuadernos de Historia de España*, 51–52 (1970), 123–44.

56. These observations, based on an examination of the texts, are supported in what is the most detailed study to date of the *Abreviada*: Diego Catalán, 'Don Juan Manuel ante el modelo alfonsí: el testimonio de la *Crónica Abreviada*', in *Juan Manuel Studies*, edited by Ian Macpherson (London, 1977), pp. 17–51. Catalán analyses the structure of the three 'libros' into which Juan Manuel divides his work, and the nature of the *Crónica Manuelina*, which is its presumed source. He shows that Juan Manuel's divisions are reflected in a number of chronicle MSS, and are the result of the state of the compilation of different parts of the *EE*. Pattison, 'The "Afrenta de Corpes"', pp. 136–38, shows that in some ways the *Abreviada* agrees both with the *PCG* and with the *CRC* in its account of this episode, and suggests that the *Manuelina* may have predated and influenced both.

CHAPTER 3

1. MSS of the *CRC* are more numerous than those of other chronicles. In the sixteenth century, the *CRC* account was superseded by a still more novelesque one, that of the *Crónica popular*. It should not be forgotten, however, that the *CVR* has a very novelesque account of the last days of Fernando I, which shows that its contents reflect its sources rather than exceptionally sober taste on the part of its author.

2. Early references to the *CVR* are: Nicolás Antonio, *Bibliotheca Hispana Vetus*, 2 vols (Rome, 1696), II, 7, 72; F. de Berganza y Arce, *Antigüedades de Castilla*, 2 vols (M., 1719–21), I, 420. See Pidal, *Catálogo* (1918), pp. 68, 108.

3. Modern studies devoted principally to the *CVR* are: Theodore Babbitt, 'Observations on the *Crónica de once reyes*', *HR*, 2 (1934), 202–16, 'Twelfth-Century Epic Forms in Fourteenth-Century Chronicles', *RR*, 26 (1935), 128–36, and *La CVR*; Jose Gómez Pérez, 'La *Estoria de España* alfonsí'; Larry L. Collins, 'An Unknown Manuscript of the *CVR*', *Sc*, 28 (1974), 51–60, and 'The Historiographical Background of the *CVR*', *Revue d'Histoire des Textes*, 4 (1974), 339–57; Nancy Joe Dyer, '*El PMC* in the *CVR* Prosification: a Critical Edition and Study' (unpublished doctoral dissertation, University of Pennsylvania, 1975).

4. Eight out of twelve MSS refer to 'once reyes'; see Appendix A.

5. Three MSS begin with Ramiro II. The monarchs after him in N are: Ordoño III, Sancho I, Ramiro III, Bermudo II, Alfonso V, Bermudo III, Fernando I, Sancho II, Alfonso VI, Alfonso VII, Sancho 'el seguno' (*sic*, = III), Alfonso VIII, Enrique I, Fernando III.

6. See Lang, 'Contributions', pp. 40–42, where he argues that Sancho II was the eleventh monarch, which he would be if two kings were placed before those listed in note 5. Babbitt, *La CVR*, p. 115, suggested a break at the death of Alfonso VI. Cintra, *A Crónica Geral*, pp. ccxxxiii–ccxxxvi, pointed out the relationship between the *CVR* and *CRC*, but also that the *CVR* does not radically change its style or methods of compilation until the reign of Fernando III. Catalán, *De Alfonso X*, pp. 241–88, showed that, when the *CVR* and *CRC* coincide, the *CVR* has some additions on Portuguese affairs.

7. Babbitt used 'once reyes' as the name of the chronicle for a time, but eventually used *CVR* (see note 3). Catalán, *De Alfonso X*, passim, vacillated between the two, but has since used *CVR*.

8. Confusingly *CVR* MS Esc. X-i-6, J, begins: 'Aqui comiença la segunda e terçera partes de los reyes que ovo en Castilla e en Leon', fol. 1r, and does not mention the 'cuarta parte'. The *Crónica abreviada* also refers to three 'partes' (see Chapter 2, II, *E*, iii).

9. The name 'Versión amplificada de la *PCG*' was coined by Catalán, *De Alfonso X*. For the *PMC* in the *PCG*, see Chapter 2, note 27.

10. Further examples of extra material in the *CVR* based on the *PCG* can be seen in Catalán, 'Crónicas generales y cantares de gesta', pp. 301–04. Earlier, Catalán thought the *CVR* depended on the *PCG* for the first 'cantar'; see 'El taller historiográfico alfonsí', pp. 367–68. So did Pidal, *CMC*, p. 134, echoed more recently by J. Horrent, 'Notes de critique textuelle sur le *CMC*', in *Mélanges offerts à M. Delbouille* (Gembloux, 1964), II, 275–89. However, there is no reason to think that the *CVR* knew or used the *PCG*.

11. The form in which the collected source material for Alfonso X's *EE* existed is uncertain. Although very similar in their versions of the first 'cantar' of the *PMC*, the *CVR* and *PCG* begin to diverge soon after the end of the first 'cantar', and well before the 1289 text is interrupted by the interpolated section, which deals only with the Cid. Thus, the *CVR* and *PCG* may have used a common prose source for the first 'cantar', but this did not include all the material on the Cid which the two chronicles use after the end of the 'cantar', and well before substantial use is made of more of the poem. On differences in this section of the *CVR* and *PCG*, see Babbitt, *La CVR*, pp. 87–93, and note 17, below.

12. There is more variety in the chronological information supplied in earlier parts of the *PCG*; see J. Gómez Pérez, 'Fuentes y cronología en la *PCG* de España', *RABM*, 65 (1959), 615–34. On the Caesarean or Spanish 'era', see C. Torres Rodríguez, 'La era hispánica', *RABM*, 79 (1976), 733–56. Annals as historical records have existed from the earliest times, and were frequent in the early Middle Ages; see Harry E. Barnes, *A History of Historical Writing*, second edition (New York, 1962); Sánchez Alonso, *Historia de la historiografía*; Denys Hay, *Annalists and Historians* (London, 1977).

13. The ten chapters placed in the same year are in the prosification of the first 'cantar' of the *PMC*, Chapters 7–16 of the reign of Alfonso VI in the *CVR*, MS N, fols 112d–19d. The series of six chapters devoted to six separate years are Chapters 20–25, fols 122a–25a.

14. The *PCG* 1289 text has the same chronology as the *CVR* in their parallel versions of the *PMC*, but the two disagree later, from the eighth year of the reign onwards; see Catalán, 'Crónicas generales', pp. 210–11. The first part of the 1289 text breaks off in the year 1087 (see *PCG*, Ch. 890), and resumes after the burial of the Cid, in 1104 (*PCG*, Ch. 963). There is no chronological information in the intervening interpolated section. The *CRC* in the *Particular* places the exile and the death of the hero in the fourth year and thirty-second year of the reign, which are given as 1073 (fol. xxvii) and 1098 (fol. xciv)! As can be deduced from this, the *CRC* is unreliable as far as chronology is concerned. Its annalistic information is incomplete and erratic. The *CVR* places the knighting of the Cid by Fernando I in the period 1033–39, at the siege of Coimbra (fol. 75a), while the *CRC* dates it in 1024 (fol. v).

15. Chapter headings are often in different coloured ink from the standard black of the text, sometimes red or occasionally blue. The description of the contents in chapter headings of *CVR* MSS are normally accurate, but other MSS occasionally have errors. The first initial of the text of a chapter is decorated with line drawings in very many chronicle MSS, frequently with coloured inks. Capital letters at the start of a chapter's text may be restricted to the first letter or the first word, or may fill the first line. N has first initials decorated in blue and red, and a line of large letters at the start of each chapter.

16. The numeration of chapters in N does not run completely smoothly. Between the two main parts of the prosification of the *PCG*, there is a series of chapters numbered 47, 48, 47, 48, 49, later corrected by 55, 57 . . . 63, 65. *CVR* MS J has the identical erroneous series. In comparison with the seventy-six chapters of the *CVR*, the printed *PCG* has 103, and the *Particular* no less than 191, which is a result of both additional material and a shortening of the average length of chapters. Other MSS of the *CRC* will have a different number of chapters and different chapter divisions, but all will have many more than the *CVR*; see Armistead, '*La Gesta*', Appendix II.

17. See Babbit *La CVR*, pp. 87–93, on the differences between the *CVR* and *PCG* after the first 'cantar'; see also Catalán, 'Crónicas generales', pp. 210–14. Very approximately, the content of the *CVR*, N, Chapters 20–48, corresponds to the chapters of the *PCG* in the following sequence: 862, 863, 866, 864, 865, 867, 877, 870–72, 878–82, 871–75, 886–95. However, compared to the *PCG*, the *CVR* has new information, and has a different form and organization of the information common to both. The account in the *CVR* is clear and logical, with none of the confusions that mar the 1289 text before it breaks off in Chapter 896 (whose content is not reached in *CVR* until seven chapters further on). See the chapter headings of this part of *CVR* in Appendix B.

18. Chapter 76 contains in addition thirty-five lines of chronicle text corresponding to the lacuna in *PMC*, ll. 2337–38. Chapter 82 contains twenty-five additional lines corresponding to the lacuna in *PMC*, ll. 3507–08. On chapters in the Alphonsine chronicles, see Armistead, '*La Gesta*', Appendix II; Babbitt, *La CVR*, p. 25, where he states: 'It is curious how the chapter seems to be the basic unit, capable of being shifted about integrally, or with the change of a date or two.' *CVR*, N, Chapters 37 and 74 have virtually the same content but a different date.

19. The anonymity of chronicle composition and transmission is one of the keys to Pidal's theory of a 'popular' tradition of chronicle writing; see Chapter 2, II, *A*, and note 17.

20. The Cid's attention to an omen in the third 'cantar' is recounted by the *CVR* without comment (fol. 158a; ll. 2615–16). In other parts of *CVR* and *PCG*, other examples of 'dizen' are found in contexts of contradiction or doubt. Before the events surrounding the partition of the kingdom by Fernando I (which is in fols 81b–87c of N), we find: 'dizen que le dio una lançada' (fol. 73d; *PCG*, p. 485.b.12); 'Algunos dizen . . . otros dizen' (fol. 79a, *PCG*, p. 491.a.30; fol. 79c, *PCG*, p. 491.b.19–20). In the *CSZ* in the *CVR*, we find: 'Pero dizen algunos' (fol. 95b; but compare *PCG*, p. 503.1.16), 'dizen que' (fol. 102a; *PCG*, p. 511.b.7). 'Otros dizen de otra guisa' (fol. 105d), when discussing different versions of Alfonso VI's escape from Toledo (see *PCG*, pp. 514–15), and 'e dizen algunos' (fol. 109b) on the effect of Urraca's influence in Alfonso's reign (see *PCG*, p. 518.b) have no equivalents in the *PCG*. Compare also the *PCG* account of the story of Bernardo del Carpio (e.g. p. 375.a.27 and b.23). For a different use of 'dizen', see *PCG*, p. 538.a.17–18 and 24, p. 546.b.44–49. See Pidal, *Reliquias*, p. liii.

21. References to 'cantares', 'gestas', 'joglares' are found in the *PCG* and the *CVR*, but no such term is used in those sections dependent on the *PMC*. For such terms, see *Reliquias*, pp. l–liii; *PCG*, pp. 351.a, 355.b, 371.a, 385.b, 471.a, 509.a. In the *CVR*, in the reign of Fernando I, see *Reliquias*, pp. 242, 243. In the *CSZ* in the *CVR* there are some interesting quotations not found in the *PCG*, which shed a great deal of light on the attitudes to the task of writing history behind the composition of the *CVR*, as well as containing terms discussed immediately above: 'Mas comoquier que en el cantar del rey don Sancho diga que luego fue sobre el rey don Garçia, fallamos en las estorias verdaderas que cuentan y el arçobispo don Rodrigo e don Lucas de Tuy e don Pedro Marquez cardenal de Santiago que ovieron sabor de escudriñar las estorias por contar verdaderamente la estoria de España que sobre el rey don Alfonso fue luego que estava en comedio, e esta fue la verdad. Mas porque vos non [*sic*, omit?] queremos contar aqui conplidamente la estoria del rey don Sancho assi como la cuentan los joglares, dexaremos aqui de contarla assi como la cuentan el arçobispo e los otros sabios' (fol. 90.c–d; after *PCG*, p. 498.b.7). 'Mas esto, comoquier que lo cuentan asi los joglares, non fue asi verdad. Ca fallamos en las estorias verdaderas que . . .' (fol. 93d; after *PCG*, p. 502.a.29). 'Mas esto non fue assi nin es de creer . . . pero quesimos lo poner aqui porque ffallamos que lo cuentan assi algunos, e por que escoja cada uno aquello que le semeja que es mas con guisa e mas con verdad' (fol. 106b; *PCG*, Chapter 840 rearranged). The identity of 'don Pedro Márquez, Cardenal de Santiago' and the extent and nature of his 'estoria', referred to in the first of these quotations and in one other place in this part of the *CVR* (as 'Pero Marcos', fol. 89c) are uncertain.

22. For the 'estoria' as *HR*, see below, Section IV, and note 28. 'Estoria' was the term used by Alfonso X for his history of Spain, see Chapter 2, II, *A*. See its use in the quotations in the preceding note. There is a brief study of its use in the *PCG* in, L. Chalon, 'De quelques vocables utilisés par la *PCG de España*', *MA*, 77 (1971), 79–84.

23. For 'estoria' in the first 'cantar' of the *PMC* in the *PCG*, see p. 527.a.18–19 and 42–43, p. 529.a.1–4, p. 530.b.42–44, p. 531.b.29–32 and 42–44, p. 533.b.19–20. It is easy to find in the 'refundición' in the *PCG*, and in the *Particular*. It also appears several times in the *Leyenda de Cardeña* chapters. In the *CRC* especially, the phrase 'cuenta la estoria' is often used in the middle of chapters to introduce unusual or amazing things. MSS B.N. 8817, 1347, and 10210 of the *CRC* seem to use it especially often.

24. For examples, see *PCG*, p. 527.a.25, p. 530.a.37–40, p. 531.a.7 and b.21, etc.; later p. 593.a.27, p. 602.b.50, p. 606.b.51, etc.; *Particular*, fols xxxi–xxxii, etc. For the range of vocabulary, compare *PMC*, ll. 899, 1310, 1603. In the reigns of Fernando I and Sancho II, we find more variety than in the prosification of the *PMC*: for example, 'Agora sabed aqui los que esta estoria oydes' (fol. 75a; *Reliquias*, p. 244,), 'assi como avemos contado . . . adelante lo contaremos . . . como lo avemos prometido' (fol. 103b); see also the quotations in note 21. For more general consideration of oral–aural words in medieval texts, see Chalon, 'De quelques vocables'; H. J. Chaytor, *From Script to Print* (Cambridge, 1945); G. B. Gybbon-Monypennny, 'The Spanish *Mester de Clerecía* and its Intended Public', in *Medieval Miscellany presented to Eugène Vinaver* (Manchester, 1965), pp. 230–44; M. Tyss-

ens, 'Le jongleur et l'écrit', in *Mélanges offerts à René Crozet*, I (Poitiers, 1966), pp. 685–95; Pidal, *Poesía juglaresca*.

25. On Ben Alcama's history, see Pidal, *EDC*, pp. 886–906; Lévi Provençal, 'La toma de Valencia'. Chapter 26 of the *CVR* begins: 'Las primeras cosas que movieron guerra por que Valençia fue perdida fue . . .' (fol. 126r; see *PCG*, p. 547.b.45–47). This seems like the beginning of a source or of a new volume perhaps of a source, in this case Arabic. There is a detailed list of sources for each chapter of the *PCG*, see especially *PCG*, pp. clxxiv–cxci, but the *CVR* and *PCG* coincide for Chapters 849–63 only (see note 17).

26. There are more than twenty-nine folios of N between the end of the first 'cantar' and the end of the siege of Valencia, where the *PMC* again becomes the principal source (fols 122a–151d). More than half of these are devoted to the deeds of the Cid, mainly to his prolonged campaign to capture Valencia (fols 122a–23a, 124c–25c, 138c–151d). Parts of these folios which seem to use the *PMC* are transcribed in Appendix B, along with the chapter headings of the whole section of the chronicle.

27. El Toledano names Búcar in the context of a battle before the capture of Valencia (see Chapter 2, I, *B*, and note 5). The *Linaje* relates the death of fourteen Moorish kings in a battle, also before the capture of Valencia (see Chapter 1, II, *E*). The name 'Cuarte' by which this battle has come to be known is from a modern Valencian name for part of their city walls compared with the *HR* and the chronicles; see Pidal, *CMC*, II, 813, 879–82. Chalon, *L'Histoire*, p. 258, fails to notice the use of the *HR* as a source in this episode.

28. Pidal, *La CG Discurso*, p. 53, quotes an example of amplification of el Toledano's Latin by the *PCG*: 'obiit' becomes 'adoleçio et fino'.

29. Russell, 'San Pedro de Cardeña and the Heroic History of the Cid', suggests that the *CVR*'s 'estoria' was a lost monastic work, but there seems no evidence for this in the *CVR*. In the *PCG*, on the other hand, the interpolated text of the Cid's life from the siege of Valencia onwards talks of the 'estoria que conpuso Abenalfarax' (*PCG*, p. 633.a.24–25), which may well be of monastic origin, but of which there is no trace in the *CVR*. The *CRC* talks of the same source too: 'la hystoria que compuso Abenalfange' (*Particular*, fol. xciid). On this 'estoria del Cid' often identified with the *Leyenda de Cardeña* see Chapter 2, II, *B*, ii, and note 31. Russell, 'San Pedro de Cardeña', p. 74, and Michael, *PMC*, p. 309, note to l. 3726, suggest the end of the extant *PMC* is truncated because of the influence of this monastic 'estoria'. It seems, however, that the *CVR*, or its source, knew the *PMC* with an ending like that of the extant manuscript, and the *CVR* shows no sign of any influence of an 'estoria', except of the *HR*.

30. The idea that there lies behind the *CVR* an 'abreviación perdida' of an Alphonsine original compilation, a theory instigated by Pidal, *Catálogo* (1918), and revived by Chalon, *L'Histoire*, pp. 256–76, is something of a red herring. *PCG* 1289 text is admittedly an expanded version of its sources. The 'normal version', of which the *PCG* is an expansion, may well be at the root of the *CVR*; but it is wrong to think of the 'normal version' as an abbreviation of anything else, or of the *CVR* as an abbreviation of it.

CHAPTER 4

1. On the *PMC* and the chronicles, see Pidal, 'El *Poema del Cid* y las crónicas generales' and *CMC*, particularly the notes to his critical edition; A. Coester, 'Compression in the *PMC*', *RH*, 15 (1906), 98–211; Lang 'Contributions'; Catalán, 'Crónicas generales'; Horrent, 'Notes de critique textuelle'; Smith, *PMC*, pp. 172–76; and, from a different viewpoint, Thomas Montgomery, 'The *PMC*: Oral Art in Transition', in *'Mio Cid' Studies*, pp. 91–112.

2. See A. Badía Margarit, 'Dos tipos de lengua cara a cara', in *Studia philologica. Homenaje ofrecido a Dámaso Alonso*, I (M., 1960), 115–39, 'La frase de la *PCG*', *RFE*, 42 (1958–59), 179–210, 'Los *Monumenta Germaniae Historica* y la *PCG* de Alfonso el Sabio', *AS*, 16 (1962), 69–75; Pidal, *La CG Discurso*; F. Lázaro Carreter, 'Sobre el *modus interpretandi* alfonsí', *Ibérida*, 6 (1961), 97–114; E. von Richthofen, 'Tradicionalismo, individualismo y positivismo en el estudio de la épica y la novela primitivas', *Prohemio*, 1 (1970), 397–435; Morris, 'Medieval Spanish Epic Style'. On the style and language of other Alphonsine works, see A. G. Solalinde, 'Intervención de Alfonso X'; María Rosa Lida de Malkiel, 'La *GE*: notas literarias y filológicas', *RPh*, 12 (1958–59), 111–42, and *RPh*, 13 (1959–60), 1–30; G. Menéndez Pidal, 'Como trabajaron'; Catalán, 'El taller historiográfico'; S. L. Hartman, 'Alfonso el Sabio and the Varieties of Verb Grammar', *HBalt*, 57 (1974), 48–55. See also the introductory study in Grismer, *Crónica Abreviada*.

3. The style and language of the *CVR* have been distinguished from that of the *PCG* by their comparative brevity and lack of rhetorical amplification. Pidal's theories of an 'abreviación

170

perdida' and 'versión vulgar' of the *EE* reflect this view. See Pidal on the chronicles in *Leyenda*, pp. 67–71, and later studies. See, on the *CVR*, Lang, 'Contributions', and Babbitt *La CVR*; see also Chapter 2, II, *A–C*, and notes.

4. Some of the more important studies on the style and language of the *PMC* are: Pidal, *CMC*, I and II; E. de Chasca, *El arte juglaresco en el 'CMC'*, which is an expanded version of *Estructura y forma en el 'PMC'* (Iowa, 1955); de Chasca, *Registro de fórmulas verbales en el 'CMC'* (Iowa, 1968); S. Gilman, *Tiempos y formas temporales en el 'PMC'*; R. Hamilton, 'Epic Epithets in the *PMC*'; Smith, *PMC*, pp. xliv–lx; L. H. Allen, 'A Structural Analysis of the Epic Style of the *Cid*', in *Structural Studies on Spanish Themes*, edited by H. R. Kahane and A. Pietrangeli (Salamanca, 1959), pp. 341–414.

5. The section from the accession of Fernando I to the throne of León until the beginning of the partition scenes (fols 71r–81r) has less than four per cent direct speech. The partition scenes themselves (fols 81r–87r) have forty per cent. The scenes at the siege of Zamora (fols 97r–104v) have over forty per cent. The figures for the prosification of the *PMC* in the *PCG* are interesting: for the first 'cantar' (1289 text) thirty-one per cent, for the second and third (in the Cidian interpolation, henceforth *PCG Refundición*) twenty-three and twenty-nine per cent respectively. The figures for the chronicle texts are approximate owing to the difficulties of counting lines precisely (chapter headings are excluded, initials included as one line), but the figures are so different for poetic sources and non-poetic sources that minor statistical inconsistencies could not alter the balance.

6. See Dámaso Alonso, 'El anuncio del estilo directo en el *PMC* y en la épica francesa', in *Mélanges . . . Lejeune*, I (Gembloux, 1969), 379–93; Smith, *PMC*, p. liii; de Chasca, *El arte juglaresco*, pp. 213–15.

7. Compare, however, *PCG*, p. 527.a.28–29. Omission of introductory words to speech is a feature of the Spanish ballads. The repetition of 'dixo' as an introduction can be seen, for example, in the prose version of the 'partición de los reinos' (e.g. *Reliquias*, pp. 252–55).

8. On word order in the *PMC*, see Pidal, *CMC*, I, 398–420; F. Hanssen, 'La colocación del verbo en el *PMC*', *BH*, 14 (1912), 47–59. More generally, see H. Ramsden, *Weak-Pronoun Position in the Early Romance Languages* (Manchester, 1963).

9. Examples of the types of inversion listed may easily be found in non-epic sections: see in the *CVR*, for example, 'que siete años la tovo çercada' (fol. 75a), 'lo que en dubda es' (fol. 79c); see also *PCG*, p. 22, for further examples. Type 2 on my list is, in fact, occasionally found in modern Spanish, although it is not normal. I am grateful to John England of the University of Sheffield for pointing this out to me.

10. Other examples of such parallel word order: fol. 121b, ll. 990; fol. 159c–d, ll. 3146–47; fol. 159d, l. 3665; fol. 159a, l. 2910; fol. 115b, l. 451; fol. 120c–d, l. 948; fol. 153b, l. 1457; fol. 116d, ll. 628–29; fol. 154b, l. 1849.

11. For other examples, see fol. 153a, l. 1423; fol. 155b, l. 2089; fol. 158c, l. 2781; fol. 159a, l. 3119; fol. 160b, l. 3279; fol. 160c, l. 3309; fol. 160c, l. 3315; fol. 161b, l. 3465.

12. Inversions may be found in other epic sections of the chronicles; see *Reliquias*, pp. 246.10–11, 248.17, 255.2: *PCG*, pp. 506.b.8–9, 511.a.3–4, 519.b.9 and 18–19, etc.

13. The term 'pairs' is from Smith, *PMC*, pp. xlviii–xlix; as 'doubles' they are discussed in Morris, 'Medieval Spanish Epic Style', Chapter 5; as 'elementos geminales' in de Chasca, *El arte juglaresco*, Chapter 10; most recently, see Smith, *Estudios cidianos*, Chapter 7.

14. See Badía Margarit, 'La frase', where he cites the translation 'fidem' to 'esfuerço e coraçon'; Pidal, *La CG Discurso*, quotes the translation of el Toledano's 'obiit' to 'adoleçio et fino'; see Lázaro Carreter, 'Sobre el *modus interpretandi*'; Lida, 'La *GE*: notas'.

15. Those pairs, that is, which are found in chronicle and poem. Many pairs in the poem are, no doubt, individual creations of the poet. The origins of popular pair phrases may have deep roots: see Smith, *Estudios cidianos*, where it is suggested that the use of pairs has origins in such necessities as precise religious, social, and legal terminology.

16. There are pairs in virtually all the texts studied in the preparation of this dissertation. For the *HR*, see Chapter 1, II, *B*. There are some interesting examples among the number of well over one hundred pairs in the *CSZ* in the *PCG* (normally found also in the *CSZ* in the *CVR*): 'oro et plata' (pp. 495.b, 496.a), 'moros et cristianos' (pp. 496.a (twice), 497.a, 506.a), 'cavalleros et peones' (pp. 499.b, 505.b), etc. Amongst some new pairs here the two most frequent are: 'por aver o por camio' (pp. 506.a, 506.b, 507.a, 507.b (twice), 508.a), 'bueno et leal' (pp. 497.b, 500.a, 508.a, 508.b, 509.b, 512.b (twice)); see also Diego Ordóñez's challenge to the people of Zamora (*PCG*, p. 513.b, *CVR*, fol. 104c). Rhetorical pairs, however, dominate all parts of the *CVR* and the *PCG*. For pairs in other medieval Spanish texts, see: Smith, *Estudios cidianos*; J. Artiles, *Los recursos literarios de Berceo* (M., 1964), pp. 110–18; Roger M. Walker, *Tradition and Technique in 'El Libro del Cavallero Zifar'* (London, 1974), Chapter 6.

17. On phrases with the past participle, see Smith, *PMC*, p. xlvii; on the gerund, see S. Lyer, 'La Syntaxe du gérondif dans le *Poema del Cid*', *RFE*, 19 (1932), 1–46.
18. Other examples of the use of the gerund are: *CVR*, fols 115b, 116c–d, 117c–d, 156c, 160d, 161a, 161c; *PMC*, ll. 762, 773, 920, 1287, 1712, 1749, 2032, 2153, 2676, 2967, 3174, 3205, 3482. Other parts of the chronicles tend to provide more expressions using past participles. The *PCG* 1289 text in its prose version of the first 'cantar' adds 'Dichas estas razones' to what is in the *CVR* (*PCG*, p. 533.a.11; *CVR*, fol. 120d), and later 'Despues desto' (fol. 121c) becomes 'Esto librado alli desta guisa que dicho es' (p. 533.b.25). More striking expressions can be seen in the *Refundición* in the *PCG*: see pp. 602.a.44–45, 616.b.18–19, 627.a.17, 631.a.10.
19. *Admiratio* phrases based on '¿Quién podría . . . ?' abound in the *Refundición* in the *PCG* and in the *CRC* in the *Particular*, particularly with reference to emotions; see *PCG*, pp. 595.b.40, 602.b.15, 606.a.43, etc.; *Particular*, fols lxixd, lxxxd, lxxxviib, etc. No examples have been noted in other chronicle sections, however. See Smith, *PMC*, p. 121, note to l. 699.
20. A similar expression with 'omne' can be seen in *Reliquias*, p. 245.14–15, in the partition scenes, where another phrase is also used: 'el mayor llanto del mundo' (p. 247.15).
21. There are two examples of clear *oppositum* in the *CSZ*: *PCG*, p. 500.b.37–38, *CVR*, fol. 92c; *PCG*, p. 513.a.29–30, *CVR*, fol. 104a. The device is frequent in the *Refundición*, with several examples repeated in the *Particular*: e.g. p. 600.b.27–28, fol. lxxiib; p. 602.a.30–31, fol. lxxiib; pp. 616.a.17–19, 620.b.6–7, 625.b.21–22, fol. lxxxviiia.
22. Proverbial expressions may be seen in other poetic sections; see *Reliquias*, p. 249.17; *PCG*, p. 507.a.19, *CVR*, fol. 98a; p. 510.a.2–3, fol. 100c. The second of the two examples in the *CSZ* prosification underlines the typical medieval respect for the *sententia* by referring to 'lo que dixo el sabio' before stating the proverb.
23. That is assonance words preserved where the *CVR* is prosifying the appropriate lines of the poem. The version of the first 'cantar' found in the *PCG* keeps approximately sixteen per cent of the assonances, showing the rather fuller use made of the poem there.
24. Most editors emend the line to place 'fue' as the assonance word; 'fue' is omited by the *CVR*. See Pidal, *CMC*, p. 1054, note, Smith, *PMC*, p. 24.
25. Pairs of assonances in the first 'cantar' include: fol. 114a, ll. 11–12; fol. 115a, ll. 415–16; fol. 118b, ll. 816–17; fol. 118d, ll. 852–53; fol. 120d, ll. 951–52. The twelve words in Alfonso's speech are: 'Miñaya, graçia, semanas, ganançia, cavalgada, batalla, Miñaya, graçia, graçia, nada, graçia, armas, vayan'; see *PMC*, ll. 882–83–84–85–87–88, when the *PMC* changes assonance. The *PCG* 1289 text preserves more series of assonances; see in *PCG*, pp. 523.a–534.b; *PMC*, ll. 525–27, 553–56, 583–86, 673–77, 701–04, 822–25, 1020–22.
26. Pairs of assonances in the *CVR* are: fol. 149c, ll. 1127–28; fol. 151d, ll. 1224–25; fol. 153c, ll. 1613–14; fol. 154c, ll. 1862–63; fol. 154d, ll. 1894–95. The misleading words in the Cid's speech are: 'mar, llegastes, presentar, estad, ayades, traen' (fol. 154a; compare ll. 1647–56).
27. For *PMC*, ll. 3105–485, the court scenes, the number of assonances preserved in the *CVR* jumps to approximately twenty per cent. There are seventeen pairs of assonances which have been noted in the prosification of the final 'cantar' as a whole; fifteen are in the above lines. See, for example, fol. 159c, ll. 3929–30; fol. 159d, ll. 3186–87; fol. 160b, ll. 3272–73; fol. 160c, ll. 3327–28; fol. 160d, ll. 3383–84; fol. 161b, ll. 3454–55. For examples of misleading words of the same assonance as the poem, in the third 'cantar', see fol. 161a–b (ll. 3392–421), where thirteen words in *ó* appear, only five of which are assonances of the poem (ll. 3396–97, 3407–18–21).
28. Dyer, '*El PMC*', Chapter 6, takes a different view, seeking out every possible assonance word in the *CVR* and seeing their origin in another version of the *PMC*. I see no justification for this approach. The situation is different in the case of other chronicles, where poetic rhythms have not been so thoroughly destroyed as in the *CVR*. Thus, Pidal's suggestions for *PMC*, ll. 14–15 and 1615–16 (see *CMC*, III, 1026, 1086) are difficult to support, while his creation of the Infantes de Lara story from other texts (see *Leyenda*, pp. 421–32, *Reliquias*, pp. 199–239) is somewhat more convincing. His lines before the start of his critical edition of the *PMC* have some credibility too, but not as part of the original of the extant *PMC*. They would be from a later version of the whole poem, which is used in the *CRC*; see *CMC*, III, 1025, and Chapter 2, II, *D*, below.
29. Epithets in the *PMC* are studied in de Chasca, *El arte juglaresco*, Chapter 9; R. Hamilton, 'Epic Epithets in the *PMC*'; Ian Michael, 'A Comparison of the Use of Epic Epithets in the *PMC* and the *Libro de Alexandre*', *BHS*, 38 (1961), 32–41; R. H. Webber, 'Un aspecto estilístico del *PMC*', *AEM*, 2 (1965), 485–96; R. L. Hathaway, 'The Art of the Epic Epithets in the *CMC*', *HR*, 42 (1974), 311–21. See also Deyermond, *Epic Poetry and the Clergy*, pp. 163–65.

30. Epithets in the *PCG* 1289 text are like those in the *CVR*. In the *Refundición*, however, several appear, attached to new characters: e.g. 'Martin Ferrandez, natural de Burgos' (p. 610.a.40–41), 'Venito Perez su repostero mayor el qual era natural de Sigueça' (p. 615.b.27–28); and others based on the formula 'que poblo' (e.g. p. 615.a; see also *Particular*, fol. lxxxi). In the prose *CSZ*, there are not many examples, but a few are of note: e.g. 'Alvar Hannez, un cavallero muy bueno que era sobrino del Çid' (*PCG*, p. 498.b.19–21; see *CVR*, fol. 91a), 'el conde don Garçia de Cabra . . . el crespo de Grannon' (p. 512.a.21–23; *CVR*, fol. 102d).

31. According to Allen, 'A Structural Analysis', 'Campeador' is used 187 times in the *PMC*, compared to 454 appearances of 'Cid'. In all parts of the *CVR*, and in other vernacular chronicles, 'el Cid' is the normal name used, whatever the source, and 'Ruy Díaz' is frequent. 'Campeador' appears once in the *CSZ*, at Golpejera (*PCG*, p. 502.b.31–32; *CVR*, fol. 94b), and no less than four times in *CVR*, fols 88c–89a, two short chapters which have no equivalent in the *PCG*. In the *PCG Refundición*, it is found on over a dozen occasions, e.g. pp. 606.a.47, 607.a.21–22, 610.b.18, 25, and 51, 623.a.25 and b.5–6.

32. Thus, all the epithets referring to the Cid's good fortune are lost in the *CVR*. The *PCG* 1289 text does offer 'el que era echado de Castiella' (p. 532.b.44–45; compare l. 955; not in the *CVR*). The *CSZ* offers 'Çide, el bien aventurado' (*CVR*, fol. 93b; *PCG*, p. 501.b.40). The *PCG Refundición* is most 'poetic', for, apart from 'el Çid de Bivar', used scornfully by the Infantes de Carrión (p. 609.a.29–30; *Particular*, fol. lxxviib), it has 'el que en buena ora nasçio' (p. 600.b.20–21), and in the *Leyenda de Cardeña* section 'Çid Ruy Diaz el Campeador, el meior cristiano nin mas honrrado que çinxo espada nin cavalgo cavallo de mill annos aca' (p. 628.b.12–15; *Particular*, fol. xca).

33. 'Mio Çid' is comparatively frequent in the *CSZ*: e.g. *PCG*, pp. 501.b.34–35, 502.a.24–25, 503.a.21–22, 519.a.22 and 27; *CVR*, fols 88c, 89b, 94b. It is, however, rare in the *PCG Refundición*: see pp. 599.b.27, 602.a.37.

34. See C. C. Smith and J. Morris, 'On Physical Phrases in Old Spanish Epic and Other Texts', *PLPLS Literary and Historical Section*, 12 (1967), 129–90, and on performance, D. Alonso, 'Estilo y creación en el *PMC*', in *Ensayos sobre poesía española* (Buenos Aires, 1944), pp. 69–111.

35. See Smith and Morris, 'Physical Phrases', pp. 169–74; for the poem, see Pidal, *CMC*, II, 593–94. The word does not have a wide range of meaning in the *CVR*. It appears fairly often in the *CSZ* with some extra contexts, in addition to those found in the *CVR*: e.g. p. 500.a.30–32 (not in *CVR*, fol. 92a); in the *PCG Refundición*, it also has a varied range: e.g. pp. 599.a.38–40, 601.a.16, 605.a.7–8, 608.a.42–43.

36. See *Reliquias*, pp. 244, 246, 247, for example: the *CSZ* in the *PCG* has ten references to kissing the hand; the *PCG Refundición* has at least fourteen. See Smith and Morris, 'Physical Phrases', pp. 139–49; Pidal, *CMC*, II, 506–09. The kissing of the hand was presumably still a recognized sign of humility for the chroniclers, but it would not normally appear in an historical text (though see *HR*, 34).

37. References to the hand are frequent in the other epic parts of the chronicles; see examples from the *CSZ* in *PCG*, p. 497.b.45–46, *CVR*, fol. 90b; p. 500.a.38–39, fol. 92a; p. 513.a.38–39, fol. 104b; p. 516.a.31, fol. 107b; examples from the *PCG Refundición* are pp. 610.b.10, 618.a.43–44, 618.b.6–8, 623.b.34. See *Particular*, passim.

38. See Pidal, *CMC*, II, 494–99, Adiciones, II, 1213–14; Smith and Morris, 'Physical Phrases', pp. 161–62.

39. For the original oath, see fol. 152a where the *CVR* adds 'cabello', perhaps misreading the poem, ll. 1238–41. For the clutching of the beard and the swearing by it, see fol. 157c, l. 2476; fol. 158d, ll. 2829–32; fol. 159d, ll. 3185–86; and in the exchange of insults, fol. 160b, ll. 3270–90. The *CVR* also refers to the pulling of Count García's beard in the account of the battle of Cabra, adding it to the main source; the *HR*; see *CMC*, III, 1023; *CVR*, fol. 113b.

40. In the chronicles studied, the Cid's beard does not appear outside the period covered by the *PMC*. In the *PCG Refundición*, its power is exaggerated, so that the sight of it can frighten; see pp. 618.b.6–8, 621.b.34. In the *Leyenda de Cardeña*, an attempt to pull it causes a miracle; see p. 642.b.

41. On 'cuerpo', see Smith and Morris, 'Physical Phrases', pp. 164–68, and on tautological verb–noun expressions, 'Physical Phrases', passim. 'Dezir de la boca' is found in *PCG Refundición*, pp. 605.b.9, 620.a.49, 621.a.2–3. 'Llorar de los ojos' is found in *PMC*, ll. 1, 18, 265, 277, 370, etc.; and also in the *CSZ*, *PCG*, p. 507.b.2, *CVR*, fol. 98c; p. 516.b.16, fol. 107b; and *PCG Refundición*, pp. 594.b.11, 611.a.14–15.

42. It has proved impossible to see a pattern in the chroniclers' use of 'divine' phrases. As well as omitting many references, the *CVR* also ignores prayers by the Cid (ll. 52–54, 215–25), Ximena (239–41, 327–65), and Alvar Fáñez (1394–95). Other 'poetic' parts of the chronicles

have phrases similar to the *CVR*. The *PCG Refundición* uses them frequently and more wordily; e.g. pp. 597.a.41–45, 612.a.12–15, 613.a.37–38, 620.a.37–38. See also the *Particular*.

43.   The *PCG* 1289 text has a little more of the first 'cantar' in it than the *CVR* has, but the differences are small. Its use of the style and language of the *PMC* is substantially the same The prose *CSZ* occasionally seems to have more poetic detail than the prose *PMC* (see notes 16, 30, 32, 33, 35, 41). The amount of detail is not very substantial, but it suggests that the *CSZ* was prosified less thoroughly than the *PMC*. The *PCG Refundición* has some striking poetic details as well as rhetorical amplification (see notes 30, 31, 32, 36, 41). There must have been an original poetic source behind it, but its total content is uncertain (see Chapter 2, note 31). Even in these cases, however, the reconstitution of poetic lines from the prose is not a feasible proposition. If lines were created, they are unlikely to be the same as those of the poetic original.

CHAPTER 5

1.   Studies of the *PMC* and the *CVR* are listed in Chapter 4, note 1. The section of the *PMC* most severely reduced in the *CVR* is from the opening lines until the Cid's departure from Cardeña (ll. 1–390; fol. 114a–d). Then, the remainder of the first 'cantar' is prosified at proportionately greater length than the other two 'cantares'. For a crude comparison, the third 'cantar', of 1446 lines of poetry, is prosified in six and a half folios of the *CVR*; the final 695 lines of the first 'cantar' take up more than seven folios.

2.   Coester, 'Compression in the *PMC*', and Dyer '*El PMC*', for example, see in the additions of the chronicles a longer form of the poem, which was quite different from the extant *PMC*. Pidal, of course used the chronicles in his critical edition, *CMC*, III, 1024–164. For additions of fact to the surviving poem, see particularly II, *C*, below. For a consideration of changes introduced by chroniclers, see Pattison, 'The "Afrenta de Corpes"'.

3.   It must be remembered that the extant *PMC* is in a MS of a date later than the date of composition of the *CVR*. There are, therefore, two lines of manuscript transmission in which possible copyist's errors might have occurred, MSS of the poem and MSS of the chronicle. The closeness of the *PMC* and the *CVR* in details is, then, all the more remarkable. The *CVR* is represented by MS N, of course. Other MSS, such as Ll, are not as reliable as it is; see Appendixes A and B.

4.   For Pidal's comments, see 'El *PdelC* y las crónicas generales', p 459. The information does not seem likely to be from an original of the *HR* either, except that later texts have neither the names nor any other details from the *HR*; see *PCG Refundición*, pp. 596–98, *Particular*, fols lxviii–lxx, where Búcar appears in a new role.

5.   Pidal, *CMC*, III, 1137–38, ingeniously fits the extra names into his poem. The Cid's daughters and the Infantes de Carrión are also named in the *CVR* near the start of the *CSZ*, in a passage not in the *PCG*: 'ovo el Çid . . . dos fijas doña Elvira e doña Sol que fueron despues casadas con Ferrand Gonçalez e Diego Gonçalez, condes de Carrion' (fol. 89b–c).

6.   For other omissions, see fol. 115b, ll. 442–43; fol. 154a, l. 1719; fol. 155a, ll. 1991–99; fol. 159c, ll. 3063–71. The *PCG* 1289 text names the money-lenders of Burgos, 'Rachel et Bipdas' (p. 523.b.44), but otherwise has the same names as the *CVR*. Later versions have different names and different characters, especially for the second half of the story in the *PMC*.

7.   See Pidal, *CMC*, I, 34–76; J. Horrent, 'Localisation du *CMC*', *Mélanges . . . Crozet*, I (Poitiers, 1966), 609–15; P. E. Russell, 'Where was Alcocer?', in *Homenaje ofrecido a J. A. Van Praag* (Amsterdam, 1956), pp. 101–07; M. Criado de Val, 'Geografía, toponimia e itinerarios del *CMC*', *ZRP*, 86 (1970), 83–107; Ian Michael, 'Geographical Problems in the *PMC*: I. The Exile Route', in *Medieval Hispanic Studies . . . Hamilton*, pp. 117–28, and '. . . II. The Corpes Route', in '*Mio Cid' Studies*, pp. 83–89. The edition 'corrected' by use of the *PMC* is Pidal's *PCG*, where the actual forms of the 1289 MS are emended in many cases and replaced in others; e.g. p. 526a–b, see notes as well as asterisked forms.

8.   In *CVR*, N, at least. 'Castrejon' is the form adopted in J, Ll, *PCG* and in later texts. 'Torpes' is used for 'Corpes' once in J, Ll (see N, fol. 157d), and is found in later texts, e.g. *Particular*, fols lxxvi ff. *PCG* 1289 MS has 'Alcaçar' for Alcocer, emended in Pidal's edition.

9.   N is consistently the best MS for these names, except that J does have 'Teca' as in the *PMC*; see footnotes to Appendix B. The *PCG* 1289 text is of variable accuracy: for example, it has 'Theca' but also 'Angrita', 'Cenqua' (for 'Çetina') (pp. 526–27, etc.) The *PCG Refundición* is difficult to compare with the *CVR*. It does have 'Xurquera' for 'Gujera' (p. 598.a.26–27), but its own itineraries elsewhere, e.g. p. 608b. The *Particular* is similar, see fol. lxxviia. The

name of the town Teruel appears with minor variations in the *PMC*, *CVR* and *PCG* 1289 text. Pidal believed this was an error in the MS of the *PMC* (*CMC*, II, 864), and emended the name to Terrer in the *PMC* and *PCG* (*PMC*, ll. 571, 585, 625, 632, 773, 842; *PCG*, pp. 526, 527, 529, 530). The *CVR* confirms that the name in both the MSS of the *PMC* was Teruel (fols 116b–18a). The one case of 'Terer' in the MS of the *PMC*, in line 860 (though see the note to the line in *CMC*, III, 965) is part of an omission in *CVR*, fol. 119a, and is represented as 'Theca' in *PCG*, p. 530.a.31. Ubieto, *El CMC y algunos problemas*, pp. 95, 192, argues that Terrer was changed to Teruel by the copyist of the extant *PMC*, c.1350. The presence of the form Teruel in the *CVR* disproves this theory.

10. In the *PCG Refundición*, Alvar Fáñez finds Alfonso VI in Palencia, coming out from Mass (p. 593.b). The first naming of Atienza in the *CVR* leads Pidal to emend the *PMC*, but in a complex way which is hardly justified by the *CVR* (see *CMC*, III, 1040; I, 42).

11. The use of numbers in the *PMC* and their significance is studied in de Chasca, *El arte juglaresco*, pp. 236–66. The *PCG* 1289 text differs over the first number (p. 524.b.1, note), but agrees with the second. The *PCG Refundición* differs over the third (p. 593.b.38), agrees with the fourth (p. 598.a.22), and seems to have no trace of the last one (p. 619.b).

12. The differences of only one Roman numeral between the texts (MMMDC, MMMCC; XX, XXX; VII, VIII) suggest they result from copyists' errors. The *PCG Refundición* has a different number for the first of these examples (p. 592.b.44–46), and no equivalent for the other two sentences (pp. 601, 606).

13. The *PCG* 1289 text specifies the number in Fariz and Galve's army as in the *PMC* (p. 527.a.46). It has two other numbers omitted by the *CVR* (p. 528.a.17, l. 686; p. 528.b.35, l. 723), and the *CVR* has one number not in the *PCG* (fol. 116c, l. 605). The *CVR* has one number of unknown source, the 'siete reyes' killed at the battle with Yucef (fol. 154a; see Chapter 3, IV, and note 4, above).

14. See D. Alonso, 'Estilo y creación en el *PMC*'; E. de Chasca, *El arte juglaresco*, pp. 123–44, and 'The King-Vassal Relationship in the *PMC*', *HR*, 21 (1953), 183–92; G. Correa, 'El tema de la honra en el *PMC*', *HR*, 20 (1952), 185–99; T. Montgomery, 'The Cid and the Count of Barcelona', *HR*, 30 (1962), 1–11; H. Moon, 'Humour in the *PMC*', *HBalt*, 46 (1963), 700–04; P. Salinas, 'El *PMC*, poema de la honra', in *Ensayos de literatura hispánica* (M., 1958), pp. 27–44, and 'La vuelta al esposo: ensayo sobre estructura y sensibilidad en el *CMC*', *Ensayos*, pp. 45–57; Smith, *PMC*, pp. lxvii–lxxiii; Roger M. Walker, 'The Role of the King and the Poet's Intentions in the *PMC*', in *Medieval Hispanic Studies . . . Hamilton*, pp. 257–66.

15. Pidal created an extra line of the poem from the chronicles to express the Cid's confidence: see *CMC*, III, 1026. However, there is no sign of the extant lines 13–14 of the *PMC* in the *CVR* (or *PCG*, p. 523.b.25), and the conclusion must be that the Cid's reaction has been changed entirely, by the chronicle. For different interpretations of line 14, see Miguel Garci Gómez, *'Mio Cid': estudios de endocrítica* (M., 1975), pp. 58–61; Michael, *PMC*, p. 77.

16. This episode is one place in which the *CVR* and the *PCG* 1289 text are quite different. In the *PCG*, although the episode is still shorter than in the *PMC*, the plan is the Cid's and he meets the 'mercaderos' as in the *PMC* (pp. 523b–24a). The changes, therefore, are an initiative of the *CVR*. On this episode in the *PMC*, see C. C. Smith, 'Did the Cid Repay the Jews?', *Romania*, 86 (1965), 520–38, and Smith, *PMC*, pp. 115–16. The *PCG Refundición* and the *Particular* have the Cid repay the Jews, with apologies for the deceit; see p. 594.a.32–37, fol. lxviic.

17. The *PCG* is substantially the same as the *CVR* in this episode. On it, see T. Montgomery, 'The Cid and the Count of Barcelona', where Montgomery mentions how the *PCG* changes the tone of the episode.

18. Moderation is not, of course, associated with the epic stories about the Cid in later chronicles, or indeed in other parts of the *CVR*. But there is a progression from the verisimilitude of the character portrayed in the poem, through the less credible features that the chroniclers create in the prosification of the *PMC*, to the obviously incredible features of other tales, in which it is action, not characters, that dominates. For suggested reasons for changes made by chroniclers, see Pattison, 'The "Afrenta de Corpes"', pp. 138–39.

19. In the *PCG* 1289 text, the intervention of the family is the same as in the *CVR*. In the *PCG Refundición* and in the *Particular*, however, more space is given to the reactions of Ximena especially (Ximena Gómez in the *Particular*), and of the daughters, although the tone is nothing like that of the *PMC*. See, for example, *PCG*, pp. 594.b–95.b, 596.a–b, 600.a, 607.b, etc.; *Particular*, fols lxviid–xviiib, lxviiid–lxixa, lxxia, etc.

20. The *PCG* 1289 text is little different from the *CVR* in its treatment of the Cid's knights. The *PCG Refundición* and the *Particular*, however, have an enormous number of new names and some extra roles for old names in their text, although their characterization is not at all

subtle. Words and actions tend to be brutal and extreme. Important new characters include Ordoño Bermúdez, 'sobrino' of the Cid, who rescues one Infante from a Moor, takes the place of Feliz Muñoz at Corpes, and challenges the wrong Infante at the King's court (*PCG*, pp. 606, 608–12, 620; *Particular*, fols lxxv, lxxvi ff., lxxxv. The *Particular* does not have the mistake over the name of the cowardly Infante); and Fernant Alfonso 'criado del Cid' who takes the Cid's 'escaño' to the court, and is involved in an altercation with García Ordóñez (pp. 615–16; fols lxxxi–lxxxii). They are added to in the *Particular* by Martín Peláez, el asturiano (lxi–lxii, etc.). Increased intervention in the story is given to Ansur González, who becomes adviser to the Infantes in Valencia, and to Pero Bermúdez, who attacks García Ordóñez and ten other counts at Alfonso's court (pp. 604, 606, 621; fols lxxiii–lxxv, lxxxv).

21. Another Moor, Aladraf, is named in the *CVR* in the section corresponding to the lacuna near the beginning of the third 'cantar' (fol. 157a; ll. 2337–38). The name is omitted in the *PCG* and the *Particular* (p. 606; fol. lxxv). When Tamin is named in the *PCG* 1289 text, the chroniclers add a note on other information at their disposal (p. 527.a.42–43).

22. In the *PCG* 1289 text, the references to Moorish activity omitted in the *CVR* are included in detail, see pp. 527a, 528a, 530b, which means that the omissions reflect the particular prejudices of the compilers of the *CVR*.

23. Abengalbón's part in the *CVR* is especially reduced because he so often appears in connection with the Cid's family (see II, *B*, above). The *PCG Refundición* and the *Particular* give more space to him and to his generosity, but omit the Infantes' scheming against his life (pp. 595a–96c, 608b, 613b–14b; fols lxviii, lxxvii, lxxx). A Moslem character given space in these later texts is the messenger of the Sultan of Persia; the Orient provides the Cid's embalming fluid (pp. 627–28; fols lxxxix–xc). Another is the supposed author, Alhuacaxi, whom the Cid coverts to Christianity as Gil Díaz (p. 632a–c; fol. xcii, Alfaxati).

24. Pidal, and other scholars, believed that other material must have come from the older poetic manuscript, but given the closeness of the *CVR* to the extant *PMC* shown in the current chapter, given the frequent existence of misleading words of parallel assonance to the poem (see Chapter 4, II, *A*), and given the chroniclers ability to create additions themselves (see below), the bases for believing in and identifying such material are very shaky. For additions by Pidal, see his critical edition, *CMC*, III, 1024–164; see also Smith *PMC*, p. 174–76; Dyer, '*Él PMC*', Chapter 6 and Appendix 4.

25. There are further oddities surrounding this episode, even in the *PMC*. The first blows granted to the Infantes in the lacuna and referred to later by Pero Bermúdez (l. 3317), are granted by the Cid to Bishop Jerónimo (fol. 157b; ll. 2370–82). The pre-battle skirmish, which Fernando is involved in is strange, too, when the real battle does not begin until much later (fol. 157b; l. 2386). In the *PCG Refundición*, there is confusion over which Infante ran from the Moor; Fernando flees, but Diego is accused (see note 20; compare the *PCG* MS F). In the *Particular*, Diego has taken over in both places. In both texts, the name of the Moor is omitted, but the display of cowardice has been moved to the battle itself. In both texts too, the scene of the Cid and Búcar's messenger is considerably expanded, and the messenger is given a name (pp. 604–05; fol. lxxiiii). On the lacuna, see Pidal *CMC*, III, 1113–14; Smith, *PMC*, p. 72.

26. There is not enough material in the *CVR* to fill the folio that seems to be missing, but it can be imagined that poetic descriptions of horse, rider, and audience would have filled out the original. Later texts expand the scene (*PCG*, p. 624; *Particular*, fol. lxxxvii). See Pidal, *CMC*, III, 1156.

27. See Pidal, 'El *PdelC* y las crónicas generales', p. 468, v. 3479, wrongly numbered. Pidal, in this article, lists a number of the additions in the *PCG* and the *CVR*, but by no means all of them. Other examples of similar expansions include: fol. 116c, l. 590; fol. 118c, l. 824; fol. 152c, l. 1332; fol. 158d, l. 2833; fol. 162a–b, l. 3645, etc.

28. Further examples include: fol. 115b, ll. 457–58; fol. 115d, l. 506; fol. 118b–c, ll. 815–19; fol. 151d, ll. 1230–31; fol. 154b, ll. 1803–04; fol. 156c–d, ll. 2305–07; fol. 157b, l. 2380; fol. 161b, l. 3426.

29. Marks of silver for Abbot Sancho (fol. 153a, l. 1422; compare l. 1285), Yuçef's tent for King Alfonso (fol. 154b, ll. 1813–14; fol. 154c, l. 1854; compare ll. 1789–90), Abengalbón's identity (fol. 158c, l. 2647). It would be very hazardous to claim that any of these were omissions from the extant MS of the *PMC*; but see Pidal, 'El *PdelC* y las crónicas generales', and his critical edition in *CMC*, III.

30. Such conclusions are applicable also to the *PCG* 1289 text, where there are a few more additions than in the *CVR*. The *PCG Refundición* is not at all comparable with the *CVR* in this respect, since it is telling a changed story.

31. See also fol. 118a, l. 798; fol. 158d, l. 2829. The Count of Barcelona's absurd reaction to the Cid (fol. 122a, l. 1049) has been referred to earlier, see II, *A*.

176

32. For other examples, see fol. 118c, ll. 835–34–32–33; fols 119d–20a, ll. 901–07; fol. 149c, ll. 1148–47–49; fol. 157c, ll. 2431–32–30, fol. 161a, ll. 3407–06; fol. 161b, ll. 3461–59–62. Some of these, and others, are discussed by Pidal, 'El *PdelC* y las crónicas generales', and *CMC*, III.

APPENDIX B

The First 'Cantar'

1. Ll dixoles, 'Amigos, el rey manda salir de su tierra', y que nol dava.
2. J Ferrandez.
3. J, Ll oquier.
4. J, Ll guisa.
5. J vio, Ll torno.
6. Ll tornaredes.
7. J vega, Ll iglesia.
8. Ll [Ça . . . çibdad].
9. J conpaña e que le mandase dar, Ll conpaña para mantenella y quel manlediese . . . manledar.
10. J levase sobre aquellas.
11. Ll [sallio . . . e].
12. J, Ll [marcos].
13. J, Ll [una].
14. Ll pesar.
15. Ll pasar en la tierra de nieves.
16. Ll tierra.
17. J, Ll quisiere buscar.
18. J, Ll Castrejon (passim).
19. Ll [dixo el].
20. J, Ll [en alguna cosa].
21. Ll [su espada en la mano].
22. Ll presa.
23. Ll bien aventurado, plugo.
24. Ll que lidiemos y yo del.
25. J fuertes
26. J, Ll gelo viniesen a conprar
27. Ll conpañas salieron aquel dia de Castrejon a las.
28. Ll Tarançо.
29. J, Ll e llegaron a Uerca e dende Atiença.
30. J Salaror (later Salon).
31. J, Ll prenden.
32. J riendas.
33. Ll [en pos ssi].
34. J, Ll fizo un ademan.
35. J, Ll andemos mas.
36. J entro el Çid e Alvar Fañez entre ellos e el castillo, Ll buelta entre el Çid y Alvar Fañez al castillo.
37. J Teca, Ll Deda.
38. J que le avernia eso mesmo que a ellos, Ll que les vernie eso mesmo que a ellos.
39. Ll que Faris y Galve avien nonbre.
40. Ll con ellos cada dia.
41. Ll [de todas partes].
42. J Amigos, non querades fazer.
43. Ll No.
44. Ll [Nuestro Señor].
45. J, Ll o grand ganançia faremos.
46. Ll las armas.
47. J [dos señas cabdales de los].
48. Ll como buenas armas traya.
49. J [que acabdellavan las conpañas].
50. Ll Minaya . . . Nuño . . . Martin, J Martin Muñoz.
51. Ll Estos todos lidiaron.

52. J, Ll desa yda.
53. Ll [mal].
54. J [en el canpo] aun e.
55. Ll levantando.
56. Ll paso.
57. Ll contra sus.
58. Ll Peruer.
59. Ll y aver en el canpo muy grande ademas.
60. J allegaron, Ll juntaron.
61. Ll llevavan.
62. J les fuera partidos, Ll bien fueran partidos y dando.
63. J, Ll yvan.
64. Ll que de los otros moros ganara.
65. Ll queria trabajar si pudiese.
66. Ll cavallos destos mejores que.
67. J ganadme.
68. Ll en esa tierra vuestra de Burgos.
69. J, Ll lugar.
70. Ll [de Alcoçer].
71. J, Ll quito todas sus conpañas con aquel aver e mandoles.
72. Ll que dizen, 'quien.
73. Ll guiase la su buena andança y que.
74. Ll que saliendo del.
75. J arroyo.
76. Ll Media y a Tribel.
77. Ll Çelsa la del Canal.
78. J, Ll [el].
79. Ll cosa començo a preguntar el rrey a Minaya.
80. J el.
81. J ende a vos, Señor, Ll en don a vos, Señor.
82. Ll [Miñaya].
83. Ll acorrerle.
84. Ll [que teniades].
85. Ll para mio Çid yr.
86. J e las aheredades e los averes.
87. Ll ca por esta merçed nos fazedes y agora.
88. Ll [Albet].
89. Ll [e de Alvar Fanez] e fablaremos.
90. J Çid Ruy Diaz.
91. J [el dia . . . aquel logar].
92. Ll a otro lugar.
93. Ll rey tan buenas nuevas como aquellas plugole.
94. J e sospiro e sonrriose.
95. Ll Alcaniz.
96. Ll años y de la.
97. Ll Almudafar.
98. J reyno asy que sy Çulema.
99. J Remonte Berenguel, Ll Remon Berenguel.
100. Ll presa. Y sono aquella cavalleria.
101. Ll para tras [mañana].
102. Ll en un puerto que dizen Alocat.
103. J, Ll [fechos].
104. Ll e yo en el de su fienança en el torne.
105. J de christianos e de moros.
106. J de.
107. J Remonte, Ll Remont.
108. J de fazer aquello, Ll de fazer lo.
109. j enxêco (sic), Ll exerçito.
110. Ll antes que lleguemos al.
111. Ll fuyran los otros'.
112. J derechamente e ellos fizieronlo asy e firieron muy.
113. J, Ll [e].
114. J, Ll otros e vençio.

115. J tierra, Ll [e mandole guardar muy bien].
116. Ll [de comer muy bien por fazer].
117. J por fazer al conde plazer.
118. Ll oyo.
119. Ll hazienda y salir de vuestra prision. Y si lo non fizierdes, en toda vuestra vida non saldreys ende ni.
120. Ll El conde don Rremon le dixo, 'Comed.
121. Ll dicha.
122. J salvo.
123. Ll el Çid mando como.
124. Ll oyo, ovo gran duelo del, y dixo al conde, 'Bien.
125. J, Ll fuese ya que mas.
126. Ll lo lazeran.
127. J, Ll e comio con aquellos.
128. Ll lo ovo comido.
129. Ll [muy bien].
130. J primero lugar dispidiendose el Çid.

The Second 'Cantar'

1. J [e correr tierra], Ll a correr tierra de Xeria (compare *PMC*, l. 1092).
2. Ll todas las cosas y tierras que dizen de Burriana, J de Burruena (compare *PMC*, ll. 1090–93).
3. J arravales, Ll comarcas (compare *PMC*, ll. 1097–98).
4. J, Ll Çebolla.
5. J Onda, Ll Euda y Almenara.
6. (Compare *PMC*, ll. 1150, 1092).
7. J Monviedro (passim. From this point on, compare *PMC*, ll. 1095–171).
8. J a Abdalcauf e a Ondra, Ll Abdalaçarif e a Ondra.
9. Ll conpañas e a amigos, 'Si nos.
10. Ll todos armados y guisados.
11. Ll faremos todo quanto dezides de buena voluntad quanto vos mandaredes.
12. J Çiguera, Ll Xinguera.
13. J, Ll villa.
14. (Compare *PMC*, ll. 1181–82).
15. (Compare *PMC*, ll. 1187–90).
16. (Compare *PMC*, l. 1199).
17. J, Ll villa.
18. (Compare *PMC*, ll. 1201–04).
19. (Compare *PMC*, ll. 1214–15).
20. J, Ll villa (compare *PMC*, ll. 1209–10).
21. (*CVR* returns to the poem as its principal source, see *PMC*, ll. 1222 ff.).
22. Ll e alcanço.
23. Ll çinquenta.
24. Ll [dezir].
25. Ll vuestros.
26. Ll [e dixole].
27. J, Ll Ruy Diaz Çid.
28. l rruega a vos le perdonedes alguna querella que avedes del.
29. Ll Cadiella.
30. J, Ll cavallos que y gano en.
31. J mucho me sirve mejor que vos.
32. Ll dixo, 'Rrey señor.
33. J, Ll bien e.
34. Ll torne.
35. J vernie en pro.
36. Ll el [casamiento porque non era].
37. J del lugar que.
38. Ll [estonces tres cavalleros al Cid que le].
39. Ll fueronse camino.
40. Ll Nuño.
41. Ll Gustiez, Anton Antolinez.

42. Ll Albarrazin desi a Molana.
43. J, Ll pasaron.
44. Ll Nuño Gustoz.
45. Ll bien tres lugares.
46. J, Ll villa (passim).
47. J veynte e nueve, Ll treynta y nueve.
48. J Yuçef (but later Yuçaf), Ll Yuçaf (passim).
49. J, Ll el Quarto (passim).
50. Ll [vinieron y].
51. Ll fueron.
52. Ll Ximena Gomez.
53. J yre lidiar, Ll yre a lidiar.
54. J Çiguera, Ll Çaguera.
55. J, Ll [don Alfonso].
56. J, Ll batalla que ovo con.
57. J creer.
58. Ll que ave el tanto bien, nos.
59. J ha de algun mal, Ll del gran mal.
60. Ll dixo, 'Yo hize mucho mal al Çid. Ovieron su acuerdo de demandarle las hijas, y haziendome . . .'.
61. Ll pues asi que se venga.
62. Ll [lo que le enbiastes, e grades-].
63. Ll su amor convusco.
64. Ll [non].
65. J, Ll Levad suso, Çid.
66. J oyan.
67. J, Ll Ordoñez.
68. J, Ll casadas e honrradamente e yo quiero que gelas.
69. J tomaron.
70. Ll [muy buenos . . . frenos e] de silla.
71. J Çid Ruy Diaz.
72. Ll dueñas.
73. Ll donovos yo estas dueñas.
74. J la santa, Ll la mandre santa.
75. J donzellas.
76. J mucho.
77. Ll prez.

The Third 'Cantar'

1. Ll Fernan.
2. Ll estrado.
3. J del lugar.
4. Ll frio.
5. Ll rebate.
6. J, Ll E pero que ellos.
7. J profazar, Ll porfazer.
8. J, Ll el Quarto.
9. Ll [las fijas del Çid, mas non a].
10. Ll Nuño Gustoz.
11. Ll enemigo.
12. Ll Fernando (passim with minor variations).
13. J, Ll por yr ferir.
14. J dos dellos.
15. Ll [Alli . . . vençio el Çid].
16. J de me veer nunca mas contigo.
17. J [a poder].
18. J [Despues que Bucar fue muerto].
19. Ll [e mando coger el canpo].
20. Ll [e graçias por quanto bien me as fecho].
21. Ll [Desto que ellos dixieron].
22. (Sic N, Ll) J profazavan.

23. J, Ll Torpes.
24. Ll Tizona e a la otra Colada.
25. J conpaña, Ll cavalleria ca viendo por.
26. Ll [e vio].
27. J, Ll Albarrazin . . . Salon . . . el Axaria.
28. J, Ll pasaron.
29. J, Ll consejo.
30. J, Ll Salon.
31. Ll Corpos.
32. Ll [muy mal].
33. Ll [con la conpaña a].
34. J salio.
35. J [le], Ll lo que ovieran las.
36. Ll [e dixo].
37. Ll mucho por esto.
38. Ll Anton.
39. J e nos [con el], Ll e vos [con el].
40. J [Las dueñas]. Quando las vieron.
41. Ll [que vinien].
42. Ll Nuño Gustiez que le denostase.
43. Ll Nuño Gustiez (passim with minor variations).
44. Ll Rremon.
45. Ll Birvon.
46. Ll Ansier . . . Ansuarez . . . Ansuarez.
47. J [don Pero Ançurez].
48. Ll mas onrra sera agora en mi.
49. J e vestir los pellotes e que, Ll e vestir de suso sobre las armas los pellotes e que.
50. J Remondo, Ll Rremon.
51. Ll agradezco las cortes que hazes por amor de mi.
52. J Cospes, Ll Torpes.
53. J, Ll ya.
54. (Sic) J les, Ll [le].
55. Ll querien.
56. J damos nos por ello, Ll damos nos nada.
57. Ll tengo.
58. J [casados].
59. J, Ll [agora].
60. Ll contra el.
61. Ll so.
62. Ll saliste de miedo del fuera del corral e fuystete meter so la viga.
63. (Sic N, J) Ll parastes.
64. Ll Anton.
65. Ll Asur.
66. J Baratarie, Ll Baratien.
67. Ll entender.
68. Ll vayas a oraçion hazet ni amigo que ayas.
69. J [de Navarra e el otro del infante].
70. J el uno Miarra, Ll Ojarran y el otro Yeñego Yemenez.
71. Ll tomen por sus mujeres a ley e a bendiçion.
72. Ll E digo e si.
73. Ll tales como las que yo digo.
74. J Tomez Pelaez.
75. Ll [cras].
76. J [El rey dixo estonçes al Çid].
77. Ll si.
78. J, Ll quando llegaron a Çocadover, el Çid yendo en.
79. J, Ll Rodrigo, fe que devedes que arremetades.
80. J, Ll tomose.
81. Ll muchos onbres guisados para.
82. Ll trabajen.
83. Ll Anton.
84. Ll de mañana.
85. Ll Anton.

86. Ll bolviosele.
87. Ll Bustoz.
88. (Other matters until the end of the chapter).
89. J, Ll [deste dicho año].
90. J enbargar, Ll menguar.
91. (The chronicle continues with other matters).

BIBLIOGRAPHICAL NOTE

There are a number of items included in the Bibliography following this note, which were published or came to my attention after the completion of the main text and the footnotes to it. The most important of these are discussed briefly below, with reference to the parts of this work to which they are most relevant. They are identified in abbreviated form, fuller details being found in the Bibliography.

Chapter 1, I, *A*. María Eugenia Lacarra, in *El PMC*, produces further evidence in favour of the date of 1207 for the composition of the *PMC*. However, Rafael Lapesa, in 'Sobre el *CMC*', declares objections to some of the arguments previously proposed in favour of that date. The date of 1207, or shortly before, still seems to me to be the likely date of composition of the poem.

Chapter 1, I, *B*. Lacarra, in *El PMC*, and David Hook, in 'On Certain Correspondences', both add substantial evidence in support of the contention that the author of the *PMC* had specialized legal knowledge. Lacarra goes much further in arguing that he could have been a legal expert attached to the household of the important noble family, the Laras. She suggests that the poem was written specifically to praise the Cid as ancestor of the Lara family, and to run down the Cid's enemies as ancestors of the powerful rival family, the Castros. The lack of any overt genealogical references in the *PMC* seems to me to cast some doubt on her case. It is certainly not proven.
   Two articles discuss the possibility of the influence of classical Latin texts on the *PMC*. David Hook, in 'Pedro Bermúdez and the Cid's Standard', suggests that there is a source in Caesar's *De Bello Gallico* for the episode recounted in *PMC*, lines 704–11, while admitting the possibility of independent invention of the tale by the poet. Louis Chalon, in 'Le Poète du *CMC*', offers a detailed rebuttal of Colin Smith's arguments in favour of the use of Sallust as a source by the author of the poem, proposing instead that that episode was independently invented. The importance of parallels with the French epic is more firmly established. David Hook, in 'The Opening Laisse of the *PMC*', notes similarities between the beginning of the *PMC* and part of *Garin Le Loheren*. He also records differences between them, concluding that use of the French work as a direct source is possible, but not certain. Other articles demonstrate parallels between French epic and the *PMC*, and conclude that the latter has been strongly influenced, without arguing for the use of specific texts as sources. Kenneth Adams, in 'Possible French Influence on the Use of the Historic Present', P. E. Russell, in 'El *PMC* como documento de información caminera' and 'La oración de doña Jimena', cite such similarities in use of verbs, in itineraries, and in Jimena's long prayer, but the differences that exist are listed, too, emphasizing the individuality of the Spanish text. I would argue that the influence of French epic which is demonstrable in the *PMC* worked primarily through a Spanish epic tradition. Of course, the author of the poem may have known French and may have heard or read French works, but I

do not think it is necessary to suppose this to be the case in order to explain the similarities.

Meanwhile, Colin Smith has pursued his case in favour of the uniqueness of the *PMC*. In 'La métrica del *PMC*', he suggests that Per Abbat, as author of the *PMC*, invented the written epic genre in Castilian, and invented the metre that he uses, imitating, but not copying the French. All other epics in Spanish, he argues, derive from this invention. I differ from these views for reasons outlined in my original text.

Chapter 1, II, *D*.   Derek Lomax, in 'La fecha de la *Crónica najerense*', produces evidence, which shows that the chronicle was composed after 1174. This brings forward the date of composition by a number of years, and means that the *Najerense* should not be bracketed chronologically with the *CAI*. This change does not, however, affect the essentials of my account of the development of the legend of the Cid.

Chapter 1, II, *E*, note 49.   Tom Drury, in 'Diego Ruiz, Son of the Cid?', reviews the scanty evidence for and against the existence of Diego Ruiz, and decides that it is inconclusive.

Chapter 2, I, *B*, note 9.   Colin Smith, in 'Sobre la difusión del *PMC*', argues that the story of Búcar derives from the *PMC*, which was known in a variant version to those works that relate that Búcar was not killed by the Cid. If I am correct in stating that el Tudense and el Toledano did not know the *PMC*, then the story of Búcar and the Cid, as well as several other stories about the Cid, was known independently of the poem. I believe that the Latin histories and the poem drew on a tradition of such stories, in different ways and with different results.

Chapter 4, Chapter 5, passim.   In the first article for some years to consider in depth the prosification of the *PMC* in the *CVR*, Nancy Joe Dyer, in '*CVR* Use of the Cid Epic', repeats and expands several points made in her doctoral dissertation, '*El PMC*'. She coincides with many of my conclusions; for example, she notes the importance of direct speech in preserving parts of the poem, the restricting of the role of the family by the chroniclers, and she accepts that some alterations such as those in the story of the chests of sand as found in the *CVR*, are due to interference by the chroniclers. However, she differs fundamentally from me in explaining most of the variations between the *CVR* and the *PMC* by supposing the existence of another version of the poem to which these variations can be attributed. This supposition seems to me to be unnecessary. I argue that almost all the differences are due to the processes of prosification and to the intervention of the chroniclers. My reasons for reaching this conclusion are explained in Chapters 4 and 5. This is not the place to respond in greater detail to Professor Dyer's article.

BIBLIOGRAPHY

Adams, Kenneth, *'Pensar de*: another Old French Influence on the *PMC* and other Medieval Spanish Poems', *La Corónica*, 7 (1978–79), 8–12

——, 'Possible French Influence on the Use of the Historic Present in the *PMC*', *MLR*, 75 (1980), 781–96

——, 'The Metrical Irregularity of the *CMC*: a Restatement Based on the Evidence of Names, Epithets, and Some Other Aspects of Formulaic Diction', *BHS*, 49 (1972), 109–19

——, 'The Yugoslav Model and the Text of the *PMC*', in *Medieval Hispanic Studies Presented to Rita Hamilton* (London, 1976), pp. 1–10

Aguirre, J. M., 'Épica oral y épica castellana: tradición creadora y tradición repetitiva', *Romanische Forschungen*, 80 (1968), 13–43

——, '*PMC*: Rima y oralidad', *La Corónica*, 7 (1978–79), 107–08

Allen, Louise H., 'A Structural Analysis of the Epic Style of the "Cid"', in *Structural Studies on Spanish Themes*, edited by H. R Kahane and A. Pietrangeli, AS 12, no. 3 (Salamanca and Urbana, 1969), pp. 341–414

Alonso, Dámaso, 'El anuncio del estilo directo en el *Poema del Cid* y en la épica francesa', in *Mélanges offerts à Rita Lejeune*, 2 vols (Gembloux, 1969), I, 379–93

——, 'Estilo y creación en el *Poema del Cid*', in *Ensayos sobre poesía española* (Buenos Aires, 1944), pp. 69–111

——, 'La tradición épica castellana en la obra de Menéndez Pidal', *La Torre*, 18–19 (1970–71), 15–49

Amador de los Ríos, José, *Historia crítica de la literatura española*, 7 vols (M., 1861–65; reprinted M., 1969)

Antonio, Nicolás, *Bibliotheca Hispana Vetus*, 2 vols (Rome, 1696), second edition, edited by F. Pérez Bayer (M., 1788)

Armistead, Samuel G., 'A Lost Version of the "Cantar de gesta de las mocedades de Rodrigo" Reflected in the Second Redaction of Rodríguez de Almela's "Compendio historial"', *University of California Publications in Modern Philology*, 38 (1963), 299–336

——, 'An Unnoticed Epic Reference to Doña Elvira, Sister of Alfonso VI', *RPh*, 12 (1958–59), 143–46

——, '*La gesta de las mocedades de Rodrigo*: Reflections of a Lost Epic Poem in the *Crónicas de los reyes de Castilla* and *de 1344*' (unpublished doctoral dissertation, Princeton University, 1955)

——, 'Manuscript Z of the *Crónica de Castilla*: Lost and Found', *La Corónica*, 6 (1977–78), 118–22

——, 'New Perspectives in Alfonsine Historiography', *RPh*, 20 (1966–67), 204–17

——, 'Para el texto de la *Refundición de las Mocedades de Rodrigo*', *AEM*, 3 (1966), 529–40

——, 'The Earliest Historiographic References to the *MR*', in *Estudios literarios de hispanistas norteamericanos dedicados a Helmut Hatzfeldt* (Barcelona, 1974), pp. 25–34

——, 'The Enamoured Doña Urraca in Chronicles and Balladry', *RPh*, 11 (1957–58), 26–29

——, 'The *MR* and Neo-Individualist Theory', *HR*, 46 (1978), 313–27

——, 'The Structure of the *Refundición de las Mocedades de Rodrigo*', *RPh*, 17 (1963–64), 338–45

Artigas, M. and E. Sánchez Reyes, *Catálogos de la Biblioteca de Menéndez Pelayo*, I, Manucritos (Santander, 1957)

Artiles, Joaquín, *Los recursos literarios de Berceo* (M., 1964)

Ashton, J. R., 'Putative *Heroides* Codex AX as a Source of Alfonsine Literature', *RPh*, 3 (1949–50), 275–89

Ayerbe-Chaux, Reinaldo, 'El uso de *exempla* en la *EE* de Alfonso X', *La Coronica*, 7 (1978–79), 28–32

Babbitt, Theodore, *La CVR* (New Haven, 1936)

——, 'Observations on the "Crónica de once reyes"', *HR*, 2 (1934), 202–16

——, 'Twelfth-Century Epic Forms in Fourteenth-Century Chronicles', *RR*, 26 (1935), 128–36

Badía Margarit, A., 'Dos tipos de lengua cara a cara', in *Studia Philologica: Homenaje a Dámaso Alonso*, 3 vols (M., 1960–63), I, 115–39

——, 'La frase de la *PCG* en relación con sus fuentes latinas', *RFE*, 42 (1958–59), 179–210

——, 'Los *Monumenta Germaniae Historica* y la *PCG* de Alfonso el Sabio', *AS*, 16 (1962), 69–75

Ballesteros Beretta, A., *Alfonso X el Sabio* (Barcelona and Murcia, 1963)

Bandera Gómez, C., *El PMC: poesía, historia, mito* (M., 1969)

Barceló, Miguel, 'Algunas observaciones al *Carmen Campidoctoris*', *Saitabi*, 16 (1965), 37–58

——, 'En torno a la primera lid singular del Campeador', *Príncipe de Viana*, 102–03 (1966), 109–26

——, 'Sobre dos textos cidianos', *BRABLB*, 32 (1967–68), 15–25

——, 'Una nota en torno al Destierro del Cid', *Ligarzas*, 1 (1968), 127–40

Barnes, Harry E., *A History of Historical Writing*, second edition (New York, 1962)

Bédier, C. M. J., *La Chanson de Roland*, edited, with a modern French translation (Paris, 1922)

——, *Les Légendes épiques*, 4 vols (Paris, 1908–13)

Bello, Andrés, *Obras completas*, Volume II, *Poema del Cid* (Santiago de Chile, 1881)

Belus, R., *Rerum Hispanicarum Scriptores* (Frankfurt, 1579)

Benito Ruano, Eloy, 'La historiografía en la alta edad media española', *CHE*, 17 (1952), 50–104

Berganza y Arce, Francisco de, *Antigüedades de España*, 2 vols (M., 1719–21)

Bernhard, E., 'Abstractions médiévales ou critique abstraite?', *Studi mediolatini e volgari*, 9 (1961), 19–70

Bonilla y San Martín, A., 'Las gestas del Cid Campeador', *BRAH*, 59 (1911), 161–257

Bowra, C. M., *From Virgil to Milton* (London, 1945)

——, *Heroic Poetry* (London, 1952)

Brewer, W. B., 'A "*loísta*" passage of the *PCG*', *HBalt*, 52 (1969), 430–33

Brey Mariño, M., *Alfonso X, rey de Castilla: Lapidario* (M., 1968)

Bricquet, C. M., *Les Filigranes. Dictionnaire historique des marques de papier*

186

(Geneva, 1907), reprinted with an introduction by A. Stevenson (Amsterdam, 1968)

Burshatin, I. G., and B. B. Thomson, '*PMC* line 508: the Cid as a Rebellious Vassal', *La Corónica*, 5 (1976–77), 90–92

Cabanes Pecourt, M. D., *Crónica latina de los reyes de Castilla* (Valencia, 1964)

CMC, edited by Ramón Menéndez Pidal, in *CMC*, III, 909–1016

Carmen Campidoctoris, edited by Ramón Menéndez Pidal, in *La España del Cid*, II, 882–86

Castro, Américo, 'Acerca del castellano escrito en torno de Alfonso el Sabio', *Filologia Romanza*, 1, no. 4 (1954), 1–11

Catalán, Diego, 'Crónicas generales y cantares de gesta. El *PMC* de Alfonso X y el del pseudo Ben-Alfaraŷ', *HR*, 31 (1963), 195–215, 291–306

——, *De Alfonso X al Conde de Barcelos* (M., 1962)

——, 'Don Juan Manuel ante el modelo alfonsí: el testimonio de la *Crónica Abreviada*', in *Juan Manuel Studies*, edited by Ian Macpherson (London, 1977), pp. 17–51

——, 'El taller historiográfico alfonsí. Métodos y problemas en el trabajo compilatorio', *Romania*, 84 (1963), 354–75

——, 'El Toledano romanzado y las estorias del fecho de los godos del siglo XV', in *Estudios dedicados a J. Homer Herriot* (Valencia, 1966), pp. 9–101

——, *Gran Crónica de Alfonso XI*, 2 vols (M., 1977)

——, 'La Estoria de los reyes del señorío de Africa del maestro Gilberto o Sujulberto: una obra del siglo XIII perdida', *RPh*, 17 (1963–64), 346–53

——, *La tradición manuscrita en la 'Crónica de Alfonso XI'* (M., 1974)

——, 'La versión portuguesa de la *Crónica general*', *RPh*, 13 (1959–60), 67–75

——, 'Poesía y novela en la historiografía castellana de los siglos XIII y XIV', in *Mélanges offerts à Rita Lejeune*, 2 vols (Gembloux, 1969), I, 423–41

—— and María Soledad de Andrés, *La Crónica de 1344 que ordenó el conde de Barcelos, don Pedro Alfonso*, I (M., 1971); no further volume published

Chalon, Louis, 'A propos des filles du Cid', *MA*, 73 (1967), 217–37

——, 'Comment travaillaient les compilateurs de la *PCG de España*', *MA*, 82 (1976), 289–300

——, 'De quelques vocables utilisés par la *PCG de España*', *MA*, 77 (1971), 79–84

——, 'Le Poète du *CMC* s'est-il inspiré de Salluste?', *MA*, 84 (1978), 479–90

——, 'Le Roi Búcar du Maroc dans l'histoire et dans la poésie épique espagnole', *MA*, 75 (1969), 39–49

——, *L'Histoire et l'épopée castillane du Moyen Age* (Paris, 1976)

——, '*Por onrra del Cid e de la sua seña*', in *Études de Philologie Romane et d'Histoire Littéraire offertes à Jules Horrent* (Liège, 1980), pp. 57–62

Chanson de Roland, edited by C. M. J. Bédier

Chaplin, Margaret, 'Oral-Formulaic Style in the Epic: a Progress Report', in *Medieval Hispanic Studies presented to Rita Hamilton* (London, 1976), pp. 11–20

Chaytor, H. J., *From Script to Print* (Cambridge, 1945)

CAI, edited by Luis Sánchez Belda (M., 1950)

Cintra, Luís Filipe Lindley, *Crónica Geral de Espanha de 1344*, 3 vols (Lisbon, 1951–61)

——, 'Sobre o "Sumario de Crónicas até ao año 1368" da Biblioteca Real de Madrid', *Boletim de Filologia*, 9 (1948), 299–320

Cirot, Georges, 'Biographie du Cid par Gil de Zamora', *BH*, 16 (1914), 80–86

——, '"Cantares" et "romances"', *BH*, 47 (1945), 5–25, 169–86

187

——, 'La Chronique générale et le poème du Cid', *BH*, 40 (1938), 306–09
——, 'La Chronique léonaise et la chronique dite de Silos', *BH*, 16 (1914), 15–34
——, 'La Chronique léonaise et les chroniques de Pélage et de Silos', *BH*, 18 (1916), 141–54
——, 'Le "Carmen Campidoctoris"', *BH*, 33 (1931), 144–49
——, 'L'Épisode des Infants de Carrión dans le *Mio Cid* et la *Chronique générale*', *BH*, 47 (1945), 124–33, and 48 (1946), 64–74
——, 'Le Rhythme du "Carmen Campidoctoris"', *BH*, 33 (1931), 247–52
——, *Les Histoires générales d'Espagne entre Alphonse X et Philippe II* (Bordeaux and Paris, 1905)
——, 'Une Chronique latine inédite des rois de Castille', *BH*, 14 (1912), 30–46, 109–18, 224–74, 353–74, and 15 (1913), 18–37, 178–87, 268–83, 411–28
——, 'Une Chronique léonaise inédite', *BH*, 11 (1909), 259–82, and 13 (1911), 133–56, 381–439
Clarke, Dorothy C., 'The Cid and His Daughters', *La Corónica*, 5 (1976–77), 16–21
Coester, Alfred, 'Compression in the *Poema del Cid*', *RH*, 15 (1906), 98–211
Collins, Larry L., 'An Unknown Manuscript of the *CVR*', *Sc*, 28 (1974), 51–60
——, 'The Historiographical Background of the *CVR*', *Revue d'Histoire des Textes*, 4 (1974), 339–57
Cooper, Louis, *Liber Regum. Estudio lingüístico* (Zaragoza, 1960)
Corbató, H., 'La sinonimia y la unidad del *PMC*', *HR*, 9 (1941), 327–47
Correa, Gustavo, 'El tema de la honra en el *PMC*', *HR*, 20 (1952), 185–99
Criado de Val, Manuel, 'Geografía, toponimia, e itinerarios del *CMC*', *ZRP*, 86 (1970), 83–107
Crónica abreviada, edited by R. L. Grismer and M. B. Grismer (Minneapolis, 1958)
Crónica del Cid, see *Crónica particular*, *Crónica popular*, and *Crónica rimada*
C1344, edited in part by Luís Felipe Lindley Cintra, *Crónica geral*, vols II and III
Crónica najerense, edited by Antonio Ubieto Arteta (Valencia, 1966)
Crónica particular del Cid, published by Juan de Velorado (Burgos, 1512)
Crónica popular del Cid, edited by R. Foulché-Delbosc, *RH*, 20 (1909), 316–428
Crónica rimada del Cid, another name for the *MR*
Cummins, J. G., 'The Chronicle Texts of the Legend of the *Infantes de Lara*', *BHS*, 53 (1976), 101–16
Curtius, Ernst Robert, *European Literature and the Latin Middle Ages*, translated by W. Trask (London, 1953)
——, 'Zur Literarästhetik des Mittelalters', *ZRP*, 58 (1938), 1–50, 129–232, 433–79
Dearing, V. A., *A Manual of Textual Analysis* (Berkeley, 1959)
de Chasca, Edmund, 'Composición escrita y oral en el *Poema del Cid*', *Filología*, 12 (1966–67), 77–94
——, *El arte juglaresco en el CMC* (M., 1967)
——, *Estructura y forma en el PMC* (Mexico and Iowa, 1955)
——, *Registro de fórmulas verbales en el CMC* (Iowa, 1967)
——, 'The King–Vassal Relationship in the *PMC*', *HR*, 21 (1953), 183–92
——, *The Poem of the Cid* (New York, 1976)
——, 'Toward a Redefinition of Epic Formula in the Light of the *CMC*', *HR*, 38 (1970), 251–63
Delbouille, Maurice, 'Les Chansons de geste et le livre', in *La Technique littéraire*

188

des chansons de geste. Actes du colloque de Liège, 1957 (Paris, 1959), pp. 295–407

Deyermond, Alan D., *Epic Poetry and the Clergy: Studies on the 'MR'* (London, 1969)

——, 'La decadencia de la epopeya española: las *MR'*, *AEM*, 1 (1964), 607–17

——, 'Medieval Spanish Epic Cycles: Observations on their Formation and Development', *KRQ*, 23 (1976), 281–303

——, 'Structural and Stylistic Patterns in the *CMC'*, in *Medieval Studies in Honor of Robert White Linker* (M., 1973), pp. 55–71

——, 'Tendencies in "Mio Cid" Scholarship, 1943–73', in *'Mio Cid' Studies*, edited by A. D. Deyermond (London, 1977), pp. 13–47

——, *A Literary History of Spain*, Vol. I, *The Middle Ages* (London and New York, 1971)

——, 'The *MR* as a Test Case: Problems of Methodology', *La Corónica*, 6 (1977–78), 108–12

——, 'The Singer of Tales and Mediaeval Spanish Epic', *BHS*, 42 (1965), 1–8

—— and Margaret Chaplin, 'Folk-Motifs in the Medieval Spanish Epic', *Philological Quarterly*, 51 (1972), 36–53

—— and David Hook, 'Doors and Cloaks: Two Image Patterns in the *CMC'*, *Modern Language Notes*, 94 (1979), 366–77

Díaz y Díaz, M. C., 'La Circulation des manuscrits dans le Péninsule Ibérique du VIIIe au XIe siècle', *Cahiers de Civilisation Médiévale*, 12 (1969), 219–41, 383–92

——, *Index Scriptorum Latinorum Medii Aevi Hispanorum* (M., 1959)

Docampo, see Ocampo

Donald, Dorothy, 'Suetonius in the *PCG* through the *Speculum Historiale'*, *HR*, 11 (1943), 95–115

Dorfman, Eugene, *The Narreme in Medieval Romance Epic* (Manchester, 1970)

Drury, Tom, 'Diego Ruiz, Son of the Cid?', *KRQ*, 27 (1980), 265–72

——, 'Martin Peláez, aquel tímido asturiano', *HBalt*, 64 (1981), 41–52

Dubler, C. E., 'Fuentes árabes y bizantinas en la *PCG'*, *Vox Romanica*, 12 (1952), 120–80

Duggan, Joseph J., 'Formulaic Diction in the *CMC* and in the Old French Epic', *FMLS*, 10 (1974), 260–69

——, *The Song of Roland: Formulaic Style and Poetic Craft* (Berkeley, 1973)

Dunn, Peter N., 'Levels of Meaning in the *PMC'*, *Modern Language Notes*, 85 (1970), 109–19

——, '*PMC* vv. 23–48: Epic Rhetoric, Legal Formula, and the Question of Dating', *Romania*, 96 (1975), 255–65

——, 'Theme and Myth in the *PMC'*, *Romania*, 83 (1962), 348–69

Dyer, Nancy Joe, '*CVR* Use of the Cid Epic: Perspectives, Method, and Rationale', *RPh*, 33 (1979–80), 534–44

——, '*El PMC* in the *CVR* Prosification, a Critical Edition and Study' (unpublished doctoral dissertation, University of Pennsylvania, 1975)

Eisenberg, D., 'The *GE*, Sources and Source Treatment', *ZRP*, 89 (1973), 206–27

Elliot, Alison G., 'The *Triumphus Sancti Remalci*: Latin Evidence for Oral Composition', *RPh*, 32 (1978–79), 292–98

England, John, 'The Second Appearance of Rachel and Vidas in the *PMC'*, in *Hispanic Studies in Honour of Frank Pierce* (Sheffield, 1980), pp. 51–58

Entwistle, W. J., '*La estoria del noble varón, el Cid Ruy Díaz el Campeador, sennor que fue de Valencia'*, *HR*, 15 (1947) 206–11

——, 'My Cid — Legist', *Bulletin of Spanish Studies*, 6 (1929), 9–15

——, 'On the *Carmen de Morte Sanctii Regis*', *BH*, 30 (1928), 204–19

——, 'Remarks Concerning the Historical Account of Spanish Epic Origins', *RH*, 81 (1933), 352–77

——, 'Remarks Concerning the Order of the Spanish "Cantares de Gesta"', *RPh*, 1 (1947–48), 113–23

——, 'The *Cantar de gesta* of Bernardo del Carpio', *MLR*, 23 (1928), 307–22, 432–52

Faulhaber, Charles, 'Neo-Traditionalism, Formulism, Individualism, and Recent Studies on the Spanish Epic', *RPh*, 30 (1976–77), 83–101

Ferrari, A., 'Artificios septenarios en la *CAI* y el *Poema de Almería*', *BRAH*, 153 (1963), 19–67

——, 'El cluniacense Pedro de Poitiers y la *CAI* y el *Poema de Almería*', *BRAH*, 153 (1963), 153–204

Finnegan, Ruth H., *Oral Poetry* (Cambridge, 1977)

Fletcher, Richard, 'Diplomatic and the Cid Revisited: the Seals and Mandates of Alfonso VII', *Journal of Medieval History*, 2 (1976), 305–38

Flórez, Henrique, *España Sagrada*, 29 vols (M., 1745–75)

——, *Memorias de las Reynas Catholicas*, second edition, 2 vols (Madrid, 1770)

Foulché-Delbosc, R., *'Suma de las cosas maravillosas que fizo en su vida el buen cavallero, Cid Ruy Diaz'* (an edition of the *Crónica popular del Cid*), *RH*, 20 (1909), 316–428

——, *'Gesta Roderici Campidocti'*, *RH*, 21 (1909), 412–59

Fradejas Lebrero, José, *Estudios épicos: el Cid* (Ceuta, 1962)

Fraker, Charles F., 'Alfonso X, the Empire, and the *Primera crónica*', *BHS*, 55 (1978), 95–102

——, 'Sancho II: Epic and Chronicle', *Romania*, 95 (1974), 467–507

——,· 'The *Fet des Romains* and the *PCG*', *HR*, 46 (1978), 199–220

Franklin, A. B., 'A Detail Concerning Scribal Peculiarities Found in Manuscript E of the *Primera Crónica*', *HR*, 6 (1938), 332–36

——, 'A Study of the Origins of the Legend of Bernardo del Carpio', *HR*, 5 (1937), 286–303

Frappier, Jean, *Les Chansons de geste du cycle de Guillaume d'Orange*, 2 vols (Paris, 1955–65)

Gallardo, B. J., *Ensayo de una biblioteca española de libros raros y curiosos*, 4 vols (M., 1863–89)

García Gómez, Emilio, 'El rey Búcar del *CMC*', in *Studi Orientalistici in Onore di Giorgio Levi Della Vida*, I (Rome, 1956), 371–77

García Romero, F., *Catálogo de los incunables existentes en la Biblioteca de la Real Academia de Historia* (M., 1921)

García Villada, Z., *Paleografía española* (M., 1923)

Garci-Gómez, Miguel, *CMC* (M., 1978)

——, 'La Afrenta de Corpes: su estructura a la luz de la retórica', *KRQ*, 24 (1977), 125–39

——, *Mio Cid. Estudios de endocrítica* (Barcelona, 1975)

Garrido, Rosa M., 'El *Cantar del rey Fernando el Magno*', *BRABLB*, 32 (1967–68), 67–95

Gayangos, Pascual de, *Catalogue of the Manuscripts in the Spanish Language in the British Museum*, 4 vols (London, 1875–93)

GE, of Alfonso X, parts I and II, edited by Antonio G. Solalinde, Lloyd A. Kasten, and Victor R. B. Oelschläger, 3 vols (Madrid, 1930–61)

Gesta Roderici, another name for the *HR*

Gibbs, Jack, 'Quelques observations sur le *Poema de Almería*', in *Société Rencesvals: IVe Congrès International. Actes et memoires* (Heidelberg, 1969), pp. 76–81

Gicovate, Bernardo, 'La fecha de composición del *PMC*', *HBalt*, 39 (1956), 419–22

Gifford, Douglas, 'European Folk-Tradition and the 'Afrenta de Corpes'', in *'Mio Cid' Studies*, pp. 49–62

Gil, Juan, '*Carmen de Expugnatione Almariae Urbis*', *Habis*, 5 (1974), 45–64

Gilman, Stephen, 'The Poetry of the *Poema* and the Music of the *Cantar*', *Philological Quarterly*, 51 (1972), 1–11

——, *Tiempo y fórmulas temporales en el 'Poema del Cid'* (M., 1961)

Gimeno Casalduero, Joaquín, 'Sobre la "oración narrativa" medieval: estructura, origen, supervivencia', in *Estructura y diseño en la literatura castellana medieval* (M., 1975), pp. 11–29

——, 'Sobre las numeraciones de los reyes de Castilla', in *Estructura y diseño*, pp. 65–101

——, 'El Cid echado de tierra', in *Estudios de literatura española* (M., 1962), pp. 28–58

Gómez Moreno, M., 'Las primeras crónicas de la Reconquista: el ciclo de Alfonso III', *BRAH*, 100 (1932), 562–628

Gómez Pérez, José, 'Elaboración de la *PCG* de España y su trasmisión manuscrita', *Sc*, 17 (1963), 233–76

——, 'El historiador Jiménez de Rada y las tierras de Soria', *Celtiberia*, 10 (1955), 159–76

——, 'Fuentes y cronología en la *PCG*', *RABM*, 65 (1959), 615–34

——, 'Jiménez de Rada y su traductor Domingo Pascual', *Celtiberia*, 23 (1962), 119–29

——, 'La estoria de España alfonsí de Fruela II a Fernando III', *Hispania*, 25 (1965), 485–520

——, 'La más antigua traducción de las crónicas del Toledano', *Hispania*, 22 (1962), 357–71

——, 'Manuscritos del Toledano, I', *RABM*, 60 (1954), 189–213

——, 'Manuscritos del Toledano, II', *RABM*, 63 (1957), 157–74

——, 'Solalinde y la *PCG* de España', *RABM*, 62 (1956), 405–10

Gormly, Sister Francis, *The Use of the Bible in Representative Works of Medieval Spanish Literature, 1250–1300* (Washington D.C., 1962)

Gorosterraztu, Javier, *Don Rodrigo Jiménez de Rada* (Pamplona, 1925)

Gransden, Antonia, *Historical Writing in England, c. 550 to c.1307* (London, 1974)

Grieve, Patricia E., 'Shelter as an Image Pattern in the *CMC*', *La Corónica*, 8 (1979–80), 44–49

Grismer, R. L. and M. B. Grismer, editors, *Juan Manuel. Crónica Abreviada* (Minneapolis, 1958)

Gybbon-Monypenny, Gerald B., 'The Spanish 'Mester de Clerecía' and its Intended Public: Concerning the Validity as Evidence of Passages of Direct Address to the Audience', in *Medieval Miscellany Presented to Eugène Vinaver* (Manchester, 1965), pp. 230–44

Hamilton, Rita, 'Epic Epithets in the *PMC*', *RLC*, 36 (1962), 161–78

Hanssen, F., 'La colocación del verbo en el *Poema del Cid*', *BH*, 14 (1912), 47–59

——, 'Notas al *Poema del Cid*', *Anales de la Universidad de Chile*, 128 (1911), 211–63

Hart, Thomas R., 'Characterization and Plot Structure in the *PMC*', in *'Mio Cid' Studies*, pp. 63–72

——, 'Hierarchical Patterns in the *CMC*', *RR*, 53 (1962), 161–73

——, 'La "Afrenta de Corpes", novela psicológica', *NRFH*, 13 (1959), 291–304

——, 'The Infantes de Carrión', *BHS*, 33 (1956), 17–24

——, 'The Rhetoric of (Epic) Fiction: Narrative Technique in the *CMC*', *Philological Quarterly*, 51 (1972), 23–35

Hartman, S. L., 'Alfonso, el Sabio, and the Varieties of Verb Grammar', *HBalt*, 57 (1974), 48–55

Harvey, L. P., 'Oral Composition and the Performance of Novels of Chivalry in Spain', *FMLS*, 10 (1974), 270–86

——, 'The Metrical Irregularity of the *CMC*', *BHS*, 40 (1963), 137–43

Hathaway, R. L., 'The Art of the Epic Epithets in the *PMC*', *HR*, 42 (1974), 311–21

Hay, Denys, *Annalists and Historians* (London, 1977)

Henríquez Ureña, Pedro, *Estudios de versificación española* (Buenos Aires, 1961)

Herrero Llorente, V. J., 'Influencia de Lucano en la obra de Alfonso el sabio. Una traducción anónima e inédita', *RABM*, 65 (1959), 697–715

Herslund, Michael, 'Le *CMC* et la chanson de geste', *Revue Romane*, 9 (1974), 69–121

Hills, E. C., 'Irregular Epic Metres: a Comparative Study of the Metre of the *Poem of the Cid* and of Certain Anglo-Norman, Franco-Italian, and Venetian Epic Poems', in *Homenaje ofrecido a Ramón Menéndez Pidal*, 3 vols (M., 1925), I, 759–77

——, 'The Unity of the *Poem of the Cid*', *HBalt*, 12 (1929), 113–18

Hinojosa y Naveros, Eduardo de, 'El derecho en el *Poema del Cid*', in *Homenaje ofrecido a Menéndez y Pelayo*, 2 vols (M., 1899), I, 541–81

Historia Gothica, another name for the *DRH* of Rodrigo Ximénez de Rada, El Toledano

Historia Roderici, edited by Ramón Menéndez Pidal, in *La España del Cid*, II, 921–71

Hogberg, Paul, 'La Chronique de Lucas de Tuy', *RH*, 81 (1933), 404–20

Hook, David, 'On Certain Correspondences between the *PMC* and Contemporary Legal Instruments', *Iberoromania*, 11 (1980), 31–53

——, 'Pedro Bermúdez and the Cid's Standard', *Neophilologus*, 63 (1979), 45–53

——, 'Some Observations upon the Episode of the Cid's Lion', *MLR*, 71 (1976), 553–65

——, 'The Conquest of Valencia in the *CMC*', *BHS*, 50 (1973), 120–26

——, 'The Opening Laisse of the *PMC*', *RLC*, 212 (1979), 490–501

Horrent, Jules, 'Chroniques latines primitives et chansons de geste espagnoles', in *Mélanges offerts à E-R. Labande* (Poitiers, 1974), pp. 407–15

——, *Historia y poesía en torno al 'Cantar del Cid'* (Barcelona, 1973)

——, 'La Jura de Santa Gadea. Historia y poesía', in *Studia Philologica: Homenaje ofrecido a Dámaso Alonso*, 3 vols (M., 1960–63), II, 241–65; reprinted in *Historia y poesía*, pp. 157–93

——, 'La Prise de Castejón: Remarques littéraires sur un passage du *CMC*', *MA*, 69 (1963), 289–97; reprinted in *Historia y poesía*, pp. 331–40

——, 'Les Chroniques espagnoles et les chansons de geste', *MA*, 53 (1947), 271–302

——, 'Les Chroniques espagnoles et les chansons de geste', *MA*, 62 (1956), 279–99

——, 'Localisation du *CMC*', in *Mélanges offerts à René Crozet*, 2 vols (Poitiers, 1966), I, 609–15, reprinted in *Historia y poesía*, pp. 313–29

——, 'Note sur le Cid, héros chrétien', *Revue Belge de Philologie et d'Histoire*, 54 (1976), 769–72

——, 'Notes de critique textuelle sur le *CMC*', in *Mélanges offerts a Maurice Delbouille*, 2 vols (Gembloux, 1964), II, 275–89; reprinted in *Historia y poesía*, pp. 197–218

——, 'Observations textuelles sur une édition récente du *CMC*', *Les Lettres Romanes*, 32 (1978), 3–51 (on the edition in Colin Smith, *PMC*)

——, 'Sur deux témoignages espagnols de la *Chanson de Roland*', *BH*, 48 (1956), 48–50

——, 'Sur le *Carmen Campidoctoris*', in *Studi in onore di Angelo Monteverdi*, I (Modena, 1959), pp. 334–52; reprinted in *Historia y poesía*, pp. 91–122

——, 'Tradition poétique du *CMC* au XIIe siècle', *Cahiers de Civilisation Médiévale*, 7 (1964), 451–77; reprinted in *Historia y poesía*, pp. 243–311.

Huber, D. V. A., *Crónica del famoso cavallero Cid Ruydiez Campeador* (Marburg, 1844)

Huici Miranda, Ambrosio, *Historia musulmana de Valencia y su región*, 3 vols (Valencia, 1969–70)

——, 'Las luchas del Cid Campeador con los almorávides y el enigma de su hijo, Diego', *Hesperis Tamuda*, 6 (1965), 79–114

Impey, Olga T., 'Un dechado de la prosa literaria alfonsí, el relato cronístico de los amores de Dido', *RPh*, 34 (1980–81), 1–27

Jonxis-Henkemans, W. J., *Bijdrage tot de Bronnenstudie der 'PCG'* (Rotterdam, 1947)

Kienast, W., 'Zur Geschichte des Cid', *Deutsches Archiv für Geschichte des Mittelalters*, 3 (1939), 57–114

Kinkade, R. P., *Los lucidarios españoles* (M., 1968)

Lacarra, María Eugenia, *El PMC: Realidad histórica e ideología* (M., 1980)

——, 'El *PMC* y el monasterio de San Pedro de Cardeña', in *Homenaje ofrecido a D. José María Lacarra de Miguel*, II (Zaragoza, 1977), pp. 79–94

Lang, H. R., 'Contributions to the Restoration of the *Poema del Cid*', *RH*, 66 (1926), 1–509

——, 'The Metrical Forms of the *Poema del Cid*', *PMLA*, 42 (1927), 523–603

Lapesa, Rafael, 'La lengua de la poesía épica en los cantares de gesta y en el romancero viejo', in *De la Edad Media a nuestros días* (M., 1967), pp. 9–28

——, 'Sobre el *CMC*. Crítica de críticas. Cuestiones lingüísticas', in *Études offertes à Jules Horrent* (Liège, 1980), pp. 213–31

Laza Palacio, Manuel, *La España del poeta de 'Mio Cid'* (Málaga, 1964)

Lázaro Carreter, Fernando, 'Sobre el "modus interpretandi" alfonsí', *Ibérida*, 6 (1961), 97–114

Letsch-Lavanchy, A., 'Éléments didactiques dans la *Crónica general*', *Vox Romanica*, 15 (1956), 231–40

Lévi-Provençal, E., *Islam d'Occident. Études d'histoire médiévale* (Paris, 1948)

——, 'La toma de Valencia por el Cid', *Al-Andalus*, 13 (1948), 97–156; reprinted from *Islam d'Occident*, pp. 187–238

——, 'Le Cid d'histoire', *Revue Historique*, 180 (1937), 58–74; reprinted in *Islam d'Occident*, pp. 155–85

—— and Ramón Menéndez Pidal, 'Alfonso VI y su hermana, Urraca', *Al-Andalus*, 13 (1948), 157–66

Liber regum, edited by M. Serrano y Sanz, in *'Cronicón villarense'*, pp. 194–215, and Henrique Flórez, in *Memorias de las reynas catholicas*, II, 492–505

Lida de Malkiel, María Rosa, 'Josefo en la *GE*', in *Hispanic Studies in Honour of I. M. González Llubera* (Oxford, 1959), pp. 163–81

——, 'La *GE*: notas literarias y filológicas, I', *RPh*, 12 (1958–59), 111–42

——, 'La *GE*: notas literarias y filológicas, II', *RPh*, 13 (1959–60), 1–30

——, 'Perduración de la literatura antigua en el Occidente (A propósito de E. R. Curtius, *Europäische Literatur und Lateinisches Mittelalter*)', *RPh*, 5 (1951–52), 99–131

Linaje del Cid, edited by Henrique Flórez, in *Memorias de las reynas catholicas*, II, 503–05, and Antonio Ubieto Arteta, *Corónicas navarras*, pp. 30–35

Linehan, Peter, *The Spanish Church and the Papacy in the Thirteenth Century* (Cambridge, 1971)

Lloyd, Paul M., 'More on the Date of Composition of the *CMC*', *HBalt*, 42 (1959), 488–91

Loaysa, Jofré de, 'Chronique des rois de Castille, 1248–1305', edited by A. Morel-Fatio, *Bibliothèque de l'École de Chartres*, 59 (1898), 325–78

Lomax, Derek W., 'La fecha de la *Crónica najerense*', *AEM*, 9 (1974–79), 405–06

——, 'The Date of the *PMC*', in *'Mio Cid' Studies*, pp. 73–81

Lord, Albert B., *The Singer of Tales* (Cambridge, Mass., 1960)

Lorenzana, Francisco Antonio de, *SS.PP. Toletanorum quotquot extant Opera*, 4 vols (M. and Rome, 1782–97)

Lorenzo, Ramón, *La traducción gallega de la Crónica general y de la Crónica de Castilla*, 2 vols (Orense, 1975–77)

Lyer, Stanislav, 'La Syntaxe du gérondif dans le *Poema del Cid*', *RFE*, 19 (1932), 1–46

Mackay, Angus and Muhammad Benaboud, 'Alfonso VI of León and Castile, "al-Imbratūr dhū-l-Millatayn"', *BHS*, 56 (1979), 95–102

Magnotta, Miguel, *Historia y bibliografía de la crítica sobre el 'PMC' (1750–1971)* (Chapel Hill, 1976)

Malkiel, Yakov, 'Towards a Reconsideration of the Old Spanish Imperfect in "-ía, -ié"', *HR*, 27 (1959), 435–81

Manuel, Juan, *Crónica abreviada*, edited by R. L. Grismer and M. B. Grismer

——, *Cronicón latino*, or *Crónica complida*, edited by Henrique Flórez, in *España Sagrada*, II, 207–16

Marden, C. Carroll, *Poema de Fernán González* (Baltimore, 1904)

Martínez, H. Salvador, *El Poema de Almería y la épica románica* (M., 1975)

——, 'Tres leyendas heroicas de la *Najerense* y sus relaciones con la épica castellana', *Anuario de Letras*, 9 (1971), 115–77

Martínez López, Ramón, *GE: versión gallega* (Oviedo, 1963)

Menéndez Pidal, Gonzalo, 'Como trabajaron las escuelas alfonsíes', *NRFH*, 5 (1951), 362–80

Menéndez Pidal, Ramón, 'Alfonso X y las leyendas heroicas', *Cuadernos hispanoamericanos*, 1 (1948), 13–37

——, *CMC: texto, gramática, y vocabulario*, fourth edition, 3 vols (M., 1964–69)

——, *Castilla. La tradición, el idioma* (Buenos Aires, 1945)

——, *Crónicas generales de España*, Catálogo de la Real Biblioteca, 1 (M., 1898); third edition, revised, Catálogo de la Real Biblioteca, 5 (M., 1918)

——, *De primitiva lírica española y antigua épica* (Buenos Aires, 1951)

——, 'Dos poetas en el *CMC*', *Romania*, 82 (1961), 145–200

194

——, 'El *Poema del Cid* y las crónicas generales de España', *RH*, 5 (1898), 435–69
——, *En torno al 'Poema del Cid'* (Barcelona, 1963)
——, *Estudios literarios* (M., 1945)
——, 'Filología e historia: de crítica cidiana', *ZRP*, 64 (1944), 211–32
——, 'Fórmulas épicas en el *Poema del Cid*', *RPh* ((1953–54), 261–67
——, *Historia y epopeya* (M., 1934)
——, *La Chanson de Roland y el neotradicionalismo* (M., 1959)
——, *La leyenda de los Infantes de Lara*, third edition (M., 1969)
——, 'La Cronica General de España que mandó componer Alfonso, el Sabio', in *Discursos leídos ante la Real Academia de Historia el día 21 de mayo de 1916* (M., 1916), pp. 10–58
——, 'La crónica general de 1404', *RABM*, 9 (1903), 34–55
——, 'La épica española y la "Literarästhetik des Mittelalters"', *ZRP*, 59 (1939), 1–9
——, *La epopeya castellana a través de la literatura española* (Buenos Aires, 1945)
——, *La España del Cid*, seventh edition, 2 vols (M., 1969)
——, 'La fecha del *CMC*', in *Studia Philologica: Homenaje a Dámaso Alonso*, III (M., 1963), 7–11
——, 'La forma épica en España y en Francia', *RFE*, 20 (1933), 345–52
——, 'La política y la Reconquista en el siglo XI', *Revista de Estudios Políticos*, 19 (1948), 1–35
——, *La PCG que mandó componer Alfonso, el Sabio, y se continuaba bajo Sancho IV en 1289*, second edition, 2 vols (M., 1955)
——, 'Los cantores épicos yugoeslavos y los occidentales. El *Mio Cid* y dos refundidores primitivos', *BRABLB*, 31 (1965–66), 195–225
——, *Los godos y la epopeya española* (M., 1956)
——, 'Poesía e historia en el *Mio Cid*: el problema de la poesía épica', *NRFH*, 3 (1949), 113–29
——, *Poesía juglaresca y orígenes de las literaturas románicas*, sixth edition (M., 1957)
——, 'Relatos poéticos en las crónicas medievales', *RFE*, 10 (1923), 329–72
——, *Reliquias de la poesía épica española* (M., 1951)
——, '*Roncesvalles*. Un nuevo cantar de gesta español del siglo XIII', *RFE*, 4 (1917), 105–204
——, 'Sobre Aluacaxí y la elegía árabe de Valencia', in *Homenaje a D. Francisco Codera* (Zaragoza, 1904), pp. 393–409
——, 'Tradicionalidad de las crónicas generales de España', *BRAH*, 136 (1955), 131–97
——, Alvaro Galmés de Fuentes, and Diego Catalán, *Como vive un romance. Dos ensayos sobre la tradicionalidad* (M., 1954)
Michael, Ian, 'A Comparison of the Use of Epic Epithets in the *PMC* and the *Libro de Alexandre*', *BHS*, 38 (1961), 32–41
——, 'Geographical Problems in the *PMC*: I. The Exile Route', in *Medieval Hispanic Studies Presented to Rita Hamilton* (London, 1976), pp. 117–28
——, 'Geographical Problems in the *PMC*: II. The Corpes Route', in '*Mio Cid' Studies*, pp. 83–89
——, *PMC*, an edition (M., 1976)
——, *The Poem of the Cid*, an edition with a translation by Rita Hamilton and Janet Perry (Manchester and New York, 1975)
Milá y Fontanals, Manuel, *De la poesía heroico-popular castellana* (Barcelona,

1874); reprinted in *Obras de Manuel Milá y Fontanals*, edited by Martín de Riquer and J. Molas, I (Barcelona, 1959)

Miletich, John S., 'Medieval Spanish Epic and European Narrative Traditions', *La Corónica*, 6 (1977–78), 90–96

Millares Carlo, A., *Tratado de paleografía española*, second edition (M., 1932)

'Mio Cid' Studies, edited by A. D. Deyermond (London, 1977)

MR, edited by A. D. Deyermond, in *Epic Poetry and the Clergy*, pp. 222–77

Montgomery, Thomas, 'Basque Models for Some Syntactic Traits of the *PMC*', *BHS*, 54 (1977), 95–99

——, 'Narrative Tense Preference in the *CMC*', *RPh*, 21 (1967–68), 253–74

——, 'The Cid and the Count of Barcelona', *HR*, 30 (1962), 1–11

——, 'The *PMC*: Oral Art in Transition', in *'Mio Cid' Studies*, pp. 91–112

Moon, Harold, 'Humour in the *PMC*', *HBalt*, 46 (1963), 700–04

Morel-Fatio, Alfonso, *Catalogue des manuscrits espagnols et des manuscrits portugais de la Bibliothèque Nationale* (Paris, 1892)

——, 'Note bibliographique sur le *Catálogo de la Real Biblioteca, Madrid* de Menéndez Pidal', *Romania*, 28 (1899), 303–07

Moreta Velayos, Salustiano, *El monasterio de San Pedro de Cardeña. Historia de un dominio monástico castellano (902–1338)* (Salamanca, 1971)

Morris, John, 'Medieval Spanish Epic Style: its Character and Development and its Influence on Other Forms of Literature' (unpublished doctoral dissertation, University of Leeds, 1961)

Moxó, S. de, 'Aproximación a la historiografía medieval española', in *Homenaje a Emilio Alarcos García*, 2 vols (Valladolid, 1965–67), II, 741–61

Myers, Oliver T., 'Assonance and Tense in the *PMC*', *PMLA*, 81 (1966), 493–98

——, 'Multiple Authorship of the *PMC*: a Final Word?', in *'Mio Cid' Studies*, pp. 113–28

Nelson, Jan A., 'Initial Imagery in the *PMC*', *Neuphilologische Mitteilungen*, 74 (1973), 382–86

Nichols, Stephen G., 'The Interaction of Life and Literature in the *Peregrinationes ad loca sancta* and the *Chansons de geste*', *Speculum*, 44 (1969), 51–77

Ocampo, Florián de, *Las quatro partes enteras de la Cronica de España que mando componer el serenissimo rey don Alonso llamado el sabio* (Zamora, 1541)

Oleza, Juan de, 'Análisis estructural del humorismo en el *Poema del Cid*', *Ligarzas*, 4 (1972), 193–234

Orduna, Germán, 'Los prólogos a la *Crónica abreviada* y al *Libro de la caza*: la tradición alfonsí y la primera época en la obra literaria de don Juan Manuel', *CHE*, 51–52 (1970), 123–44

Pardo, Aristóbulo, 'Los versos 1–9 del *PMC*: ¿no comenzaba ahí el *Poema?*', *Thesaurus*, 27 (1972), 261–92

Parry, Milman and Albert B. Lord, *Serbocroatian Heroic Songs*, I (Cambridge, Mass. and Belgrade, 1954)

Pattison, D. G., 'Legendary Material and its Elaboration in an Idiosyncratic Alphonsine Chronicle', in *Belfast Spanish and Portuguese Papers* (Belfast, 1979), pp. 173–81

——, 'The "Afrenta de Corpes" in Fourteenth-Century Historiography', in *'Mio Cid' Studies*, pp. 129–40

——, 'The Date of the *CMC*: a Linguistic Approach', *MLR*, 62 (1967), 443–50

Pellen, René, 'Le *Poème du Cid* étudié à l'ordinateur', *Cahiers de Linguistique Hispanique Médiévale*, 1 (1976), 7–99; 2 (1977), 171–251; 3 (1978), 155–267

Pérez de Urbel, Justo, and A. G. Ruiz Zorrilla, *Historia silense* (M., 1959)
Poema de Fernán Gonzalez, edited by C. Carroll Marden (Baltimore, 1904)
PMC, edited by Ramón Menéndez Pidal, in *CMC*, III, 909–1016
PCG, edited by Ramón Menéndez Pidal, in *La PCG*
Procter, Evelyn S., *Alfonso X of Castile, Patron of Literature and Learning* (Oxford, 1951)
——, 'The Scientific Works of the Court of Alfonso X of Castile', *MLR*, 40 (1945), 12–29
Puyol y Alonso, Julio, *Cantar de gesta de don Sancho II de Castilla* (M., 1911)
——, editor of a romance version of Lucas de Tuy's *Crónica de España* (M., 1926)
——, *La Crónica popular del Cid* (M., 1911)
Ramsden, H., 'The Taking of Alcocer', *BHS*, 36 (1959), 129–34
——, *Weak-Pronoun Position in the Early Romance Languages* (Manchester, 1963)
Reig, Carola, *El Cantar de Sancho II y cerco de Zamora* (M., 1947)
Reilly, B. F., 'Sources of the Fourth Book of Lucas of Tuy's *Chronicon Mundi*', *Classical Folia*, 30 (1976), 127–37
——, 'The *Historia Compostellana*: the Genesis and Composition of a Twelfth-Century Spanish *Gesta*', *Speculum*, 44 (1969), 78–85
Riaño, J. F., *La Crónica general de don Alfonso el Sabio y los elementos que concurren a la cultura de la época* (M., 1869)
Riaño Rodríguez, Timoteo, 'Del autor y fecha del *PMC*', *Prohemio*, 2 (1971), 467–500
Richthofen, Erich von, *Estudios épicos medievales*, (M., 1954)
——, 'Nuevas aportaciones críticas sobre la estructura del *PMC*', *Prohemio*, 5 (1974), 197–206
——, *Nuevos estudios épicos medievales* (M., 1970)
——, 'Problemas rolandinos, almerienses, y cidianos', *AEM*, 5 (1968), 437–44
——, *Tradicionalismo épico-novelesco* (Barcelona, 1972)
——, 'Tradicionalismo, individualismo, y positivismo en el estudio de la épica y de la novela primitivas', *Prohemio*, 1 (1970), 397–435
Rico, Francisco, *Alfonso el Sabio y la General Estoria* (Barcelona, 1972)
——, 'Las letras latinas del siglo XII en Galicia, León, y Castilla', *Abaco*, 2 (1969), 9–91
Riquer, Martín de, 'Barcelona en las leyendas épicas medievales', *Cuadernos de Arqueología e Historia de la Ciudad de Barcelona*, 10 (1967), 175–85
Risco, M. de, *La Castilla y el más famoso castellano* (M., 1792)
Rodríguez-Puértolas, Julio, 'El *PMC*: nueva épica y nueva propaganda', in *'Mio Cid' Studies*, pp. 141–59
Roncesvalles, edited by Ramón Menéndez Pidal, in *'Roncesvalles'*
Rubio García, Luis, *Realidad y fantasía en el 'PMC'* (Murcia, 1972)
Russell, J. C., 'Chroniclers of Medieval Spain', *HR*, 6 (1938), 218–35
Russell, P. E., 'El *PMC* como documento de información caminera', in *Temas de 'La Celestina'*, pp. 159–205
——, 'La oración de doña Jimena (*PMC*, vv. 325–67)', in *Temas de 'La Celestina'*, pp. 113–58
——, 'Nuevas reflexiones sobre el Alcocer del *PMC*', in *Temas de 'La Celestina'*, pp. 45–69
——, 'San Pedro de Cardeña and the Heroic History of the Cid', *Medium Aevum*, 28 (1958), 57–79; reprinted in *Temas de 'la Celestina'*, pp. 71–112

——, 'Some Problems of Diplomatic in the *PMC*', *MLR*, 47 (1952), 340–49, reprinted in *Temas de 'La Celestina'*, pp. 13–33
——, *Temas de 'La Celestina' y otros estudios del 'Cid' al 'Quijote'* (Barcelona, 1978)
——, 'Where was Alcocer?', in *Homenaje ofrecido a J. A. Van Praag* (Amsterdam, 1956), pp. 101–07; reprinted in *Temas de 'La Celestina'*, pp. 37–44
Rychner, Jean, *La Chanson de geste* (Geneva, 1955)
Sala Balust, J., 'Los autores de la *Historia Compostellana*', *Hispania*, 3 (1943), 16–69
Salinas, Pedro, *Ensayos de literatura hispánica* (M., 1958)
Sánchez, Tomás Antonio, *Colección de poesías castellanas anteriores al siglo XV*, 2 vols (M., 1779–80)
Sánchez Albornoz, Claudio, 'De nuevo sobre la *Crónica de Alfonso III* y sobre la llamada *Historia silense*', *CHE*, 37–38 (1963), 292–317
——, 'Sobre el autor de la llamada *Historia silense*', *CHE*, 23–24 (1955), 307–16
Sánchez Alonso, B., *Historia de la historiografía española*, I (M., 1947)
——, Versiones en romance de las crónicas del Toledano', *Homenaje ofrecido a Ramón Menéndez Pidal*, 3 vols (M., 1925), I, 341–54
Sánchez Belda, Luis, *Chronica Adefonsi Imperatoris* (M., 1950)
Sanchis y Sivera, José, *La diócesis valentina. Estudios históricos*, Anales del Instituto general y técnico de Valencia, 5 (Valencia, 1920)
——, *La diócesis valentina. Nuevos estudios históricos*, Anales del Instituto general y técnico de Valencia, 12 (Valencia, 1921)
Schafler, Norman, '*Sapientia et fortitudo* in the *PMC*', *HBalt*, 60 (1977), 44–50
Schottus, Andreas, *Hispaniae Bibliotheca seu de Academis ac Bibliothecis*, 3 vols (Frankfurt, 1608)
——, *Hispaniae Illustratae*, 4 vols (Frankfurt, 1605–08)
Serrano, Luciano, *El obispado de Burgos y Castilla primitiva desde el siglo VIII al XIII*, 3 vols (M., 1935–36)
Serrano y Sanz, Manuel, 'Cronicón villarense (*Liber regum*)', *BRAE*, 6 (1919), 193–220
——, 'Cronicón villarense (*Liber Regum*). Continuación y conclusión', *BRAE*, 8 (1921), 367–82
Smith, C. Colin, 'Did the Cid Repay the Jews?', *Romania*, 86 (1965), 520–38
——, *Estudios cidianos* (Barcelona, 1977)
——, 'Further French Analogues and Sources for the *PMC*', *La Corónica*, 6 (1977–78), 14–21
——, 'La métrica del *PMC*: nuevas posibilidades', *NRFH*, 28 (1979), 30–56
——, 'Latin Histories and Vernacular Epic in Twelfth-Century Spain: Similarities of Spirit and Style', *BHS*, 48 (1971), 1–19; reprinted in *Estudios cidianos*, pp. 87–106
——, 'Literary Sources of Two Episodes in the *PMC*', *BHS*, 52 (1975), 109–22; reprinted in *Estudios cidianos*, pp. 107–23
——, 'On Sound-Patterning in the *PMC*', *HR*, 44 (1976), 223–37
——, 'On the Distinctiveness of the *PMC*', in '*Mio Cid' Studies*, pp. 161–94
——, 'Per Abbat and the *PMC*', *Medium Aevum*, 42 (1973), 1–17; reprinted in *Estudios cidianos*, pp. 13–34
——, *PMC*, an edition (Oxford, 1972)
——, 'Sobre la difusión del *PMC*', in *Études de philologie romane et d'histoire littéraire offertes à Jules Horrent* (Liège, 1980), pp. 417–27

——, 'The Cid as Charlemagne in the *Leyenda de Cardeña*', *Romania*, 97 (1976), 509–31

——, 'The Diffusion of the Cid Cult: a Survey and a Little-Known Document', *Journal of Medieval History*, 6 (1980), 37–60

——, 'The Personages of the *PMC* and the Date of the Poem', *MLR*, 66 (1971), 580–98; reprinted in *Estudios cidianos*, pp. 35–62

—— and J. Morris, 'On "Physical" Phrases in Old Spanish Epic and Other Texts', *PLPLS*, 12, no. 5 (1967), 129–90; reprinted in *Estudios cidianos*, pp. 219–89

—— and Roger M. Walker, 'Did the Infantes de Carrión Intend to Kill the Cid's Daughters?', *BHS*, 56 (1979), 1–10

Smith, John D., 'The Singer or the Song? A Reassessment of Lord's "Oral Theory"', *Man: Journal of the Royal Anthropological Instutute*, 12 (1967), 141–53

Solalinde, A. G., 'Intervención de Alfonso X en la redacción de sus obras', *RFE*, 2 (1915), 283–88

——, 'Una fuente de la *PCG*: Lucano', *HR*, 9 (1941), 235–42

Spitzer, Leo, *Sobre antigua poesía española* (Buenos Aires, 1962)

——, 'Sobre el carácter histórico del *CMC*', *NRFH*, 2 (1948), 105–17; reprinted in *Sobre antigua poesía española*, pp. 9–25

Stefano, G. di, *Sincronia e diacronia nel Romanzero* (Pisa, 1967)

TCG, edited by Florián de Ocampo, in *Las quatro partes enteras*

Toledano, El, see Rodrigo Ximénez de Rada

Torres Rodríguez, C., 'La era hispánica', *RABM*, 79 (1976), 733–56

Tudense, El, see Lucas de Tuy

Tuy, Lucas de, *Chronicon Mundi*, edited by Andreas Schottus in *Hispaniae Illustratae*, IV, 1–116

Tyssens, Madeleine, 'Le Jongleur et l'écrit', in *Mélanges offerts à René Crozet*, 2 vols (Poitiers, 1966), I, 685–95

——, 'Le Style oral et les ateliers de copistes', in *Mélanges offerts à Maurice Delbouille*, 2 vols (Gembloux, 1964), II, 659–75

Ubieto Arteta, Antonio, *Colección diplomática de Pedro I de Aragón y Navarra* (Zaragoza, 1951)

——, *Corónicas navarras*, an edition (Valencia, 1964)

——, *Crónica de Alfonso III*, an edition (Valencia, 1961)

——, *Crónica de los estados peninsulares*, an edition (Granada, 1955)

——, *Crónica najerense*, an edition (Valencia, 1966)

——, *El 'CMC' y algunos problemas históricos* (Valencia, 1973); reprinted from *Ligarzas*, 4 (1972), 5–192

——, 'La *HR* y su fecha de redacción', *Saitabi*, 11 (1961), 241–46; reprinted in *El CMC*, pp. 170–76

——, 'Observaciones al *CMC*', *Arbor*, 37 (1957), 145–70

——, 'Sugerencias sobre la *CAI*', *CHE*, 25–26 (1957), 317–27

Van Emden, Wolfgang G., '"La bataille est adurée endementres": Traditionalism and Individualism in Chanson de Geste Studies', *Nottingham Medieval Studies*, 13 (1969), 3–26

Varvaro, Alberto, 'Dalla storia alla poesia epica: Alvar Fáñez', in *Studi di filologia romanza offerti a Silvio Pellegrini* (Padua, 1971), pp. 655–65

Velorado, Juan de, editor, *Cronica del famoso cavallero Cid Ruydiez Campeador* (Burgos, 1512); commonly called the *Crónica particular del Cid*; reprinted in facsimile (New York, 1967)

Victorio, Juan, 'La Chanson de geste comme moyen de propaganda', *Les Lettres Romanes*, 33 (1979), 309–28

Walker, Roger M., 'A Possible Source for the "Afrenta de Corpes" Episode in the *PMC*', *MLR*, 72 (1977), 335–47

——, 'The Infantes de Carrión and the Final Duels in the *PMC*', *La Corónica*, 6 (1977–78) 22–25

——, 'The Role of the King and the Poet's Intentions in the *PMC*', in *Medieval Studies Presented to Rita Hamilton* (London, 1976), pp. 257–66

——, *Tradition and Technique in 'El Libro del Cavallero Zifar'* (London, 1974)

Walsh, John K., 'Epic Flaw and Final Combat in the *PMC*', *La Corónica*, 5 (1976–77), 100–09

——, 'Religious Motifs in the Early Spanish Epic', *Revista Hispánica Moderna*, 36 (1970–71), 165–72

Waltman, Franklin M., *Concordance to 'PMC'* (Pennsylvania, 1972)

——, 'Divided Heroic Vision or Dual Authorship in the *PMC*', *Romance Notes*, 17 (1976), 84–88

——, 'Formula and Theme in the *CMC*', *HBalt*, 63 (1980), 20–24

——, 'Similarity in the Three Cantares of the *CMC*', *HBalt*, 59 (1976), 844–55

——, 'Synonym Choice in the *CMC*', *HBalt*, 57 (1974), 452–61

Webber, Ruth H., 'Narrative Organization of the *CMC*', *Olifant*, 1, no. 2 (1973), 21–33

——, 'Un aspecto estilístico del *CMC*', *AEM*, 2 (1965), 485–96

West, Geoffrey, 'A Proposed Literary Context for the Count of Barcelona Episode of the *CMC*', *BHS*, 58 (1981), 1–12

——, 'King and Vassal in History and Poetry: a Contrast between the *HR* and the *PMC*', in *'Mio Cid' Studies*, pp. 195–208

Whinnom, Keith, *Spanish Literary Historiography: Three Forms of Distortion* (Exeter, 1967)

Wright, Roger, 'The First Poem on the Cid: The *Carmen Campidoctoris*', in *Papers of the Liverpool Latin Seminar*, II (Liverpool, 1979), pp. 213–48

Ximénez de Rada, Rodrigo, El Toledano, *De Rebus Hispaniae*, edited by Andreas Schottus, in *Hispaniae Illustratae*, II, 25–148

——, *Opera*, edited by F. A. de Lorenzana (M., 1793); reprinted in facsimile, with indexes by M. D. Cabanes Pecourt (Valencia, 1968)

Zamora, Fray Gil de, *De Praeconiis Civitatis Numantiae*, edited by P. F. Fita, *BRAH*, 5 (1884), 131–200

——, *De Praeconiis Hispaniae*, edited by Manuel de Castro y Castro (M., 1955)

Zamora Vicente, Alonso, *PFG*, fourth edition (M., 1970)

Zarco Cuevas, J., *Catálogo de los manuscritos castellanos de la Biblioteca del Escorial*, 3 vols (M. and San Lorenzo del Escorial, 1924–29)

Zingarelli, Nicola, 'Per la genesi del *Poema del Cid*: alcuni raffronti con la *Crónica general*', *Rendiconti del Reale Istituto Lombardo di Scienze e Lettere*, 58 (1925), 705–26

INDEX